Wonder Girl
ADVENTURES OF A TEEN TITAN

ROB KANIGHER — Editors – Original Series
GEORGE KASHDAN
DICK GIORDANO
PAUL KUPPERBERG
PAUL LEVITZ
JEB WOODARD — Group Editor – Collected Editions
PAUL SANTOS — Editor – Collected Edition
STEVE COOK — Design Director – Books
SHANNON STEWART — Publication Design

BOB HARRAS — Senior VP – Editor-in-Chief, DC Comics

DIANE NELSON — President
DAN DiDIO — Publisher
JIM LEE — Publisher
GEOFF JOHNS — President & Chief Creative Officer
AMIT DESAI — Executive VP – Business & Marketing Strategy,
Direct to Consumer & Global Franchise Management
SAM ADES — Senior VP – Direct to Consumer
BOBBIE CHASE — VP – Talent Development
MARK CHIARELLO — Senior VP – Art, Design & Collected Editions
JOHN CUNNINGHAM — Senior VP – Sales & Trade Marketing
ANNE DEPIES — Senior VP – Business Strategy, Finance & Administration
DON FALLETTI — VP – Manufacturing Operations
LAWRENCE GANEM — VP – Editorial Administration & Talent Relations
ALISON GILL — Senior VP – Manufacturing & Operations
HANK KANALZ — Senior VP – Editorial Strategy & Administration
JAY KOGAN — VP – Legal Affairs
THOMAS LOFTUS — VP – Business Affairs
JACK MAHAN — VP – Business Affairs
NICK J. NAPOLITANO — VP – Manufacturing Administration
EDDIE SCANNELL — VP – Consumer Marketing
COURTNEY SIMMONS — Senior VP – Publicity & Communications
JIM (SKI) SOKOLOWSKI — VP – Comic Book Specialty Sales & Trade Marketing
NANCY SPEARS — VP – Mass, Book, Digital Sales & Trade Marketing

WONDER GIRL: ADVENTURES OF A TEEN TITAN

Originally published in single magazine form in WONDER WOMAN 105, BRAVE AND THE BOLD 60, TEEN TITANS 22, ADVENTURE COMICS 461, WONDER WOMAN 105,
113, WONDER WOMAN: DONNA TROY 1, and WONDER GIRL 1. Copyright © 1959, 1965, 1969, 1979, 1996, 1998, 2011 DC Comics. All Rights Reserved. All characters,
their distinctive likenesses and related elements featured in this publication are trademarks of DC Comics. The stories, characters and incidents featured in
this publication are entirely fictional. DC Comics does not read or accept unsolicited submissions of ideas, stories or artwork.

DC Comics
2900 West Alameda Ave., Burbank, CA 91505
Printed by LSC Communications, Kendallville, IN, USA. 07/28/17. First printing.
ISBN: 978-1-4012-7165-7

TWENTY-FOUR

Wonder Girl
ADVENTURES OF A TEEN TITAN

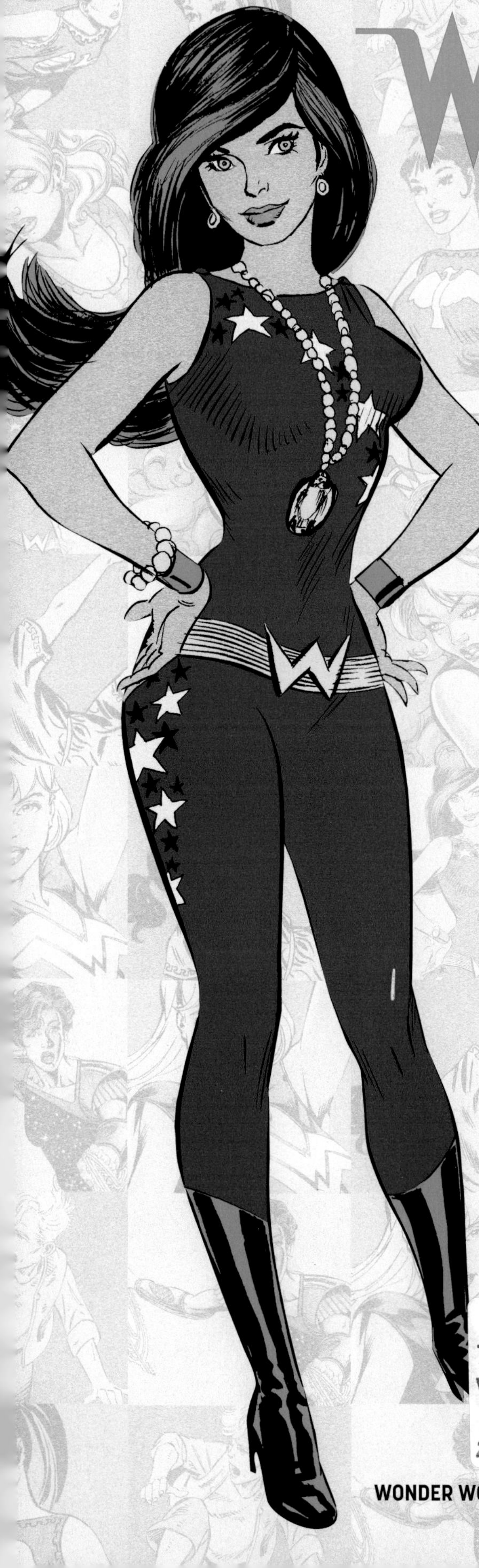

ROBERT KANIGHER
BOB HANEY
MARV WOLFMAN
JACK C. HARRIS
J.T. KRUL
Writers

JOHN BYRNE
PHIL JIMENEZ
ROSS ANDRU
BRUNO PREMIANI
GIL KANE
JACK ABEL
ADRIANA MELO
MIKE ESPOSITO
NICK CARDY
JOHN STOKES
MARIAH BENES
Artists

PATRICIA MULVIHILL
ADRIENNE ROY
JASON SCOTT JONES
MARCELO MAIOLO
Colorists

TODD KLEIN
SAL CIPRIANO
Letterers

NICOLA SCOTT and DOUG HAZLEWOOD
Collection cover art by

WONDER WOMAN created by WILLIAM MOULTON MARSTON

Table
OF CONTENTS

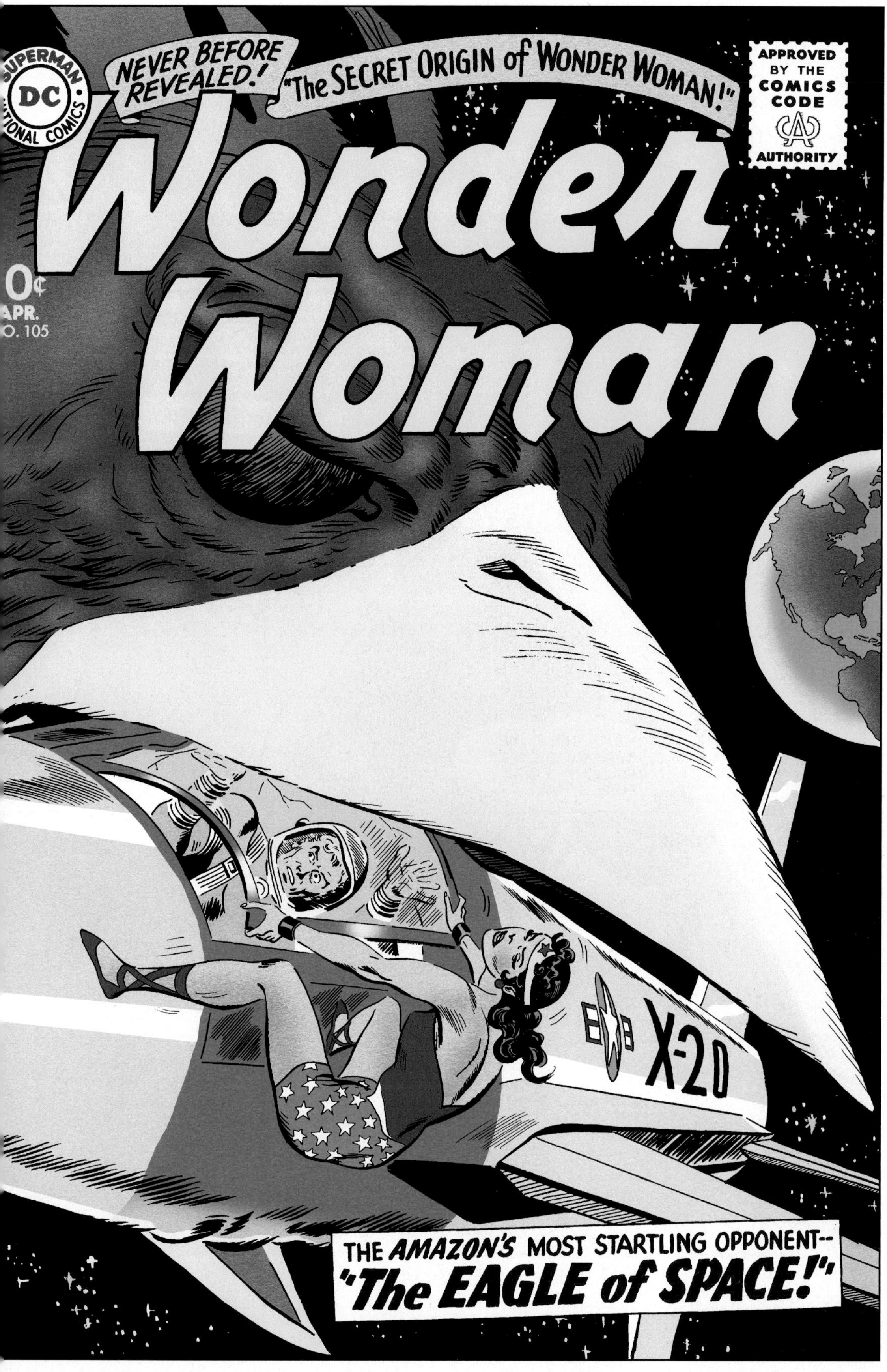
SUPERMAN DC NATIONAL COMICS
NEVER BEFORE REVEALED!
"The SECRET ORIGIN of WONDER WOMAN!"
APPROVED BY THE COMICS CODE AUTHORITY
Wonder Woman
10¢
APR.
NO. 105
X-20
THE AMAZON'S MOST STARTLING OPPONENT--
"The EAGLE of SPACE!"

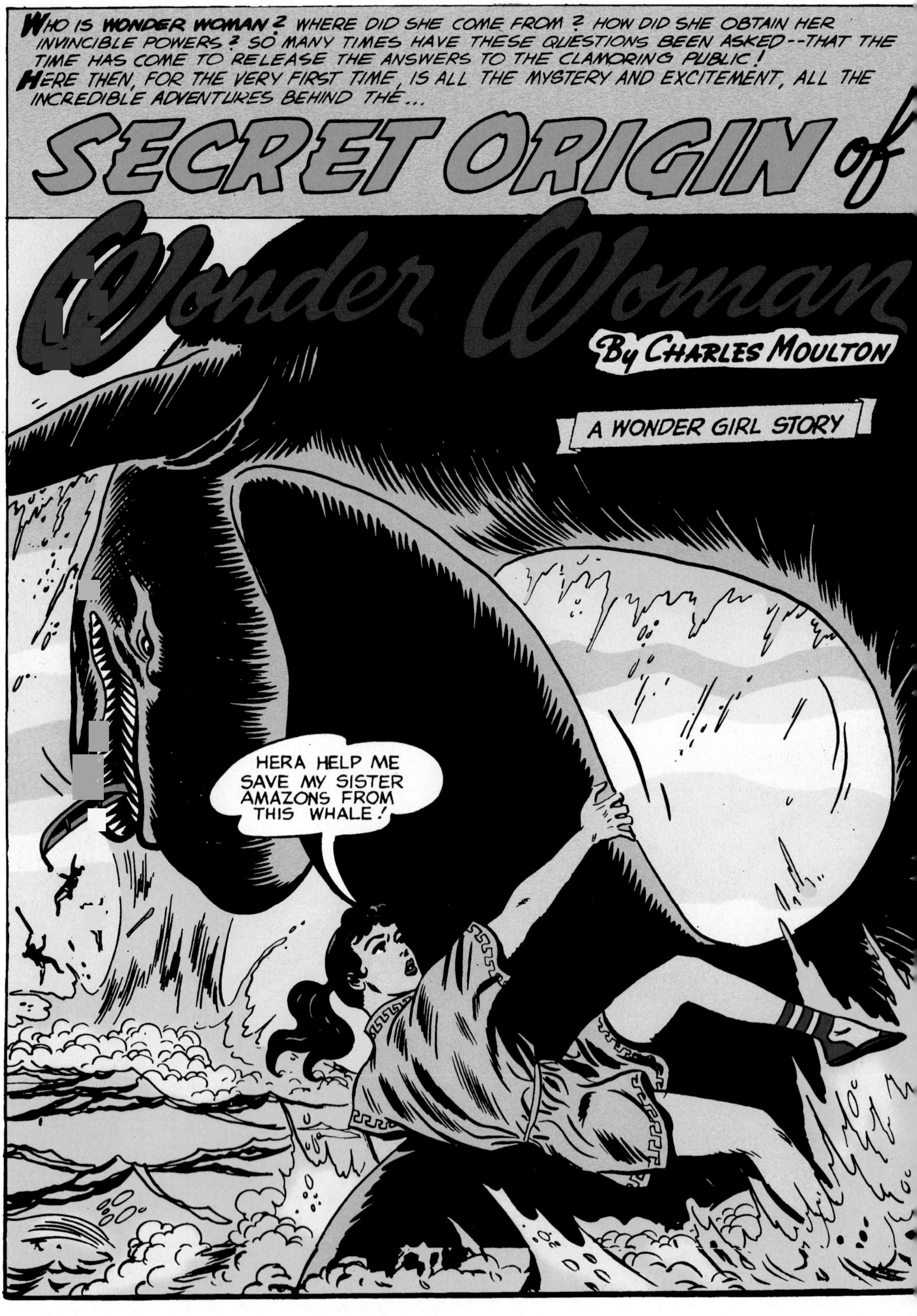
WHO IS WONDER WOMAN? WHERE DID SHE COME FROM? HOW DID SHE OBTAIN HER INVINCIBLE POWERS? SO MANY TIMES HAVE THESE QUESTIONS BEEN ASKED--THAT THE TIME HAS COME TO RELEASE THE ANSWERS TO THE CLAMORING PUBLIC!
HERE THEN, FOR THE VERY FIRST TIME, IS ALL THE MYSTERY AND EXCITEMENT, ALL THE INCREDIBLE ADVENTURES BEHIND THE...
SECRET ORIGIN of Wonder Woman
By CHARLES MOULTON
A WONDER GIRL STORY
HERA HELP ME SAVE MY SISTER AMAZONS FROM THIS WHALE!

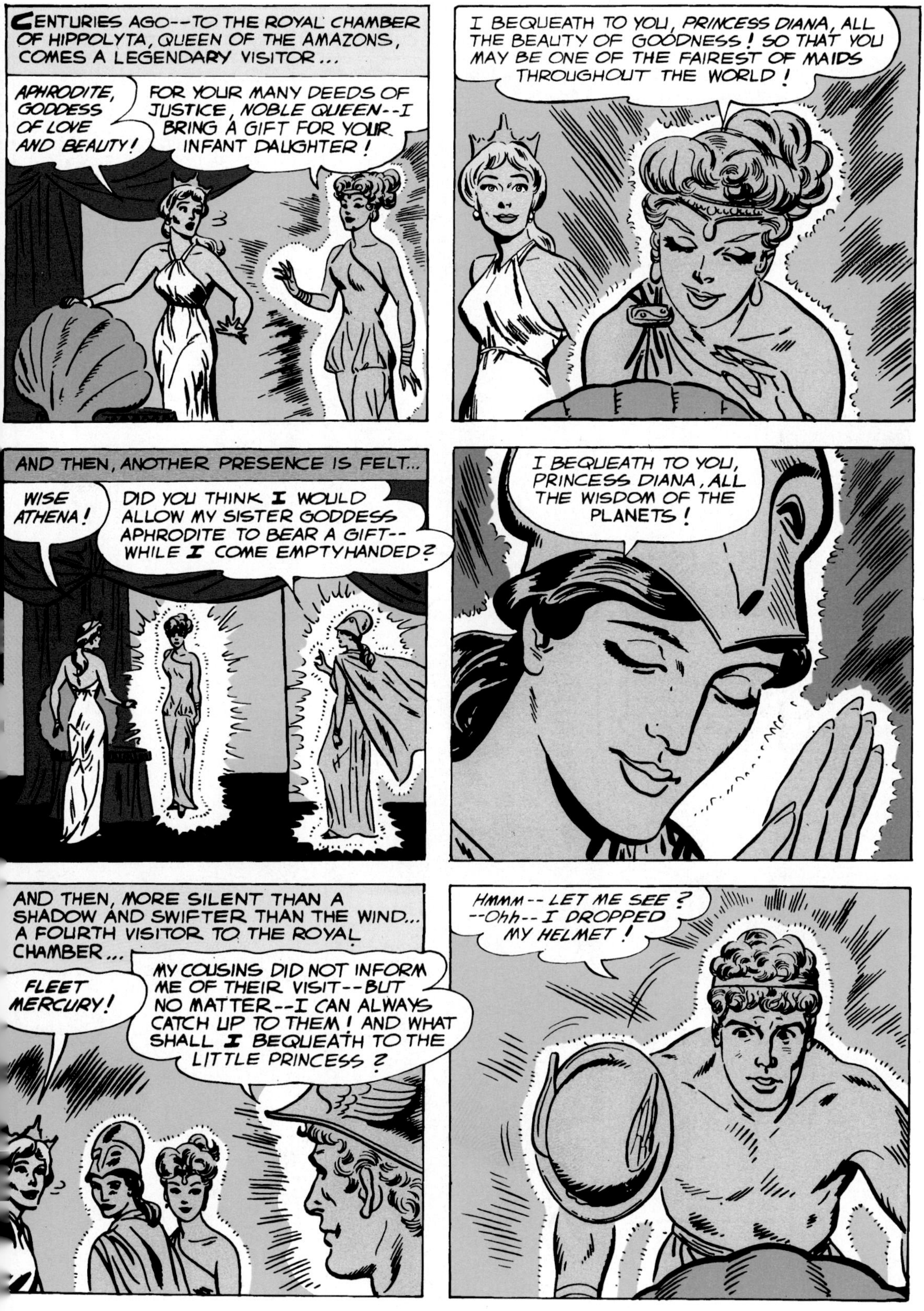
CENTURIES AGO--TO THE ROYAL CHAMBER OF HIPPOLYTA, QUEEN OF THE AMAZONS, COMES A LEGENDARY VISITOR...
APHRODITE, GODDESS OF LOVE AND BEAUTY!
FOR YOUR MANY DEEDS OF JUSTICE, NOBLE QUEEN--I BRING A GIFT FOR YOUR INFANT DAUGHTER!
I BEQUEATH TO YOU, PRINCESS DIANA, ALL THE BEAUTY OF GOODNESS! SO THAT YOU MAY BE ONE OF THE FAIREST OF MAIDS THROUGHOUT THE WORLD!
AND THEN, ANOTHER PRESENCE IS FELT...
WISE ATHENA!
DID YOU THINK I WOULD ALLOW MY SISTER GODDESS APHRODITE TO BEAR A GIFT--WHILE I COME EMPTYHANDED?
I BEQUEATH TO YOU, PRINCESS DIANA, ALL THE WISDOM OF THE PLANETS!
AND THEN, MORE SILENT THAN A SHADOW AND SWIFTER THAN THE WIND... A FOURTH VISITOR TO THE ROYAL CHAMBER...
FLEET MERCURY!
MY COUSINS DID NOT INFORM ME OF THEIR VISIT--BUT NO MATTER--I CAN ALWAYS CATCH UP TO THEM! AND WHAT SHALL I BEQUEATH TO THE LITTLE PRINCESS?
HMMM--LET ME SEE? --Ohh--I DROPPED MY HELMET!

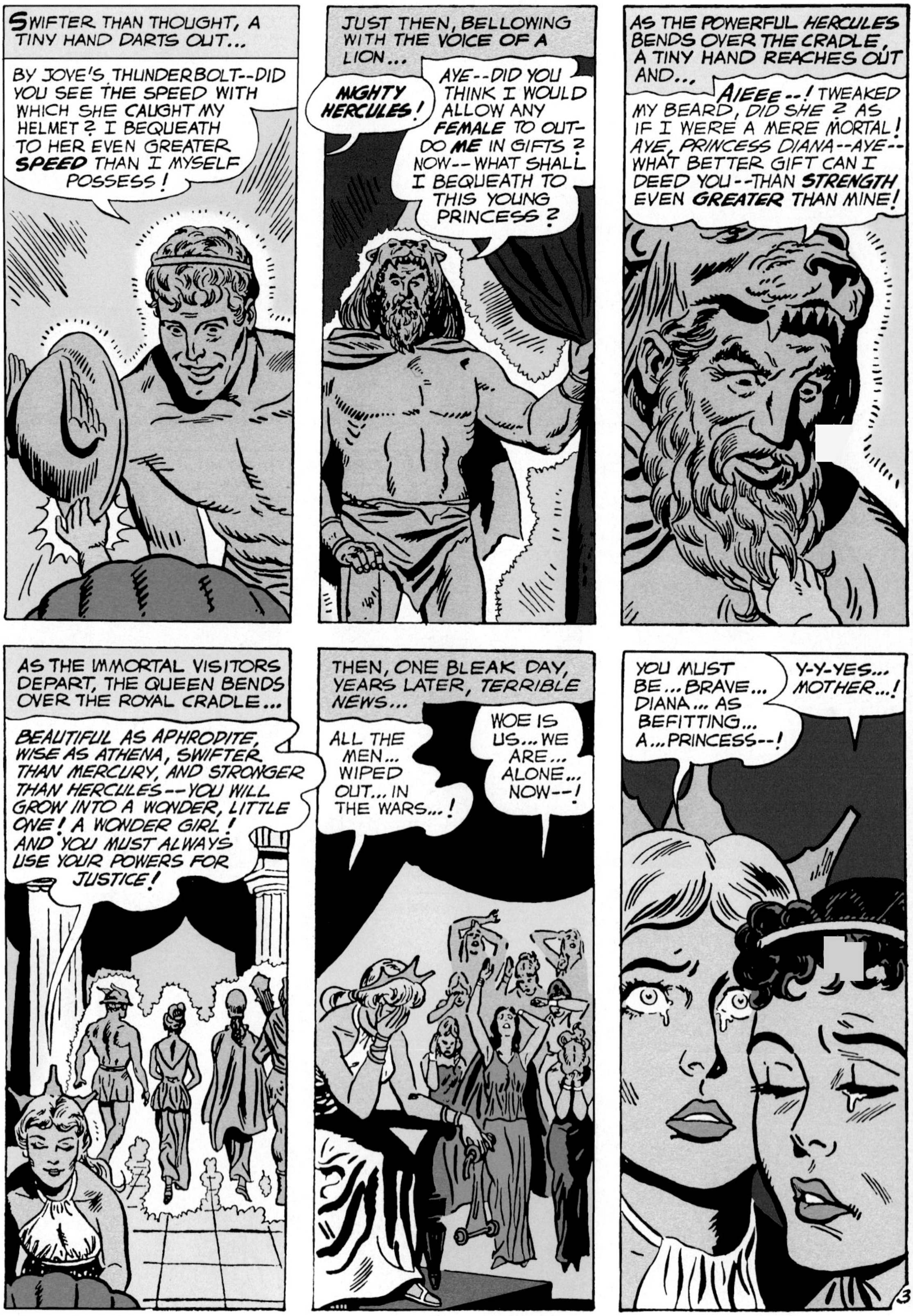

SWIFTER THAN THOUGHT, A TINY HAND DARTS OUT...
BY JOVE'S THUNDERBOLT--DID YOU SEE THE SPEED WITH WHICH SHE CAUGHT MY HELMET? I BEQUEATH TO HER EVEN GREATER SPEED THAN I MYSELF POSSESS!
JUST THEN, BELLOWING WITH THE VOICE OF A LION...
MIGHTY HERCULES!
AYE--DID YOU THINK I WOULD ALLOW ANY FEMALE TO OUT-DO ME IN GIFTS? NOW--WHAT SHALL I BEQUEATH TO THIS YOUNG PRINCESS?
AS THE POWERFUL HERCULES BENDS OVER THE CRADLE, A TINY HAND REACHES OUT AND...
AIEEE--! TWEAKED MY BEARD, DID SHE? AS IF I WERE A MERE MORTAL! AYE, PRINCESS DIANA--AYE--WHAT BETTER GIFT CAN I DEED YOU--THAN STRENGTH EVEN GREATER THAN MINE!
AS THE IMMORTAL VISITORS DEPART, THE QUEEN BENDS OVER THE ROYAL CRADLE...
BEAUTIFUL AS APHRODITE, WISE AS ATHENA, SWIFTER THAN MERCURY, AND STRONGER THAN HERCULES--YOU WILL GROW INTO A WONDER, LITTLE ONE! A WONDER GIRL! AND YOU MUST ALWAYS USE YOUR POWERS FOR JUSTICE!
THEN, ONE BLEAK DAY, YEARS LATER, TERRIBLE NEWS...
ALL THE MEN... WIPED OUT... IN THE WARS...!
WOE IS US... WE ARE... ALONE... NOW--!
YOU MUST BE... BRAVE... DIANA... AS BEFITTING... A... PRINCESS--!
Y-Y-YES... MOTHER...!

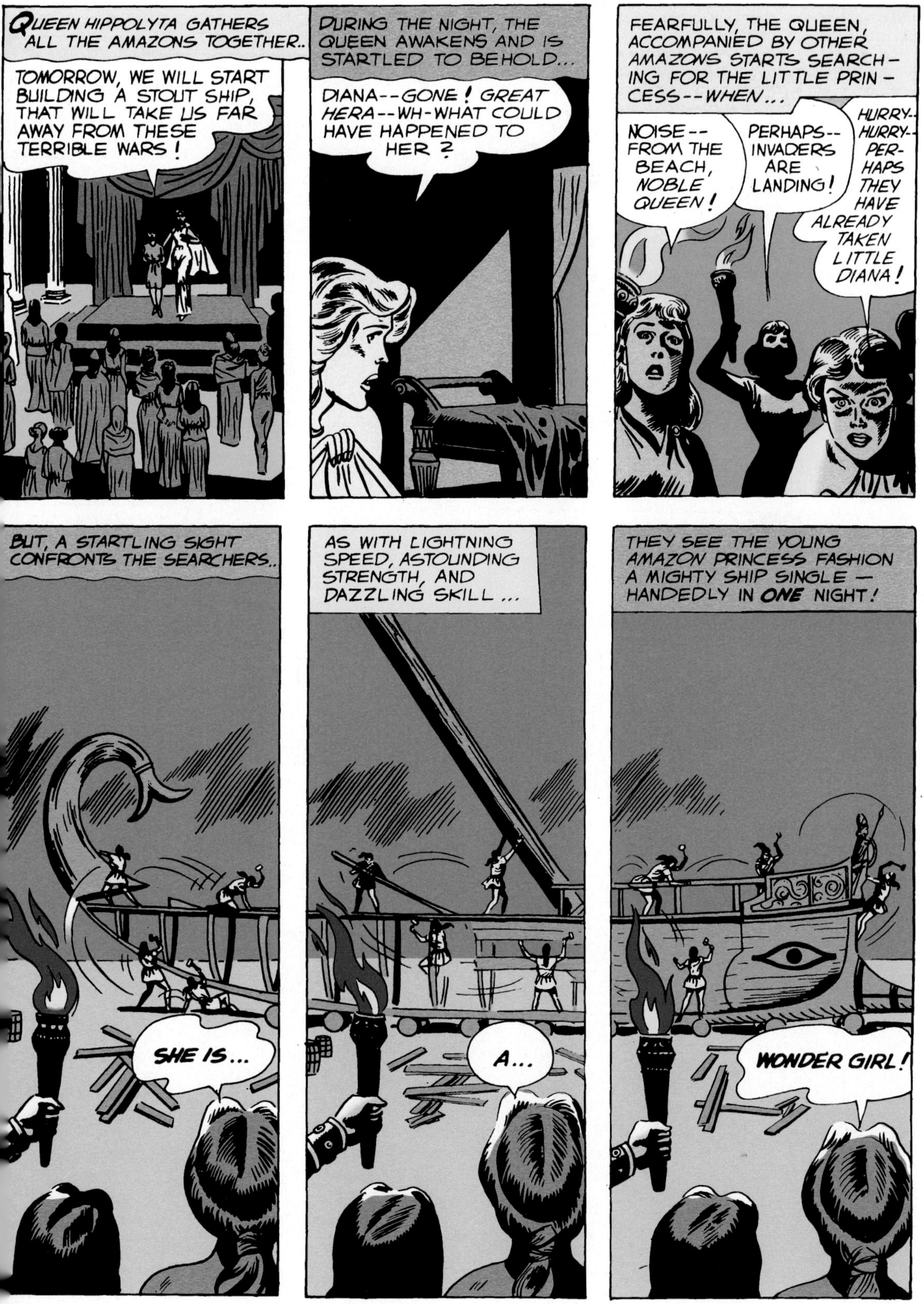
QUEEN HIPPOLYTA GATHERS ALL THE AMAZONS TOGETHER..
TOMORROW, WE WILL START BUILDING A STOUT SHIP, THAT WILL TAKE US FAR AWAY FROM THESE TERRIBLE WARS!
DURING THE NIGHT, THE QUEEN AWAKENS AND IS STARTLED TO BEHOLD...
DIANA--GONE! GREAT HERA--WH-WHAT COULD HAVE HAPPENED TO HER?
FEARFULLY, THE QUEEN, ACCOMPANIED BY OTHER AMAZONS STARTS SEARCHING FOR THE LITTLE PRINCESS--WHEN...
NOISE--FROM THE BEACH, NOBLE QUEEN!
PERHAPS--INVADERS ARE LANDING!
HURRY--HURRY--PERHAPS THEY HAVE ALREADY TAKEN LITTLE DIANA!
BUT, A STARTLING SIGHT CONFRONTS THE SEARCHERS..
SHE IS...
AS WITH LIGHTNING SPEED, ASTOUNDING STRENGTH, AND DAZZLING SKILL...
A...
THEY SEE THE YOUNG AMAZON PRINCESS FASHION A MIGHTY SHIP SINGLE-HANDEDLY IN ONE NIGHT!
WONDER GIRL!

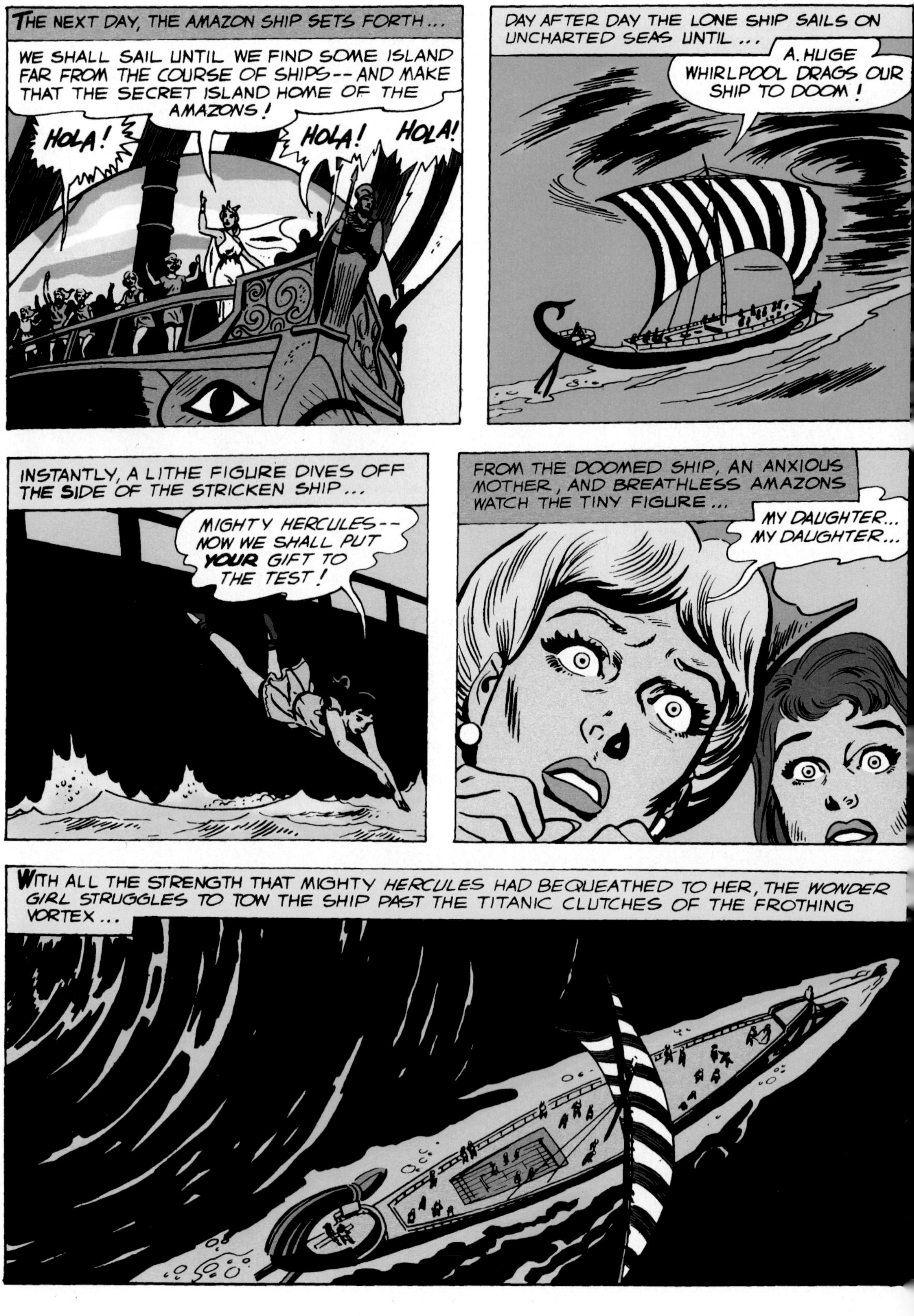
THE NEXT DAY, THE AMAZON SHIP SETS FORTH...
WE SHALL SAIL UNTIL WE FIND SOME ISLAND FAR FROM THE COURSE OF SHIPS-- AND MAKE THAT THE SECRET ISLAND HOME OF THE AMAZONS!
HOLA!
HOLA!
HOLA!
DAY AFTER DAY THE LONE SHIP SAILS ON UNCHARTED SEAS UNTIL...
A HUGE WHIRLPOOL DRAGS OUR SHIP TO DOOM!
INSTANTLY, A LITHE FIGURE DIVES OFF THE SIDE OF THE STRICKEN SHIP...
MIGHTY HERCULES-- NOW WE SHALL PUT YOUR GIFT TO THE TEST!
FROM THE DOOMED SHIP, AN ANXIOUS MOTHER, AND BREATHLESS AMAZONS WATCH THE TINY FIGURE...
MY DAUGHTER... MY DAUGHTER...
WITH ALL THE STRENGTH THAT MIGHTY HERCULES HAD BEQUEATHED TO HER, THE WONDER GIRL STRUGGLES TO TOW THE SHIP PAST THE TITANIC CLUTCHES OF THE FROTHING VORTEX...

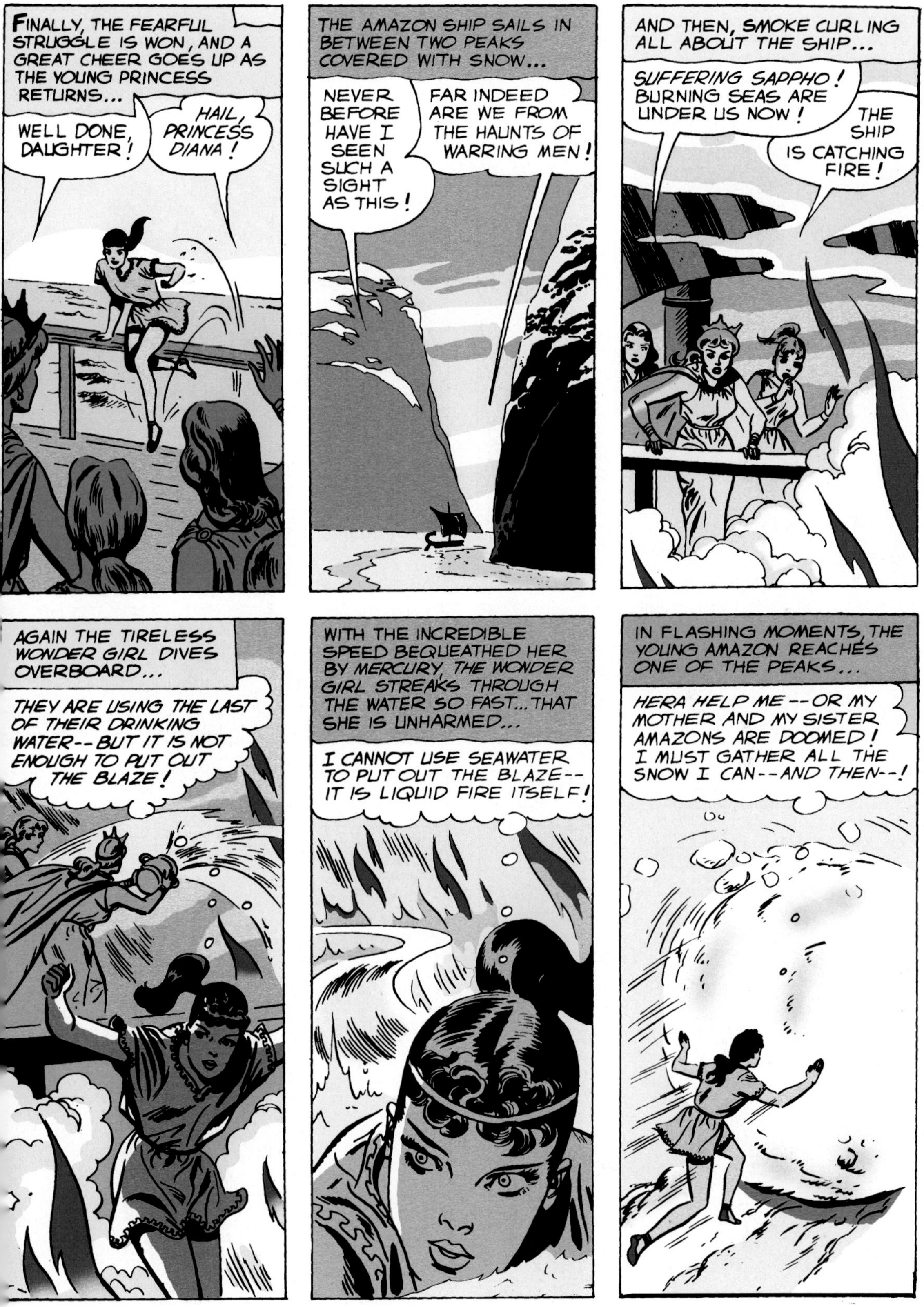
FINALLY, THE FEARFUL STRUGGLE IS WON, AND A GREAT CHEER GOES UP AS THE YOUNG PRINCESS RETURNS...
WELL DONE, DAUGHTER!
HAIL, PRINCESS DIANA!
THE AMAZON SHIP SAILS IN BETWEEN TWO PEAKS COVERED WITH SNOW...
NEVER BEFORE HAVE I SEEN SUCH A SIGHT AS THIS!
FAR INDEED ARE WE FROM THE HAUNTS OF WARRING MEN!
AND THEN, SMOKE CURLING ALL ABOUT THE SHIP...
SUFFERING SAPPHO! BURNING SEAS ARE UNDER US NOW!
THE SHIP IS CATCHING FIRE!
AGAIN THE TIRELESS WONDER GIRL DIVES OVERBOARD...
THEY ARE USING THE LAST OF THEIR DRINKING WATER--BUT IT IS NOT ENOUGH TO PUT OUT THE BLAZE!
WITH THE INCREDIBLE SPEED BEQUEATHED HER BY MERCURY, THE WONDER GIRL STREAKS THROUGH THE WATER SO FAST... THAT SHE IS UNHARMED...
I CANNOT USE SEAWATER TO PUT OUT THE BLAZE--IT IS LIQUID FIRE ITSELF!
IN FLASHING MOMENTS, THE YOUNG AMAZON REACHES ONE OF THE PEAKS...
HERA HELP ME--OR MY MOTHER AND MY SISTER AMAZONS ARE DOOMED! I MUST GATHER ALL THE SNOW I CAN--AND THEN--!

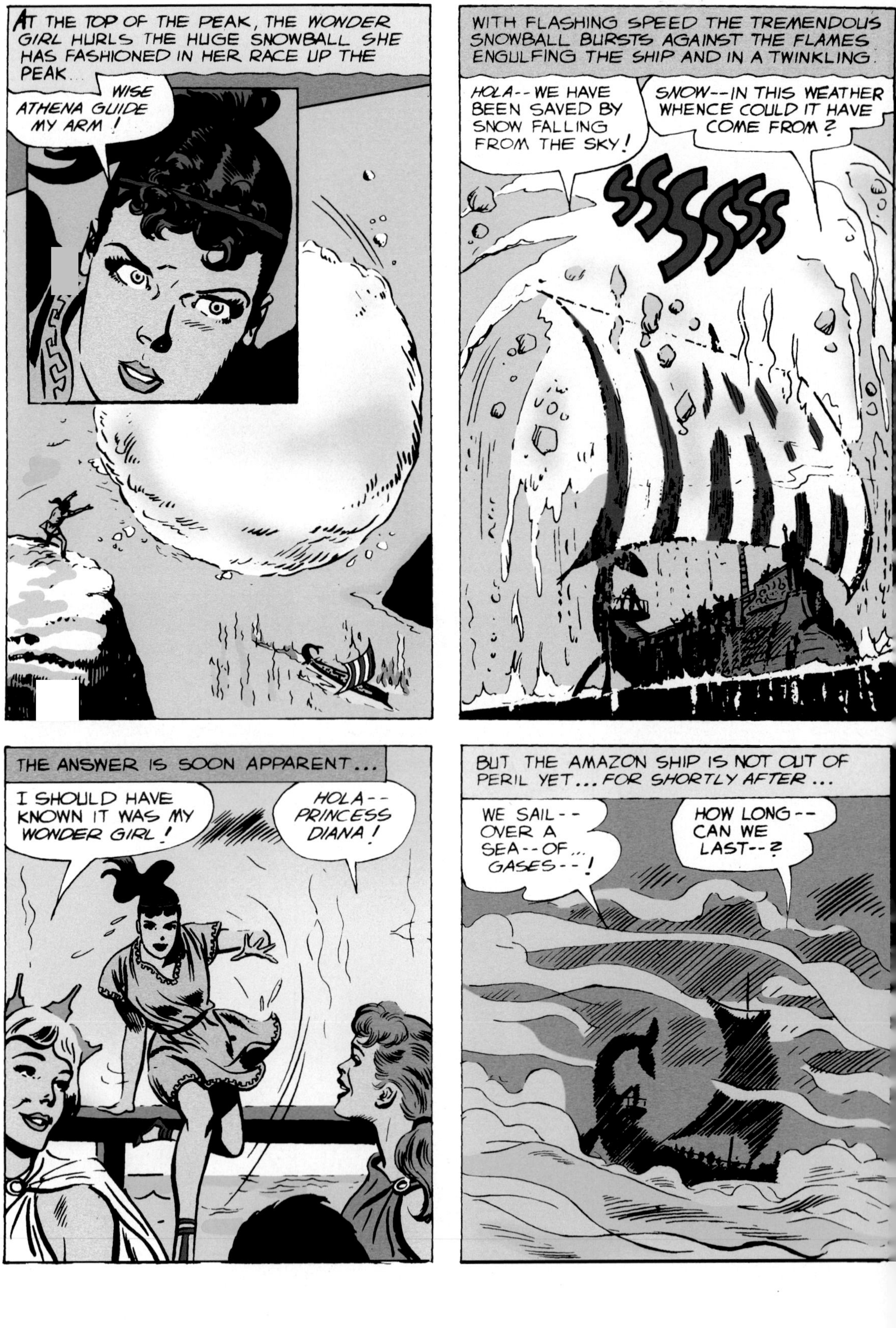
AT THE TOP OF THE PEAK, THE WONDER GIRL HURLS THE HUGE SNOWBALL SHE HAS FASHIONED IN HER RACE UP THE PEAK...
WISE ATHENA GUIDE MY ARM!
WITH FLASHING SPEED THE TREMENDOUS SNOWBALL BURSTS AGAINST THE FLAMES ENGULFING THE SHIP AND IN A TWINKLING.
HOLA--WE HAVE BEEN SAVED BY SNOW FALLING FROM THE SKY!
SNOW--IN THIS WEATHER WHENCE COULD IT HAVE COME FROM?
SSSSSS
THE ANSWER IS SOON APPARENT...
I SHOULD HAVE KNOWN IT WAS MY WONDER GIRL!
HOLA--PRINCESS DIANA!
BUT THE AMAZON SHIP IS NOT OUT OF PERIL YET... FOR SHORTLY AFTER...
WE SAIL--OVER A SEA--OF... GASES--!
HOW LONG--CAN WE LAST--?

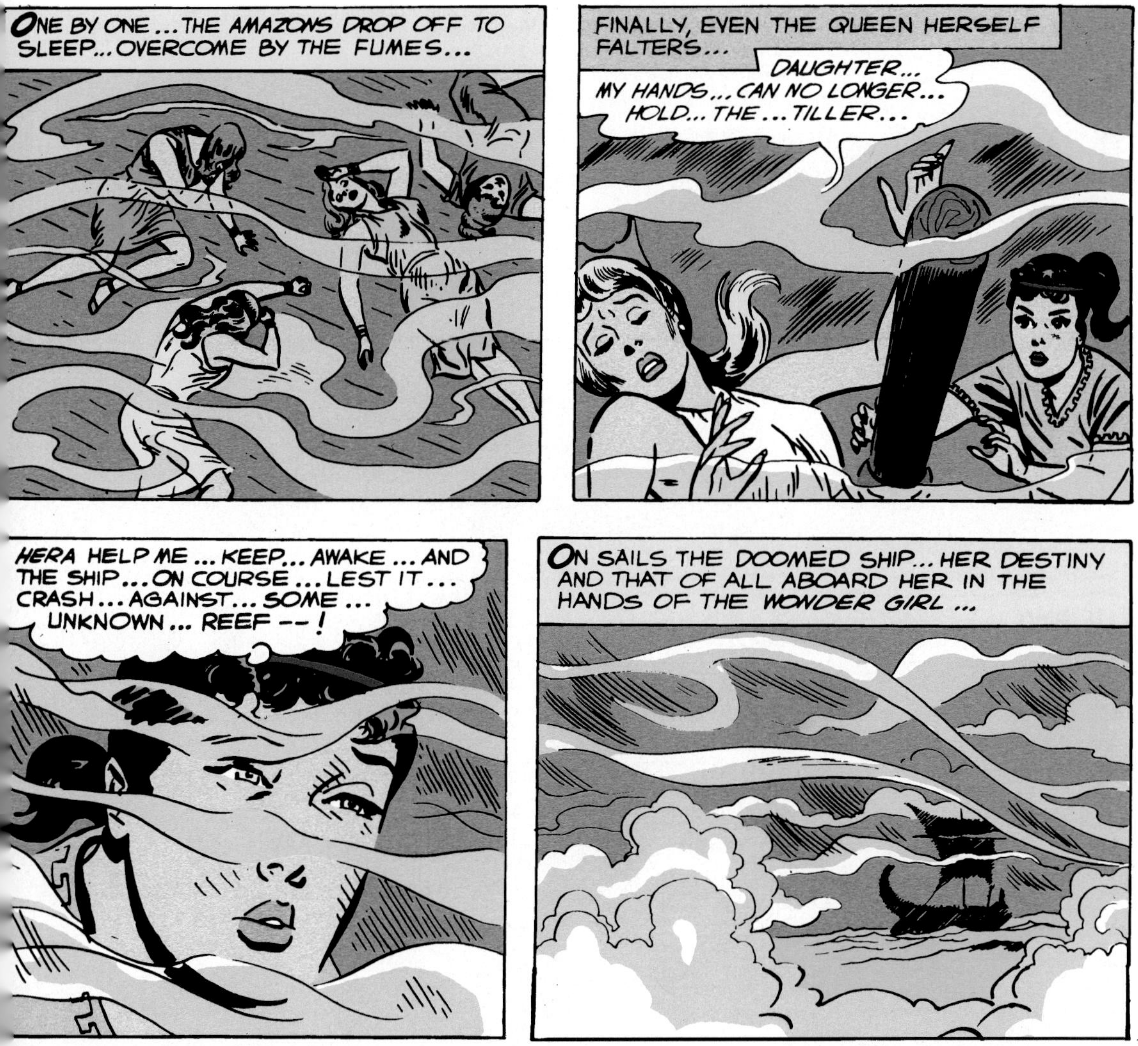
ONE BY ONE ... THE AMAZONS DROP OFF TO SLEEP... OVERCOME BY THE FUMES...
FINALLY, EVEN THE QUEEN HERSELF FALTERS...
DAUGHTER... MY HANDS... CAN NO LONGER... HOLD... THE ...TILLER...
HERA HELP ME ... KEEP... AWAKE ... AND THE SHIP... ON COURSE ... LEST IT ... CRASH... AGAINST... SOME ... UNKNOWN... REEF --!
ON SAILS THE DOOMED SHIP... HER DESTINY AND THAT OF ALL ABOARD HER IN THE HANDS OF THE WONDER GIRL ...

Wonder Girl
ADVENTURES OF A TEEN TITAN

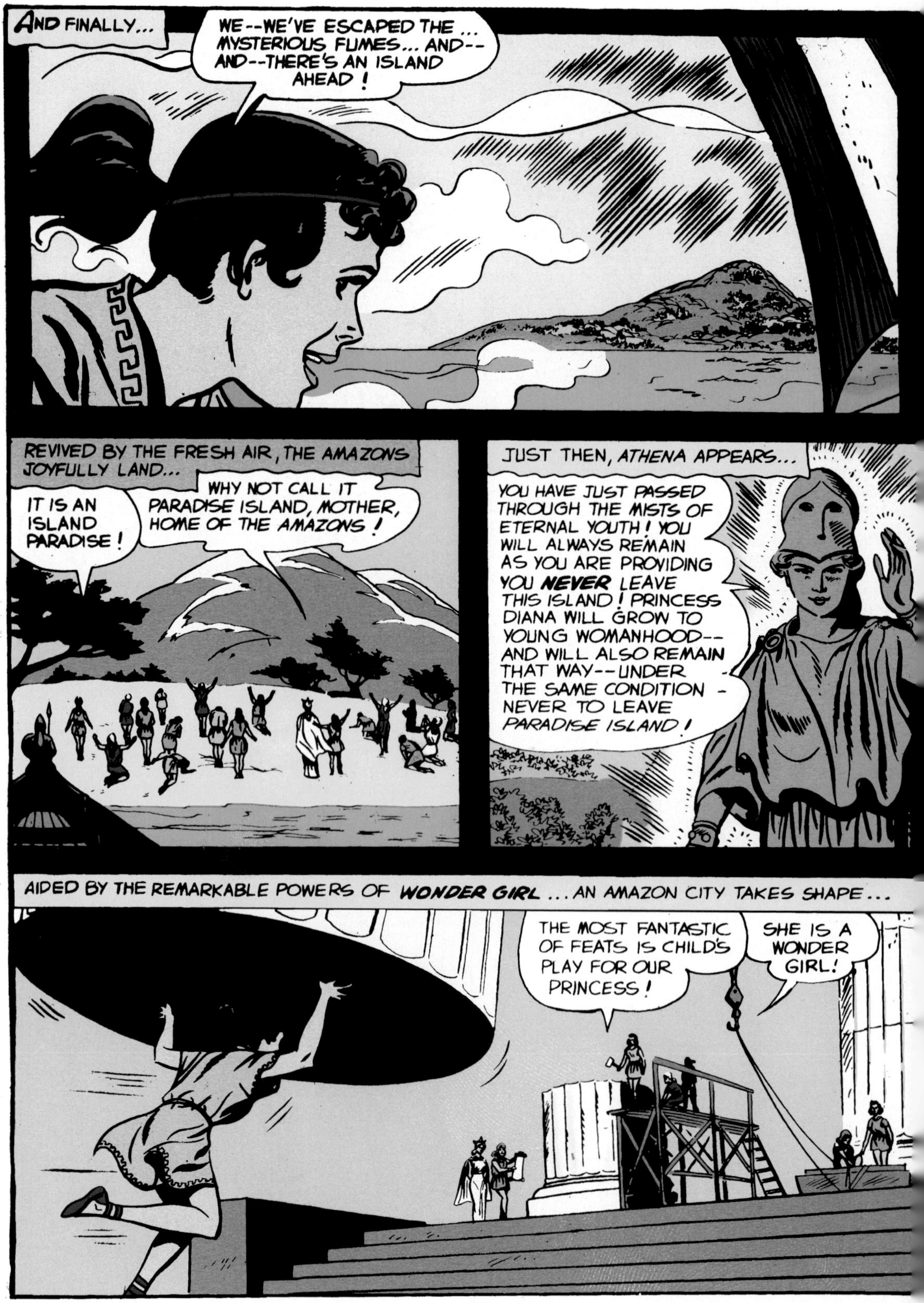
AND FINALLY...
WE--WE'VE ESCAPED THE ... MYSTERIOUS FUMES... AND--AND--THERE'S AN ISLAND AHEAD !
REVIVED BY THE FRESH AIR, THE AMAZONS JOYFULLY LAND...
IT IS AN ISLAND PARADISE !
WHY NOT CALL IT PARADISE ISLAND, MOTHER, HOME OF THE AMAZONS !
JUST THEN, ATHENA APPEARS...
YOU HAVE JUST PASSED THROUGH THE MISTS OF ETERNAL YOUTH ! YOU WILL ALWAYS REMAIN AS YOU ARE PROVIDING YOU NEVER LEAVE THIS ISLAND ! PRINCESS DIANA WILL GROW TO YOUNG WOMANHOOD--AND WILL ALSO REMAIN THAT WAY--UNDER THE SAME CONDITION - NEVER TO LEAVE PARADISE ISLAND !
AIDED BY THE REMARKABLE POWERS OF WONDER GIRL ... AN AMAZON CITY TAKES SHAPE...
THE MOST FANTASTIC OF FEATS IS CHILD'S PLAY FOR OUR PRINCESS !
SHE IS A WONDER GIRL !

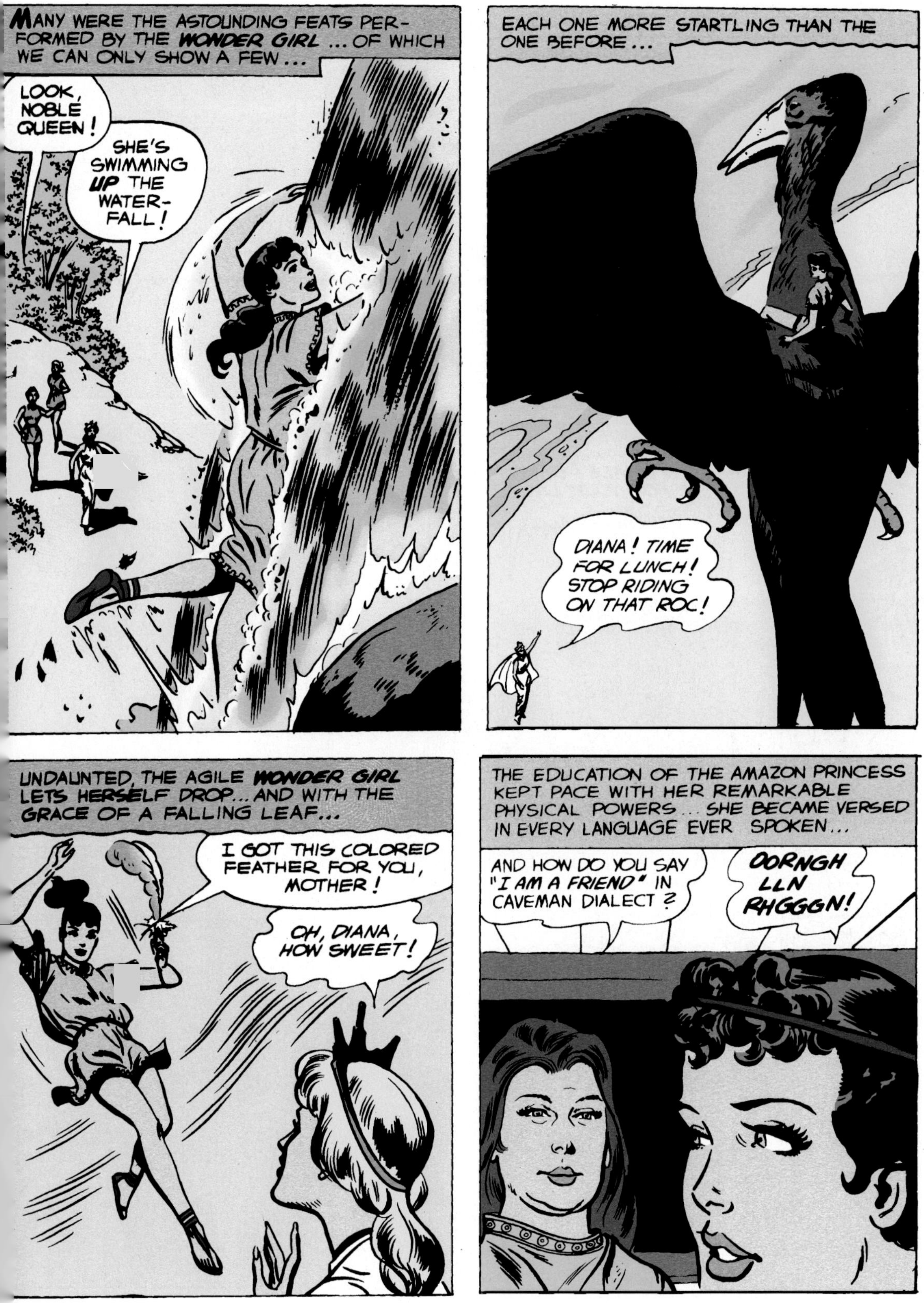
MANY WERE THE ASTOUNDING FEATS PERFORMED BY THE WONDER GIRL ... OF WHICH WE CAN ONLY SHOW A FEW ...
LOOK, NOBLE QUEEN!
SHE'S SWIMMING UP THE WATERFALL!
EACH ONE MORE STARTLING THAN THE ONE BEFORE ...
DIANA! TIME FOR LUNCH! STOP RIDING ON THAT ROC!
UNDAUNTED, THE AGILE WONDER GIRL LETS HERSELF DROP... AND WITH THE GRACE OF A FALLING LEAF...
I GOT THIS COLORED FEATHER FOR YOU, MOTHER!
OH, DIANA, HOW SWEET!
THE EDUCATION OF THE AMAZON PRINCESS KEPT PACE WITH HER REMARKABLE PHYSICAL POWERS... SHE BECAME VERSED IN EVERY LANGUAGE EVER SPOKEN...
AND HOW DO YOU SAY "I AM A FRIEND" IN CAVEMAN DIALECT?
OORNGH LLN RHGGGN!

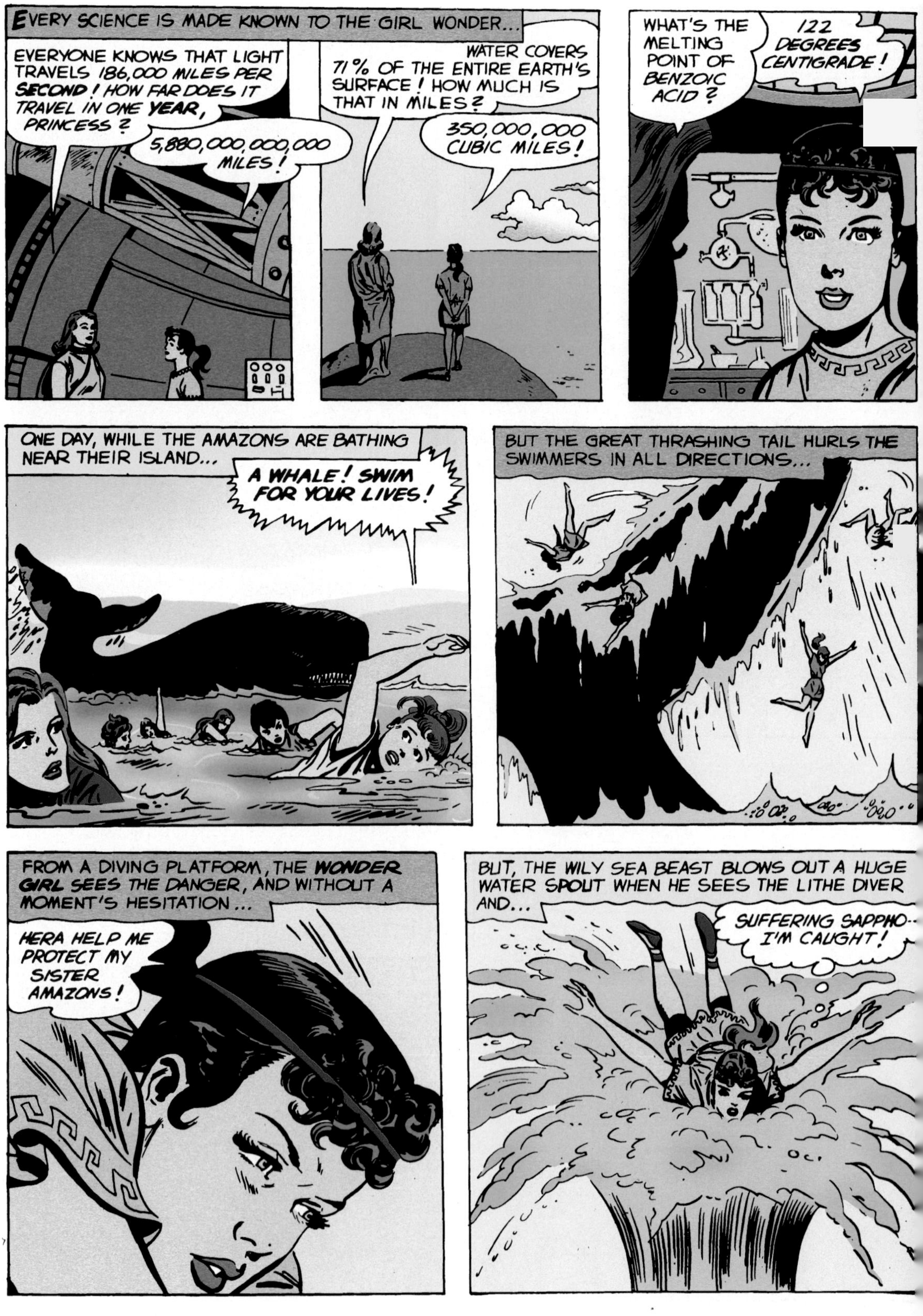

EVERY SCIENCE IS MADE KNOWN TO THE GIRL WONDER...
EVERYONE KNOWS THAT LIGHT TRAVELS 186,000 MILES PER SECOND! HOW FAR DOES IT TRAVEL IN ONE YEAR, PRINCESS?
5,880,000,000,000 MILES!
WATER COVERS 71% OF THE ENTIRE EARTH'S SURFACE! HOW MUCH IS THAT IN MILES?
350,000,000 CUBIC MILES!
WHAT'S THE MELTING POINT OF BENZOIC ACID?
122 DEGREES CENTIGRADE!
ONE DAY, WHILE THE AMAZONS ARE BATHING NEAR THEIR ISLAND...
A WHALE! SWIM FOR YOUR LIVES!
BUT THE GREAT THRASHING TAIL HURLS THE SWIMMERS IN ALL DIRECTIONS...
FROM A DIVING PLATFORM, THE WONDER GIRL SEES THE DANGER, AND WITHOUT A MOMENT'S HESITATION...
HERA HELP ME PROTECT MY SISTER AMAZONS!
BUT, THE WILY SEA BEAST BLOWS OUT A HUGE WATER SPOUT WHEN HE SEES THE LITHE DIVER AND...
SUFFERING SAPPHO-- I'M CAUGHT!

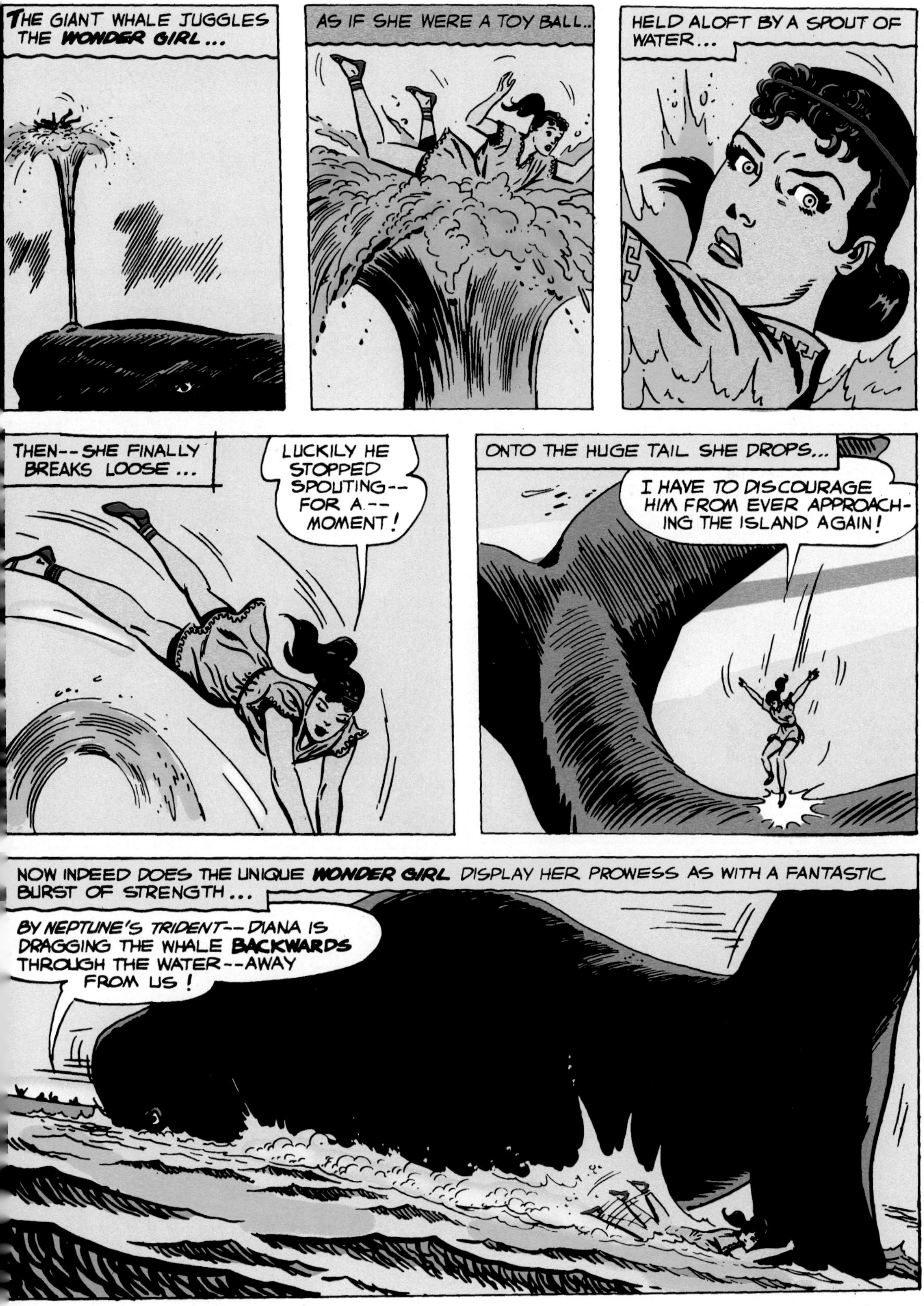
THE GIANT WHALE JUGGLES THE WONDER GIRL...
AS IF SHE WERE A TOY BALL..
HELD ALOFT BY A SPOUT OF WATER...
THEN--SHE FINALLY BREAKS LOOSE...
LUCKILY HE STOPPED SPOUTING-- FOR A-- MOMENT!
ONTO THE HUGE TAIL SHE DROPS...
I HAVE TO DISCOURAGE HIM FROM EVER APPROACHING THE ISLAND AGAIN!
NOW INDEED DOES THE UNIQUE WONDER GIRL DISPLAY HER PROWESS AS WITH A FANTASTIC BURST OF STRENGTH...
BY NEPTUNE'S TRIDENT--DIANA IS DRAGGING THE WHALE BACKWARDS THROUGH THE WATER--AWAY FROM US!

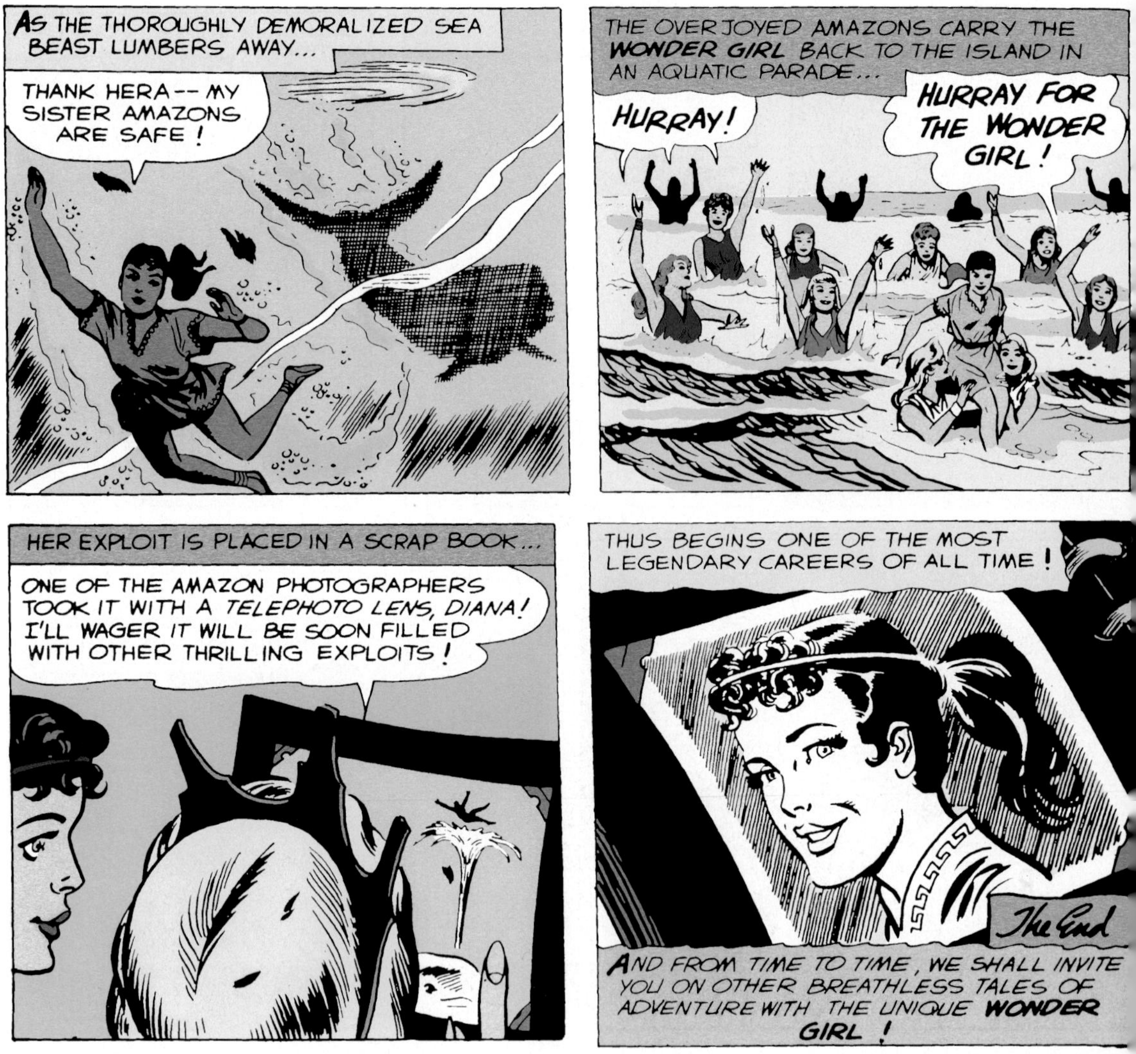
AS THE THOROUGHLY DEMORALIZED SEA BEAST LUMBERS AWAY...
THANK HERA-- MY SISTER AMAZONS ARE SAFE!
THE OVERJOYED AMAZONS CARRY THE WONDER GIRL BACK TO THE ISLAND IN AN AQUATIC PARADE...
HURRAY!
HURRAY FOR THE WONDER GIRL!
HER EXPLOIT IS PLACED IN A SCRAP BOOK...
ONE OF THE AMAZON PHOTOGRAPHERS TOOK IT WITH A TELEPHOTO LENS, DIANA! I'LL WAGER IT WILL BE SOON FILLED WITH OTHER THRILLING EXPLOITS!
THUS BEGINS ONE OF THE MOST LEGENDARY CAREERS OF ALL TIME!
The End
AND FROM TIME TO TIME, WE SHALL INVITE YOU ON OTHER BREATHLESS TALES OF ADVENTURE WITH THE UNIQUE WONDER GIRL!

Wonder Girl
ADVENTURES OF A TEEN TITAN

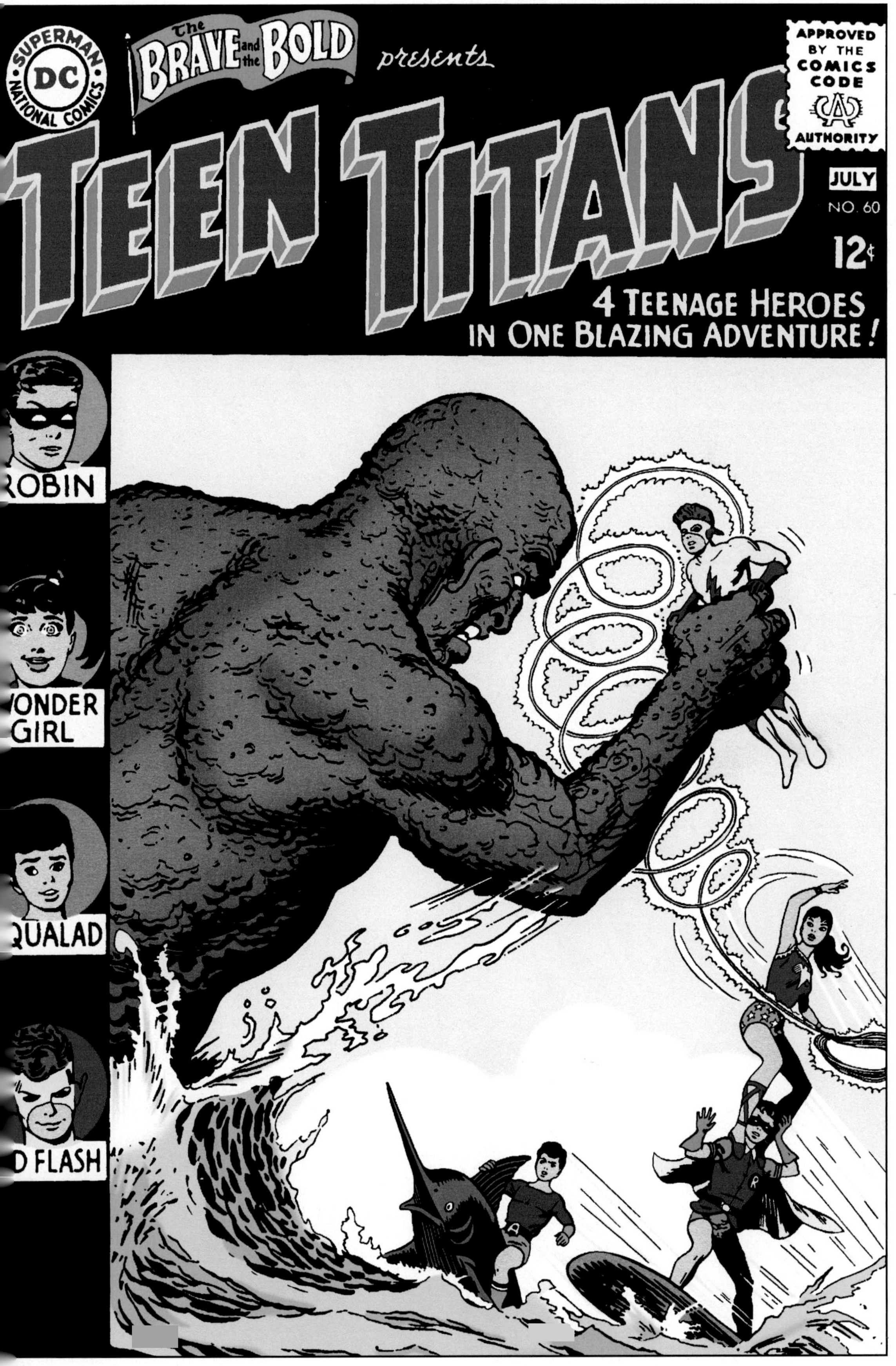

SUPERMAN
DC
NATIONAL COMICS
The BRAVE and the BOLD
presents
TEEN TITANS
APPROVED BY THE COMICS CODE AUTHORITY
JULY
NO. 60
12¢
4 TEENAGE HEROES IN ONE BLAZING ADVENTURE!
ROBIN
WONDER GIRL
QUALAD
D FLASH

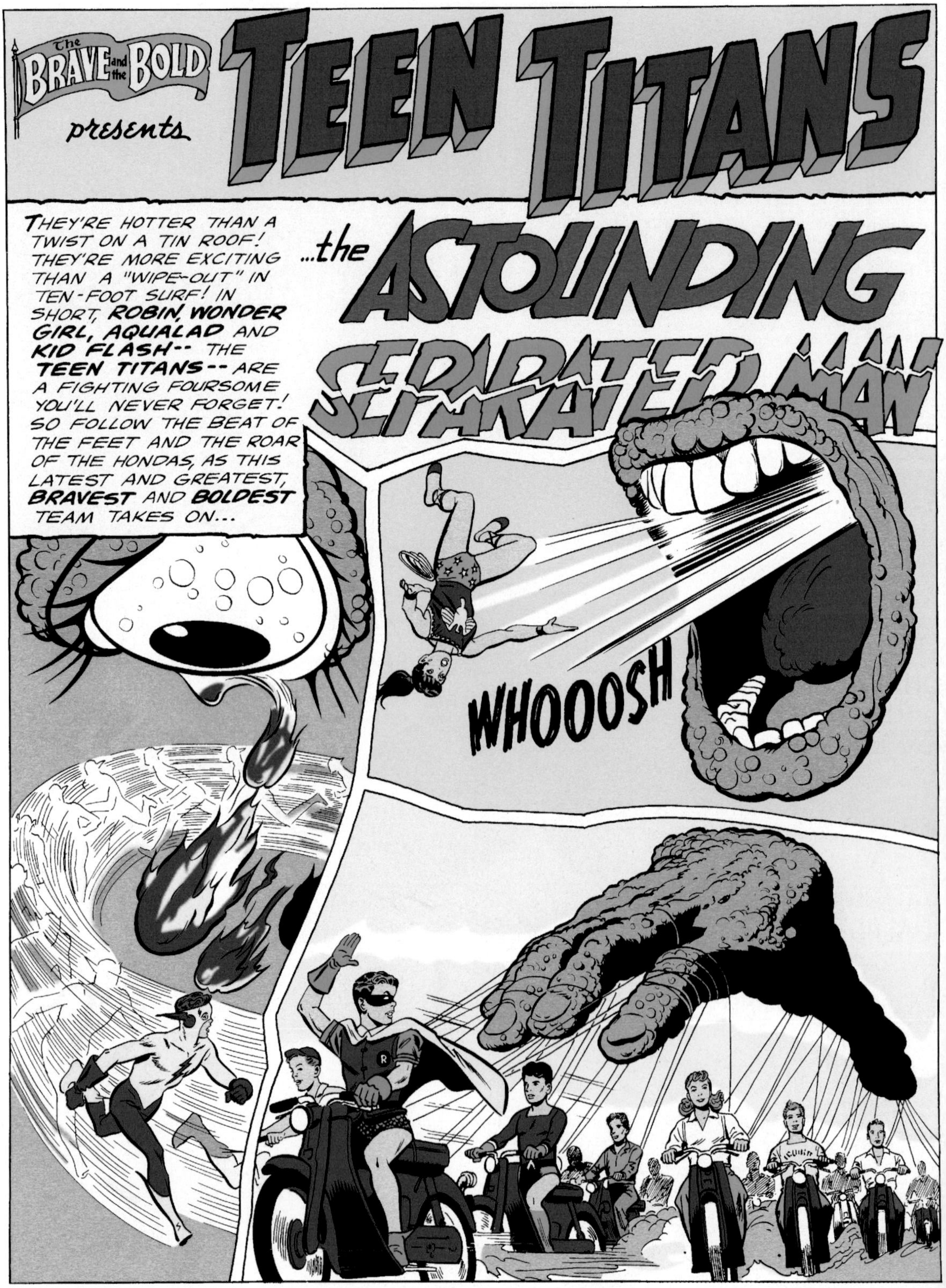
The BRAVE and the BOLD
presents
TEEN TITANS
THEY'RE HOTTER THAN A TWIST ON A TIN ROOF! THEY'RE MORE EXCITING THAN A "WIPE-OUT" IN TEN-FOOT SURF! IN SHORT, ROBIN, WONDER GIRL, AQUALAD AND KID FLASH-- THE TEEN TITANS-- ARE A FIGHTING FOURSOME YOU'LL NEVER FORGET! SO FOLLOW THE BEAT OF THE FEET AND THE ROAR OF THE HONDAS, AS THIS LATEST AND GREATEST, BRAVEST AND BOLDEST TEAM TAKES ON...
...the ASTOUNDING SEPARATED MAN
WHOOOSH

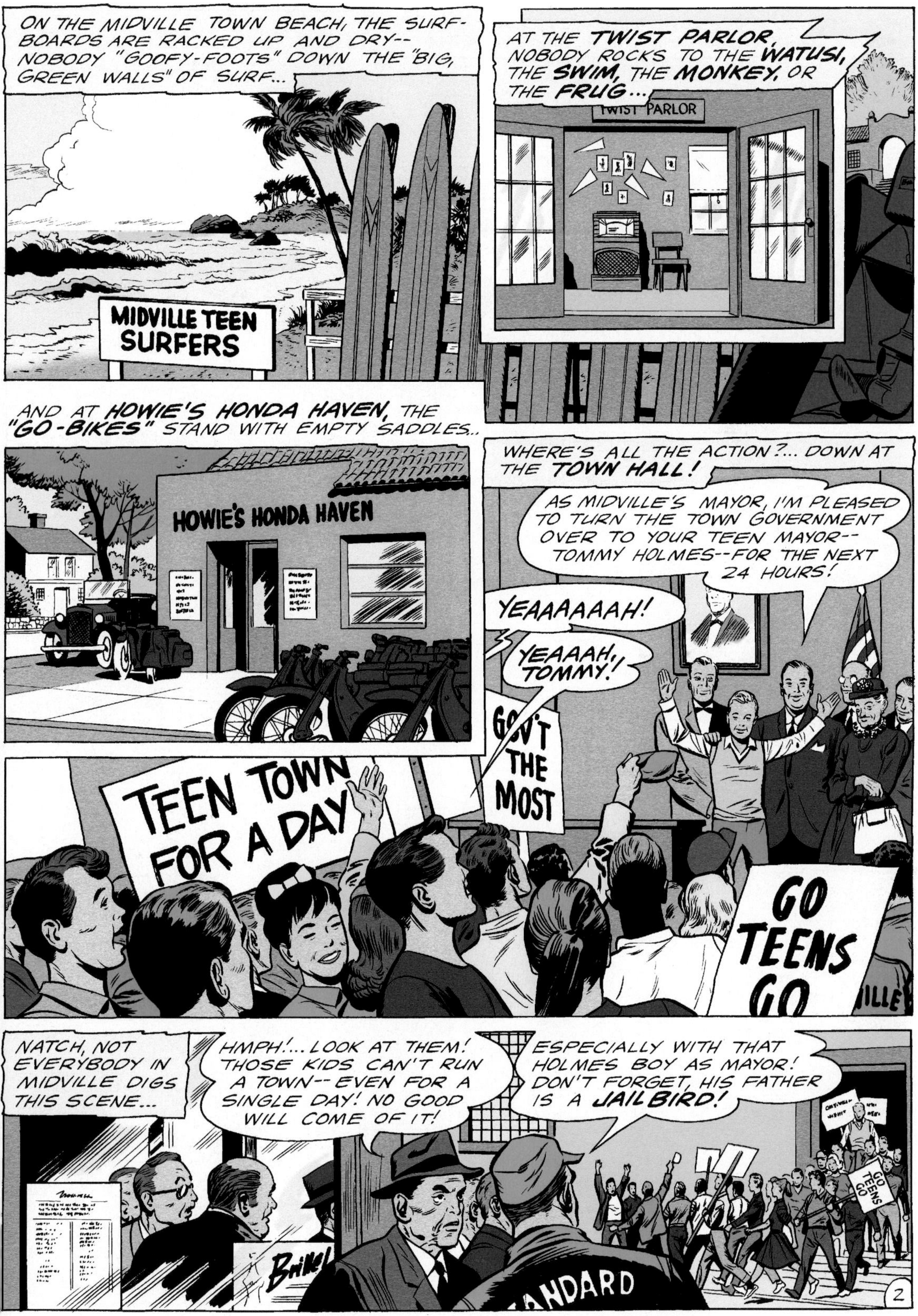
ON THE MIDVILLE TOWN BEACH, THE SURF-BOARDS ARE RACKED UP AND DRY-- NOBODY "GOOFY-FOOTS" DOWN THE "BIG, GREEN WALLS" OF SURF...
MIDVILLE TEEN SURFERS
AT THE TWIST PARLOR, NOBODY ROCKS TO THE WATUSI, THE SWIM, THE MONKEY, OR THE FRUG...
TWIST PARLOR
AND AT HOWIE'S HONDA HAVEN, THE "GO-BIKES" STAND WITH EMPTY SADDLES...
HOWIE'S HONDA HAVEN
WHERE'S ALL THE ACTION?... DOWN AT THE TOWN HALL!
AS MIDVILLE'S MAYOR, I'M PLEASED TO TURN THE TOWN GOVERNMENT OVER TO YOUR TEEN MAYOR-- TOMMY HOLMES--FOR THE NEXT 24 HOURS!
YEAAAAAAH!
YEAAAH, TOMMY!
GOV'T THE MOST
TEEN TOWN FOR A DAY
GO TEENS GO
NATCH, NOT EVERYBODY IN MIDVILLE DIGS THIS SCENE...
HMPH!... LOOK AT THEM! THOSE KIDS CAN'T RUN A TOWN-- EVEN FOR A SINGLE DAY! NO GOOD WILL COME OF IT!
ESPECIALLY WITH THAT HOLMES BOY AS MAYOR! DON'T FORGET, HIS FATHER IS A JAILBIRD!
GO TEENS GO
STANDARD

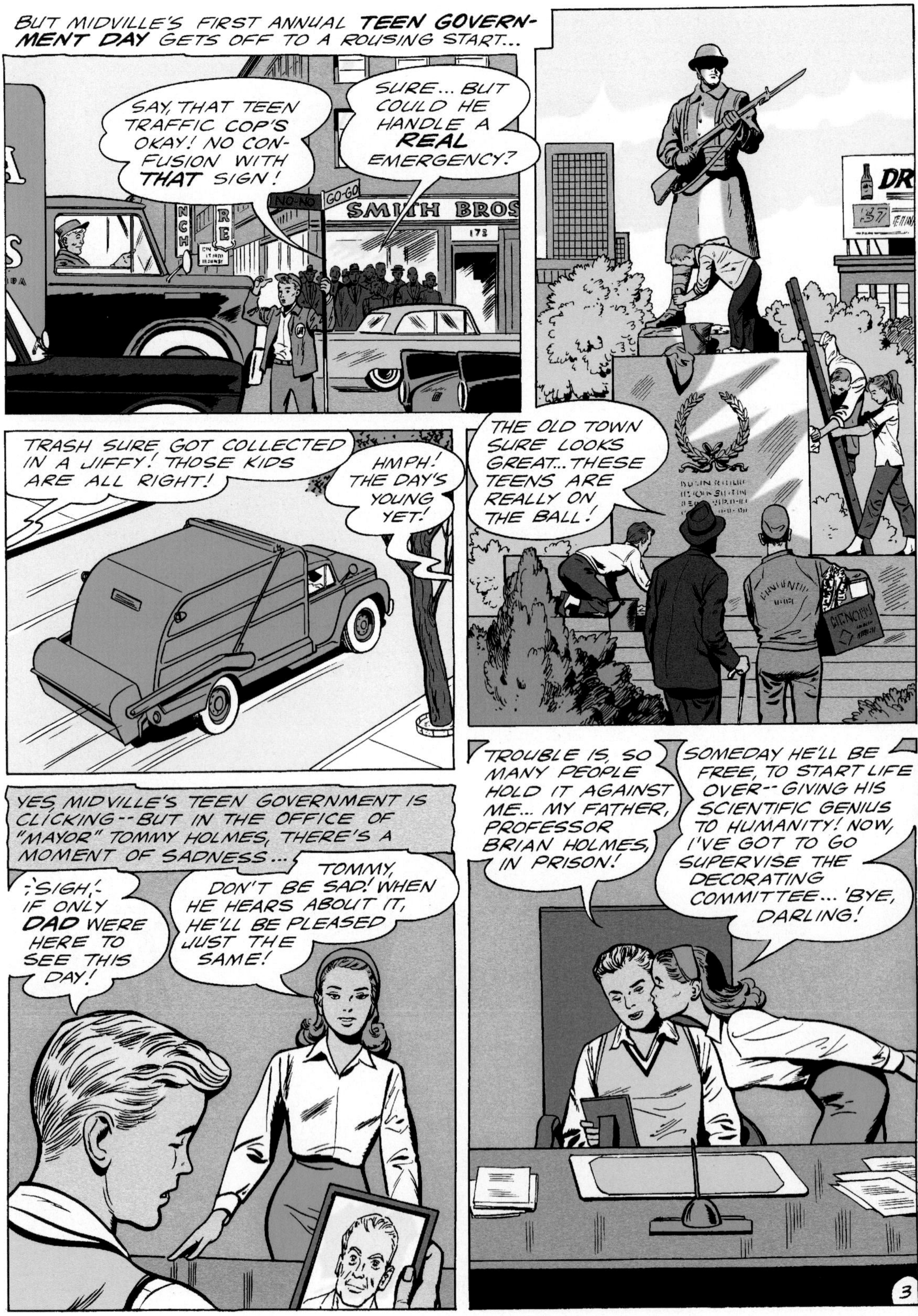

BUT MIDVILLE'S FIRST ANNUAL TEEN GOVERNMENT DAY GETS OFF TO A ROUSING START...
SAY, THAT TEEN TRAFFIC COP'S OKAY! NO CONFUSION WITH THAT SIGN!
SURE... BUT COULD HE HANDLE A REAL EMERGENCY?
NO-NO
GO-GO
SMITH BROS
TRASH SURE GOT COLLECTED IN A JIFFY! THOSE KIDS ARE ALL RIGHT!
HMPH! THE DAY'S YOUNG YET!
THE OLD TOWN SURE LOOKS GREAT...THESE TEENS ARE REALLY ON THE BALL!
YES, MIDVILLE'S TEEN GOVERNMENT IS CLICKING--BUT IN THE OFFICE OF "MAYOR" TOMMY HOLMES, THERE'S A MOMENT OF SADNESS...
-SIGH!- IF ONLY DAD WERE HERE TO SEE THIS DAY!
TOMMY, DON'T BE SAD! WHEN HE HEARS ABOUT IT, HE'LL BE PLEASED JUST THE SAME!
TROUBLE IS, SO MANY PEOPLE HOLD IT AGAINST ME... MY FATHER, PROFESSOR BRIAN HOLMES, IN PRISON!
SOMEDAY HE'LL BE FREE, TO START LIFE OVER-- GIVING HIS SCIENTIFIC GENIUS TO HUMANITY! NOW, I'VE GOT TO GO SUPERVISE THE DECORATING COMMITTEE... 'BYE, DARLING!

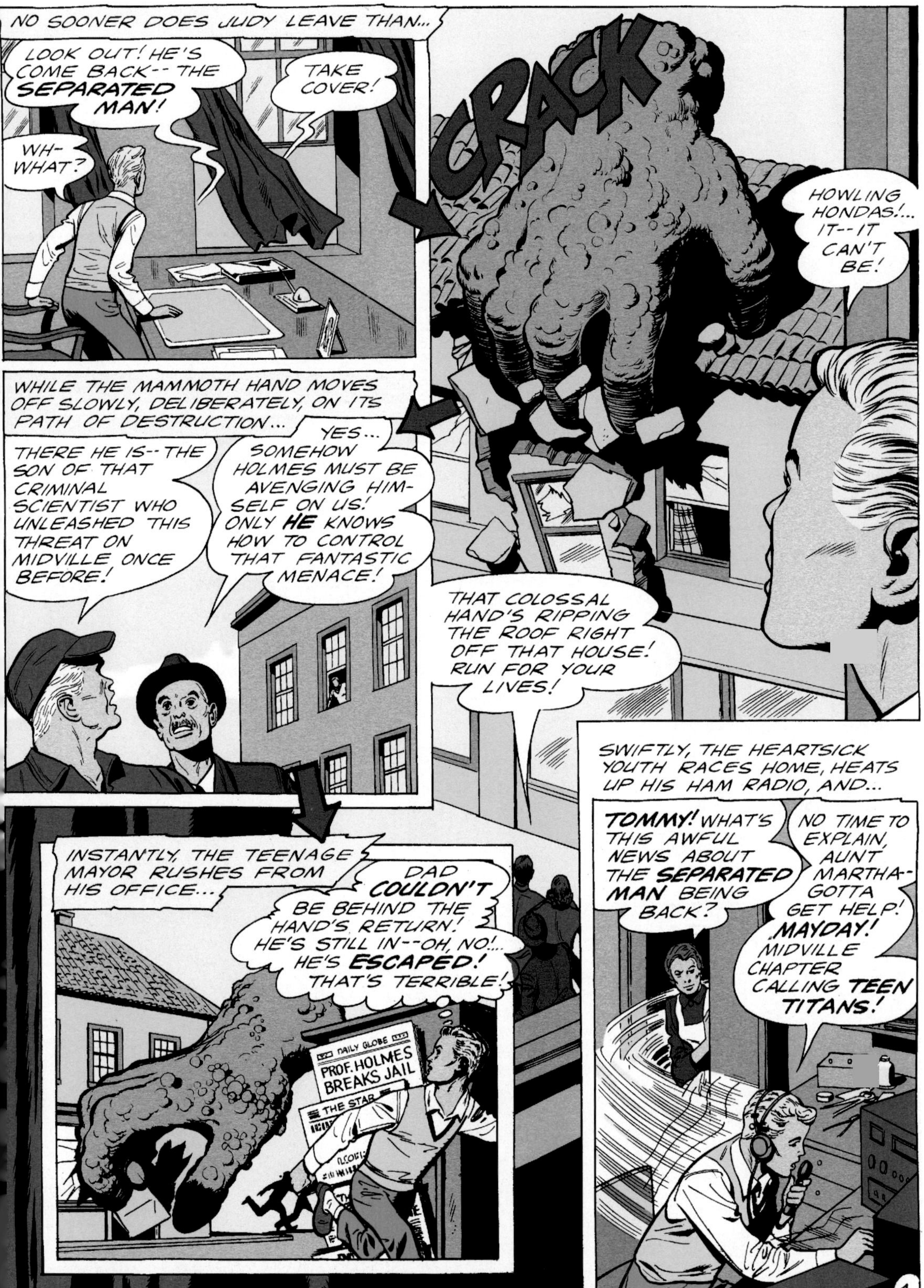
NO SOONER DOES JUDY LEAVE THAN...
LOOK OUT! HE'S COME BACK-- THE SEPARATED MAN!
TAKE COVER!
WH-WHAT?
CRACK
HOWLING HONDAS!... IT--IT CAN'T BE!
WHILE THE MAMMOTH HAND MOVES OFF SLOWLY, DELIBERATELY, ON ITS PATH OF DESTRUCTION...
THERE HE IS--THE SON OF THAT CRIMINAL SCIENTIST WHO UNLEASHED THIS THREAT ON MIDVILLE ONCE BEFORE!
YES... SOMEHOW HOLMES MUST BE AVENGING HIMSELF ON US! ONLY HE KNOWS HOW TO CONTROL THAT FANTASTIC MENACE!
THAT COLOSSAL HAND'S RIPPING THE ROOF RIGHT OFF THAT HOUSE! RUN FOR YOUR LIVES!
INSTANTLY, THE TEENAGE MAYOR RUSHES FROM HIS OFFICE...
DAD COULDN'T BE BEHIND THE HAND'S RETURN! HE'S STILL IN--OH, NO!... HE'S ESCAPED! THAT'S TERRIBLE!
DAILY GLOBE
PROF. HOLMES BREAKS JAIL
THE STAR
SWIFTLY, THE HEARTSICK YOUTH RACES HOME, HEATS UP HIS HAM RADIO, AND...
TOMMY! WHAT'S THIS AWFUL NEWS ABOUT THE SEPARATED MAN BEING BACK?
NO TIME TO EXPLAIN, AUNT MARTHA-- GOTTA GET HELP! MAYDAY! MIDVILLE CHAPTER CALLING TEEN TITANS!

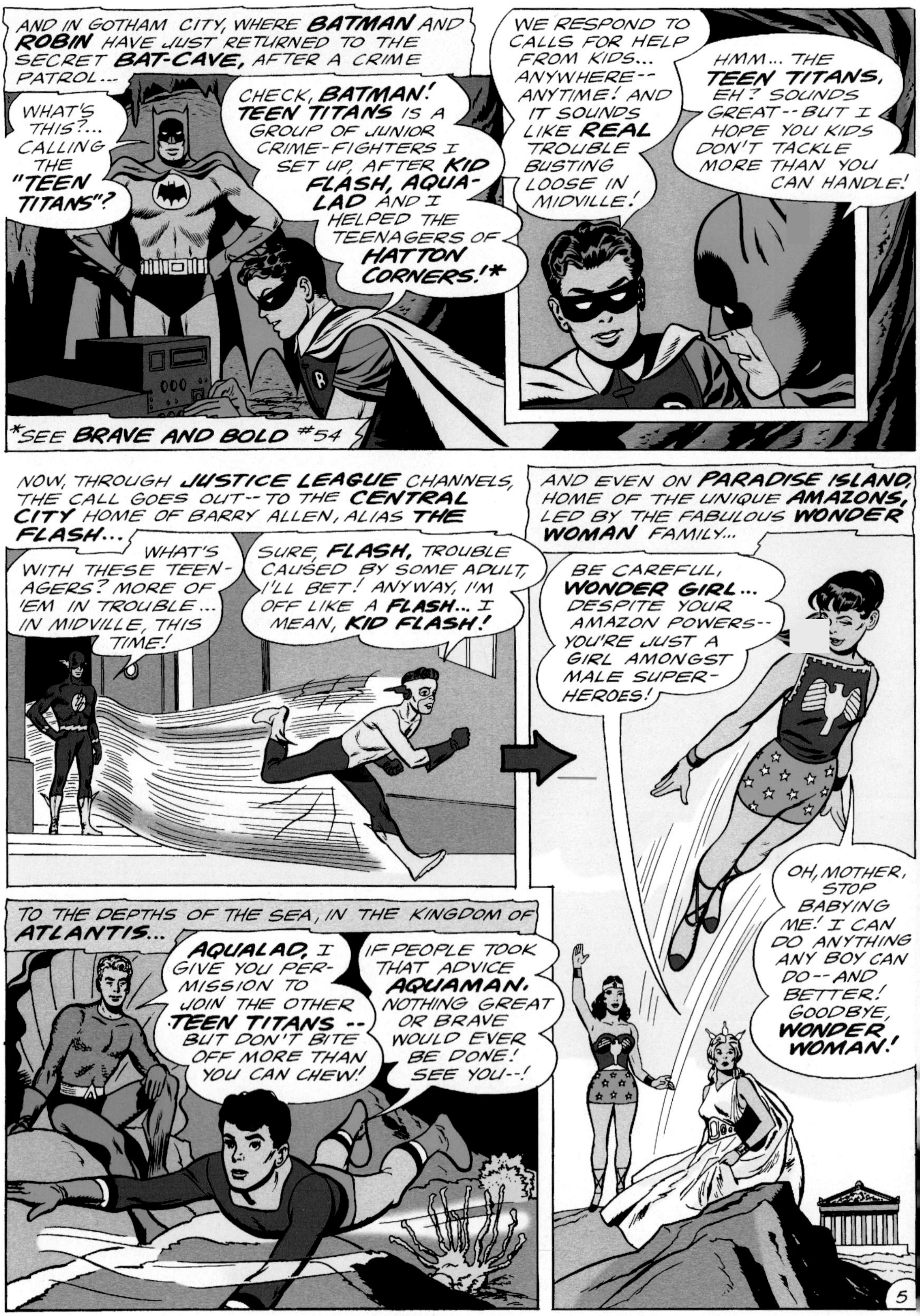
AND IN GOTHAM CITY, WHERE BATMAN AND ROBIN HAVE JUST RETURNED TO THE SECRET BAT-CAVE, AFTER A CRIME PATROL...
WHAT'S THIS?... CALLING THE "TEEN TITANS"?
CHECK, BATMAN! TEEN TITANS IS A GROUP OF JUNIOR CRIME-FIGHTERS I SET UP, AFTER KID FLASH, AQUALAD AND I HELPED THE TEENAGERS OF HATTON CORNERS!*
*SEE BRAVE AND BOLD #54
WE RESPOND TO CALLS FOR HELP FROM KIDS... ANYWHERE--ANYTIME! AND IT SOUNDS LIKE REAL TROUBLE BUSTING LOOSE IN MIDVILLE!
HMM... THE TEEN TITANS, EH? SOUNDS GREAT--BUT I HOPE YOU KIDS DON'T TACKLE MORE THAN YOU CAN HANDLE!
NOW, THROUGH JUSTICE LEAGUE CHANNELS, THE CALL GOES OUT--TO THE CENTRAL CITY HOME OF BARRY ALLEN, ALIAS THE FLASH...
WHAT'S WITH THESE TEEN-AGERS? MORE OF 'EM IN TROUBLE... IN MIDVILLE, THIS TIME!
SURE, FLASH, TROUBLE CAUSED BY SOME ADULT, I'LL BET! ANYWAY, I'M OFF LIKE A FLASH... I MEAN, KID FLASH!
AND EVEN ON PARADISE ISLAND, HOME OF THE UNIQUE AMAZONS, LED BY THE FABULOUS WONDER WOMAN FAMILY...
BE CAREFUL, WONDER GIRL... DESPITE YOUR AMAZON POWERS--YOU'RE JUST A GIRL AMONGST MALE SUPER-HEROES!
OH, MOTHER, STOP BABYING ME! I CAN DO ANYTHING ANY BOY CAN DO--AND BETTER! GOODBYE, WONDER WOMAN!
TO THE DEPTHS OF THE SEA, IN THE KINGDOM OF ATLANTIS...
AQUALAD, I GIVE YOU PERMISSION TO JOIN THE OTHER TEEN TITANS--BUT DON'T BITE OFF MORE THAN YOU CAN CHEW!
IF PEOPLE TOOK THAT ADVICE AQUAMAN, NOTHING GREAT OR BRAVE WOULD EVER BE DONE! SEE YOU--!

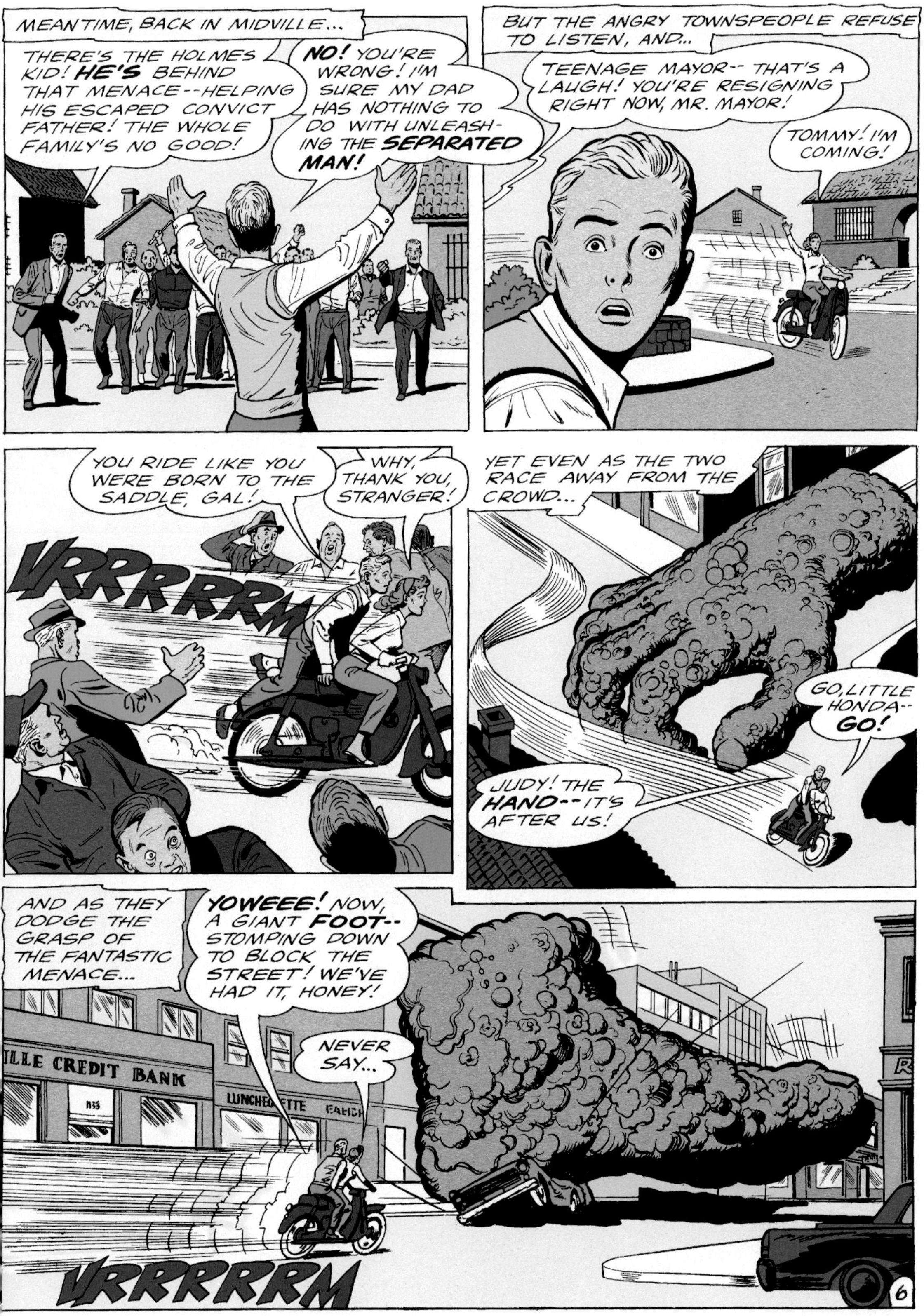
MEANTIME, BACK IN MIDVILLE...
THERE'S THE HOLMES KID! HE'S BEHIND THAT MENACE--HELPING HIS ESCAPED CONVICT FATHER! THE WHOLE FAMILY'S NO GOOD!
NO! YOU'RE WRONG! I'M SURE MY DAD HAS NOTHING TO DO WITH UNLEASHING THE SEPARATED MAN!
BUT THE ANGRY TOWNSPEOPLE REFUSE TO LISTEN, AND...
TEENAGE MAYOR-- THAT'S A LAUGH! YOU'RE RESIGNING RIGHT NOW, MR. MAYOR!
TOMMY! I'M COMING!
YOU RIDE LIKE YOU WERE BORN TO THE SADDLE, GAL!
WHY, THANK YOU, STRANGER!
VRRRRRM
YET EVEN AS THE TWO RACE AWAY FROM THE CROWD...
GO, LITTLE HONDA-- GO!
JUDY! THE HAND--IT'S AFTER US!
AND AS THEY DODGE THE GRASP OF THE FANTASTIC MENACE...
YOWEEE! NOW, A GIANT FOOT-- STOMPING DOWN TO BLOCK THE STREET! WE'VE HAD IT, HONEY!
NEVER SAY...
ILLE CREDIT BANK
LUNCHEONETTE
VRRRRRM
6

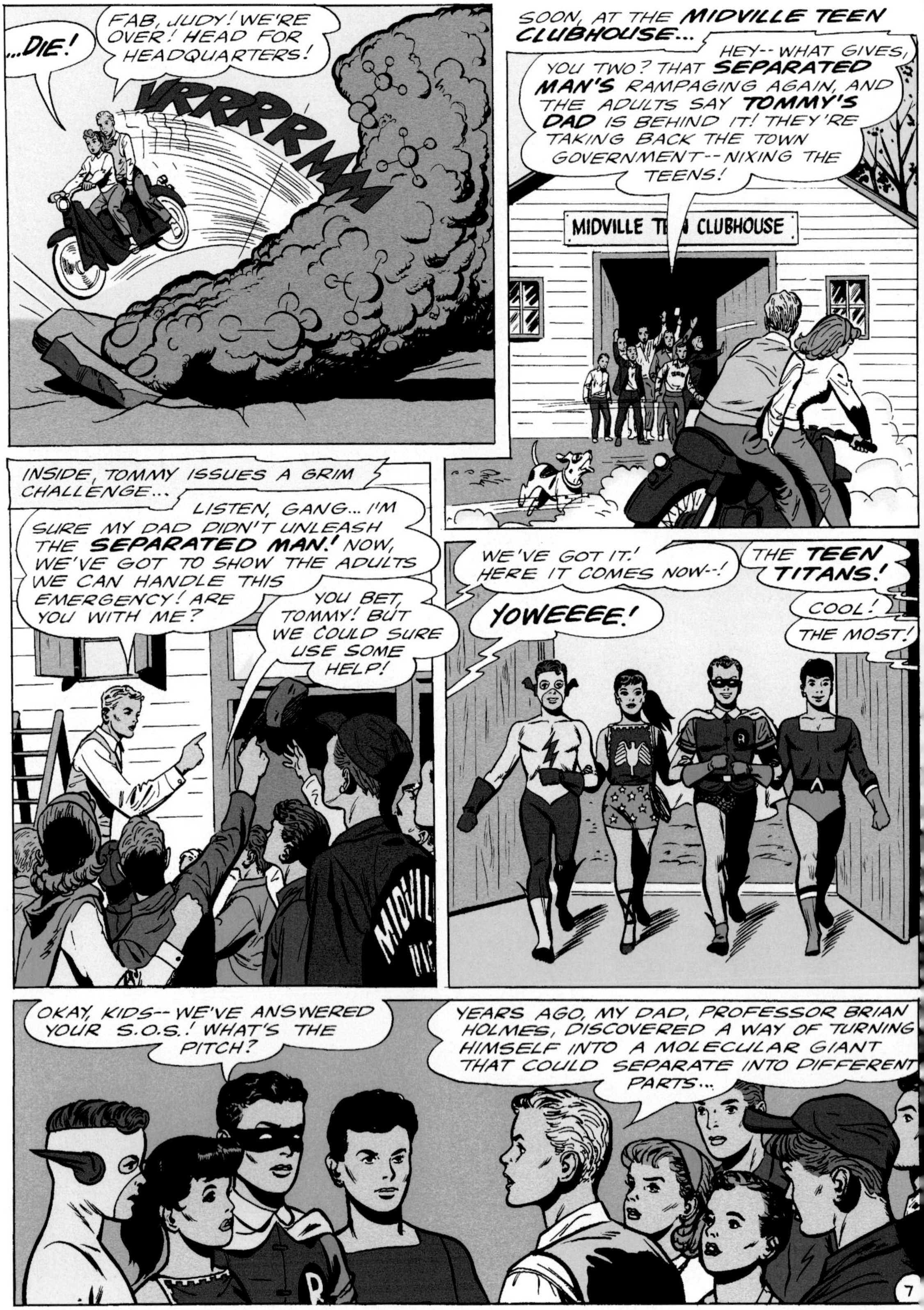
...DIE!
FAB, JUDY! WE'RE OVER! HEAD FOR HEADQUARTERS!
VRRRRMM
SOON, AT THE MIDVILLE TEEN CLUBHOUSE...
HEY-- WHAT GIVES, YOU TWO? THAT SEPARATED MAN'S RAMPAGING AGAIN, AND THE ADULTS SAY TOMMY'S DAD IS BEHIND IT! THEY'RE TAKING BACK THE TOWN GOVERNMENT-- NIXING THE TEENS!
MIDVILLE TEEN CLUBHOUSE
INSIDE, TOMMY ISSUES A GRIM CHALLENGE...
LISTEN, GANG... I'M SURE MY DAD DIDN'T UNLEASH THE SEPARATED MAN! NOW, WE'VE GOT TO SHOW THE ADULTS WE CAN HANDLE THIS EMERGENCY! ARE YOU WITH ME?
YOU BET, TOMMY! BUT WE COULD SURE USE SOME HELP!
WE'VE GOT IT! HERE IT COMES NOW--!
YOWEEEE!
THE TEEN TITANS!
COOL!
THE MOST!
OKAY, KIDS-- WE'VE ANSWERED YOUR S.O.S.! WHAT'S THE PITCH?
YEARS AGO, MY DAD, PROFESSOR BRIAN HOLMES, DISCOVERED A WAY OF TURNING HIMSELF INTO A MOLECULAR GIANT THAT COULD SEPARATE INTO DIFFERENT PARTS...

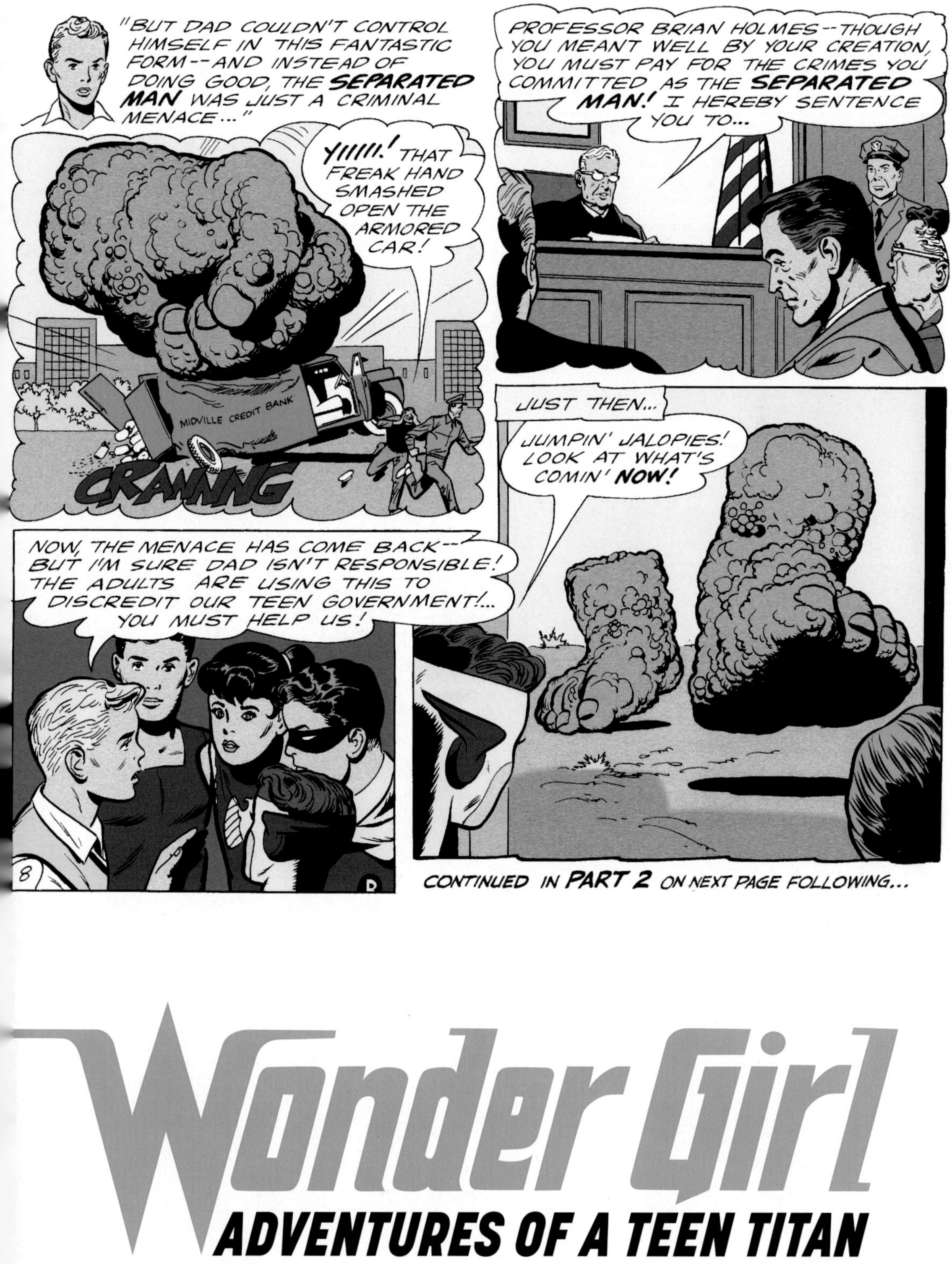
"BUT DAD COULDN'T CONTROL HIMSELF IN THIS FANTASTIC FORM--AND INSTEAD OF DOING GOOD, THE SEPARATED MAN WAS JUST A CRIMINAL MENACE..."
YIIIII.! THAT FREAK HAND SMASHED OPEN THE ARMORED CAR!
MIDVILLE CREDIT BANK
CRANNNG
PROFESSOR BRIAN HOLMES--THOUGH YOU MEANT WELL BY YOUR CREATION, YOU MUST PAY FOR THE CRIMES YOU COMMITTED AS THE SEPARATED MAN! I HEREBY SENTENCE YOU TO...
NOW, THE MENACE HAS COME BACK--BUT I'M SURE DAD ISN'T RESPONSIBLE! THE ADULTS ARE USING THIS TO DISCREDIT OUR TEEN GOVERNMENT!... YOU MUST HELP US!
8
JUST THEN...
JUMPIN' JALOPIES! LOOK AT WHAT'S COMIN' NOW!

CONTINUED IN **PART 2** ON NEXT PAGE FOLLOWING...

Wonder Girl
ADVENTURES OF A TEEN TITAN

the ASTOUNDING SEPARATED MAN PART 2

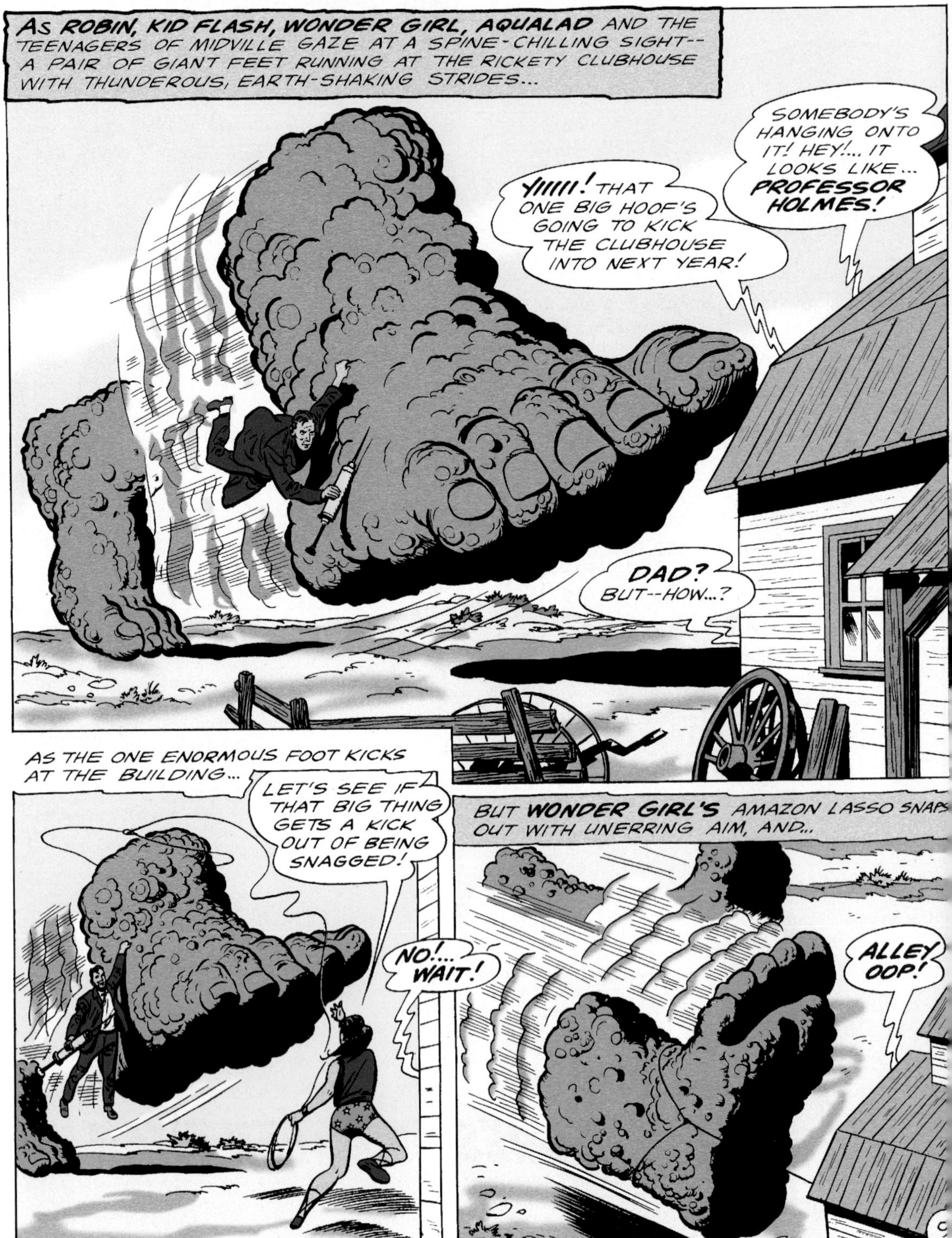

AS ROBIN, KID FLASH, WONDER GIRL, AQUALAD AND THE TEENAGERS OF MIDVILLE GAZE AT A SPINE-CHILLING SIGHT-- A PAIR OF GIANT FEET RUNNING AT THE RICKETY CLUBHOUSE WITH THUNDEROUS, EARTH-SHAKING STRIDES...
YIIIII! THAT ONE BIG HOOF'S GOING TO KICK THE CLUBHOUSE INTO NEXT YEAR!
SOMEBODY'S HANGING ONTO IT! HEY!... IT LOOKS LIKE... PROFESSOR HOLMES!
DAD? BUT--HOW...?
AS THE ONE ENORMOUS FOOT KICKS AT THE BUILDING...
LET'S SEE IF THAT BIG THING GETS A KICK OUT OF BEING SNAGGED!
NO!... WAIT!
BUT WONDER GIRL'S AMAZON LASSO SNAPS OUT WITH UNERRING AIM, AND...
ALLEY OOP!

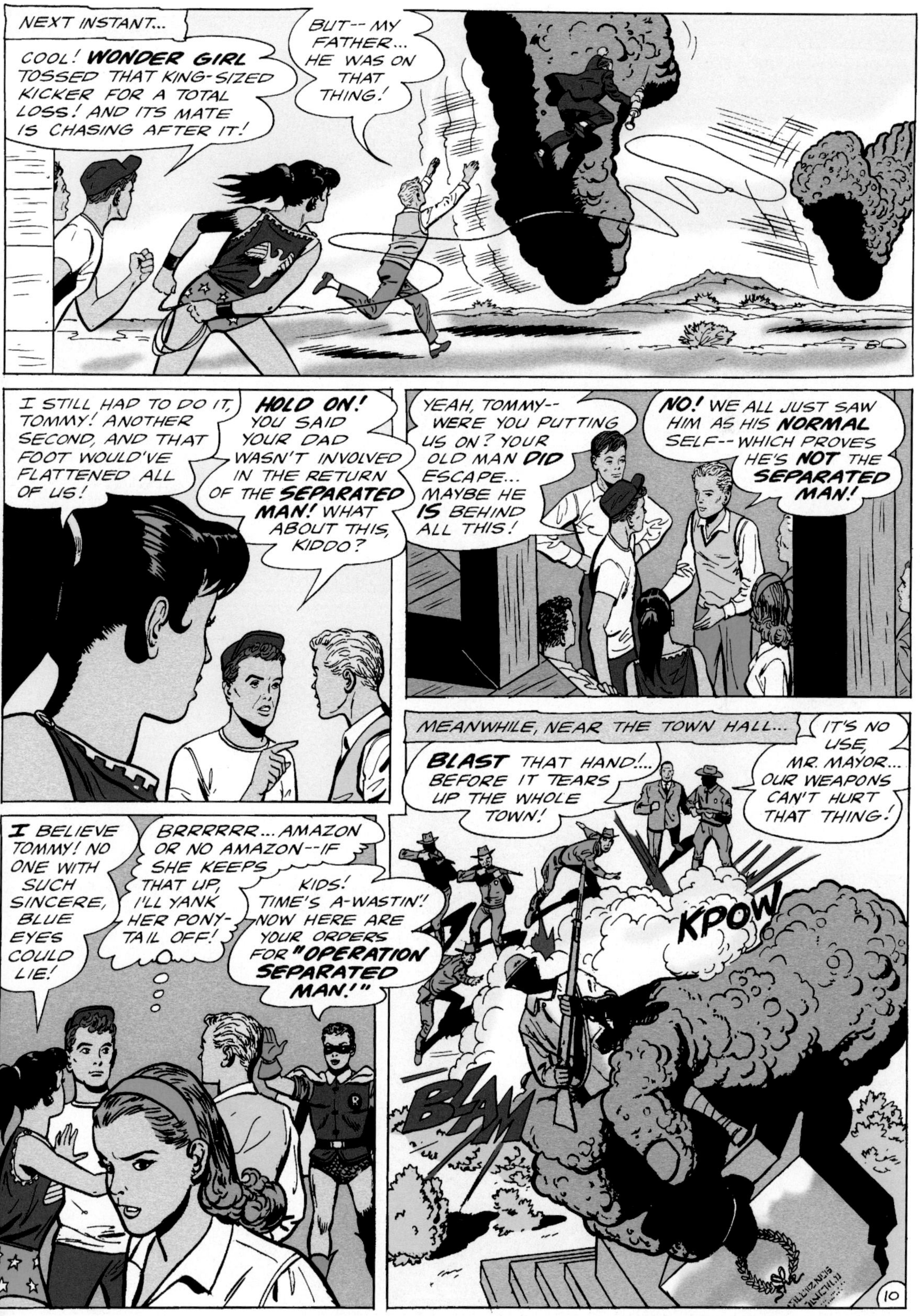
NEXT INSTANT...
COOL! WONDER GIRL TOSSED THAT KING-SIZED KICKER FOR A TOTAL LOSS! AND ITS MATE IS CHASING AFTER IT!
BUT-- MY FATHER... HE WAS ON THAT THING!
I STILL HAD TO DO IT, TOMMY! ANOTHER SECOND, AND THAT FOOT WOULD'VE FLATTENED ALL OF US!
HOLD ON! YOU SAID YOUR DAD WASN'T INVOLVED IN THE RETURN OF THE SEPARATED MAN! WHAT ABOUT THIS, KIDDO?
YEAH, TOMMY-- WERE YOU PUTTING US ON? YOUR OLD MAN DID ESCAPE... MAYBE HE IS BEHIND ALL THIS!
NO! WE ALL JUST SAW HIM AS HIS NORMAL SELF--WHICH PROVES HE'S NOT THE SEPARATED MAN!
I BELIEVE TOMMY! NO ONE WITH SUCH SINCERE, BLUE EYES COULD LIE!
BRRRRRR... AMAZON OR NO AMAZON--IF SHE KEEPS THAT UP, I'LL YANK HER PONY-TAIL OFF!
KIDS! TIME'S A-WASTIN'! NOW HERE ARE YOUR ORDERS FOR "OPERATION SEPARATED MAN!"
MEANWHILE, NEAR THE TOWN HALL...
BLAST THAT HAND!... BEFORE IT TEARS UP THE WHOLE TOWN!
IT'S NO USE, MR. MAYOR... OUR WEAPONS CAN'T HURT THAT THING!
KPOW
BLAM
10

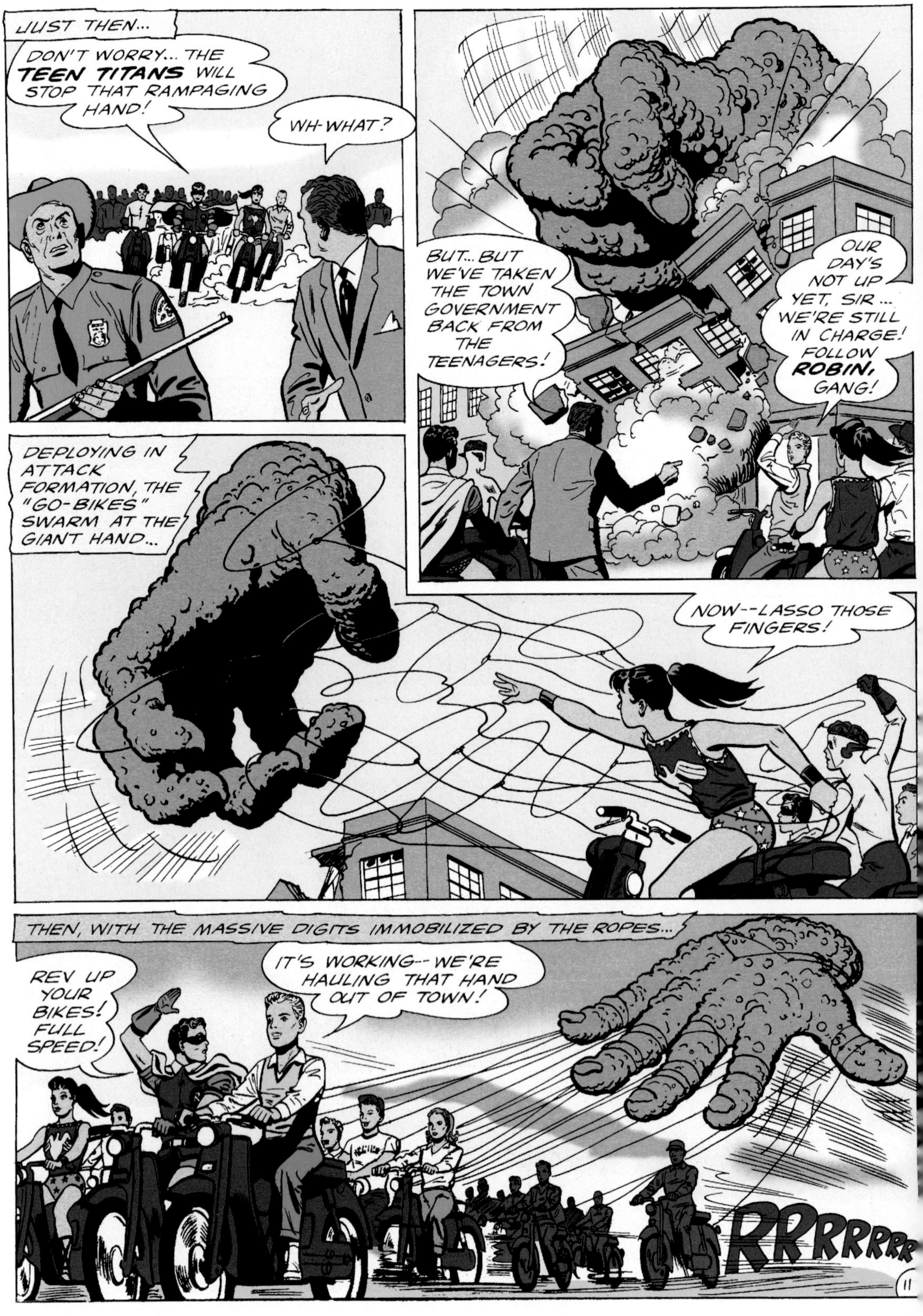
JUST THEN...
DON'T WORRY... THE TEEN TITANS WILL STOP THAT RAMPAGING HAND!
WH-WHAT?
BUT... BUT WE'VE TAKEN THE TOWN GOVERNMENT BACK FROM THE TEENAGERS!
OUR DAY'S NOT UP YET, SIR... WE'RE STILL IN CHARGE! FOLLOW ROBIN, GANG!
DEPLOYING IN ATTACK FORMATION, THE "GO-BIKES" SWARM AT THE GIANT HAND...
NOW--LASSO THOSE FINGERS!
THEN, WITH THE MASSIVE DIGITS IMMOBILIZED BY THE ROPES...
REV UP YOUR BIKES! FULL SPEED!
IT'S WORKING--WE'RE HAULING THAT HAND OUT OF TOWN!
RRRRRRRR

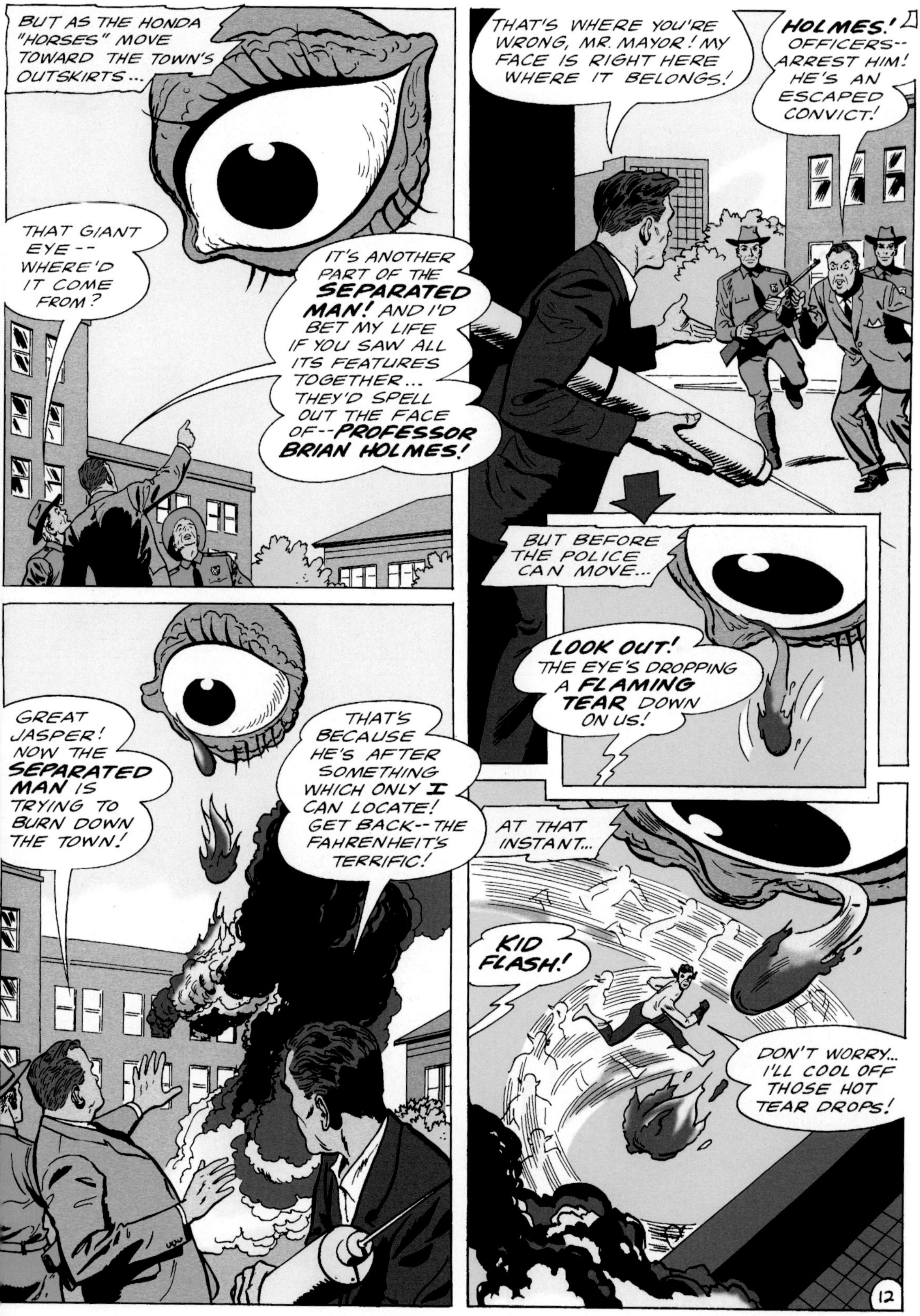

BUT AS THE HONDA "HORSES" MOVE TOWARD THE TOWN'S OUTSKIRTS...
THAT GIANT EYE -- WHERE'D IT COME FROM?
IT'S ANOTHER PART OF THE SEPARATED MAN! AND I'D BET MY LIFE IF YOU SAW ALL ITS FEATURES TOGETHER... THEY'D SPELL OUT THE FACE OF--PROFESSOR BRIAN HOLMES!
THAT'S WHERE YOU'RE WRONG, MR. MAYOR! MY FACE IS RIGHT HERE WHERE IT BELONGS!
HOLMES! OFFICERS-- ARREST HIM! HE'S AN ESCAPED CONVICT!
BUT BEFORE THE POLICE CAN MOVE...
LOOK OUT! THE EYE'S DROPPING A FLAMING TEAR DOWN ON US!
GREAT JASPER! NOW THE SEPARATED MAN IS TRYING TO BURN DOWN THE TOWN!
THAT'S BECAUSE HE'S AFTER SOMETHING WHICH ONLY I CAN LOCATE! GET BACK--THE FAHRENHEIT'S TERRIFIC!
AT THAT INSTANT...
KID FLASH!
DON'T WORRY... I'LL COOL OFF THOSE HOT TEAR DROPS!

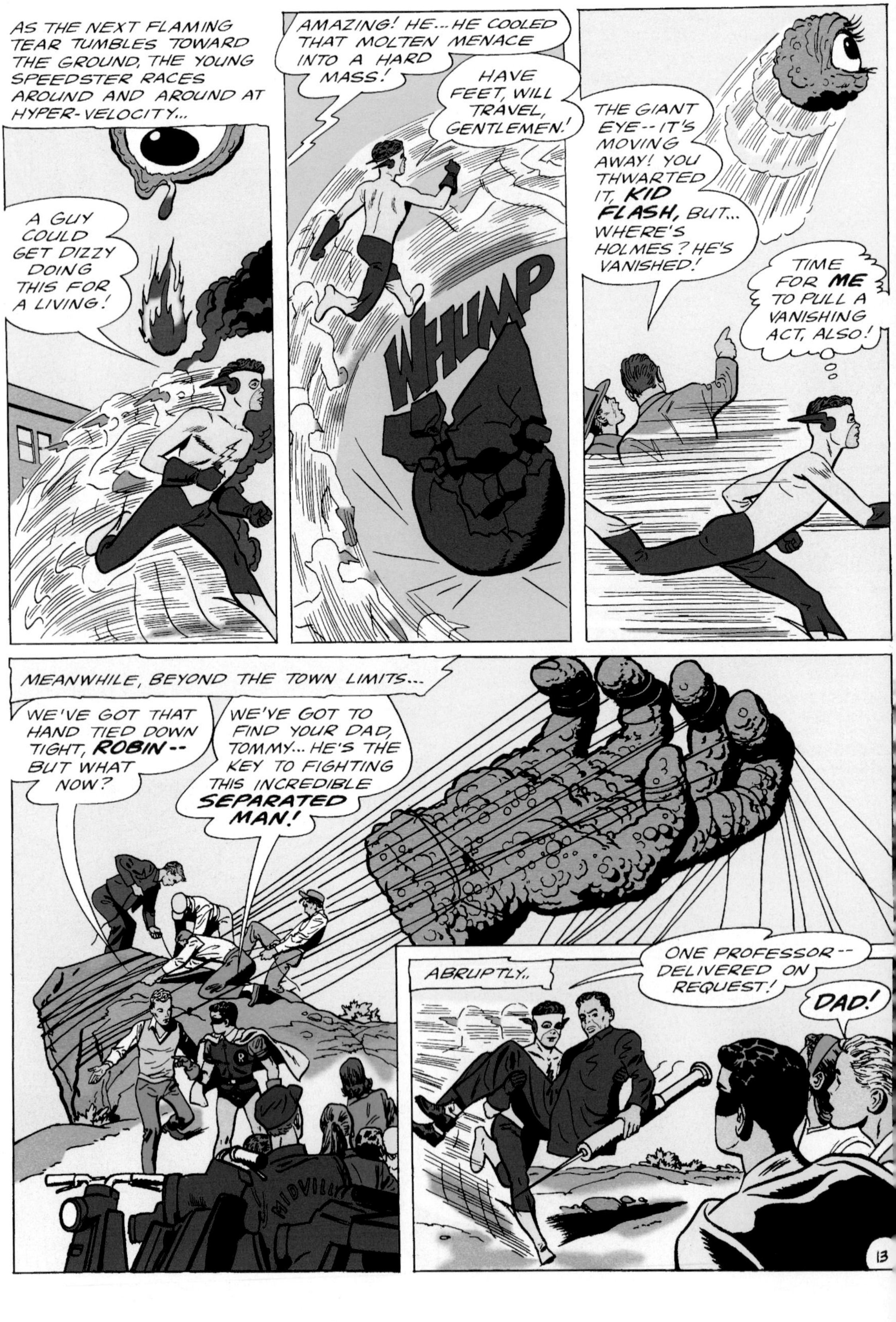
AS THE NEXT FLAMING TEAR TUMBLES TOWARD THE GROUND, THE YOUNG SPEEDSTER RACES AROUND AND AROUND AT HYPER-VELOCITY...
A GUY COULD GET DIZZY DOING THIS FOR A LIVING!
AMAZING! HE... HE COOLED THAT MOLTEN MENACE INTO A HARD MASS!
HAVE FEET, WILL TRAVEL, GENTLEMEN!
WHUMP
THE GIANT EYE -- IT'S MOVING AWAY! YOU THWARTED IT, KID FLASH, BUT... WHERE'S HOLMES? HE'S VANISHED!
TIME FOR ME TO PULL A VANISHING ACT, ALSO!
MEANWHILE, BEYOND THE TOWN LIMITS...
WE'VE GOT THAT HAND TIED DOWN TIGHT, ROBIN -- BUT WHAT NOW?
WE'VE GOT TO FIND YOUR DAD, TOMMY... HE'S THE KEY TO FIGHTING THIS INCREDIBLE SEPARATED MAN!
MIDVILLE
ABRUPTLY..
ONE PROFESSOR -- DELIVERED ON REQUEST!
DAD!

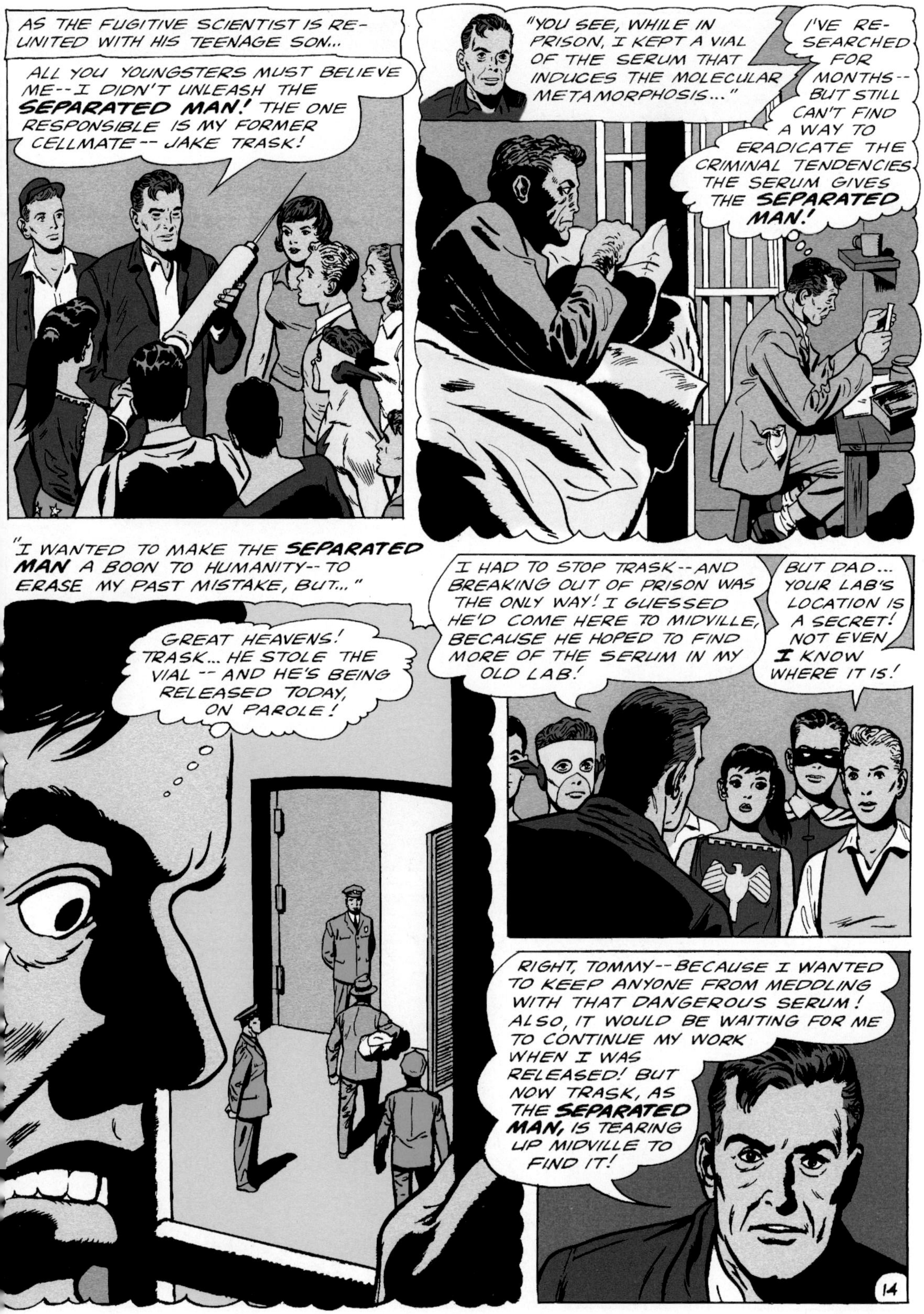

AS THE FUGITIVE SCIENTIST IS RE-UNITED WITH HIS TEENAGE SON...
ALL YOU YOUNGSTERS MUST BELIEVE ME--I DIDN'T UNLEASH THE SEPARATED MAN! THE ONE RESPONSIBLE IS MY FORMER CELLMATE-- JAKE TRASK!
"YOU SEE, WHILE IN PRISON, I KEPT A VIAL OF THE SERUM THAT INDUCES THE MOLECULAR METAMORPHOSIS..."
I'VE RE-SEARCHED FOR MONTHS-- BUT STILL CAN'T FIND A WAY TO ERADICATE THE CRIMINAL TENDENCIES THE SERUM GIVES THE SEPARATED MAN!
"I WANTED TO MAKE THE SEPARATED MAN A BOON TO HUMANITY-- TO ERASE MY PAST MISTAKE, BUT..."
GREAT HEAVENS! TRASK... HE STOLE THE VIAL -- AND HE'S BEING RELEASED TODAY, ON PAROLE!
I HAD TO STOP TRASK--AND BREAKING OUT OF PRISON WAS THE ONLY WAY! I GUESSED HE'D COME HERE TO MIDVILLE, BECAUSE HE HOPED TO FIND MORE OF THE SERUM IN MY OLD LAB!
BUT DAD... YOUR LAB'S LOCATION IS A SECRET! NOT EVEN I KNOW WHERE IT IS!
RIGHT, TOMMY--BECAUSE I WANTED TO KEEP ANYONE FROM MEDDLING WITH THAT DANGEROUS SERUM! ALSO, IT WOULD BE WAITING FOR ME TO CONTINUE MY WORK WHEN I WAS RELEASED! BUT NOW TRASK, AS THE SEPARATED MAN, IS TEARING UP MIDVILLE TO FIND IT!
14

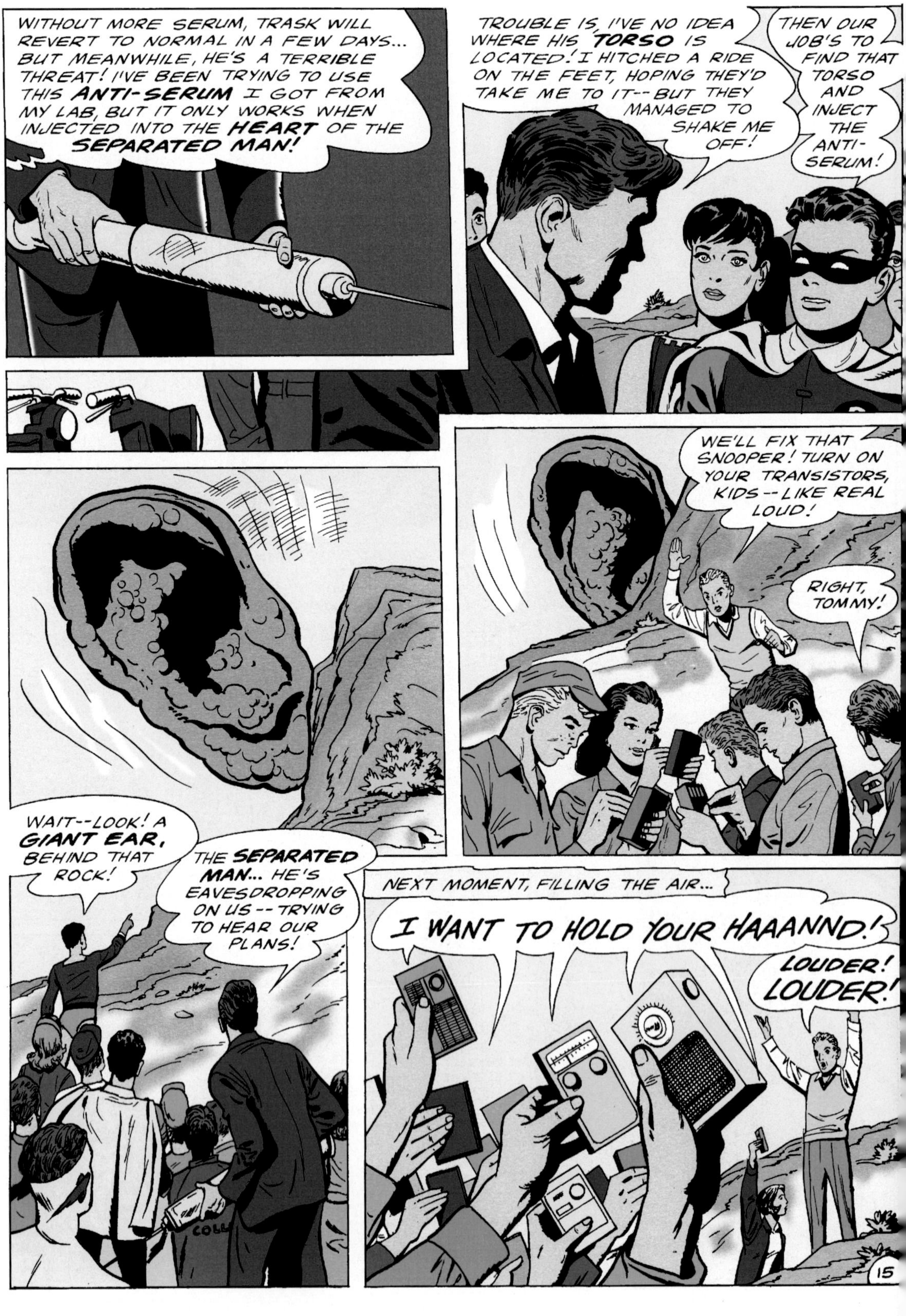
WITHOUT MORE SERUM, TRASK WILL REVERT TO NORMAL IN A FEW DAYS... BUT MEANWHILE, HE'S A TERRIBLE THREAT! I'VE BEEN TRYING TO USE THIS ANTI-SERUM I GOT FROM MY LAB, BUT IT ONLY WORKS WHEN INJECTED INTO THE HEART OF THE SEPARATED MAN!
TROUBLE IS, I'VE NO IDEA WHERE HIS TORSO IS LOCATED! I HITCHED A RIDE ON THE FEET, HOPING THEY'D TAKE ME TO IT--BUT THEY MANAGED TO SHAKE ME OFF!
THEN OUR JOB'S TO FIND THAT TORSO AND INJECT THE ANTI-SERUM!
WE'LL FIX THAT SNOOPER! TURN ON YOUR TRANSISTORS, KIDS--LIKE REAL LOUD!
RIGHT, TOMMY!
WAIT--LOOK! A GIANT EAR, BEHIND THAT ROCK!
THE SEPARATED MAN... HE'S EAVESDROPPING ON US--TRYING TO HEAR OUR PLANS!
NEXT MOMENT, FILLING THE AIR...
I WANT TO HOLD YOUR HAAANND!
LOUDER! LOUDER!

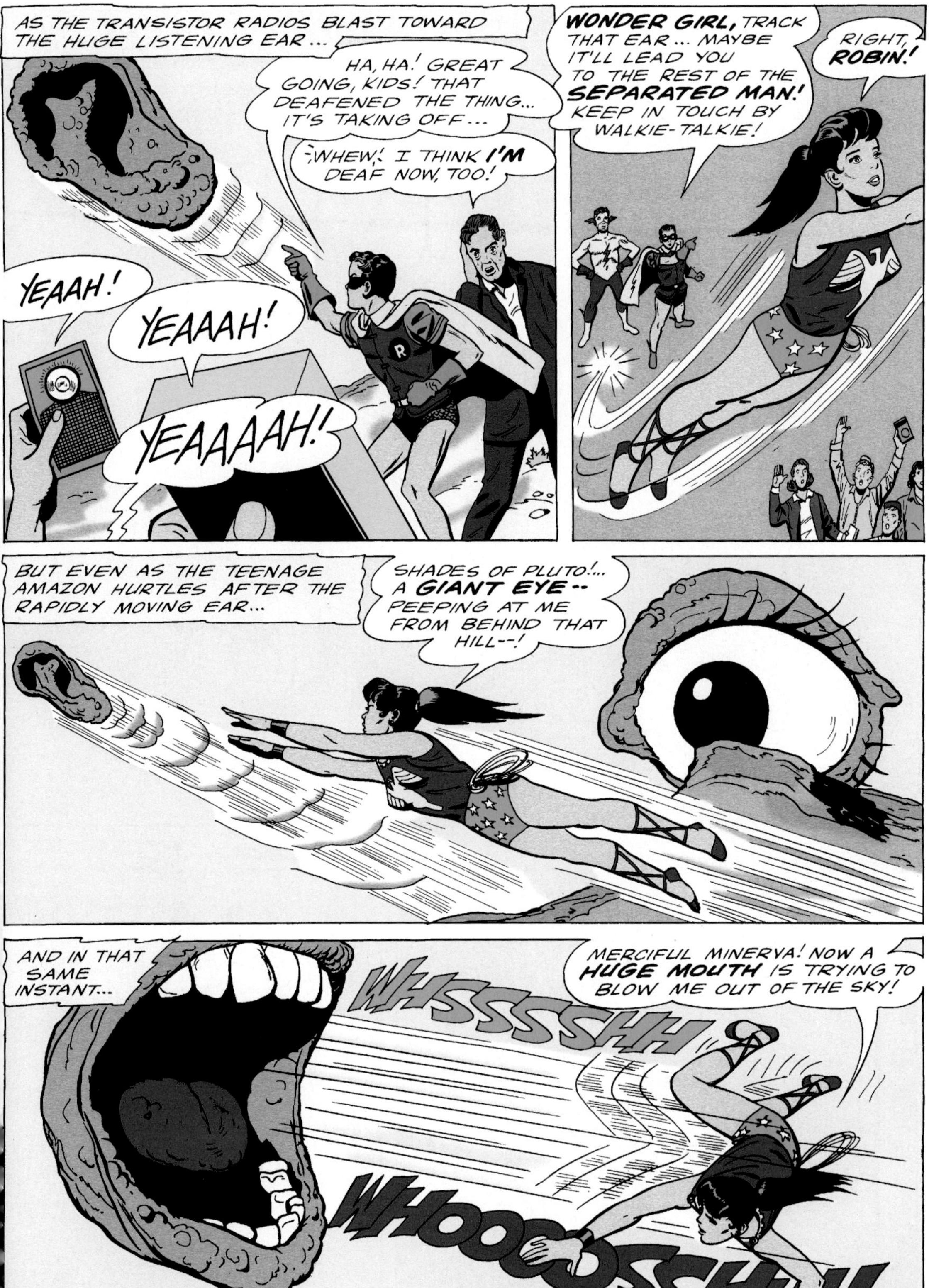

AS THE TRANSISTOR RADIOS BLAST TOWARD THE HUGE LISTENING EAR...
HA, HA! GREAT GOING, KIDS! THAT DEAFENED THE THING... IT'S TAKING OFF...
WHEW! I THINK I'M DEAF NOW, TOO!
YEAAH!
YEAAAH!
YEAAAAH!
WONDER GIRL, TRACK THAT EAR... MAYBE IT'LL LEAD YOU TO THE REST OF THE SEPARATED MAN! KEEP IN TOUCH BY WALKIE-TALKIE!
RIGHT, ROBIN!
BUT EVEN AS THE TEENAGE AMAZON HURTLES AFTER THE RAPIDLY MOVING EAR...
SHADES OF PLUTO!... A GIANT EYE-- PEEPING AT ME FROM BEHIND THAT HILL--!
AND IN THAT SAME INSTANT...
MERCIFUL MINERVA! NOW A HUGE MOUTH IS TRYING TO BLOW ME OUT OF THE SKY!
WHSSSSHH
WHOOOOSCHHH
CONTINUED IN PART 3 ON THE NEXT PAGE FOLLOWING
16

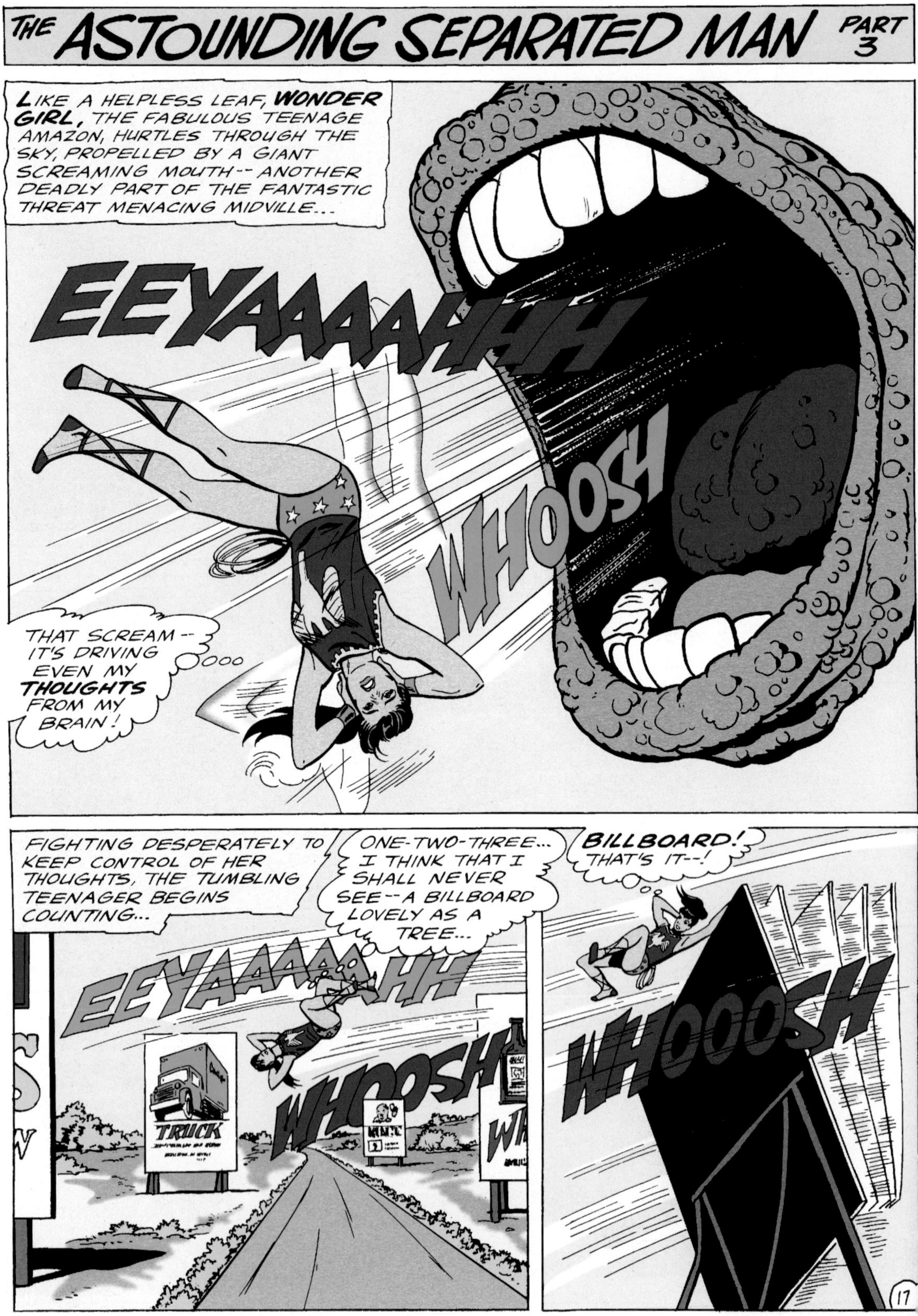

THE ASTOUNDING SEPARATED MAN PART 3
LIKE A HELPLESS LEAF, WONDER GIRL, THE FABULOUS TEENAGE AMAZON, HURTLES THROUGH THE SKY, PROPELLED BY A GIANT SCREAMING MOUTH -- ANOTHER DEADLY PART OF THE FANTASTIC THREAT MENACING MIDVILLE...
EEYAAAAAHHH
WHOOSH
THAT SCREAM -- IT'S DRIVING EVEN MY THOUGHTS FROM MY BRAIN!
FIGHTING DESPERATELY TO KEEP CONTROL OF HER THOUGHTS, THE TUMBLING TEENAGER BEGINS COUNTING...
ONE-TWO-THREE... I THINK THAT I SHALL NEVER SEE -- A BILLBOARD LOVELY AS A TREE...
EEYAAAAAHH
WHOOSH
TRUCK
BILLBOARD! THAT'S IT--!
WHOOOOSH
17

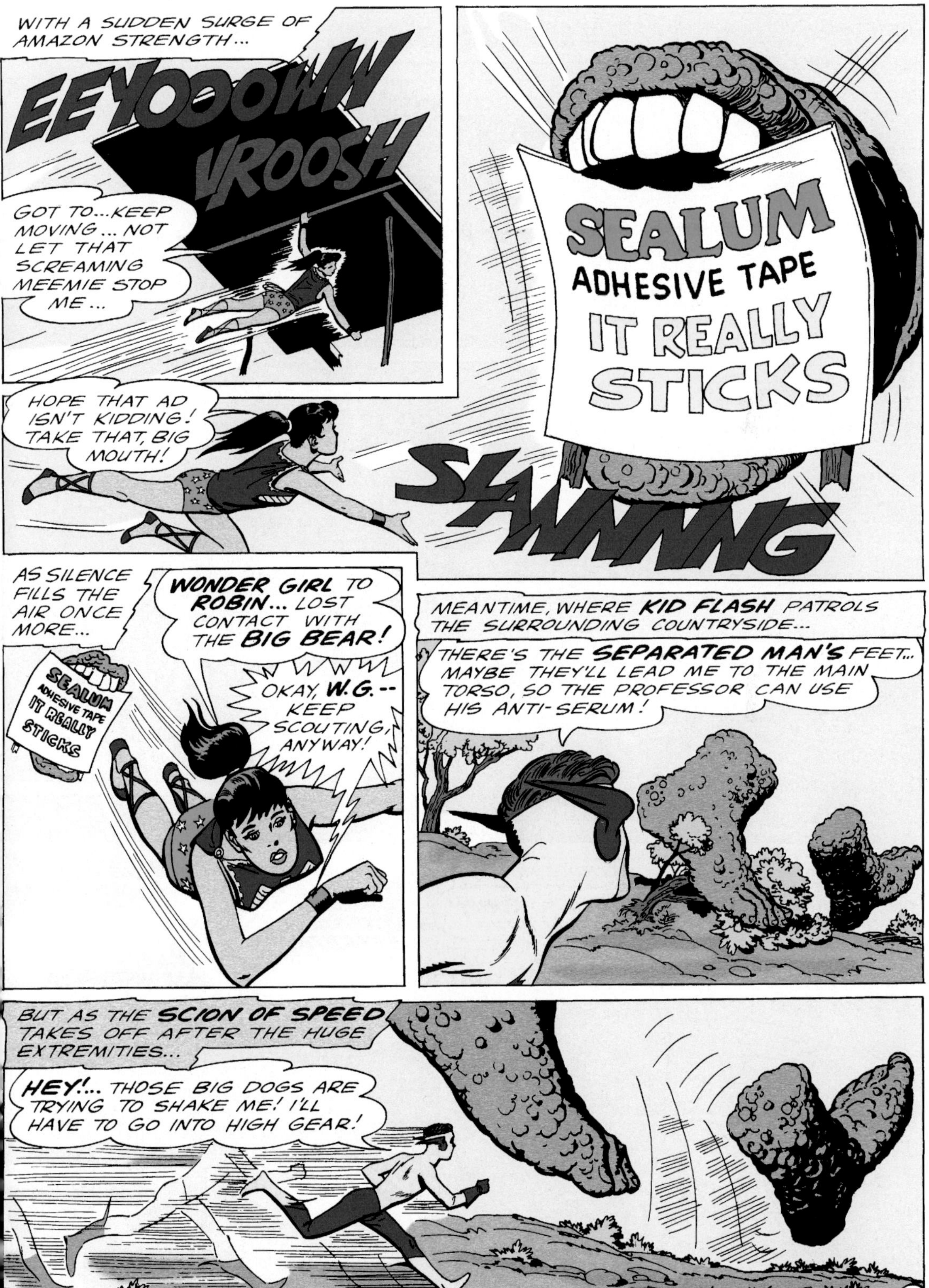

WITH A SUDDEN SURGE OF AMAZON STRENGTH...
EEYOOOWN
VROOSH
GOT TO...KEEP MOVING... NOT LET THAT SCREAMING MEEMIE STOP ME...
SEALUM
ADHESIVE TAPE
IT REALLY STICKS
HOPE THAT AD ISN'T KIDDING! TAKE THAT, BIG MOUTH!
SLANNNG
AS SILENCE FILLS THE AIR ONCE MORE...
WONDER GIRL TO ROBIN... LOST CONTACT WITH THE BIG BEAR!
OKAY, W.G.-- KEEP SCOUTING, ANYWAY!
SEALUM ADHESIVE TAPE IT REALLY STICKS
MEANTIME, WHERE KID FLASH PATROLS THE SURROUNDING COUNTRYSIDE...
THERE'S THE SEPARATED MAN'S FEET... MAYBE THEY'LL LEAD ME TO THE MAIN TORSO, SO THE PROFESSOR CAN USE HIS ANTI-SERUM!
BUT AS THE SCION OF SPEED TAKES OFF AFTER THE HUGE EXTREMITIES...
HEY!... THOSE BIG DOGS ARE TRYING TO SHAKE ME! I'LL HAVE TO GO INTO HIGH GEAR!

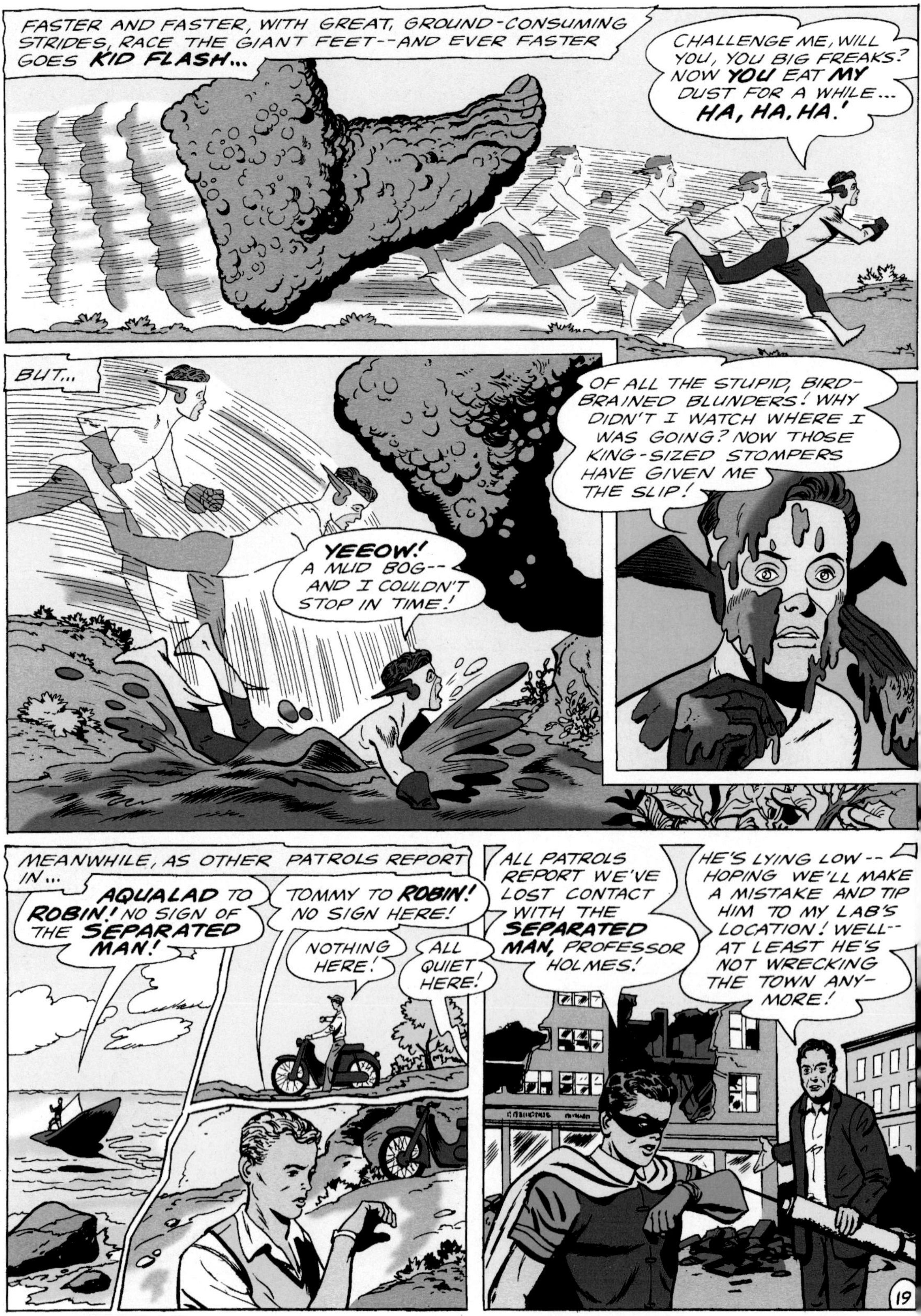
FASTER AND FASTER, WITH GREAT, GROUND-CONSUMING STRIDES, RACE THE GIANT FEET--AND EVER FASTER GOES KID FLASH...
CHALLENGE ME, WILL YOU, YOU BIG FREAKS? NOW YOU EAT MY DUST FOR A WHILE... HA, HA, HA!
BUT...
YEEOW! A MUD BOG--AND I COULDN'T STOP IN TIME!
OF ALL THE STUPID, BIRD-BRAINED BLUNDERS! WHY DIDN'T I WATCH WHERE I WAS GOING? NOW THOSE KING-SIZED STOMPERS HAVE GIVEN ME THE SLIP!
MEANWHILE, AS OTHER PATROLS REPORT IN...
AQUALAD TO ROBIN! NO SIGN OF THE SEPARATED MAN!
TOMMY TO ROBIN! NO SIGN HERE!
NOTHING HERE!
ALL QUIET HERE!
ALL PATROLS REPORT WE'VE LOST CONTACT WITH THE SEPARATED MAN, PROFESSOR HOLMES!
HE'S LYING LOW--HOPING WE'LL MAKE A MISTAKE AND TIP HIM TO MY LAB'S LOCATION! WELL--AT LEAST HE'S NOT WRECKING THE TOWN ANYMORE!

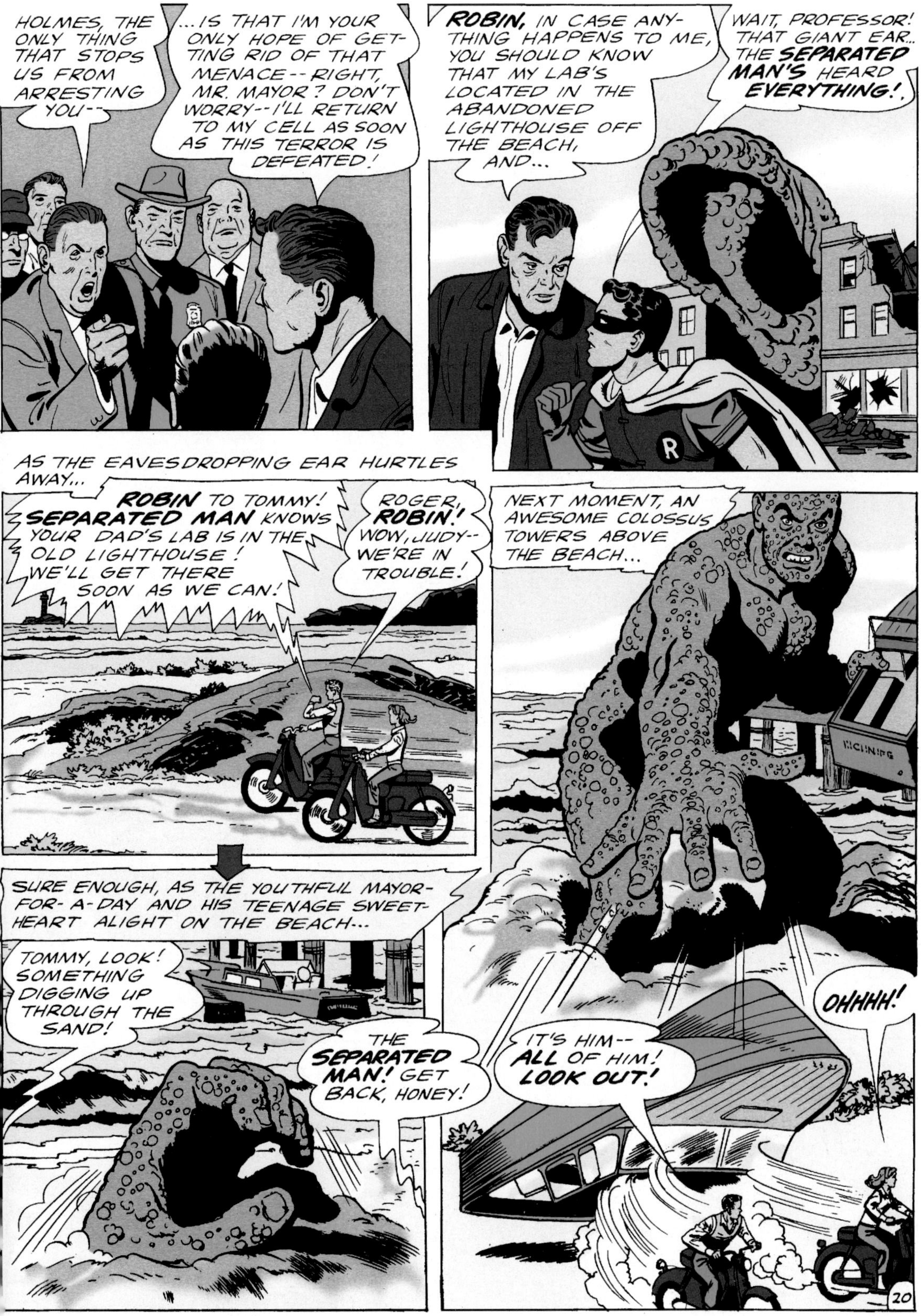
HOLMES, THE ONLY THING THAT STOPS US FROM ARRESTING YOU--
...IS THAT I'M YOUR ONLY HOPE OF GETTING RID OF THAT MENACE--RIGHT, MR. MAYOR? DON'T WORRY--I'LL RETURN TO MY CELL AS SOON AS THIS TERROR IS DEFEATED!
ROBIN, IN CASE ANYTHING HAPPENS TO ME, YOU SHOULD KNOW THAT MY LAB'S LOCATED IN THE ABANDONED LIGHTHOUSE OFF THE BEACH, AND...
WAIT, PROFESSOR! THAT GIANT EAR... THE SEPARATED MAN'S HEARD EVERYTHING!
AS THE EAVESDROPPING EAR HURTLES AWAY...
ROBIN TO TOMMY! SEPARATED MAN KNOWS YOUR DAD'S LAB IS IN THE OLD LIGHTHOUSE! WE'LL GET THERE SOON AS WE CAN!
ROGER, ROBIN! WOW, JUDY-- WE'RE IN TROUBLE!
NEXT MOMENT, AN AWESOME COLOSSUS TOWERS ABOVE THE BEACH...
SURE ENOUGH, AS THE YOUTHFUL MAYOR-FOR-A-DAY AND HIS TEENAGE SWEETHEART ALIGHT ON THE BEACH...
TOMMY, LOOK! SOMETHING DIGGING UP THROUGH THE SAND!
THE SEPARATED MAN! GET BACK, HONEY!
OHHHH!
IT'S HIM-- ALL OF HIM! LOOK OUT!
20

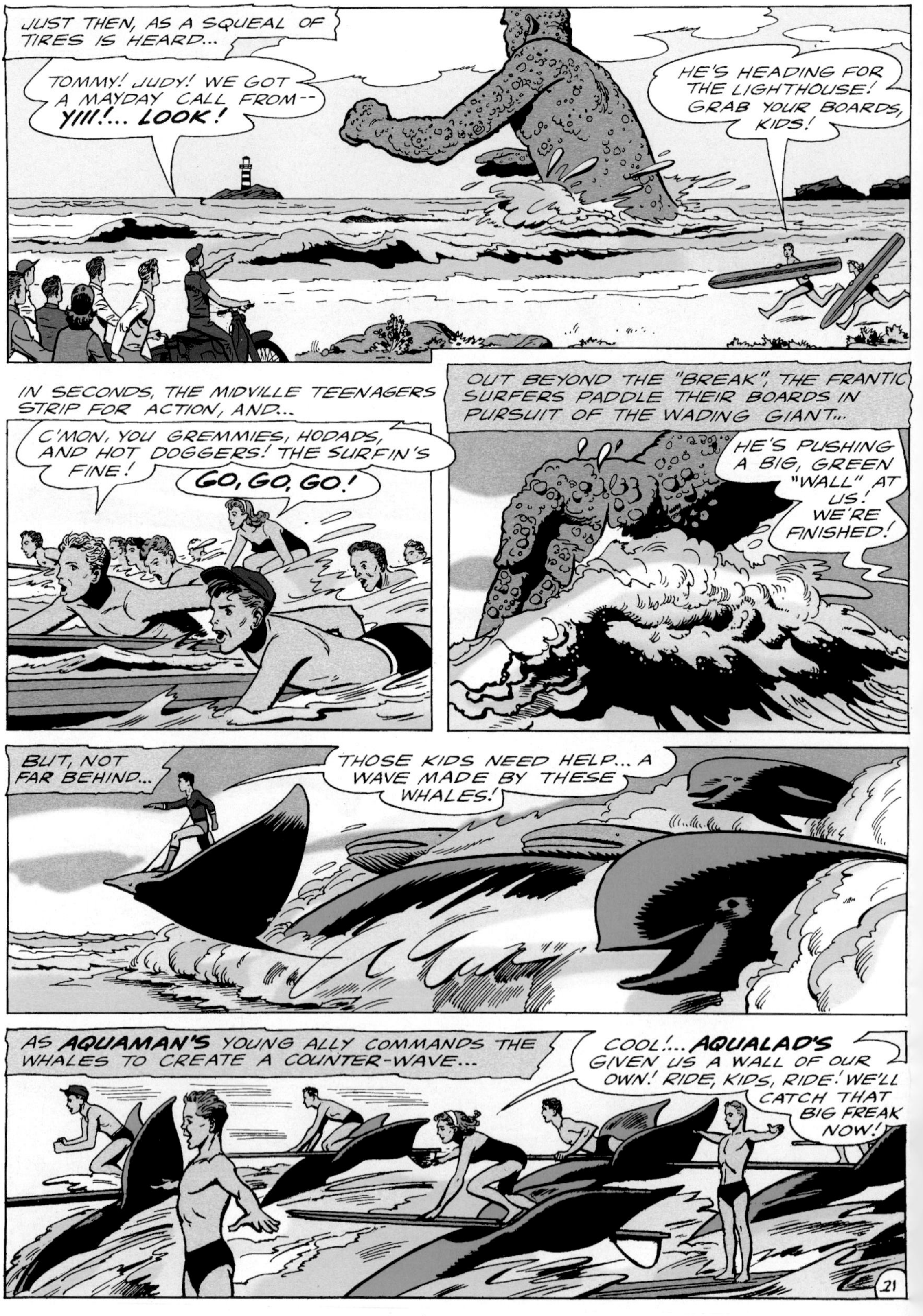
JUST THEN, AS A SQUEAL OF TIRES IS HEARD...
TOMMY! JUDY! WE GOT A MAYDAY CALL FROM-- YIII!... LOOK!
HE'S HEADING FOR THE LIGHTHOUSE! GRAB YOUR BOARDS, KIDS!
IN SECONDS, THE MIDVILLE TEENAGERS STRIP FOR ACTION, AND...
C'MON, YOU GREMMIES, HODADS, AND HOT DOGGERS! THE SURFIN'S FINE!
GO, GO, GO!
OUT BEYOND THE "BREAK", THE FRANTIC SURFERS PADDLE THEIR BOARDS IN PURSUIT OF THE WADING GIANT...
HE'S PUSHING A BIG, GREEN "WALL" AT US! WE'RE FINISHED!
BUT, NOT FAR BEHIND...
THOSE KIDS NEED HELP... A WAVE MADE BY THESE WHALES!
AS AQUAMAN'S YOUNG ALLY COMMANDS THE WHALES TO CREATE A COUNTER-WAVE...
COOL!... AQUALAD'S GIVEN US A WALL OF OUR OWN! RIDE, KIDS, RIDE! WE'LL CATCH THAT BIG FREAK NOW!
21

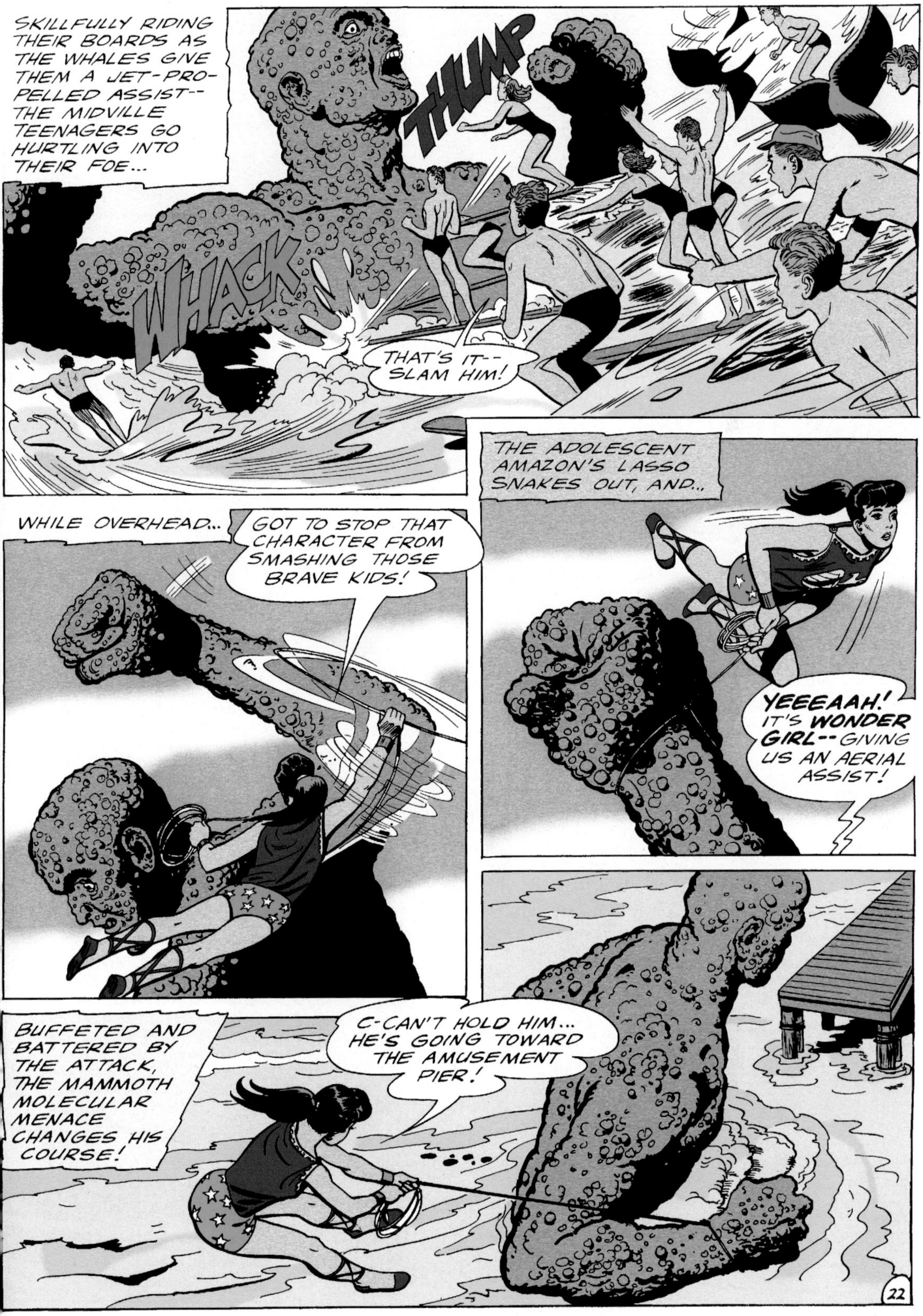
SKILLFULLY RIDING THEIR BOARDS AS THE WHALES GIVE THEM A JET-PROPELLED ASSIST-- THE MIDVILLE TEENAGERS GO HURTLING INTO THEIR FOE...
THUMP
WHACK
THAT'S IT-- SLAM HIM!
WHILE OVERHEAD...
GOT TO STOP THAT CHARACTER FROM SMASHING THOSE BRAVE KIDS!
THE ADOLESCENT AMAZON'S LASSO SNAKES OUT, AND...
YEEEAAH! IT'S WONDER GIRL-- GIVING US AN AERIAL ASSIST!
BUFFETED AND BATTERED BY THE ATTACK, THE MAMMOTH MOLECULAR MENACE CHANGES HIS COURSE!
C-CAN'T HOLD HIM... HE'S GOING TOWARD THE AMUSEMENT PIER!
22

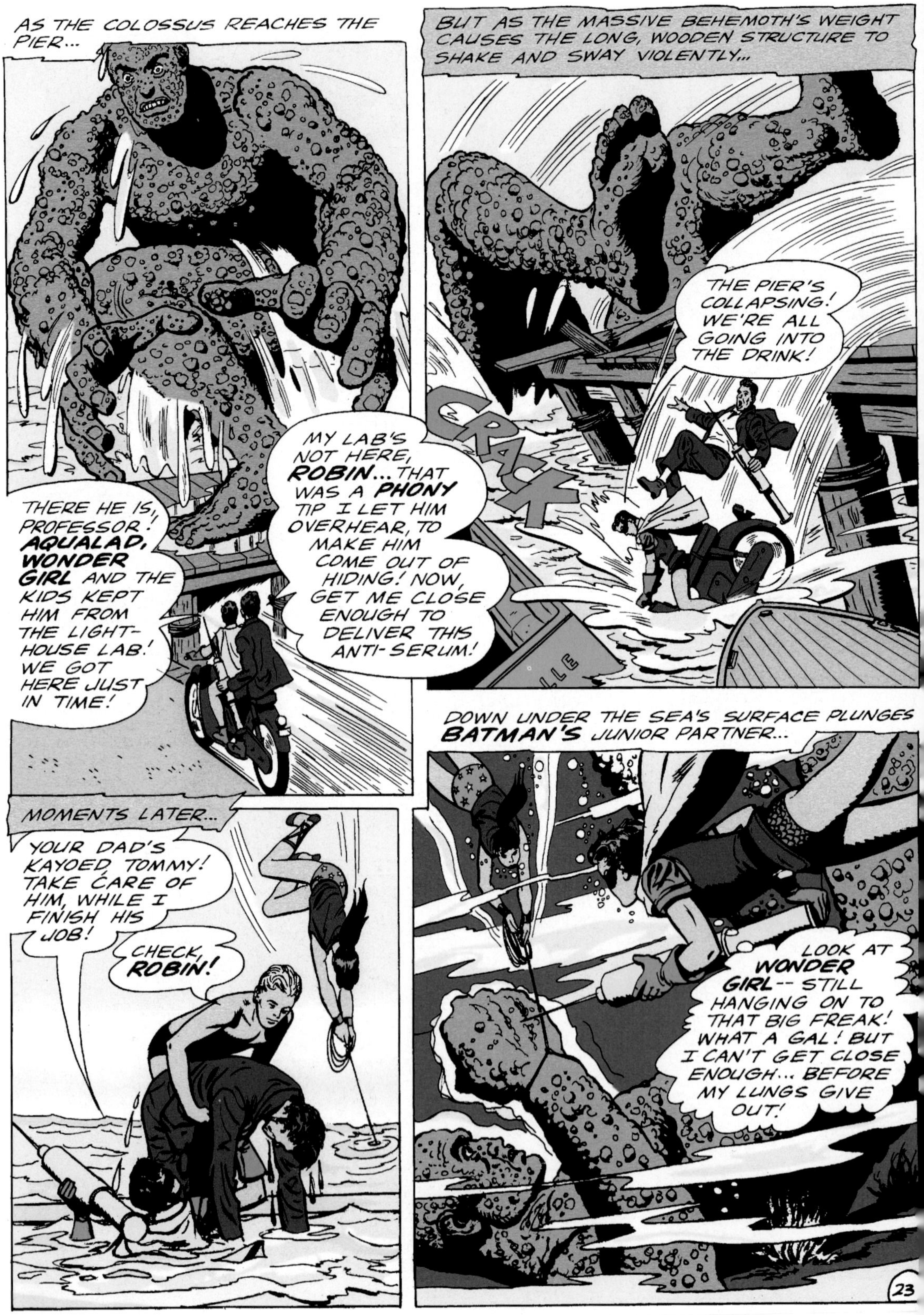
AS THE COLOSSUS REACHES THE PIER...
BUT AS THE MASSIVE BEHEMOTH'S WEIGHT CAUSES THE LONG, WOODEN STRUCTURE TO SHAKE AND SWAY VIOLENTLY...
THE PIER'S COLLAPSING! WE'RE ALL GOING INTO THE DRINK!
CRACK
THERE HE IS, PROFESSOR! AQUALAD, WONDER GIRL AND THE KIDS KEPT HIM FROM THE LIGHT-HOUSE LAB! WE GOT HERE JUST IN TIME!
MY LAB'S NOT HERE, ROBIN... THAT WAS A PHONY TIP I LET HIM OVERHEAR, TO MAKE HIM COME OUT OF HIDING! NOW, GET ME CLOSE ENOUGH TO DELIVER THIS ANTI-SERUM!
MOMENTS LATER...
YOUR DAD'S KAYOED, TOMMY! TAKE CARE OF HIM, WHILE I FINISH HIS JOB!
CHECK, ROBIN!
DOWN UNDER THE SEA'S SURFACE PLUNGES BATMAN'S JUNIOR PARTNER...
LOOK AT WONDER GIRL-- STILL HANGING ON TO THAT BIG FREAK! WHAT A GAL! BUT I CAN'T GET CLOSE ENOUGH... BEFORE MY LUNGS GIVE OUT!

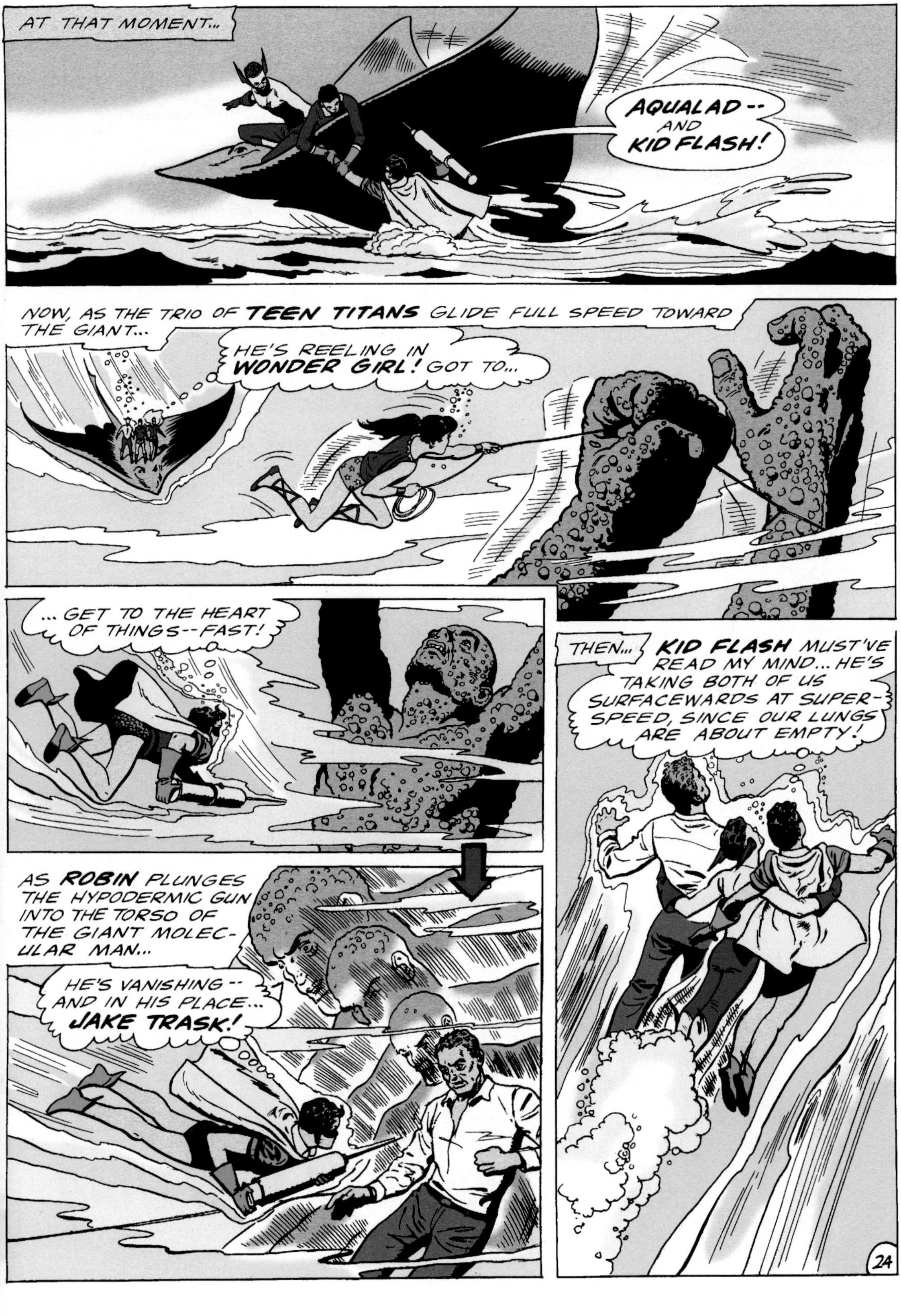
AT THAT MOMENT...
AQUALAD -- AND KID FLASH!
NOW, AS THE TRIO OF TEEN TITANS GLIDE FULL SPEED TOWARD THE GIANT...
HE'S REELING IN WONDER GIRL! GOT TO...
... GET TO THE HEART OF THINGS--FAST!
AS ROBIN PLUNGES THE HYPODERMIC GUN INTO THE TORSO OF THE GIANT MOLECULAR MAN...
HE'S VANISHING -- AND IN HIS PLACE... JAKE TRASK!
THEN...
KID FLASH MUST'VE READ MY MIND... HE'S TAKING BOTH OF US SURFACEWARDS AT SUPER-SPEED, SINCE OUR LUNGS ARE ABOUT EMPTY!
24

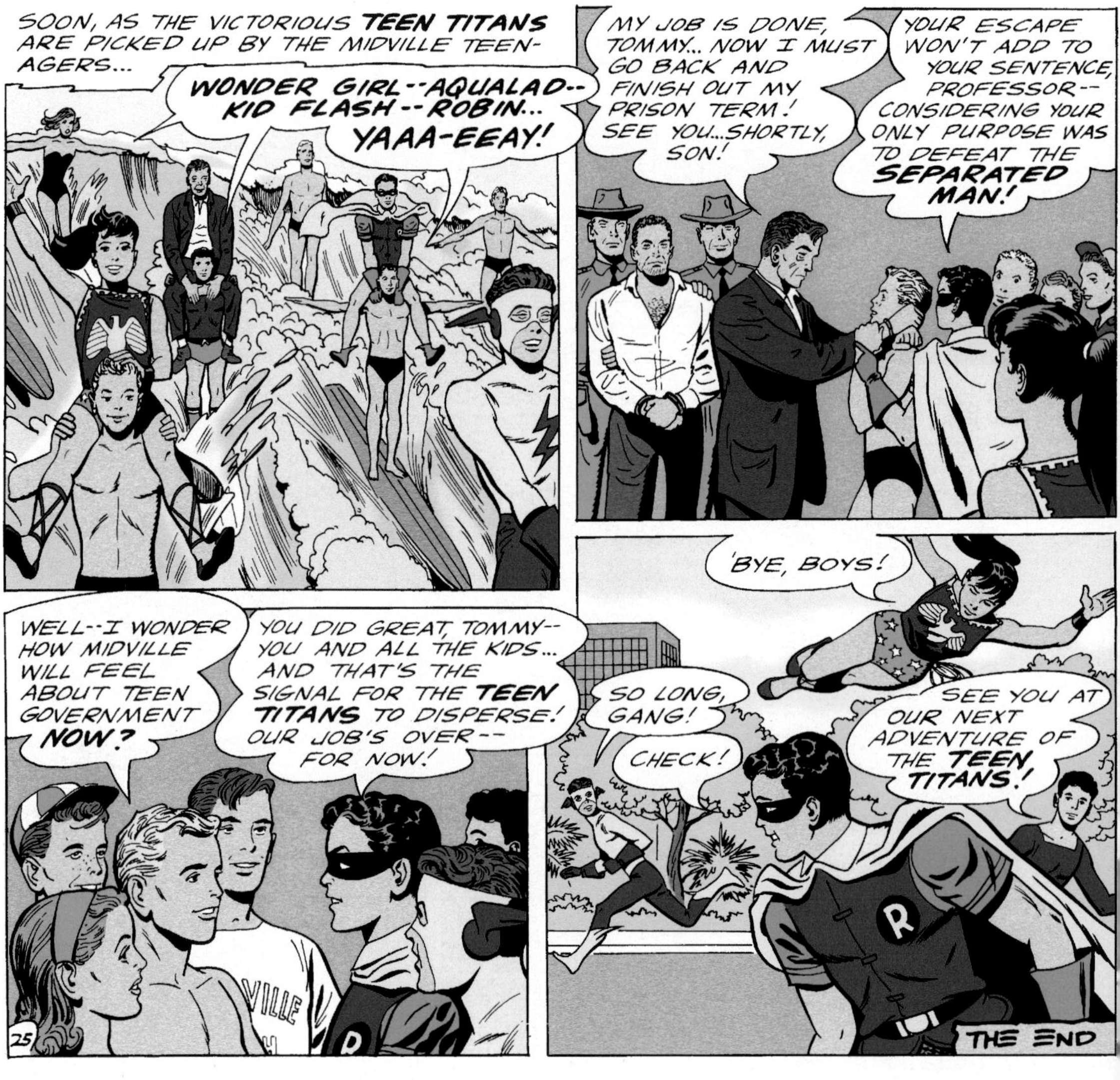
SOON, AS THE VICTORIOUS TEEN TITANS ARE PICKED UP BY THE MIDVILLE TEEN-AGERS...
WONDER GIRL--AQUALAD--KID FLASH--ROBIN... YAAA-EEAY!
MY JOB IS DONE, TOMMY... NOW I MUST GO BACK AND FINISH OUT MY PRISON TERM! SEE YOU...SHORTLY, SON!
YOUR ESCAPE WON'T ADD TO YOUR SENTENCE, PROFESSOR--CONSIDERING YOUR ONLY PURPOSE WAS TO DEFEAT THE SEPARATED MAN!
WELL--I WONDER HOW MIDVILLE WILL FEEL ABOUT TEEN GOVERNMENT NOW?
YOU DID GREAT, TOMMY--YOU AND ALL THE KIDS... AND THAT'S THE SIGNAL FOR THE TEEN TITANS TO DISPERSE! OUR JOB'S OVER--FOR NOW!
25
'BYE, BOYS!
SO LONG, GANG!
CHECK!
SEE YOU AT OUR NEXT ADVENTURE OF THE TEEN TITANS!
THE END

Wonder Girl

ADVENTURES OF A TEEN TITAN

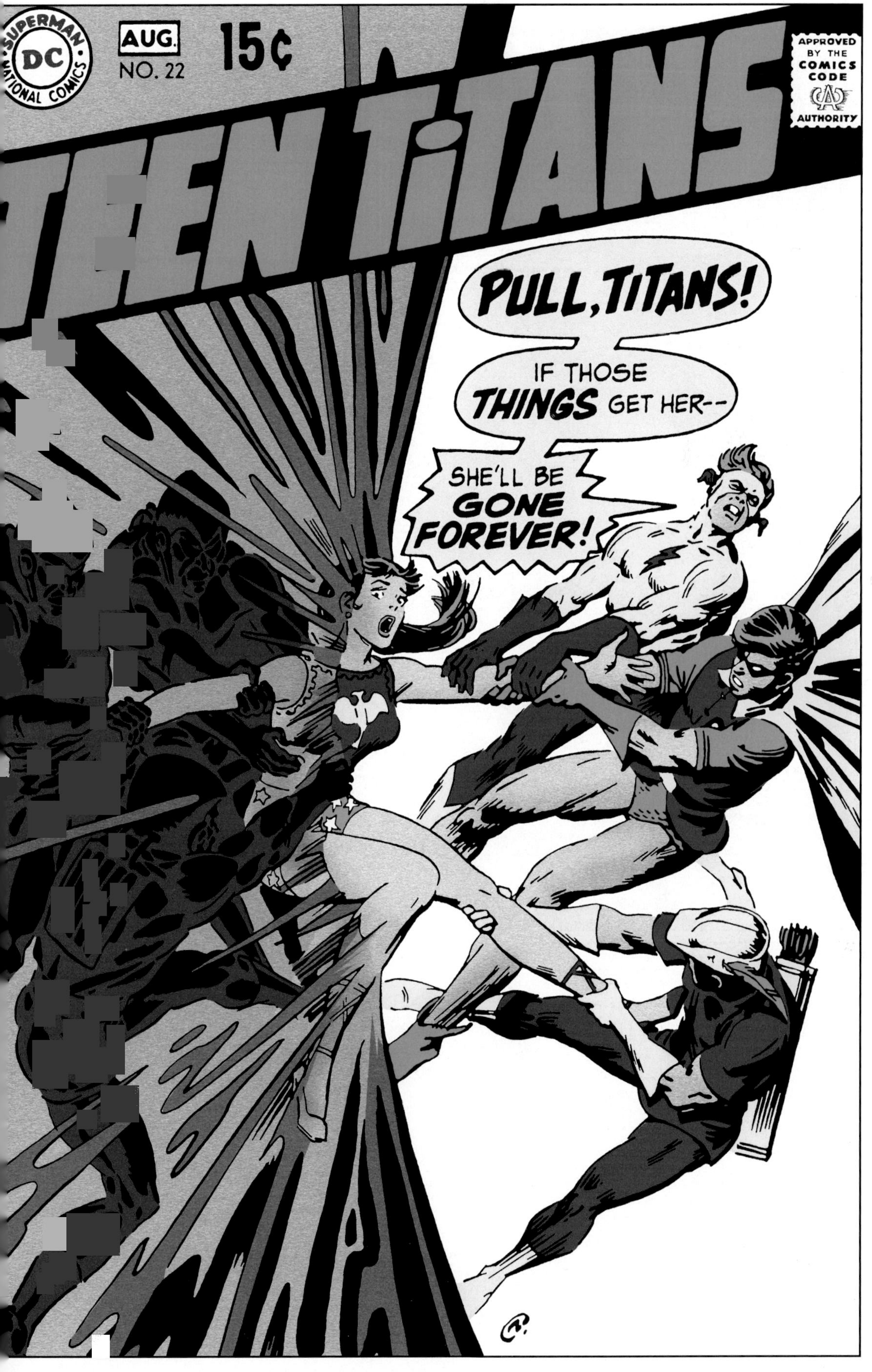
SUPERMAN DC NATIONAL COMICS
AUG.
NO. 22
15¢
APPROVED BY THE COMICS CODE AUTHORITY
TEEN TITANS
PULL, TITANS!
IF THOSE THINGS GET HER--
SHE'LL BE GONE FOREVER!

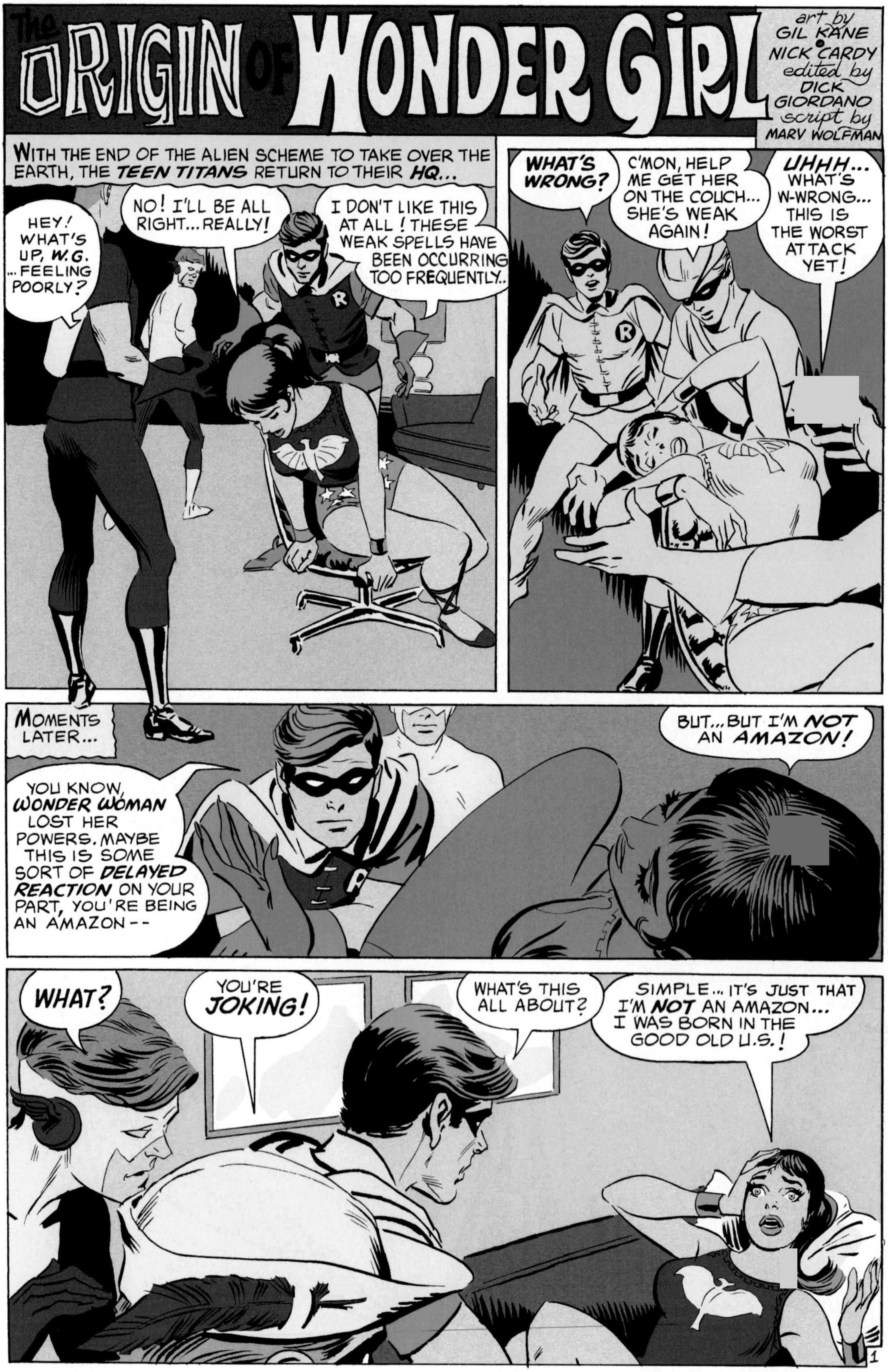
The ORIGIN OF WONDER GIRL
art by GIL KANE • NICK CARDY edited by DICK GIORDANO script by MARV WOLFMAN
WITH THE END OF THE ALIEN SCHEME TO TAKE OVER THE EARTH, THE TEEN TITANS RETURN TO THEIR HQ...
HEY! WHAT'S UP, W.G. ...FEELING POORLY?
NO! I'LL BE ALL RIGHT... REALLY!
I DON'T LIKE THIS AT ALL! THESE WEAK SPELLS HAVE BEEN OCCURRING TOO FREQUENTLY..
WHAT'S WRONG?
C'MON, HELP ME GET HER ON THE COUCH... SHE'S WEAK AGAIN!
UHHH... WHAT'S W-WRONG... THIS IS THE WORST ATTACK YET!
MOMENTS LATER...
YOU KNOW, WONDER WOMAN LOST HER POWERS. MAYBE THIS IS SOME SORT OF DELAYED REACTION ON YOUR PART, YOU'RE BEING AN AMAZON --
BUT... BUT I'M NOT AN AMAZON!
WHAT?
YOU'RE JOKING!
WHAT'S THIS ALL ABOUT?
SIMPLE... IT'S JUST THAT I'M NOT AN AMAZON... I WAS BORN IN THE GOOD OLD U.S.!
1

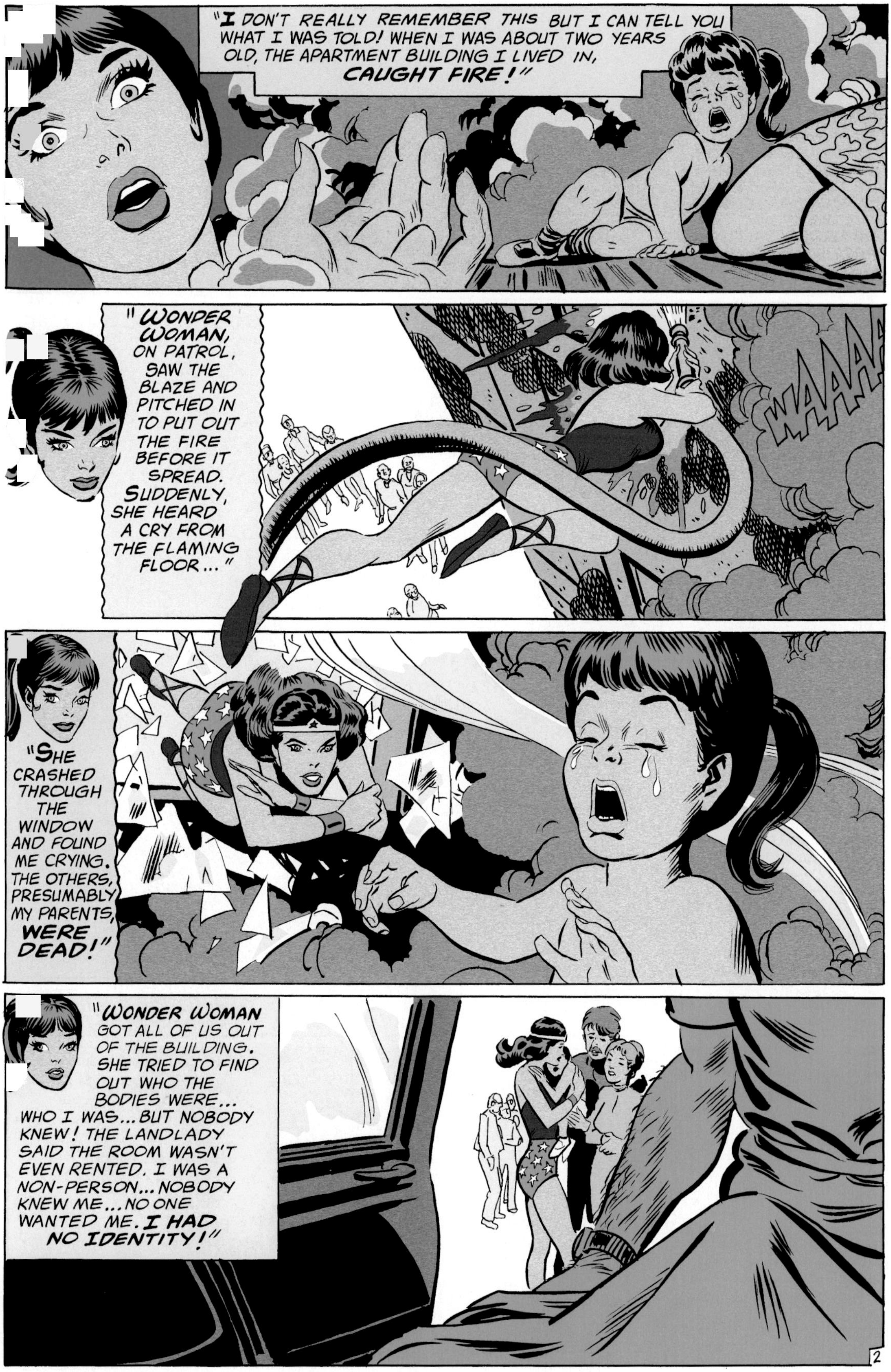
"I DON'T REALLY REMEMBER THIS BUT I CAN TELL YOU WHAT I WAS TOLD! WHEN I WAS ABOUT TWO YEARS OLD, THE APARTMENT BUILDING I LIVED IN, CAUGHT FIRE!"
"WONDER WOMAN, ON PATROL, SAW THE BLAZE AND PITCHED IN TO PUT OUT THE FIRE BEFORE IT SPREAD. SUDDENLY, SHE HEARD A CRY FROM THE FLAMING FLOOR..."
WAAAA
"SHE CRASHED THROUGH THE WINDOW AND FOUND ME CRYING. THE OTHERS, PRESUMABLY MY PARENTS, WERE DEAD!"
"WONDER WOMAN GOT ALL OF US OUT OF THE BUILDING. SHE TRIED TO FIND OUT WHO THE BODIES WERE... WHO I WAS... BUT NOBODY KNEW! THE LANDLADY SAID THE ROOM WASN'T EVEN RENTED. I WAS A NON-PERSON... NOBODY KNEW ME... NO ONE WANTED ME. I HAD NO IDENTITY!"

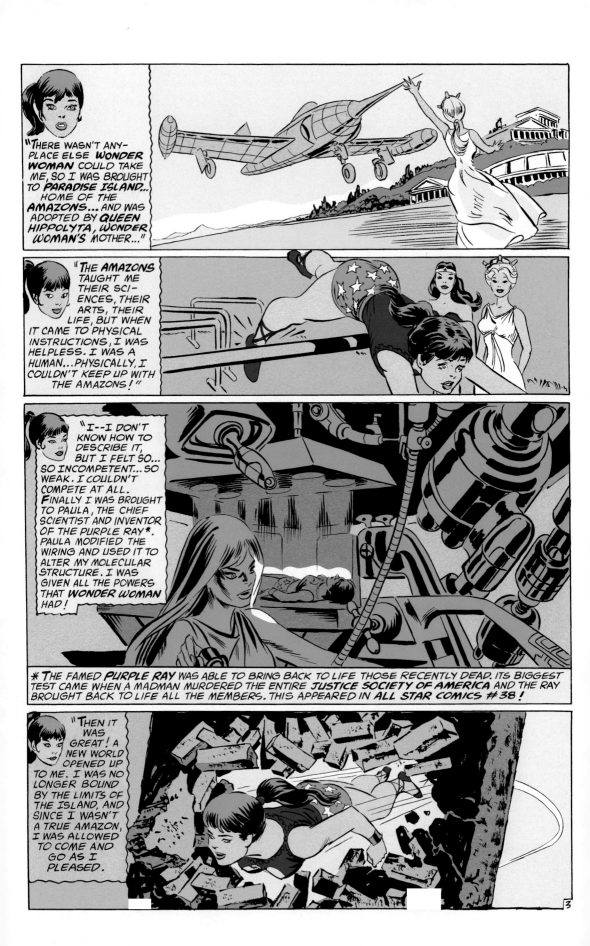

"THERE WASN'T ANYPLACE ELSE WONDER WOMAN COULD TAKE ME, SO I WAS BROUGHT TO PARADISE ISLAND... HOME OF THE AMAZONS... AND WAS ADOPTED BY QUEEN HIPPOLYTA, WONDER WOMAN'S MOTHER..."

"THE AMAZONS TAUGHT ME THEIR SCIENCES, THEIR ARTS, THEIR LIFE, BUT WHEN IT CAME TO PHYSICAL INSTRUCTIONS, I WAS HELPLESS. I WAS A HUMAN...PHYSICALLY, I COULDN'T KEEP UP WITH THE AMAZONS!"

"I--I DON'T KNOW HOW TO DESCRIBE IT, BUT I FELT SO... SO INCOMPETENT... SO WEAK. I COULDN'T COMPETE AT ALL. FINALLY I WAS BROUGHT TO PAULA, THE CHIEF SCIENTIST AND INVENTOR OF THE PURPLE RAY*. PAULA MODIFIED THE WIRING AND USED IT TO ALTER MY MOLECULAR STRUCTURE. I WAS GIVEN ALL THE POWERS THAT WONDER WOMAN HAD!"

* THE FAMED PURPLE RAY WAS ABLE TO BRING BACK TO LIFE THOSE RECENTLY DEAD. ITS BIGGEST TEST CAME WHEN A MADMAN MURDERED THE ENTIRE JUSTICE SOCIETY OF AMERICA AND THE RAY BROUGHT BACK TO LIFE ALL THE MEMBERS. THIS APPEARED IN ALL STAR COMICS #38!

"THEN IT WAS GREAT! A NEW WORLD OPENED UP TO ME. I WAS NO LONGER BOUND BY THE LIMITS OF THE ISLAND, AND SINCE I WASN'T A TRUE AMAZON, I WAS ALLOWED TO COME AND GO AS I PLEASED.

3

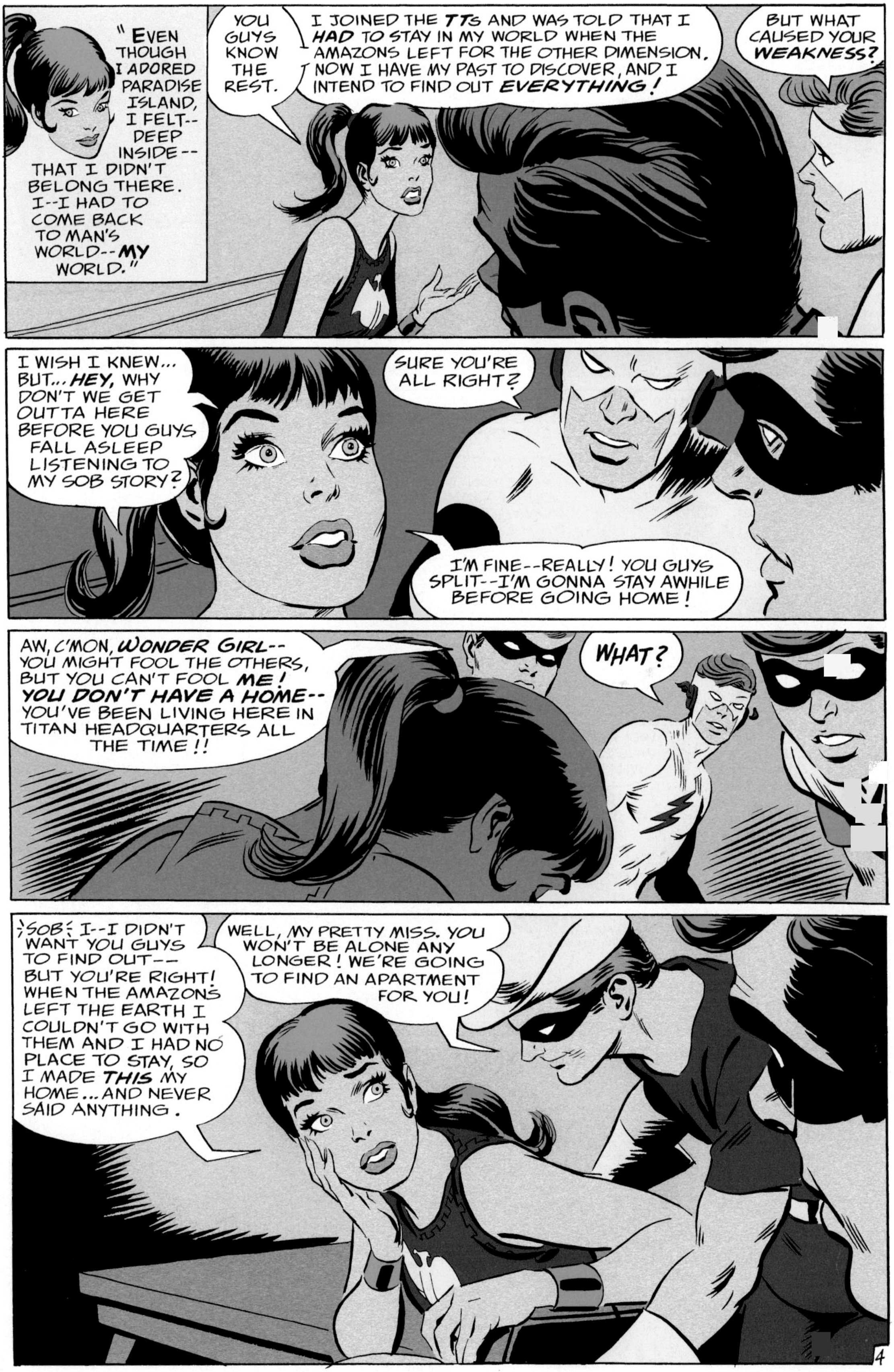
"EVEN THOUGH I ADORED PARADISE ISLAND, I FELT-- DEEP INSIDE-- THAT I DIDN'T BELONG THERE. I--I HAD TO COME BACK TO MAN'S WORLD--MY WORLD."
YOU GUYS KNOW THE REST.
I JOINED THE TTs AND WAS TOLD THAT I HAD TO STAY IN MY WORLD WHEN THE AMAZONS LEFT FOR THE OTHER DIMENSION. NOW I HAVE MY PAST TO DISCOVER, AND I INTEND TO FIND OUT EVERYTHING!
BUT WHAT CAUSED YOUR WEAKNESS?
I WISH I KNEW... BUT... HEY, WHY DON'T WE GET OUTTA HERE BEFORE YOU GUYS FALL ASLEEP LISTENING TO MY SOB STORY?
SURE YOU'RE ALL RIGHT?
I'M FINE--REALLY! YOU GUYS SPLIT--I'M GONNA STAY AWHILE BEFORE GOING HOME!
AW, C'MON, WONDER GIRL-- YOU MIGHT FOOL THE OTHERS, BUT YOU CAN'T FOOL ME! YOU DON'T HAVE A HOME-- YOU'VE BEEN LIVING HERE IN TITAN HEADQUARTERS ALL THE TIME!!
WHAT?
;SOB; I--I DIDN'T WANT YOU GUYS TO FIND OUT-- BUT YOU'RE RIGHT! WHEN THE AMAZONS LEFT THE EARTH I COULDN'T GO WITH THEM AND I HAD NO PLACE TO STAY, SO I MADE THIS MY HOME... AND NEVER SAID ANYTHING.
WELL, MY PRETTY MISS. YOU WON'T BE ALONE ANY LONGER! WE'RE GOING TO FIND AN APARTMENT FOR YOU!

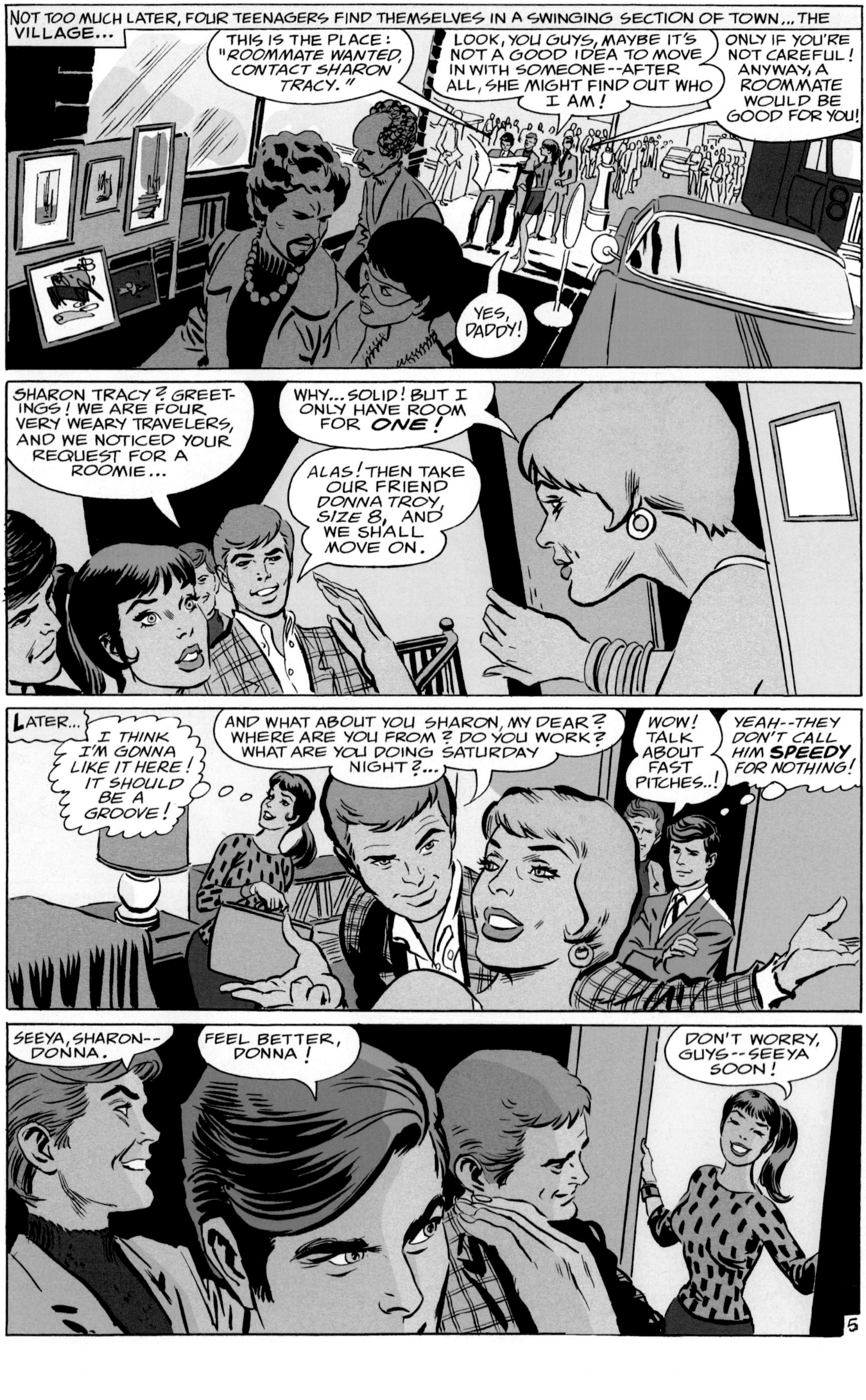
NOT TOO MUCH LATER, FOUR TEENAGERS FIND THEMSELVES IN A SWINGING SECTION OF TOWN... THE VILLAGE...
THIS IS THE PLACE: "ROOMMATE WANTED, CONTACT SHARON TRACY."
LOOK, YOU GUYS, MAYBE IT'S NOT A GOOD IDEA TO MOVE IN WITH SOMEONE--AFTER ALL, SHE MIGHT FIND OUT WHO I AM!
ONLY IF YOU'RE NOT CAREFUL! ANYWAY, A ROOMMATE WOULD BE GOOD FOR YOU!
YES, DADDY!
SHARON TRACY? GREETINGS! WE ARE FOUR VERY WEARY TRAVELERS, AND WE NOTICED YOUR REQUEST FOR A ROOMIE...
WHY... SOLID! BUT I ONLY HAVE ROOM FOR ONE!
ALAS! THEN TAKE OUR FRIEND DONNA TROY, SIZE 8, AND WE SHALL MOVE ON.
LATER...
I THINK I'M GONNA LIKE IT HERE! IT SHOULD BE A GROOVE!
AND WHAT ABOUT YOU SHARON, MY DEAR? WHERE ARE YOU FROM? DO YOU WORK? WHAT ARE YOU DOING SATURDAY NIGHT?...
WOW! TALK ABOUT FAST PITCHES..!
YEAH--THEY DON'T CALL HIM SPEEDY FOR NOTHING!
SEEYA, SHARON--DONNA.
FEEL BETTER, DONNA!
DON'T WORRY, GUYS--SEEYA SOON!

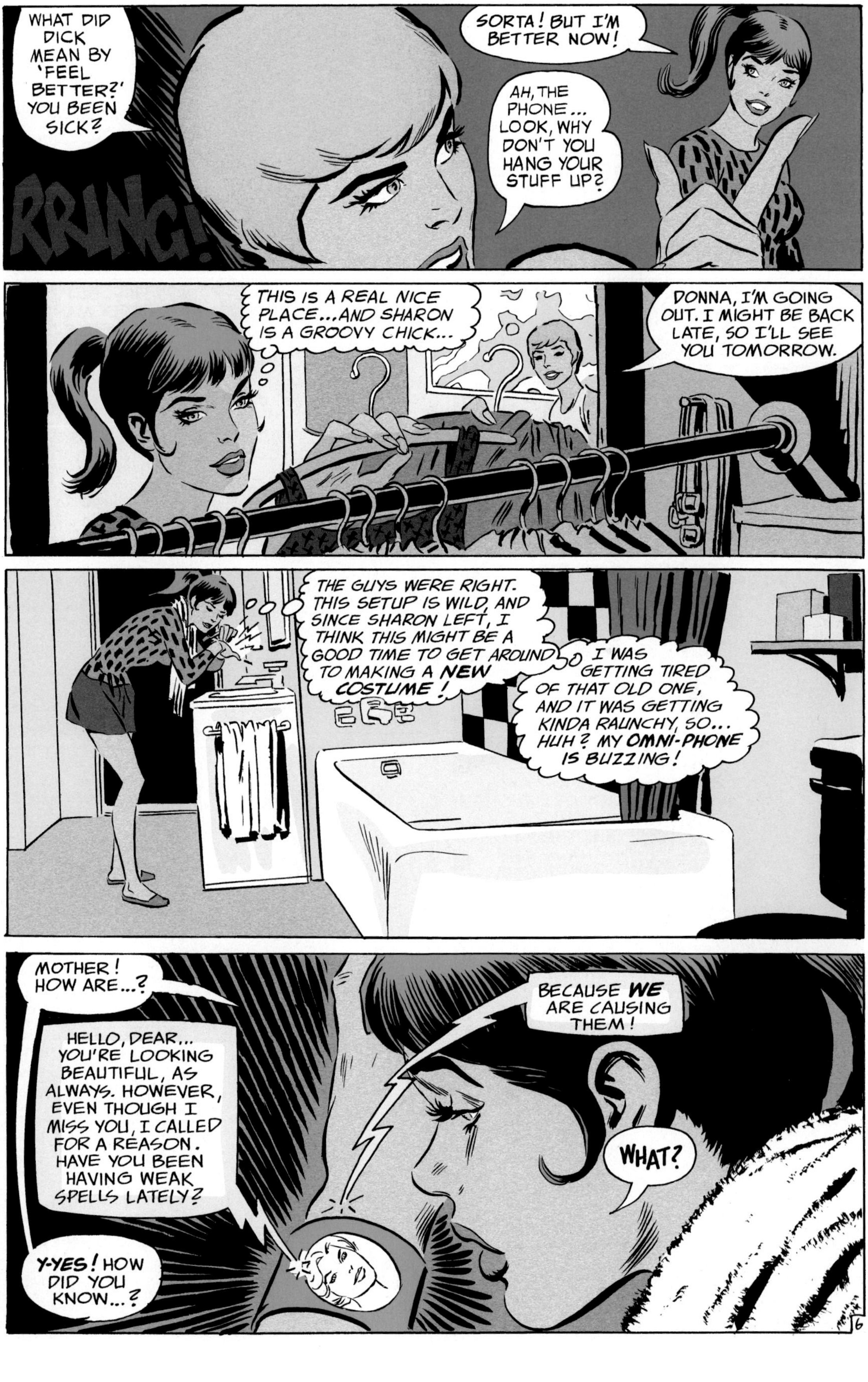

WHAT DID DICK MEAN BY 'FEEL BETTER?' YOU BEEN SICK?
SORTA! BUT I'M BETTER NOW!
RRING!
AH, THE PHONE... LOOK, WHY DON'T YOU HANG YOUR STUFF UP?
THIS IS A REAL NICE PLACE...AND SHARON IS A GROOVY CHICK...
DONNA, I'M GOING OUT. I MIGHT BE BACK LATE, SO I'LL SEE YOU TOMORROW.
THE GUYS WERE RIGHT. THIS SETUP IS WILD, AND SINCE SHARON LEFT, I THINK THIS MIGHT BE A GOOD TIME TO GET AROUND TO MAKING A NEW COSTUME!
I WAS GETTING TIRED OF THAT OLD ONE, AND IT WAS GETTING KINDA RAUNCHY, SO... HUH? MY OMNI-PHONE IS BUZZING!
MOTHER! HOW ARE...?
HELLO, DEAR... YOU'RE LOOKING BEAUTIFUL, AS ALWAYS. HOWEVER, EVEN THOUGH I MISS YOU, I CALLED FOR A REASON. HAVE YOU BEEN HAVING WEAK SPELLS LATELY?
Y-YES! HOW DID YOU KNOW...?
BECAUSE WE ARE CAUSING THEM!
WHAT?

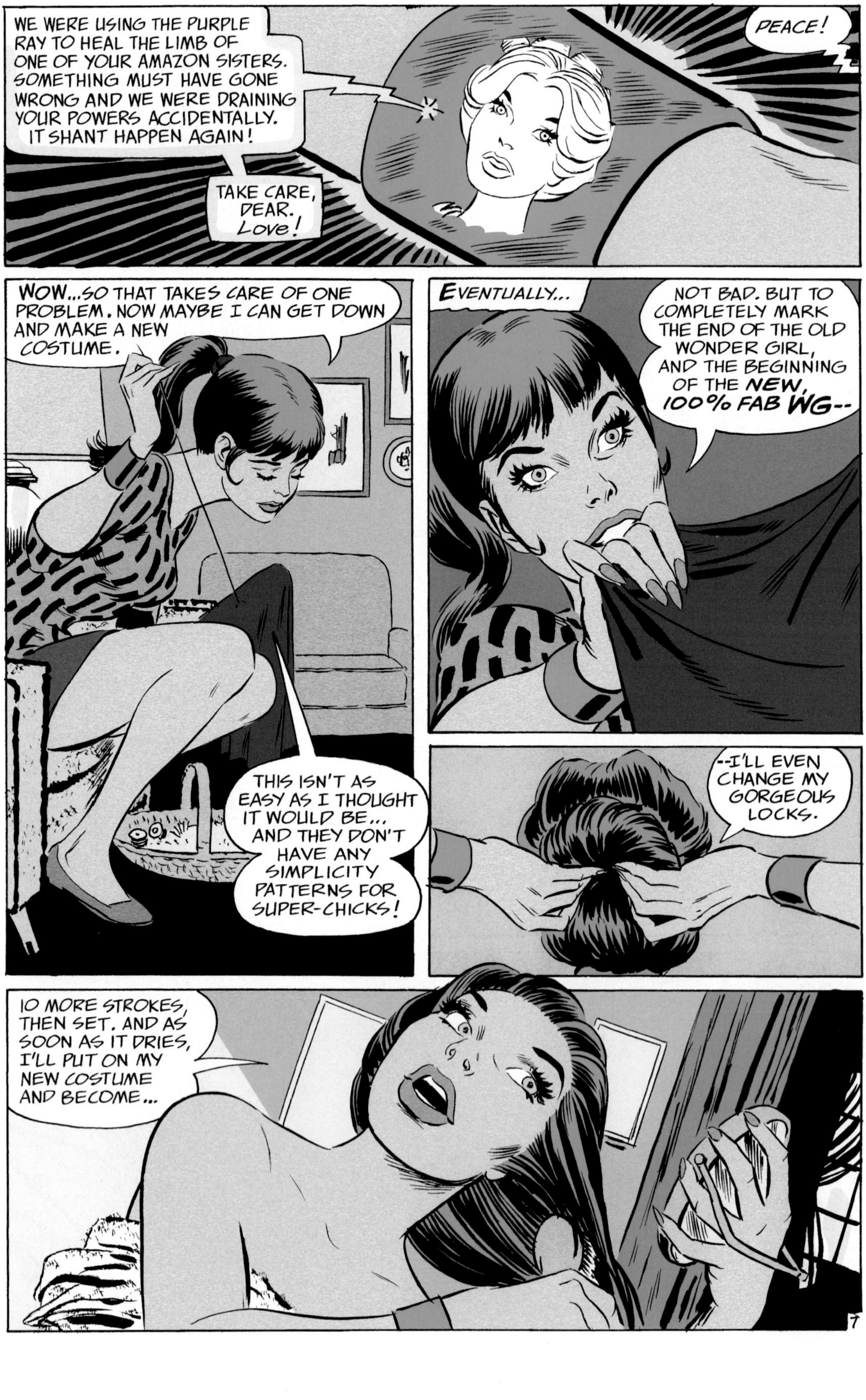
WE WERE USING THE PURPLE RAY TO HEAL THE LIMB OF ONE OF YOUR AMAZON SISTERS. SOMETHING MUST HAVE GONE WRONG AND WE WERE DRAINING YOUR POWERS ACCIDENTALLY. IT SHANT HAPPEN AGAIN!
TAKE CARE, DEAR. Love!
PEACE!
WOW...SO THAT TAKES CARE OF ONE PROBLEM. NOW MAYBE I CAN GET DOWN AND MAKE A NEW COSTUME.
THIS ISN'T AS EASY AS I THOUGHT IT WOULD BE... AND THEY DON'T HAVE ANY SIMPLICITY PATTERNS FOR SUPER-CHICKS!
EVENTUALLY...
NOT BAD. BUT TO COMPLETELY MARK THE END OF THE OLD WONDER GIRL, AND THE BEGINNING OF THE NEW, 100% FAB WG--
--I'LL EVEN CHANGE MY GORGEOUS LOCKS.
10 MORE STROKES, THEN SET. AND AS SOON AS IT DRIES, I'LL PUT ON MY NEW COSTUME AND BECOME...

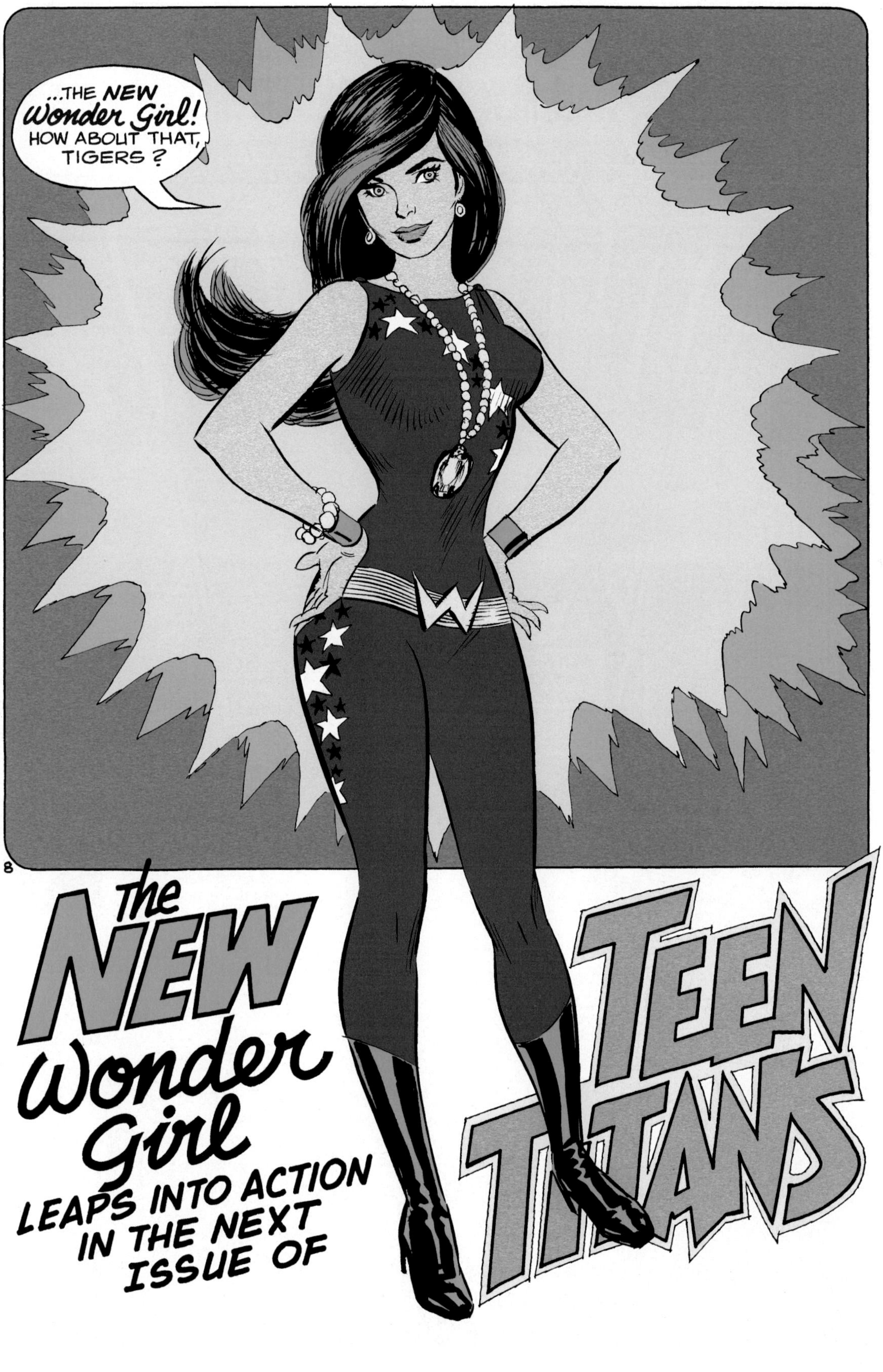
...THE NEW Wonder Girl! HOW ABOUT THAT, TIGERS?
8
The NEW Wonder Girl
LEAPS INTO ACTION IN THE NEXT ISSUE OF
TEEN TITANS

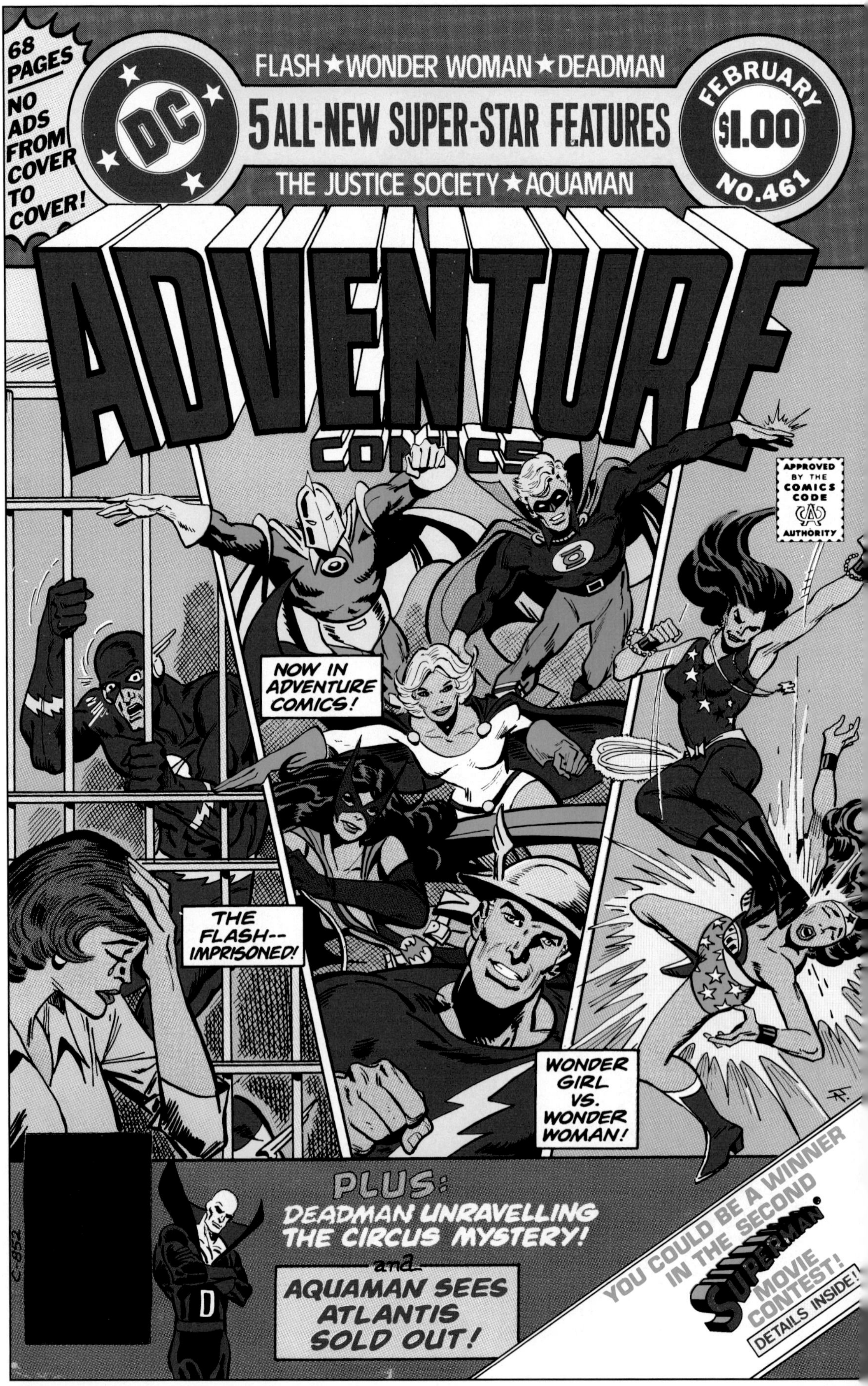
68 PAGES
NO ADS FROM COVER TO COVER!
FLASH ★ WONDER WOMAN ★ DEADMAN
5 ALL-NEW SUPER-STAR FEATURES
THE JUSTICE SOCIETY ★ AQUAMAN
FEBRUARY
$1.00
NO. 461
ADVENTURE COMICS
APPROVED BY THE COMICS CODE AUTHORITY
NOW IN ADVENTURE COMICS!
THE FLASH-- IMPRISONED!
WONDER GIRL VS. WONDER WOMAN!
PLUS:
DEADMAN UNRAVELLING THE CIRCUS MYSTERY!
and
AQUAMAN SEES ATLANTIS SOLD OUT!
YOU COULD BE A WINNER IN THE SECOND SUPERMAN MOVIE CONTEST!
DETAILS INSIDE!
C-852

STORY: JACK C. HARRIS * LETTERING: KARISHA
ART: JACK ABEL COLORING: ADRIENNE ROY
EDITOR: PAUL LEVITZ
GRANTED THE WISDOM OF ATHENA, THE STRENGTH OF HERCULES, THE SPEED OF MERCURY AND THE BEAUTY OF APHRODITE BY THE GODS, PRINCESS DIANA OF PARADISE ISLAND RENOUNCED HER IMMORTALITY AND ENTERED MANS WORLD AS THE MOST LEGENDARY AMAZON OF ALL...
Wonder Woman
CREATED BY: WILLIAM MOULTON MARSTON
SAN FRANCISCO COUNTY, CALIFORNIA IS THE LOCATION OF A CITY ON A BAY...
A CITY WITH THE AREA OF 46.3 SQUARE MILES RESTING A MERE 65 FEET ABOVE SEA LEVEL...
A CITY CALLED SAN FRANCISCO--A METROPOLIS WHEREIN ITS LATEST VISITOR WILL EXPERIENCE HER LATEST ADVENTURE...
THE WHOLE PLACE IS IN FLAMES! AND I HAVE A SUSPICION THAT THESE THREE AREN'T RUNNING FOR THEIR HEALTH!
STOP! STOP OR I'LL SHOOT!
SCHOOL OF THE AMAZOIDS

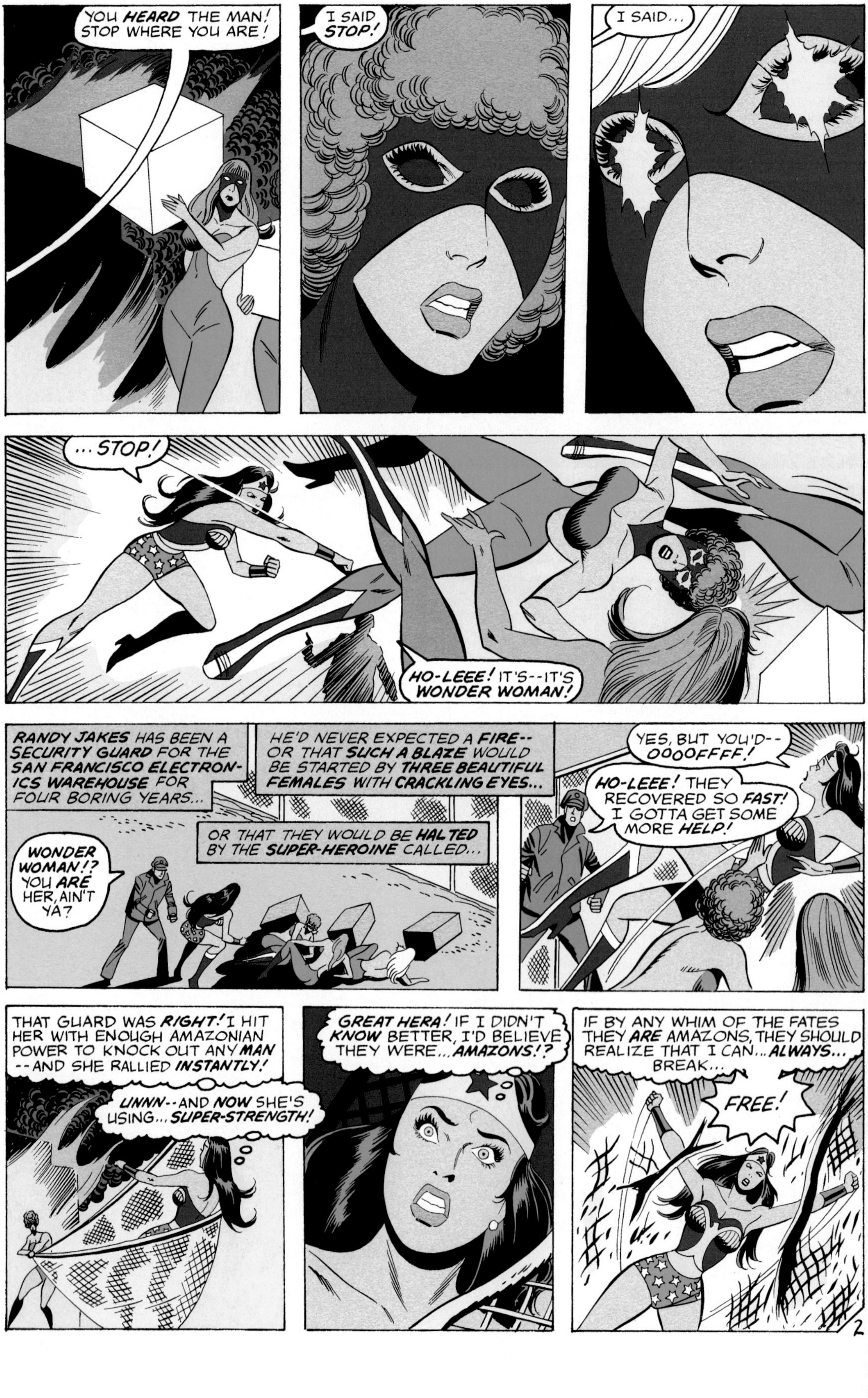
YOU HEARD THE MAN! STOP WHERE YOU ARE!
I SAID STOP!
I SAID...
...STOP!
HO-LEEE! IT'S--IT'S WONDER WOMAN!
RANDY JAKES HAS BEEN A SECURITY GUARD FOR THE SAN FRANCISCO ELECTRONICS WAREHOUSE FOR FOUR BORING YEARS...
HE'D NEVER EXPECTED A FIRE-- OR THAT SUCH A BLAZE WOULD BE STARTED BY THREE BEAUTIFUL FEMALES WITH CRACKLING EYES...
OR THAT THEY WOULD BE HALTED BY THE SUPER-HEROINE CALLED...
WONDER WOMAN!? YOU ARE HER, AIN'T YA?
YES, BUT YOU'D-- OOOOFFFF!
HO-LEEE! THEY RECOVERED SO FAST! I GOTTA GET SOME MORE HELP!
THAT GUARD WAS RIGHT! I HIT HER WITH ENOUGH AMAZONIAN POWER TO KNOCK OUT ANY MAN --AND SHE RALLIED INSTANTLY!
UNNN--AND NOW SHE'S USING...SUPER-STRENGTH!
GREAT HERA! IF I DIDN'T KNOW BETTER, I'D BELIEVE THEY WERE...AMAZONS!?
IF BY ANY WHIM OF THE FATES THEY ARE AMAZONS, THEY SHOULD REALIZE THAT I CAN...ALWAYS... BREAK...
FREE!
2

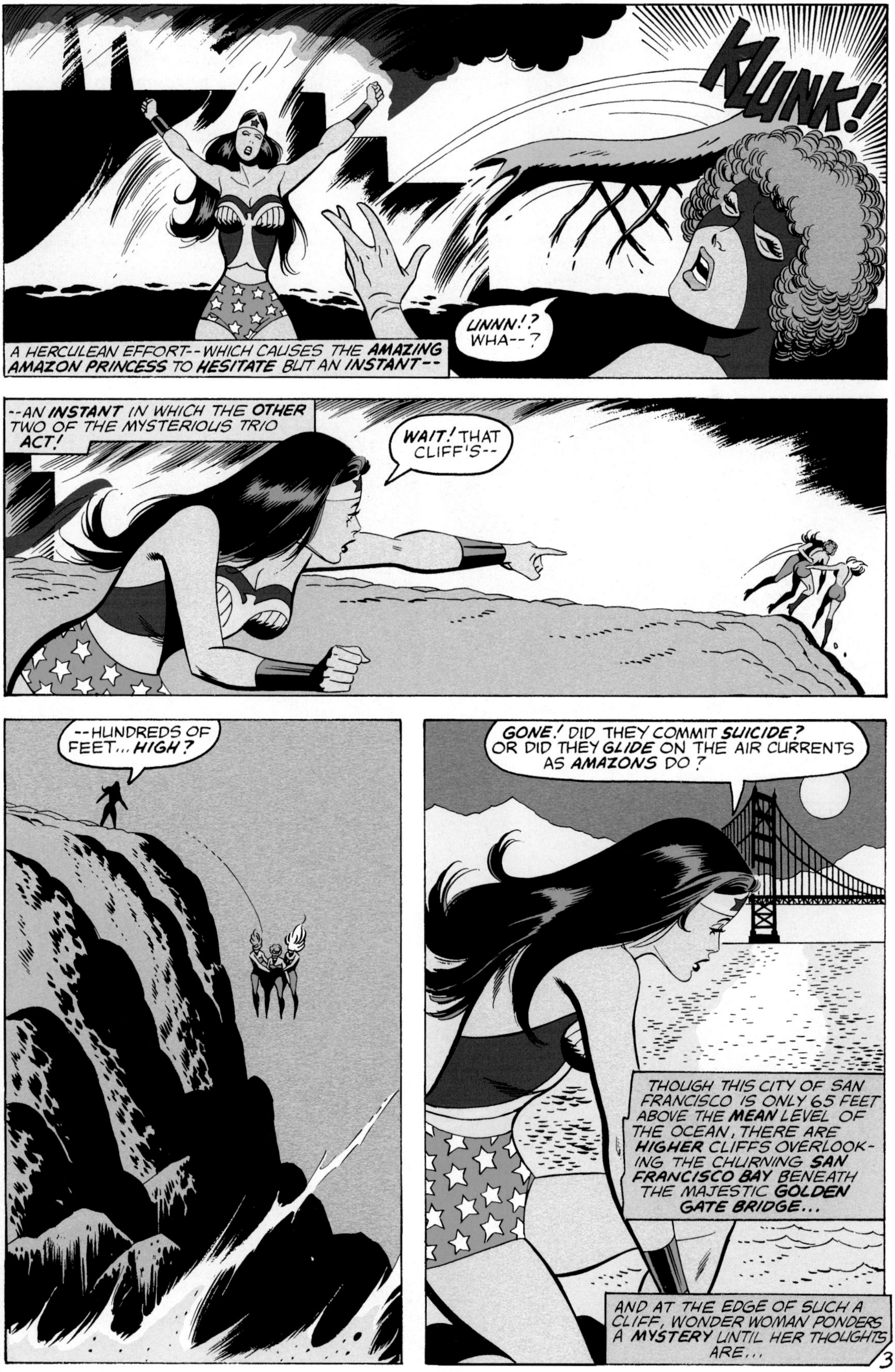
KLUNK!
A HERCULEAN EFFORT--WHICH CAUSES THE AMAZING AMAZON PRINCESS TO HESITATE BUT AN INSTANT--
UNNN!? WHA--?
--AN INSTANT IN WHICH THE OTHER TWO OF THE MYSTERIOUS TRIO ACT!
WAIT! THAT CLIFF'S--
--HUNDREDS OF FEET... HIGH?
GONE! DID THEY COMMIT SUICIDE? OR DID THEY GLIDE ON THE AIR CURRENTS AS AMAZONS DO?
THOUGH THIS CITY OF SAN FRANCISCO IS ONLY 65 FEET ABOVE THE MEAN LEVEL OF THE OCEAN, THERE ARE HIGHER CLIFFS OVERLOOKING THE CHURNING SAN FRANCISCO BAY BENEATH THE MAJESTIC GOLDEN GATE BRIDGE...
AND AT THE EDGE OF SUCH A CLIFF, WONDER WOMAN PONDERS A MYSTERY UNTIL HER THOUGHTS ARE...
3

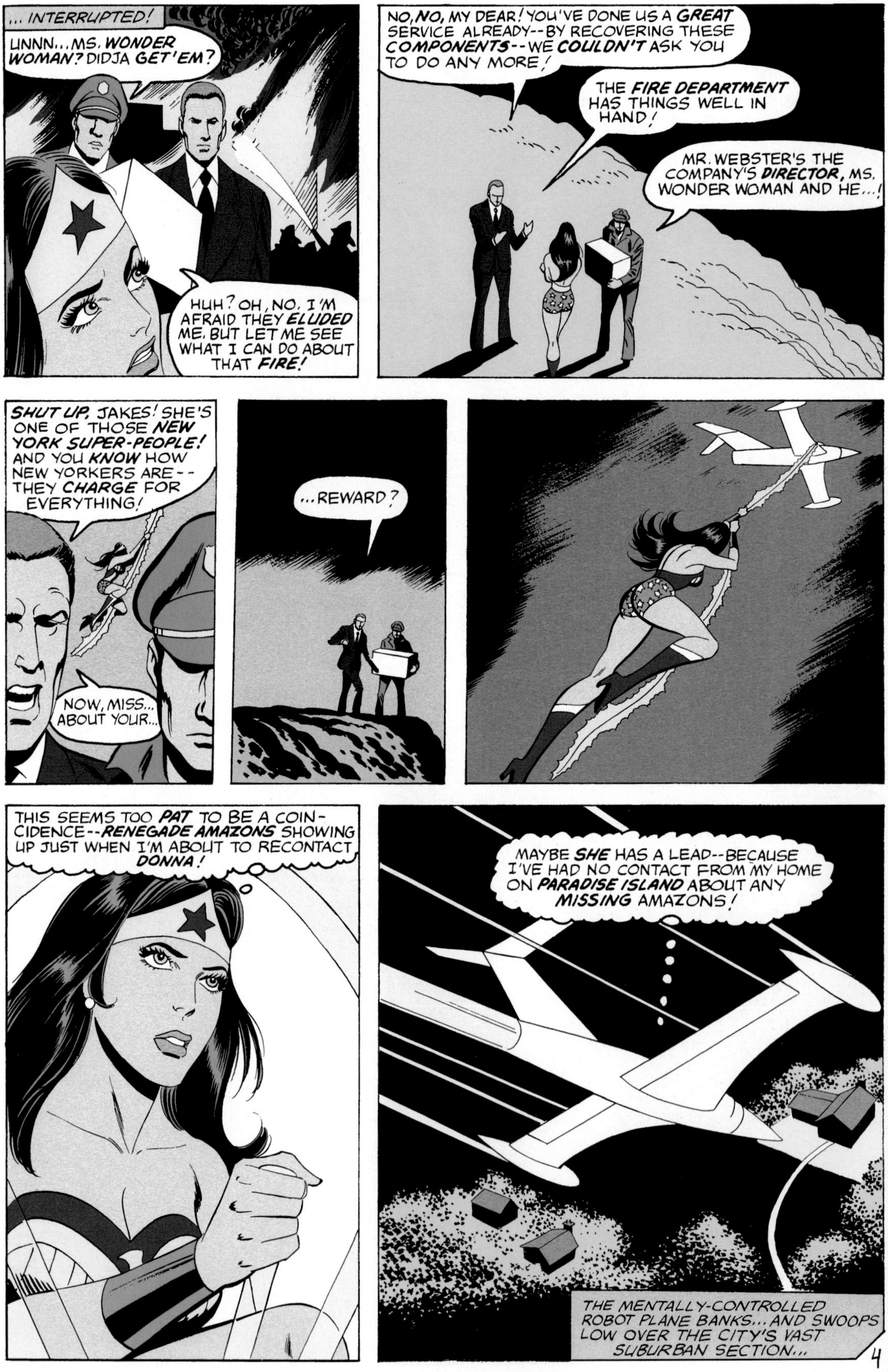

... INTERRUPTED!
UNNN... MS. WONDER WOMAN? DIDJA GET 'EM?
HUH? OH, NO. I'M AFRAID THEY ELUDED ME. BUT LET ME SEE WHAT I CAN DO ABOUT THAT FIRE!
NO, NO, MY DEAR! YOU'VE DONE US A GREAT SERVICE ALREADY--BY RECOVERING THESE COMPONENTS--WE COULDN'T ASK YOU TO DO ANY MORE!
THE FIRE DEPARTMENT HAS THINGS WELL IN HAND!
MR. WEBSTER'S THE COMPANY'S DIRECTOR, MS. WONDER WOMAN AND HE...!
NOW, MISS... ABOUT YOUR...
SHUT UP, JAKES! SHE'S ONE OF THOSE NEW YORK SUPER-PEOPLE! AND YOU KNOW HOW NEW YORKERS ARE--THEY CHARGE FOR EVERYTHING!
...REWARD?
THIS SEEMS TOO PAT TO BE A COIN-CIDENCE--RENEGADE AMAZONS SHOWING UP JUST WHEN I'M ABOUT TO RECONTACT DONNA!
MAYBE SHE HAS A LEAD--BECAUSE I'VE HAD NO CONTACT FROM MY HOME ON PARADISE ISLAND ABOUT ANY MISSING AMAZONS!
THE MENTALLY-CONTROLLED ROBOT PLANE BANKS... AND SWOOPS LOW OVER THE CITY'S VAST SUBURBAN SECTION...
4

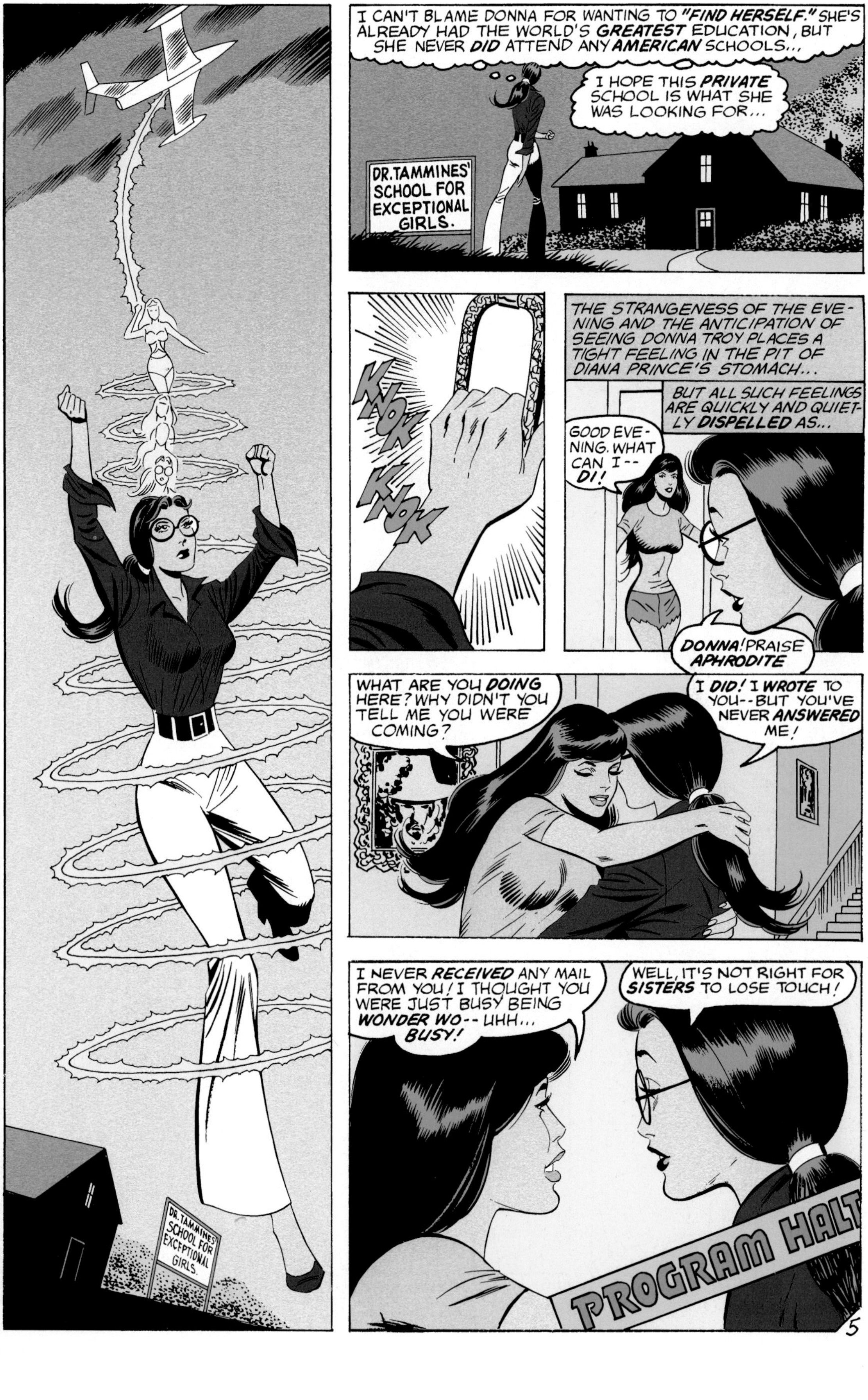

DR. TAMMINES' SCHOOL FOR EXCEPTIONAL GIRLS.
I CAN'T BLAME DONNA FOR WANTING TO "FIND HERSELF." SHE'S ALREADY HAD THE WORLD'S GREATEST EDUCATION, BUT SHE NEVER DID ATTEND ANY AMERICAN SCHOOLS...
I HOPE THIS PRIVATE SCHOOL IS WHAT SHE WAS LOOKING FOR...
DR. TAMMINES' SCHOOL FOR EXCEPTIONAL GIRLS.
KNOK KNOK
THE STRANGENESS OF THE EVENING AND THE ANTICIPATION OF SEEING DONNA TROY PLACES A TIGHT FEELING IN THE PIT OF DIANA PRINCE'S STOMACH...
BUT ALL SUCH FEELINGS ARE QUICKLY AND QUIETLY DISPELLED AS...
GOOD EVENING. WHAT CAN I-- DI!
DONNA! PRAISE APHRODITE
WHAT ARE YOU DOING HERE? WHY DIDN'T YOU TELL ME YOU WERE COMING?
I DID! I WROTE TO YOU--BUT YOU'VE NEVER ANSWERED ME!
I NEVER RECEIVED ANY MAIL FROM YOU! I THOUGHT YOU WERE JUST BUSY BEING WONDER WO-- UHH... BUSY!
WELL, IT'S NOT RIGHT FOR SISTERS TO LOSE TOUCH!
PROGRAM HALT

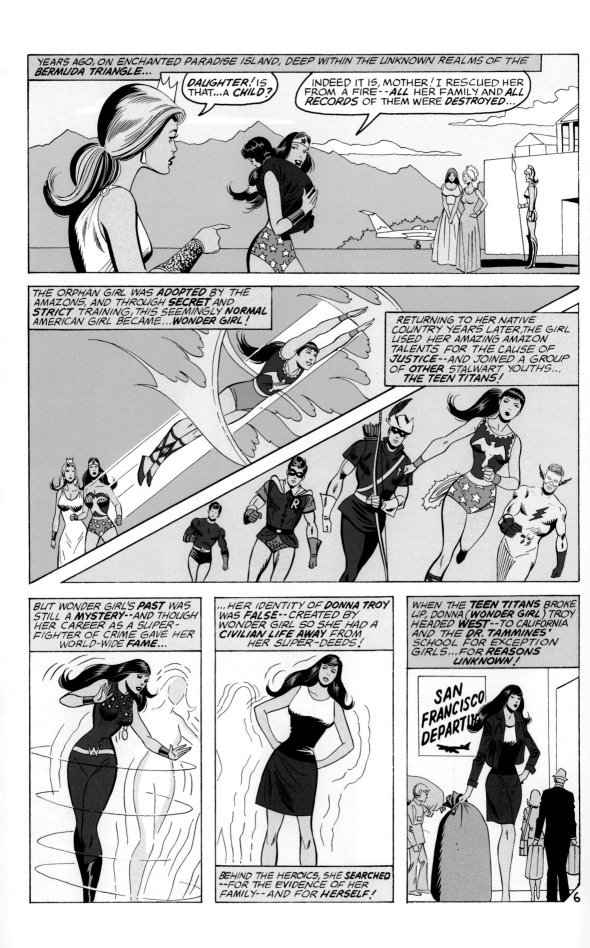

YEARS AGO, ON ENCHANTED PARADISE ISLAND, DEEP WITHIN THE UNKNOWN REALMS OF THE BERMUDA TRIANGLE...

DAUGHTER! IS THAT...A CHILD?

INDEED IT IS, MOTHER! I RESCUED HER FROM A FIRE--ALL HER FAMILY AND ALL RECORDS OF THEM WERE DESTROYED...

THE ORPHAN GIRL WAS ADOPTED BY THE AMAZONS, AND THROUGH SECRET AND STRICT TRAINING, THIS SEEMINGLY NORMAL AMERICAN GIRL BECAME...WONDER GIRL!

RETURNING TO HER NATIVE COUNTRY YEARS LATER, THE GIRL USED HER AMAZING AMAZON TALENTS FOR THE CAUSE OF JUSTICE--AND JOINED A GROUP OF OTHER STALWART YOUTHS... THE TEEN TITANS!

BUT WONDER GIRL'S PAST WAS STILL A MYSTERY--AND THOUGH HER CAREER AS A SUPER-FIGHTER OF CRIME GAVE HER WORLD-WIDE FAME...

...HER IDENTITY OF DONNA TROY WAS FALSE--CREATED BY WONDER GIRL SO SHE HAD A CIVILIAN LIFE AWAY FROM HER SUPER-DEEDS!

BEHIND THE HEROICS, SHE SEARCHED --FOR THE EVIDENCE OF HER FAMILY--AND FOR HERSELF!

WHEN THE TEEN TITANS BROKE UP, DONNA (WONDER GIRL) TROY HEADED WEST--TO CALIFORNIA AND THE DR. TAMMINES' SCHOOL FOR EXCEPTION GIRLS...FOR REASONS UNKNOWN!

SAN FRANCISCO DEPARTU

6

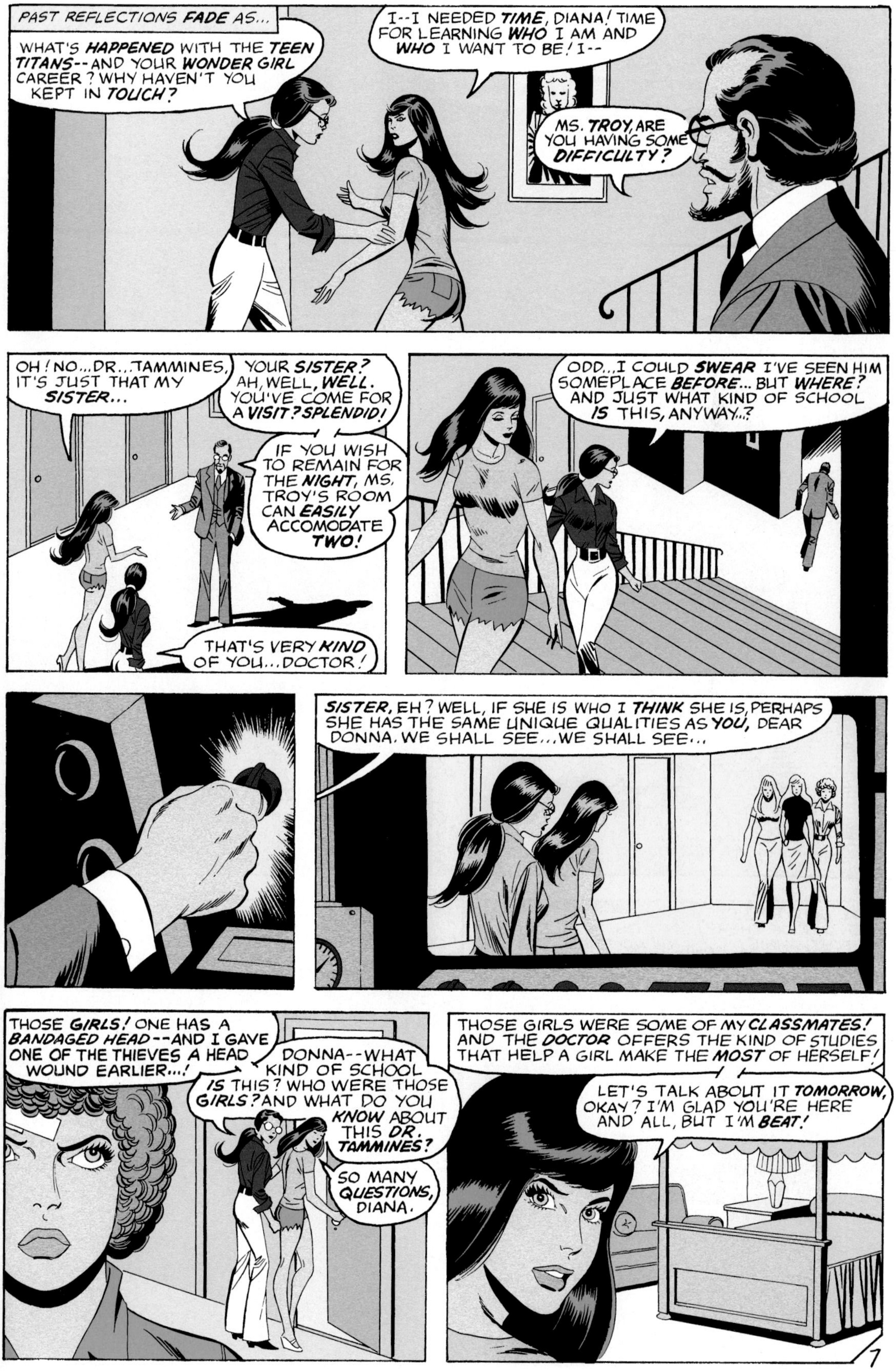
PAST REFLECTIONS FADE AS...
WHAT'S HAPPENED WITH THE TEEN TITANS--AND YOUR WONDER GIRL CAREER? WHY HAVEN'T YOU KEPT IN TOUCH?
I--I NEEDED TIME, DIANA! TIME FOR LEARNING WHO I AM AND WHO I WANT TO BE! I--
MS. TROY, ARE YOU HAVING SOME DIFFICULTY?
OH! NO...DR...TAMMINES, IT'S JUST THAT MY SISTER...
YOUR SISTER? AH, WELL, WELL. YOU'VE COME FOR A VISIT? SPLENDID!
IF YOU WISH TO REMAIN FOR THE NIGHT, MS. TROY'S ROOM CAN EASILY ACCOMODATE TWO!
THAT'S VERY KIND OF YOU...DOCTOR!
ODD...I COULD SWEAR I'VE SEEN HIM SOMEPLACE BEFORE... BUT WHERE? AND JUST WHAT KIND OF SCHOOL IS THIS, ANYWAY...?
SISTER, EH? WELL, IF SHE IS WHO I THINK SHE IS, PERHAPS SHE HAS THE SAME UNIQUE QUALITIES AS YOU, DEAR DONNA. WE SHALL SEE...WE SHALL SEE...
THOSE GIRLS! ONE HAS A BANDAGED HEAD--AND I GAVE ONE OF THE THIEVES A HEAD WOUND EARLIER...!
DONNA--WHAT KIND OF SCHOOL IS THIS? WHO WERE THOSE GIRLS? AND WHAT DO YOU KNOW ABOUT THIS DR. TAMMINES?
SO MANY QUESTIONS, DIANA.
THOSE GIRLS WERE SOME OF MY CLASSMATES! AND THE DOCTOR OFFERS THE KIND OF STUDIES THAT HELP A GIRL MAKE THE MOST OF HERSELF!
LET'S TALK ABOUT IT TOMORROW, OKAY? I'M GLAD YOU'RE HERE AND ALL, BUT I'M BEAT!

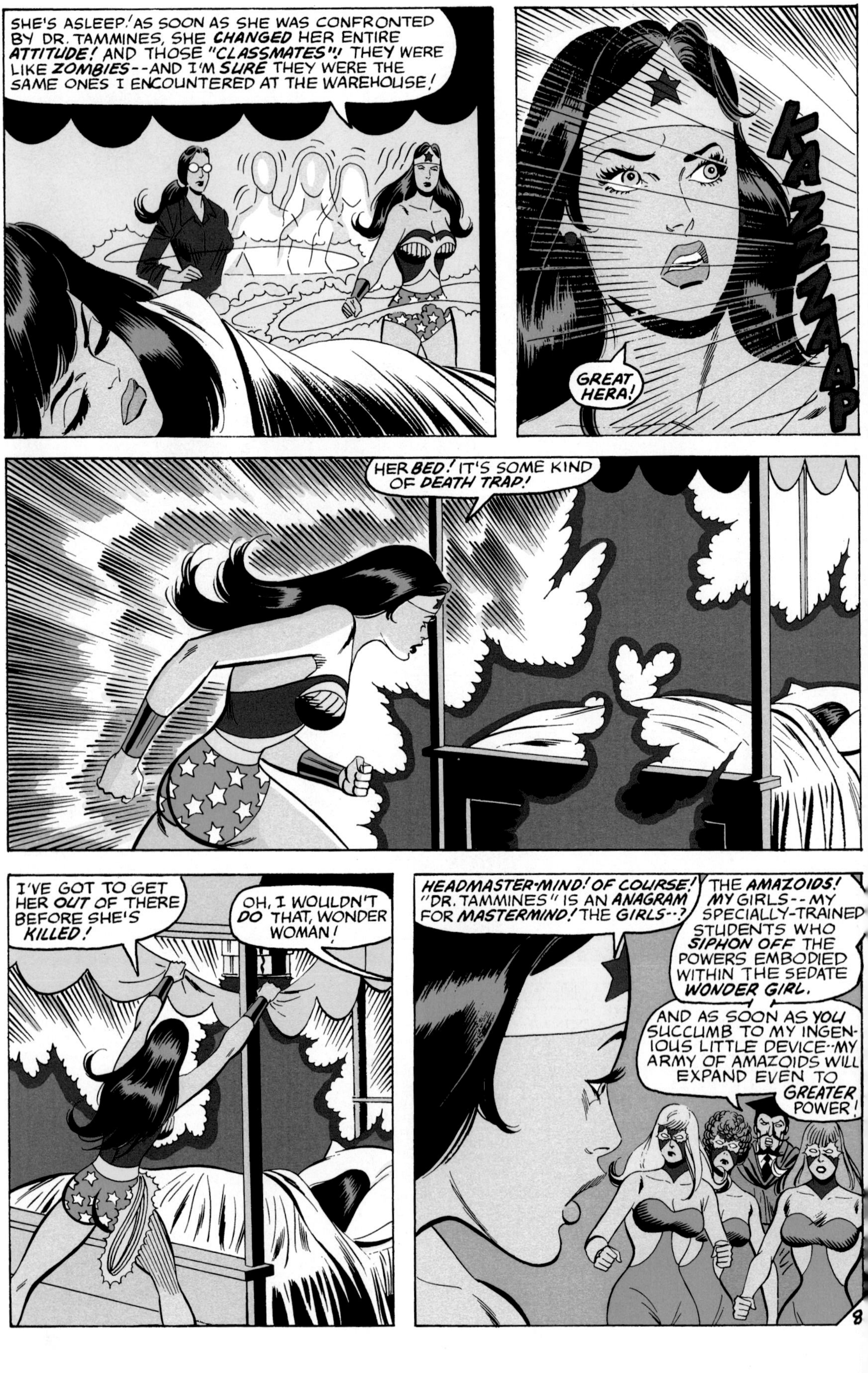
SHE'S ASLEEP! AS SOON AS SHE WAS CONFRONTED BY DR. TAMMINES, SHE CHANGED HER ENTIRE ATTITUDE! AND THOSE "CLASSMATES"! THEY WERE LIKE ZOMBIES--AND I'M SURE THEY WERE THE SAME ONES I ENCOUNTERED AT THE WAREHOUSE!
KAZZZZAAP
GREAT HERA!
HER BED! IT'S SOME KIND OF DEATH TRAP!
I'VE GOT TO GET HER OUT OF THERE BEFORE SHE'S KILLED!
OH, I WOULDN'T DO THAT, WONDER WOMAN!
HEADMASTER-MIND! OF COURSE! "DR. TAMMINES" IS AN ANAGRAM FOR MASTERMIND! THE GIRLS--?
THE AMAZOIDS! MY GIRLS--MY SPECIALLY-TRAINED STUDENTS WHO SIPHON OFF THE POWERS EMBODIED WITHIN THE SEDATE WONDER GIRL.
AND AS SOON AS YOU SUCCUMB TO MY INGENIOUS LITTLE DEVICE--MY ARMY OF AMAZOIDS WILL EXPAND EVEN TO GREATER POWER!
8

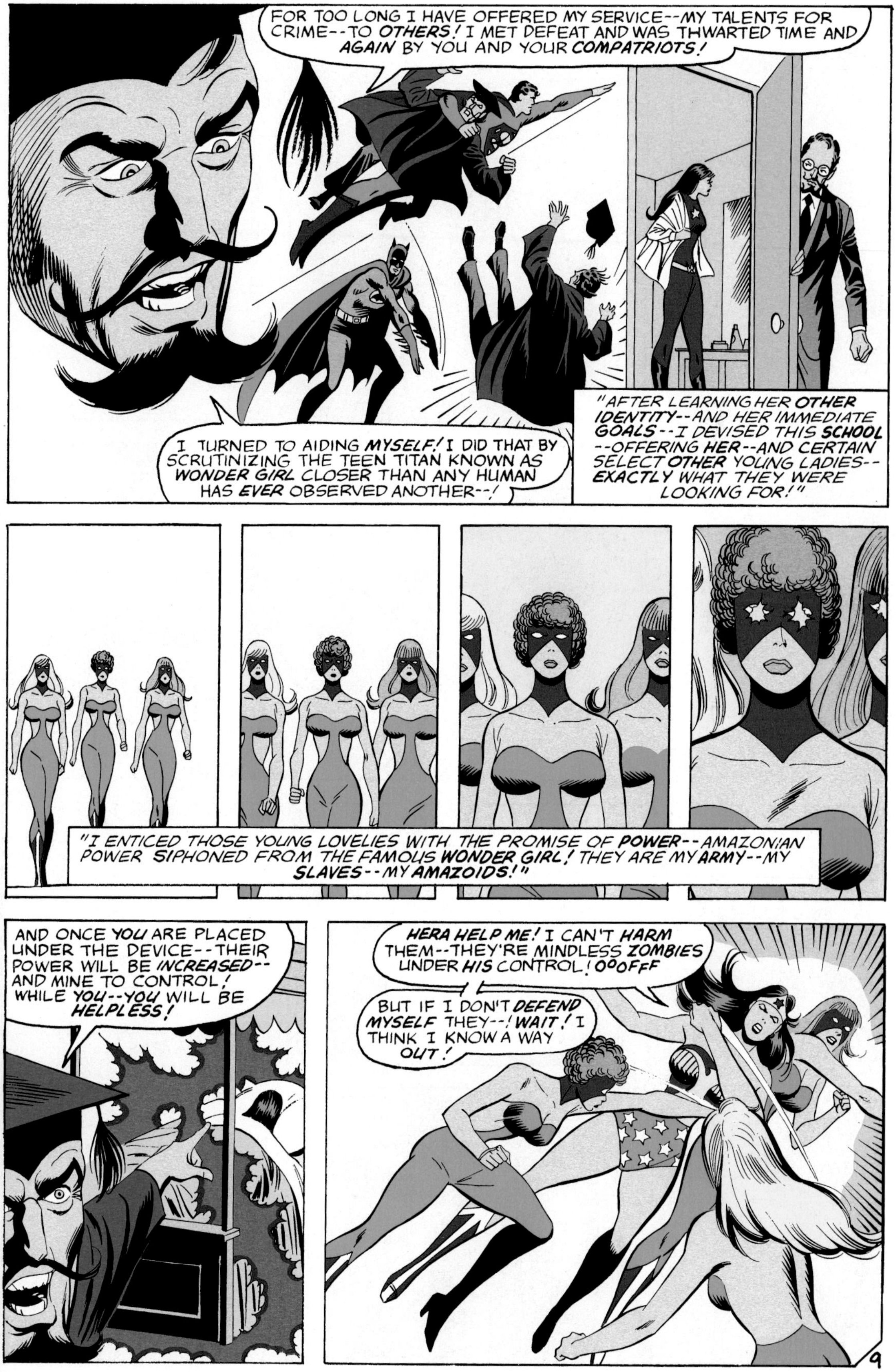
FOR TOO LONG I HAVE OFFERED MY SERVICE--MY TALENTS FOR CRIME--TO **OTHERS!** I MET DEFEAT AND WAS THWARTED TIME AND **AGAIN** BY YOU AND YOUR **COMPATRIOTS!**
I TURNED TO AIDING **MYSELF!** I DID THAT BY SCRUTINIZING THE TEEN TITAN KNOWN AS **WONDER GIRL** CLOSER THAN ANY HUMAN HAS **EVER** OBSERVED ANOTHER--!
"AFTER LEARNING HER **OTHER IDENTITY**--AND HER IMMEDIATE **GOALS**--I DEVISED THIS **SCHOOL**--OFFERING **HER**--AND CERTAIN SELECT **OTHER** YOUNG LADIES--**EXACTLY** WHAT THEY WERE LOOKING FOR!"
"I ENTICED THOSE YOUNG LOVELIES WITH THE PROMISE OF **POWER**--AMAZONIAN POWER SIPHONED FROM THE FAMOUS **WONDER GIRL!** THEY ARE MY **ARMY**--MY **SLAVES**--MY **AMAZOIDS!**"
AND ONCE **YOU** ARE PLACED UNDER THE DEVICE--THEIR POWER WILL BE **INCREASED**--AND MINE TO CONTROL! WHILE **YOU**--**YOU** WILL BE **HELPLESS!**
HERA HELP ME! I CAN'T **HARM** THEM--THEY'RE MINDLESS **ZOMBIES** UNDER **HIS** CONTROL! OOOFFF
BUT IF I DON'T **DEFEND MYSELF** THEY--! **WAIT!** I THINK I KNOW A WAY **OUT!**

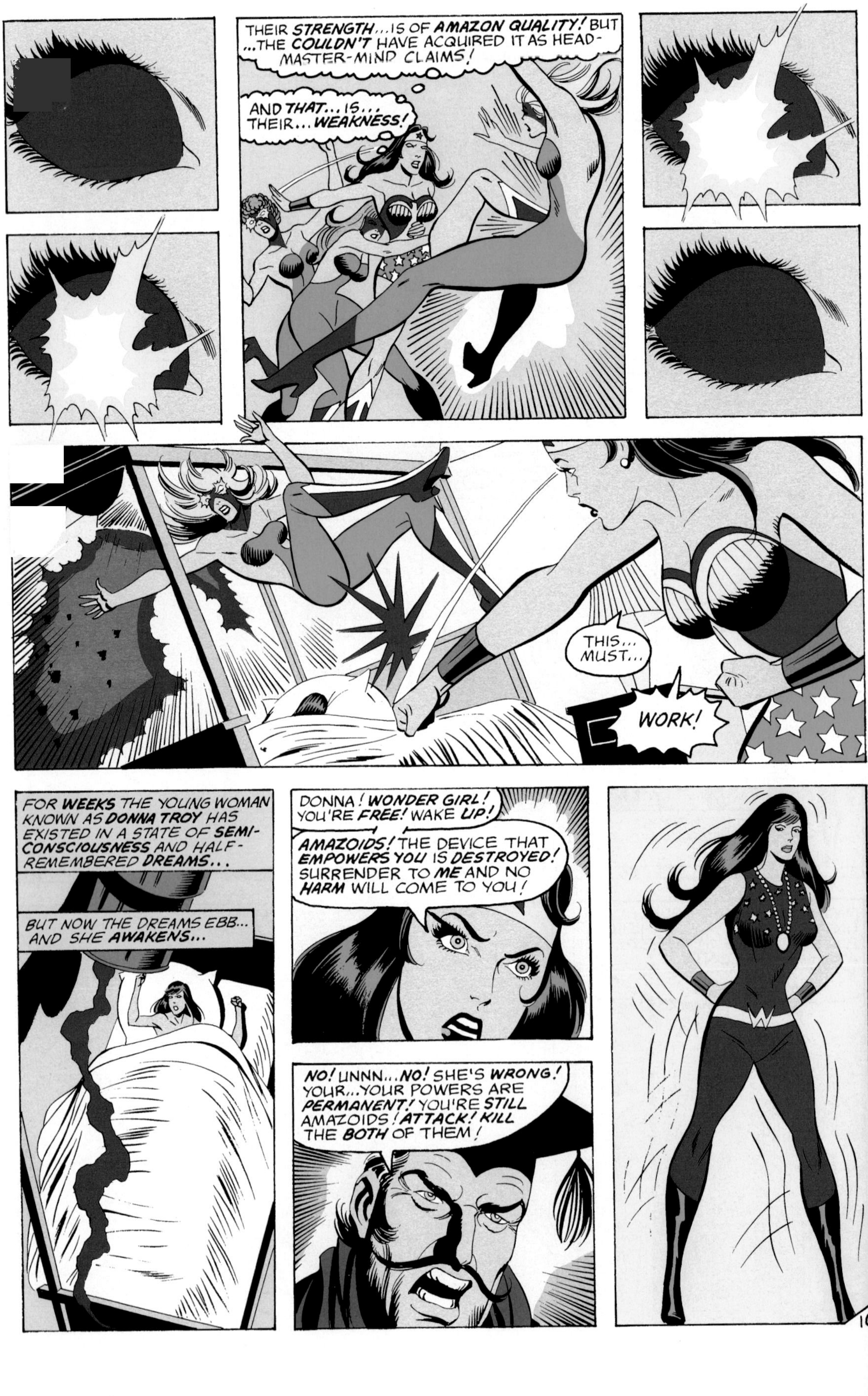

THEIR STRENGTH... IS OF AMAZON QUALITY! BUT ...THE COULDN'T HAVE ACQUIRED IT AS HEAD-MASTER-MIND CLAIMS!
AND THAT... IS... THEIR... WEAKNESS!
THIS... MUST...
WORK!
FOR WEEKS THE YOUNG WOMAN KNOWN AS DONNA TROY HAS EXISTED IN A STATE OF SEMI-CONSCIOUSNESS AND HALF-REMEMBERED DREAMS...
BUT NOW THE DREAMS EBB... AND SHE AWAKENS...
DONNA! WONDER GIRL! YOU'RE FREE! WAKE UP!
AMAZOIDS! THE DEVICE THAT EMPOWERS YOU IS DESTROYED! SURRENDER TO ME AND NO HARM WILL COME TO YOU!
NO! UNNN... NO! SHE'S WRONG! YOUR... YOUR POWERS ARE PERMANENT! YOU'RE STILL AMAZOIDS! ATTACK! KILL THE BOTH OF THEM!

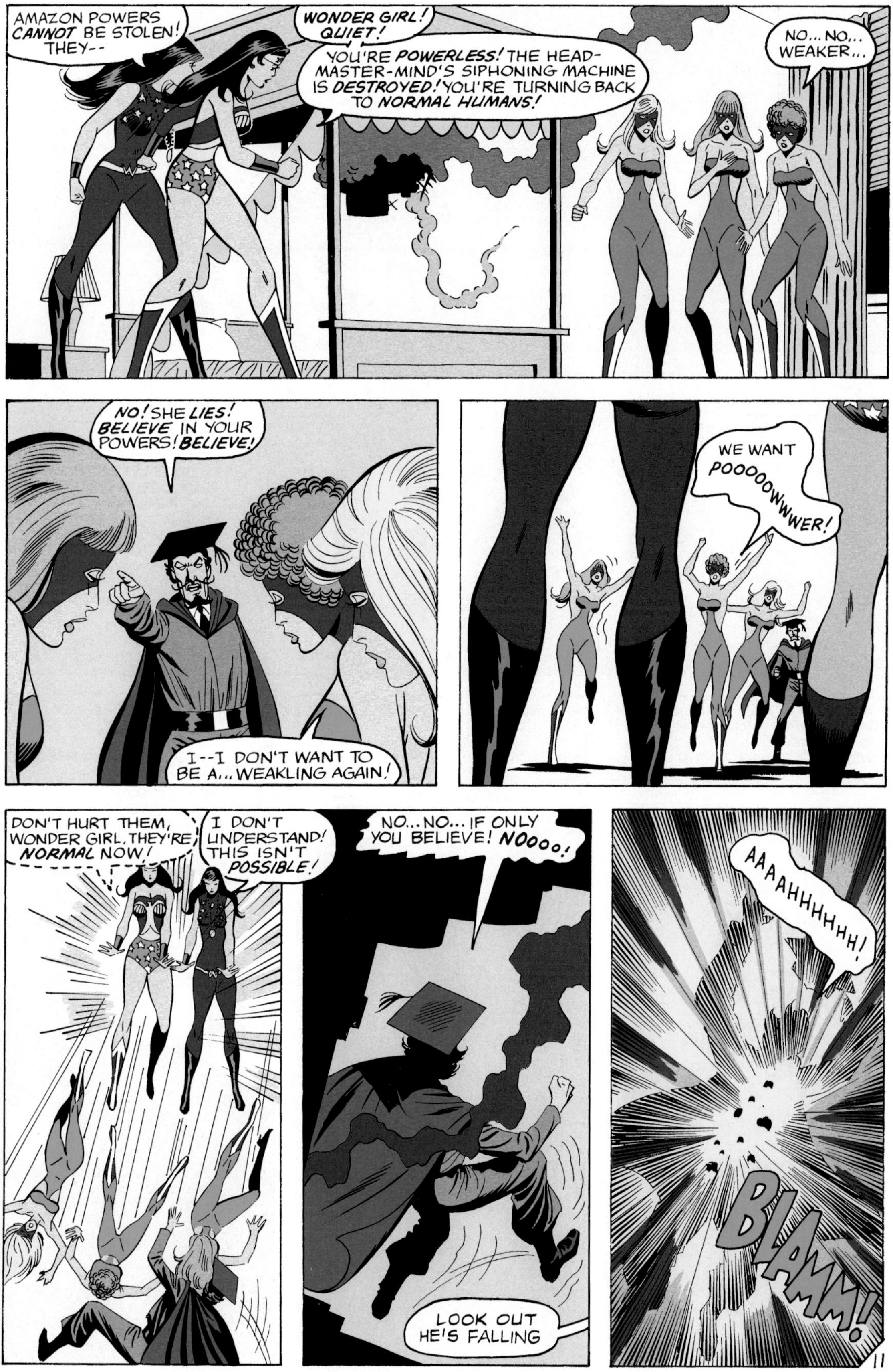
AMAZON POWERS CANNOT BE STOLEN! THEY--
WONDER GIRL! QUIET!
YOU'RE POWERLESS! THE HEAD-MASTER-MIND'S SIPHONING MACHINE IS DESTROYED! YOU'RE TURNING BACK TO NORMAL HUMANS!
NO... NO... WEAKER...
NO! SHE LIES! BELIEVE IN YOUR POWERS! BELIEVE!
I--I DON'T WANT TO BE A... WEAKLING AGAIN!
WE WANT POOOOOWWWER!
DON'T HURT THEM, WONDER GIRL, THEY'RE NORMAL NOW!
I DON'T UNDERSTAND! THIS ISN'T POSSIBLE!
NO... NO... IF ONLY YOU BELIEVE! NOOOO!
LOOK OUT HE'S FALLING
AAAAHHHHHHH!
BLAMM!

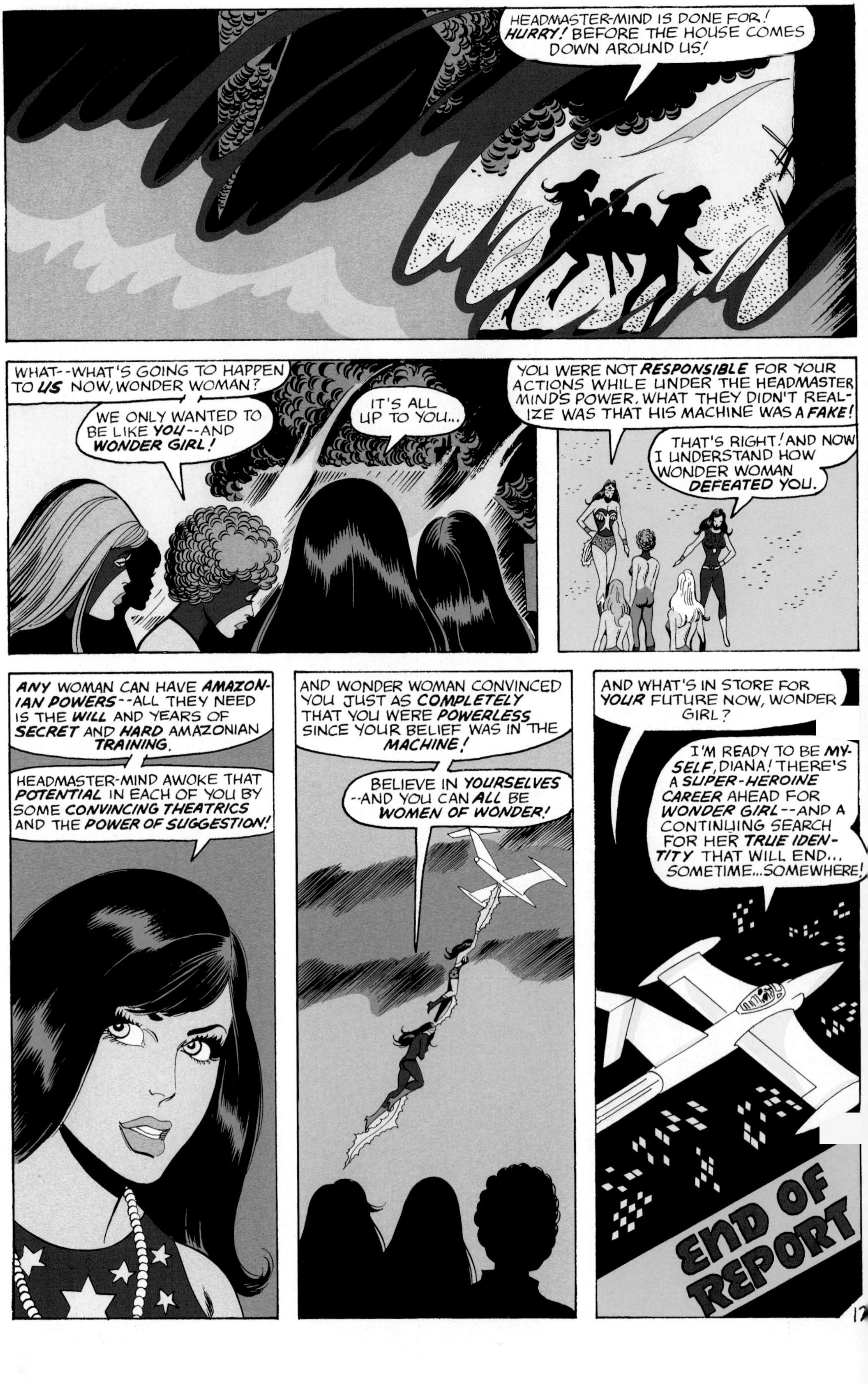
HEADMASTER-MIND IS DONE FOR! HURRY! BEFORE THE HOUSE COMES DOWN AROUND US!
WHAT--WHAT'S GOING TO HAPPEN TO US NOW, WONDER WOMAN?
WE ONLY WANTED TO BE LIKE YOU--AND WONDER GIRL!
IT'S ALL UP TO YOU...
YOU WERE NOT RESPONSIBLE FOR YOUR ACTIONS WHILE UNDER THE HEADMASTER MIND'S POWER. WHAT THEY DIDN'T REAL-IZE WAS THAT HIS MACHINE WAS A FAKE!
THAT'S RIGHT! AND NOW I UNDERSTAND HOW WONDER WOMAN DEFEATED YOU.
ANY WOMAN CAN HAVE AMAZON-IAN POWERS--ALL THEY NEED IS THE WILL AND YEARS OF SECRET AND HARD AMAZONIAN TRAINING.
HEADMASTER-MIND AWOKE THAT POTENTIAL IN EACH OF YOU BY SOME CONVINCING THEATRICS AND THE POWER OF SUGGESTION!
AND WONDER WOMAN CONVINCED YOU JUST AS COMPLETELY THAT YOU WERE POWERLESS SINCE YOUR BELIEF WAS IN THE MACHINE!
BELIEVE IN YOURSELVES --AND YOU CAN ALL BE WOMEN OF WONDER!
AND WHAT'S IN STORE FOR YOUR FUTURE NOW, WONDER GIRL?
I'M READY TO BE MY-SELF, DIANA! THERE'S A SUPER-HEROINE CAREER AHEAD FOR WONDER GIRL--AND A CONTINUING SEARCH FOR HER TRUE IDEN-TITY THAT WILL END... SOMETIME...SOMEWHERE!
END OF REPORT

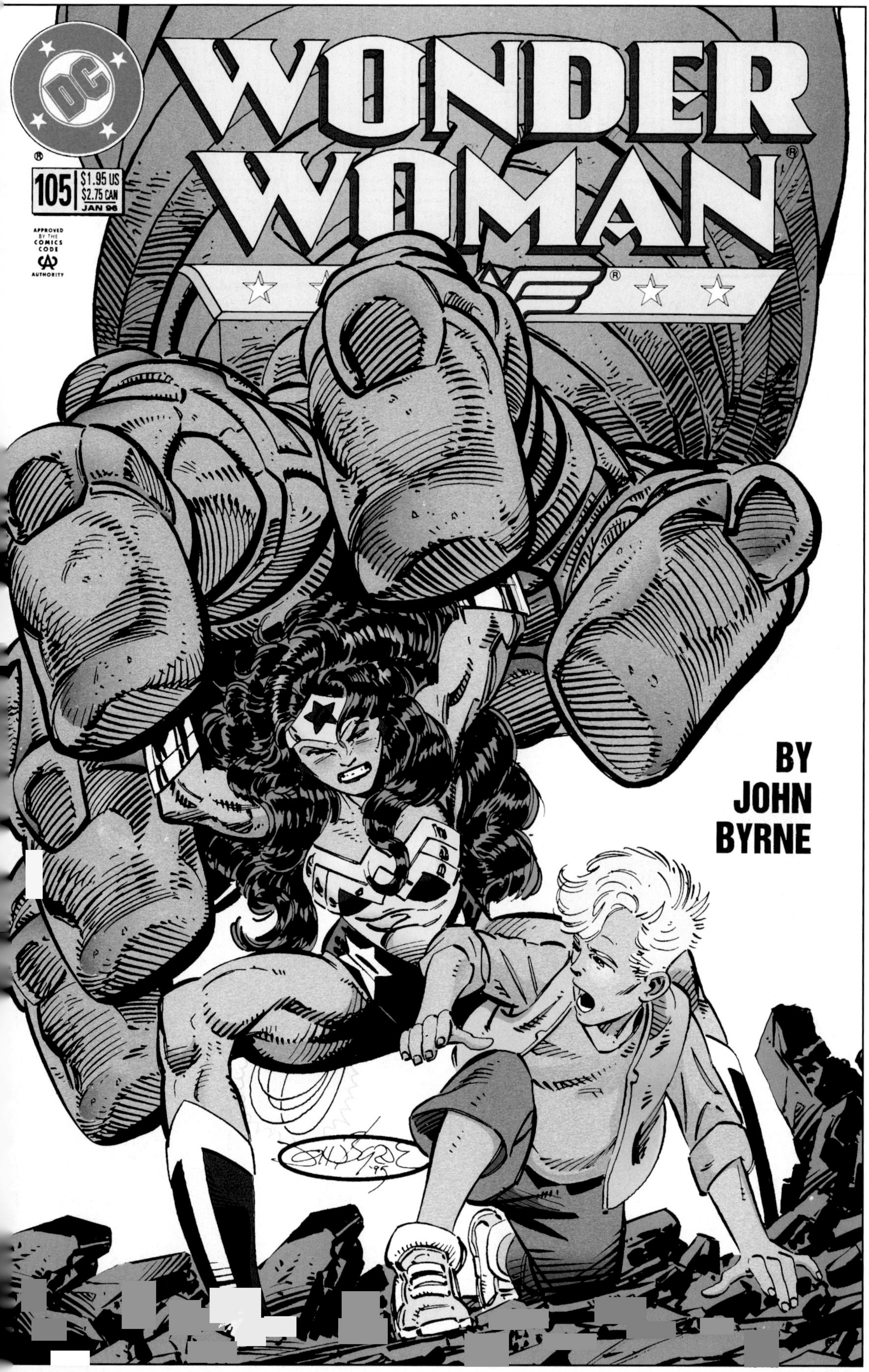
DC
WONDER WOMAN
105
$1.95 US
$2.75 CAN
JAN 96
APPROVED BY THE COMICS CODE AUTHORITY
BY JOHN BYRNE

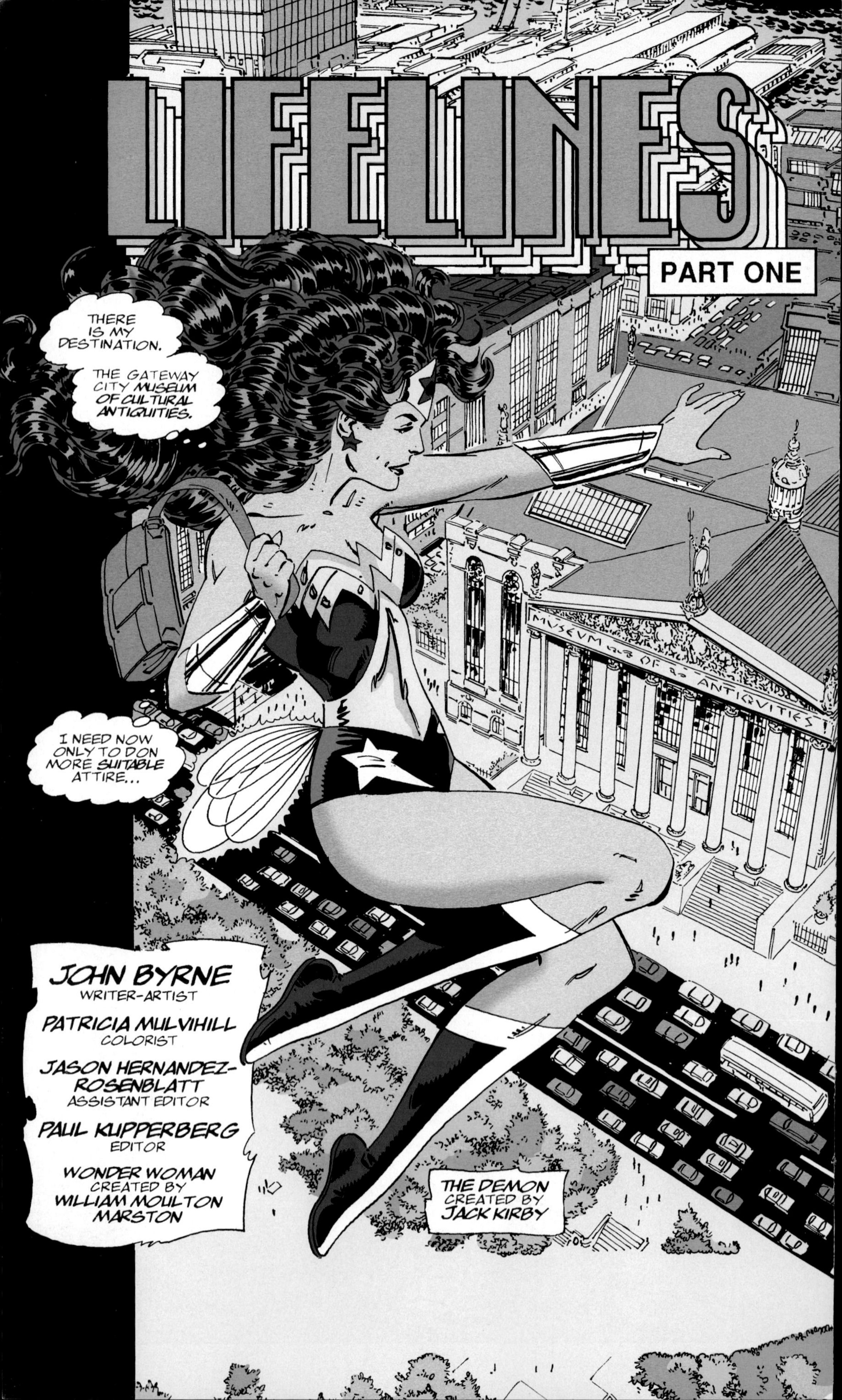
LIFELINES
PART ONE
THERE IS MY DESTINATION.
THE GATEWAY CITY MUSEUM OF CULTURAL ANTIQUITIES.
I NEED NOW ONLY TO DON MORE SUITABLE ATTIRE...
MUSEUM OF ANTIQUITIES
JOHN BYRNE WRITER-ARTIST
PATRICIA MULVIHILL COLORIST
JASON HERNANDEZ-ROSENBLATT ASSISTANT EDITOR
PAUL KUPPERBERG EDITOR
WONDER WOMAN CREATED BY WILLIAM MOULTON MARSTON
THE DEMON CREATED BY JACK KIRBY

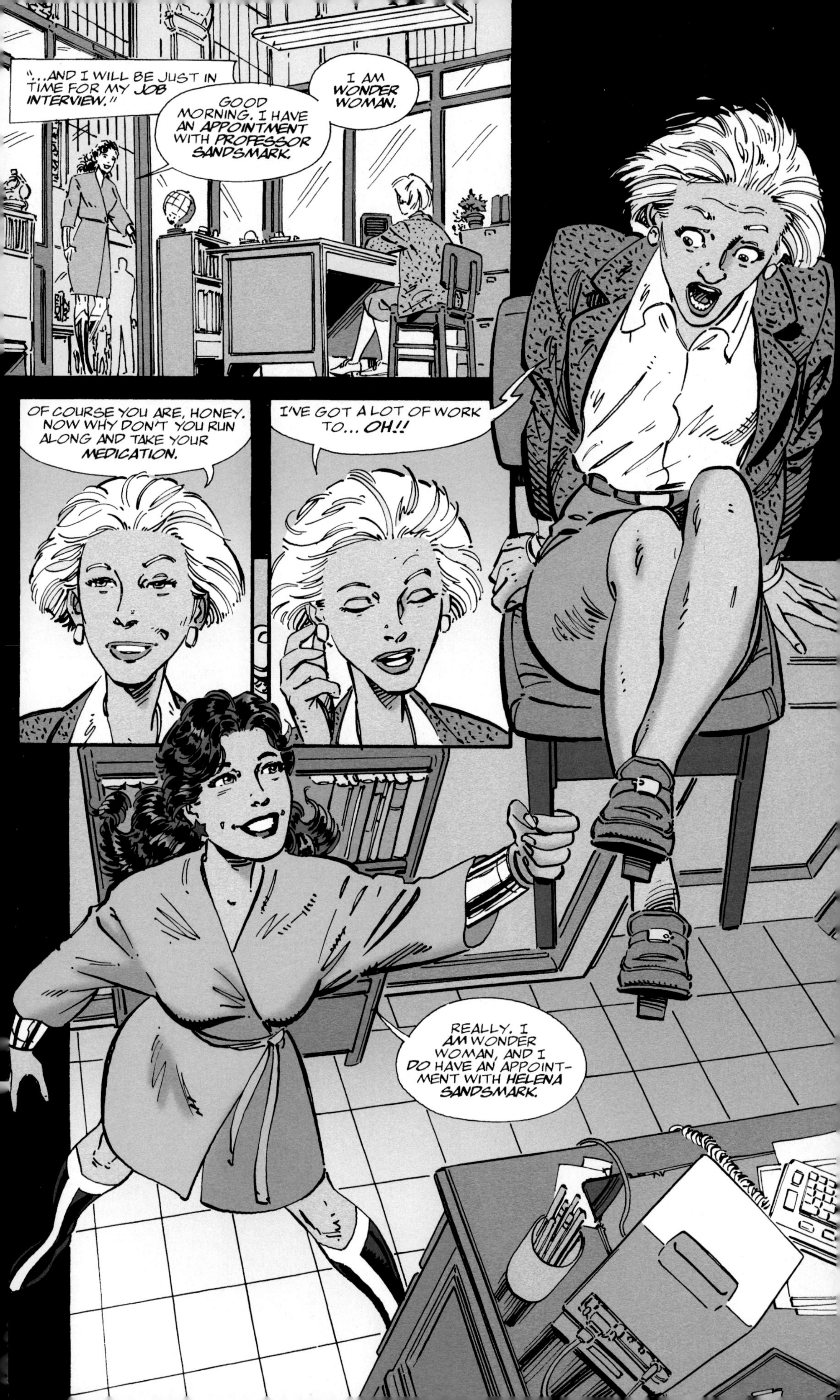
"...AND I WILL BE JUST IN TIME FOR MY JOB INTERVIEW."
GOOD MORNING. I HAVE AN APPOINTMENT WITH PROFESSOR SANDSMARK.
I AM WONDER WOMAN.
OF COURSE YOU ARE, HONEY. NOW WHY DON'T YOU RUN ALONG AND TAKE YOUR MEDICATION.
I'VE GOT A LOT OF WORK TO... OH!!
REALLY. I AM WONDER WOMAN, AND I DO HAVE AN APPOINTMENT WITH HELENA SANDSMARK.

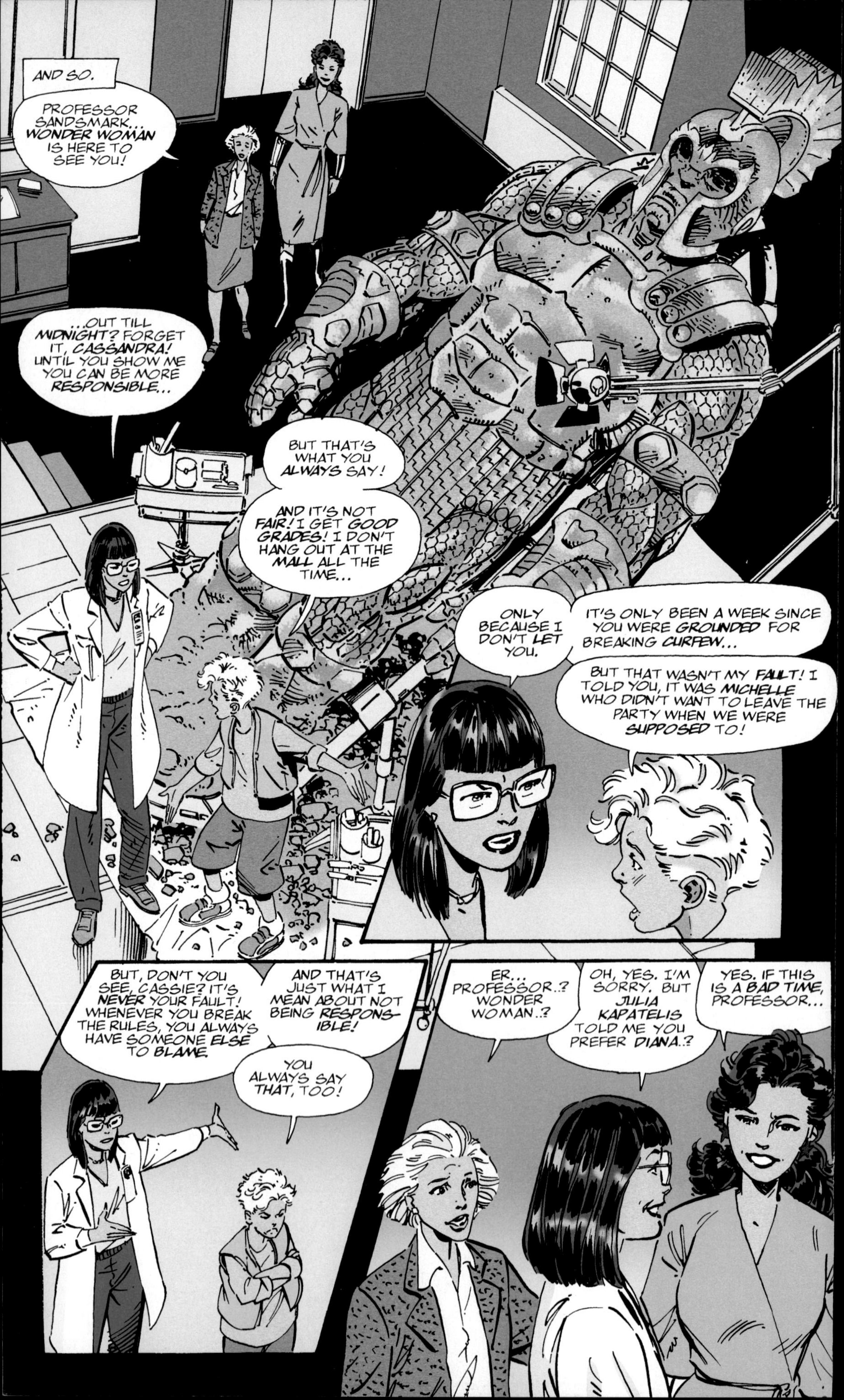
AND SO.
PROFESSOR SANDSMARK... WONDER WOMAN IS HERE TO SEE YOU!
...OUT TILL MIDNIGHT? FORGET IT, CASSANDRA! UNTIL YOU SHOW ME YOU CAN BE MORE RESPONSIBLE...
BUT THAT'S WHAT YOU ALWAYS SAY!
AND IT'S NOT FAIR! I GET GOOD GRADES! I DON'T HANG OUT AT THE MALL ALL THE TIME...
ONLY BECAUSE I DON'T LET YOU.
IT'S ONLY BEEN A WEEK SINCE YOU WERE GROUNDED FOR BREAKING CURFEW...
BUT THAT WASN'T MY FAULT! I TOLD YOU, IT WAS MICHELLE WHO DIDN'T WANT TO LEAVE THE PARTY WHEN WE WERE SUPPOSED TO!
BUT, DON'T YOU SEE, CASSIE? IT'S NEVER YOUR FAULT! WHENEVER YOU BREAK THE RULES, YOU ALWAYS HAVE SOMEONE ELSE TO BLAME.
AND THAT'S JUST WHAT I MEAN ABOUT NOT BEING RESPONSIBLE!
YOU ALWAYS SAY THAT, TOO!
ER... PROFESSOR..? WONDER WOMAN..?
OH, YES. I'M SORRY. BUT JULIA KAPATELIS TOLD ME YOU PREFER DIANA..?
YES. IF THIS IS A BAD TIME, PROFESSOR...

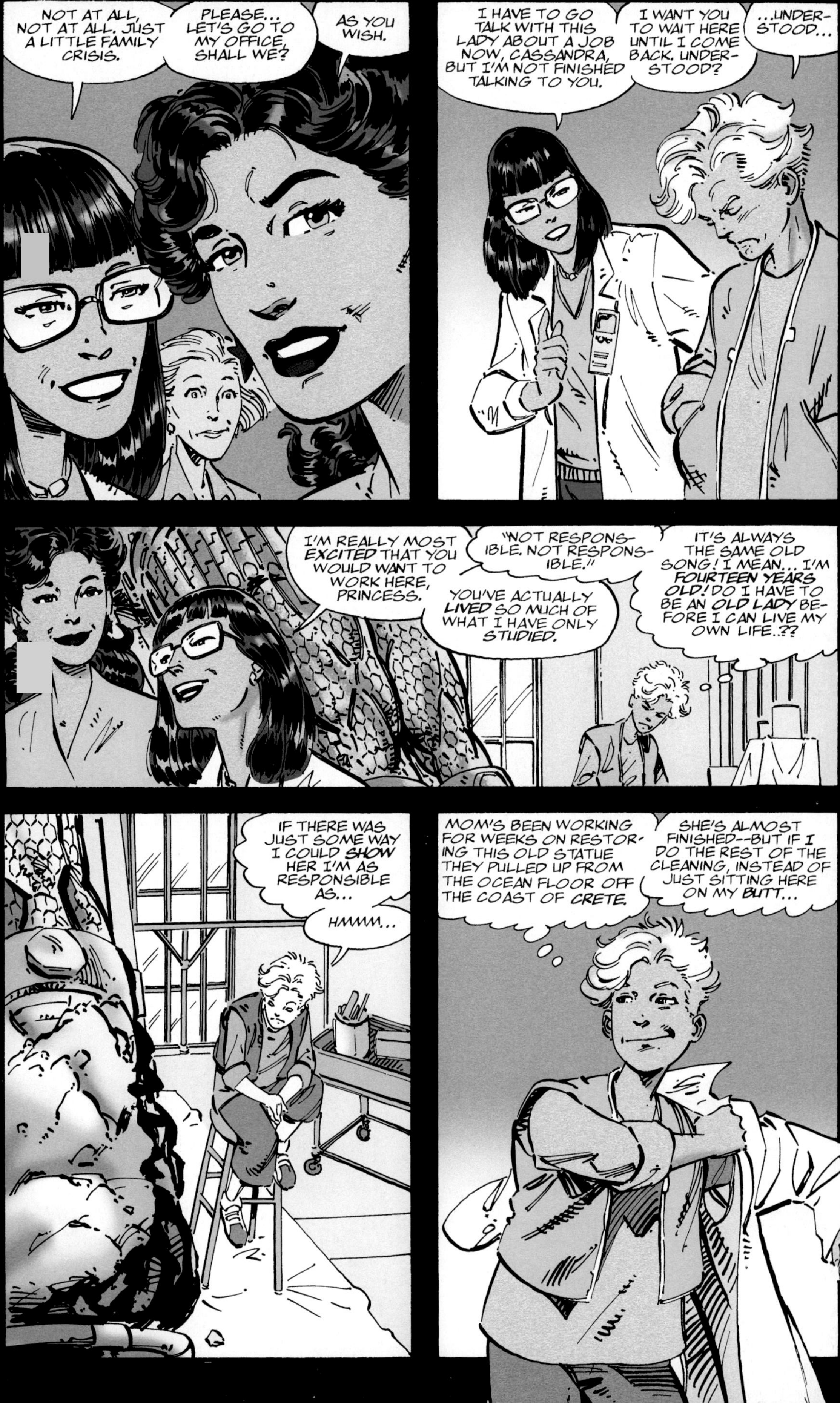
NOT AT ALL, NOT AT ALL. JUST A LITTLE FAMILY CRISIS.
PLEASE... LET'S GO TO MY OFFICE, SHALL WE?
AS YOU WISH.
I HAVE TO GO TALK WITH THIS LADY ABOUT A JOB NOW, CASSANDRA, BUT I'M NOT FINISHED TALKING TO YOU.
I WANT YOU TO WAIT HERE UNTIL I COME BACK. UNDERSTOOD?
...UNDERSTOOD...
I'M REALLY MOST EXCITED THAT YOU WOULD WANT TO WORK HERE, PRINCESS.
YOU'VE ACTUALLY LIVED SO MUCH OF WHAT I HAVE ONLY STUDIED.
"NOT RESPONSIBLE. NOT RESPONSIBLE."
IT'S ALWAYS THE SAME OLD SONG! I MEAN... I'M FOURTEEN YEARS OLD! DO I HAVE TO BE AN OLD LADY BEFORE I CAN LIVE MY OWN LIFE..??
IF THERE WAS JUST SOME WAY I COULD SHOW HER I'M AS RESPONSIBLE AS...
HMMM...
MOM'S BEEN WORKING FOR WEEKS ON RESTORING THIS OLD STATUE THEY PULLED UP FROM THE OCEAN FLOOR OFF THE COAST OF CRETE.
SHE'S ALMOST FINISHED--BUT IF I DO THE REST OF THE CLEANING, INSTEAD OF JUST SITTING HERE ON MY BUTT...

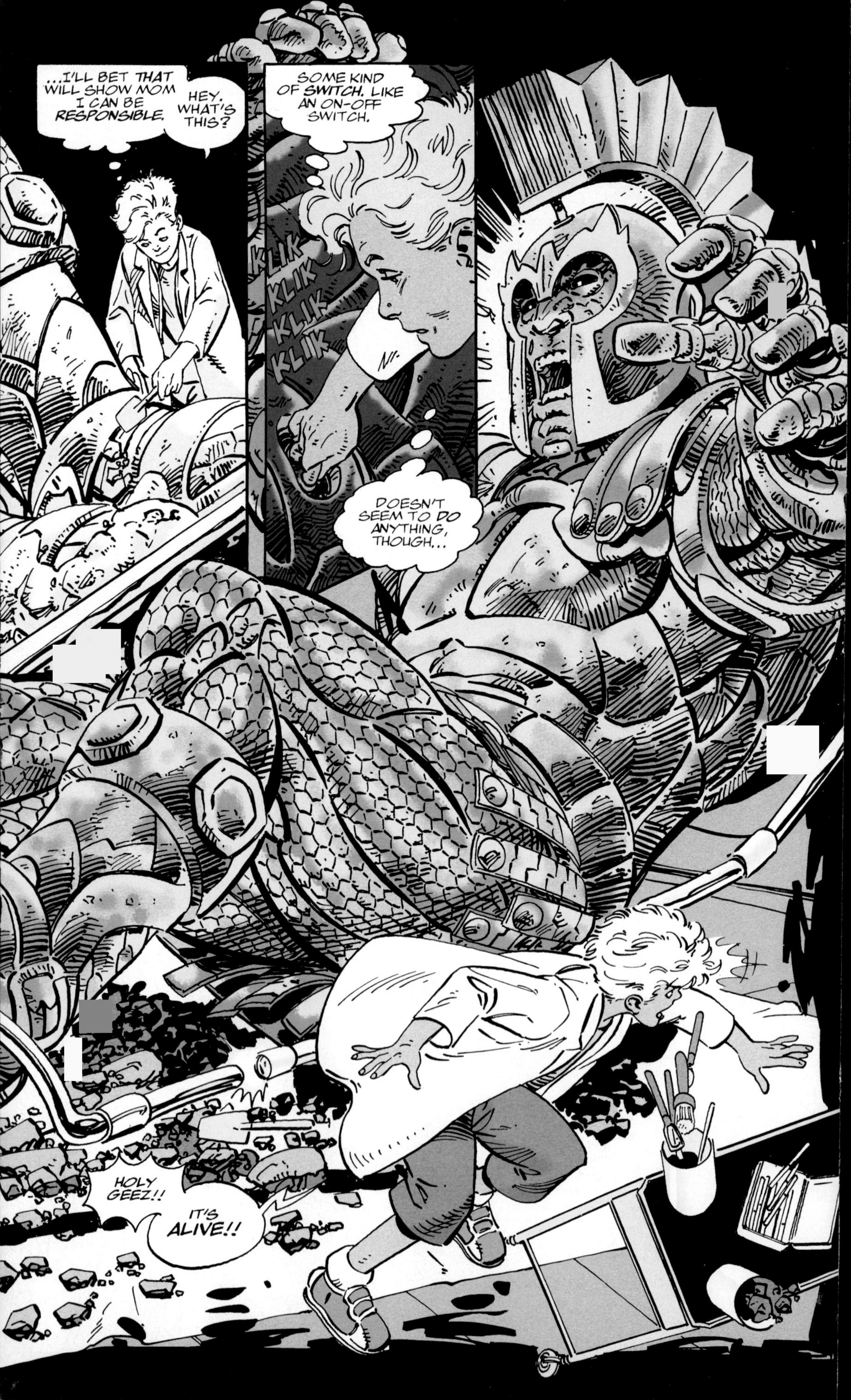

...I'LL BET THAT WILL SHOW MOM I CAN BE RESPONSIBLE.
HEY. WHAT'S THIS?
SOME KIND OF SWITCH. LIKE AN ON-OFF SWITCH.
KLIK KLIK KLIK KLIK KLIK
DOESN'T SEEM TO DO ANYTHING, THOUGH...
HOLY GEEZ!!
IT'S ALIVE!!

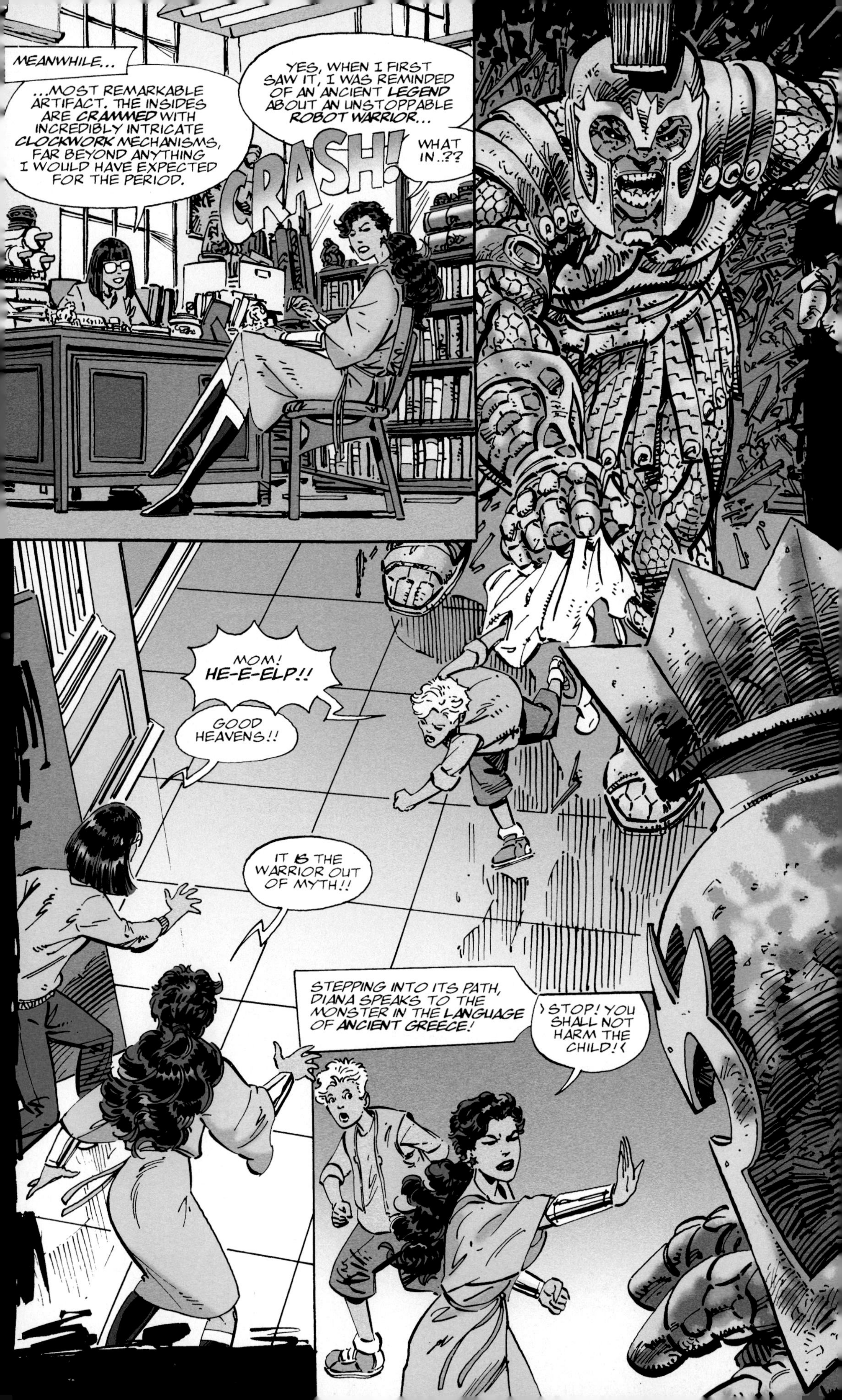
MEANWHILE...
...MOST REMARKABLE ARTIFACT. THE INSIDES ARE CRAMMED WITH INCREDIBLY INTRICATE CLOCKWORK MECHANISMS, FAR BEYOND ANYTHING I WOULD HAVE EXPECTED FOR THE PERIOD.
YES, WHEN I FIRST SAW IT, I WAS REMINDED OF AN ANCIENT LEGEND ABOUT AN UNSTOPPABLE ROBOT WARRIOR...
CRASH!
WHAT IN..??
MOM! HE-E-ELP!!
GOOD HEAVENS!!
IT IS THE WARRIOR OUT OF MYTH!!
STEPPING INTO ITS PATH, DIANA SPEAKS TO THE MONSTER IN THE LANGUAGE OF ANCIENT GREECE!
›STOP! YOU SHALL NOT HARM THE CHILD!‹

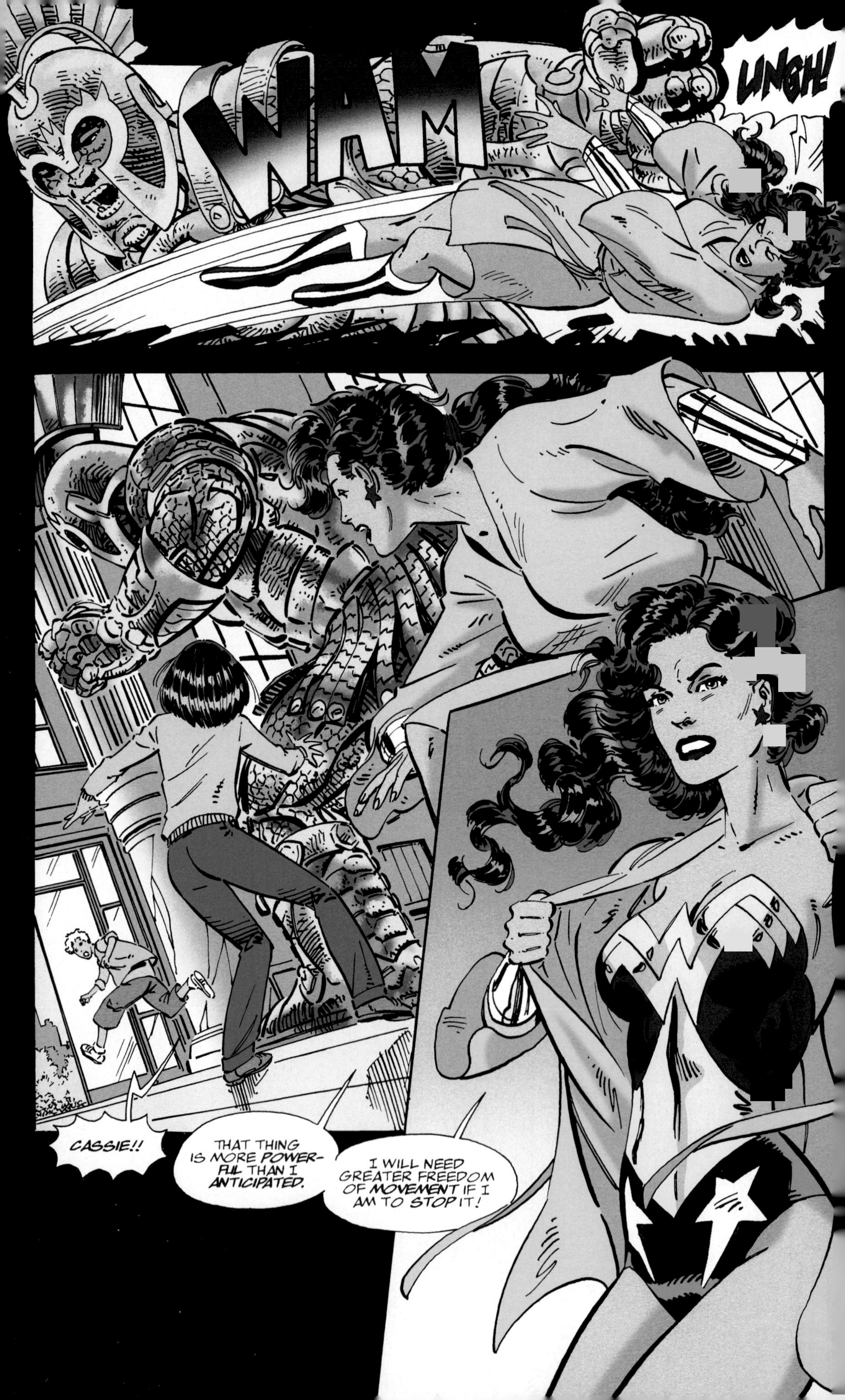
WAM
UNGH!
CASSIE!!
THAT THING IS MORE POWER-FUL THAN I ANTICIPATED.
I WILL NEED GREATER FREEDOM OF MOVEMENT IF I AM TO STOP IT!

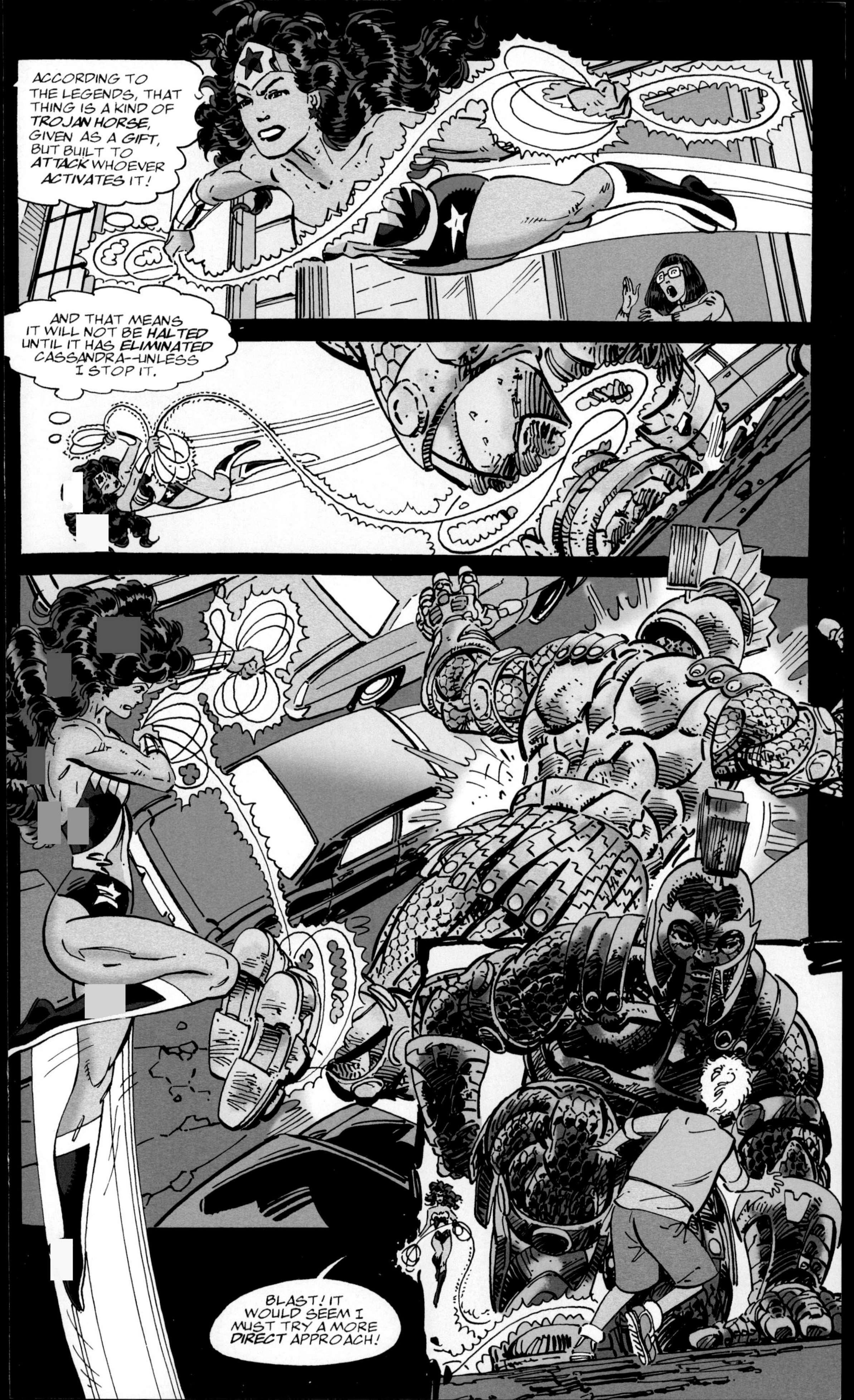
ACCORDING TO THE LEGENDS, THAT THING IS A KIND OF TROJAN HORSE, GIVEN AS A GIFT, BUT BUILT TO ATTACK WHOEVER ACTIVATES IT!
AND THAT MEANS IT WILL NOT BE HALTED UNTIL IT HAS ELIMINATED CASSANDRA--UNLESS I STOP IT.
BLAST! IT WOULD SEEM I MUST TRY A MORE DIRECT APPROACH!

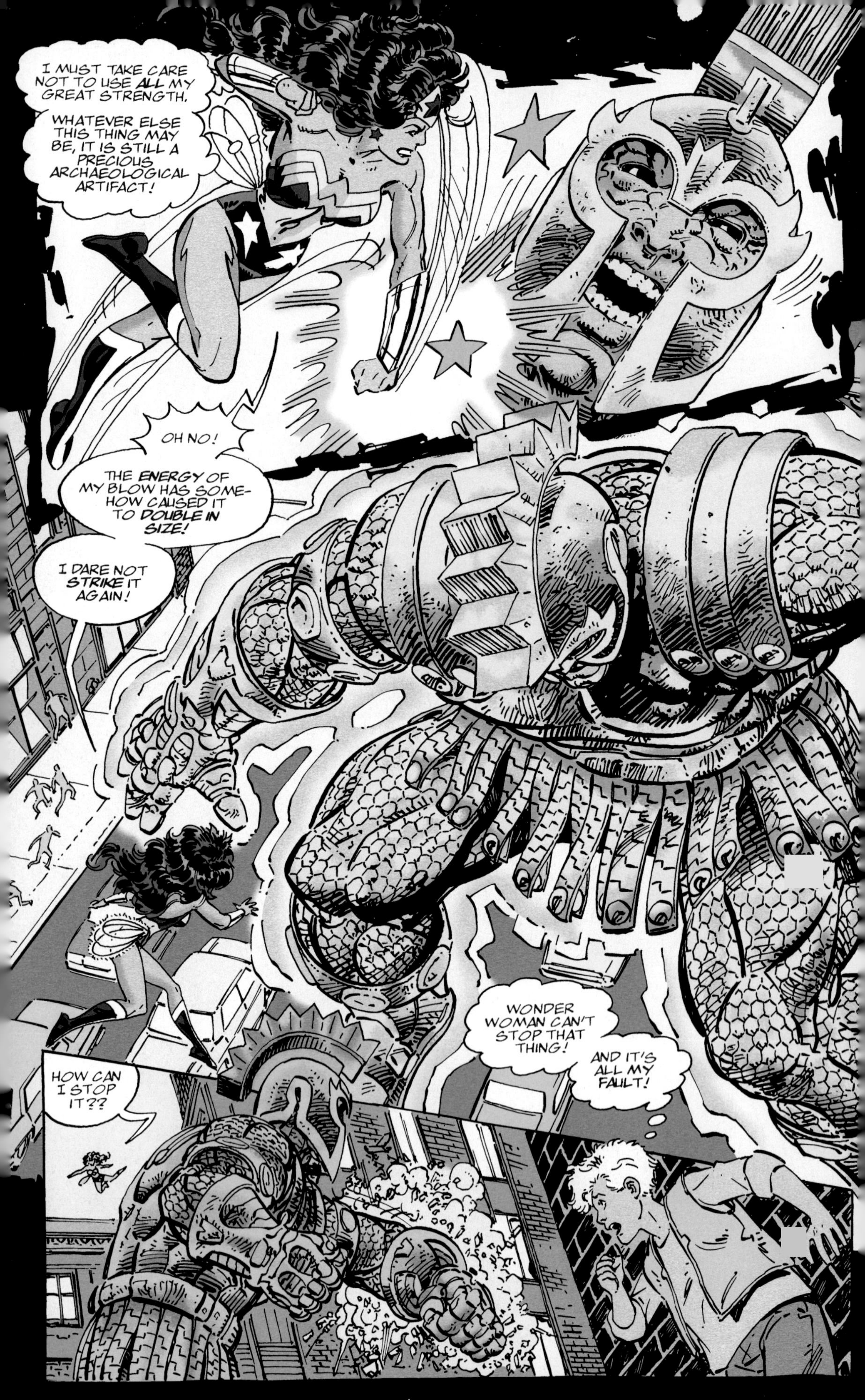
I MUST TAKE CARE NOT TO USE ALL MY GREAT STRENGTH.
WHATEVER ELSE THIS THING MAY BE, IT IS STILL A PRECIOUS ARCHAEOLOGICAL ARTIFACT!
OH NO!
THE ENERGY OF MY BLOW HAS SOMEHOW CAUSED IT TO DOUBLE IN SIZE!
I DARE NOT STRIKE IT AGAIN!
WONDER WOMAN CAN'T STOP THAT THING!
AND IT'S ALL MY FAULT!
HOW CAN I STOP IT??

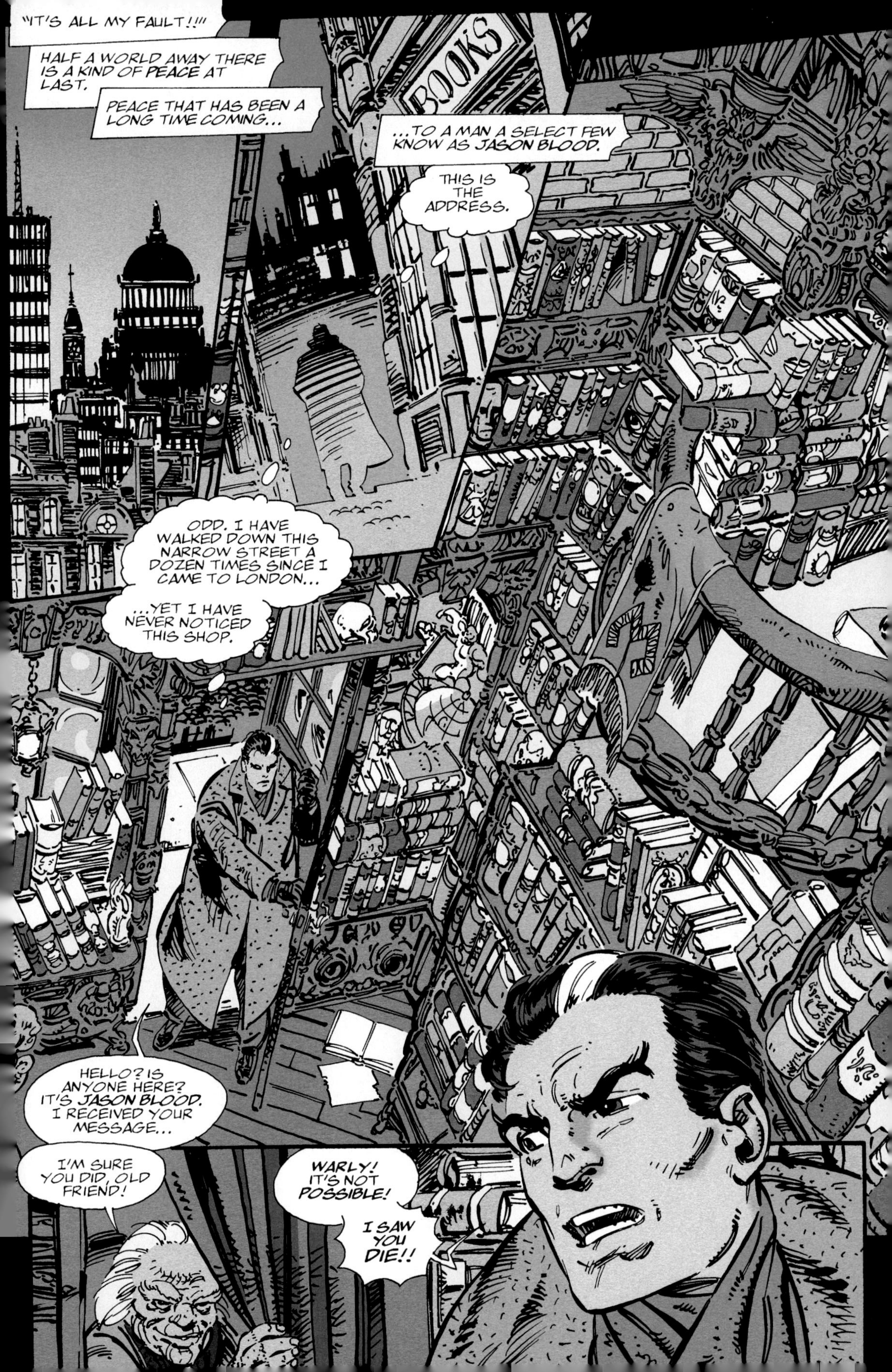
"IT'S ALL MY FAULT!!"
HALF A WORLD AWAY THERE IS A KIND OF PEACE AT LAST.
PEACE THAT HAS BEEN A LONG TIME COMING...
...TO A MAN A SELECT FEW KNOW AS JASON BLOOD.
BOOKS
THIS IS THE ADDRESS.
ODD. I HAVE WALKED DOWN THIS NARROW STREET A DOZEN TIMES SINCE I CAME TO LONDON...
...YET I HAVE NEVER NOTICED THIS SHOP.
HELLO? IS ANYONE HERE? IT'S JASON BLOOD. I RECEIVED YOUR MESSAGE...
I'M SURE YOU DID, OLD FRIEND!
WARLY! IT'S NOT POSSIBLE!
I SAW YOU DIE!!

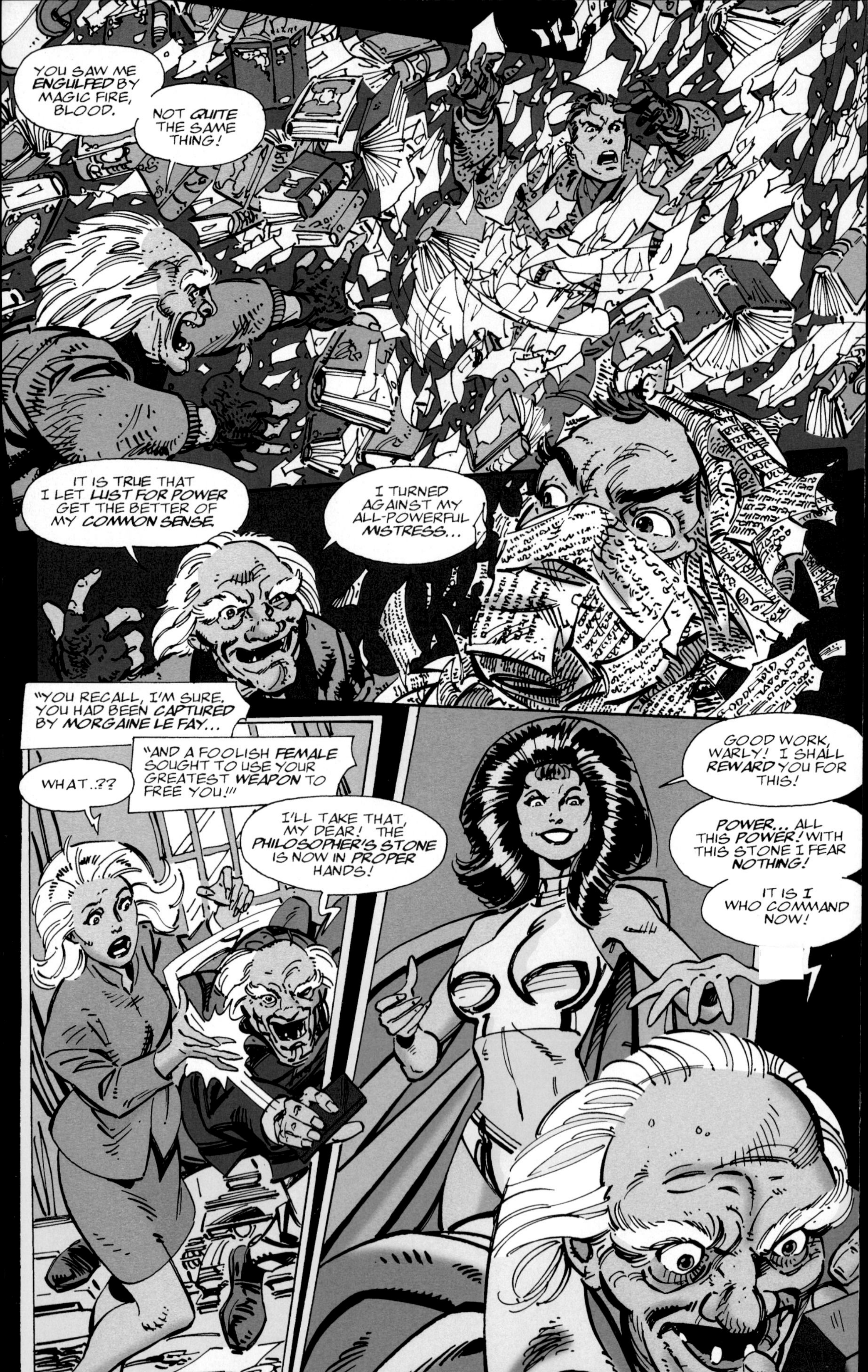
YOU SAW ME ENGULFED BY MAGIC FIRE, BLOOD.
NOT QUITE THE SAME THING!
IT IS TRUE THAT I LET LUST FOR POWER GET THE BETTER OF MY COMMON SENSE.
I TURNED AGAINST MY ALL-POWERFUL MISTRESS...
"YOU RECALL, I'M SURE. YOU HAD BEEN CAPTURED BY MORGAINE LE FAY...
"AND A FOOLISH FEMALE SOUGHT TO USE YOUR GREATEST WEAPON TO FREE YOU!"
WHAT..??
I'LL TAKE THAT, MY DEAR! THE PHILOSOPHER'S STONE IS NOW IN PROPER HANDS!
GOOD WORK, WARLY! I SHALL REWARD YOU FOR THIS!
POWER... ALL THIS POWER! WITH THIS STONE I FEAR NOTHING!
IT IS I WHO COMMAND NOW!

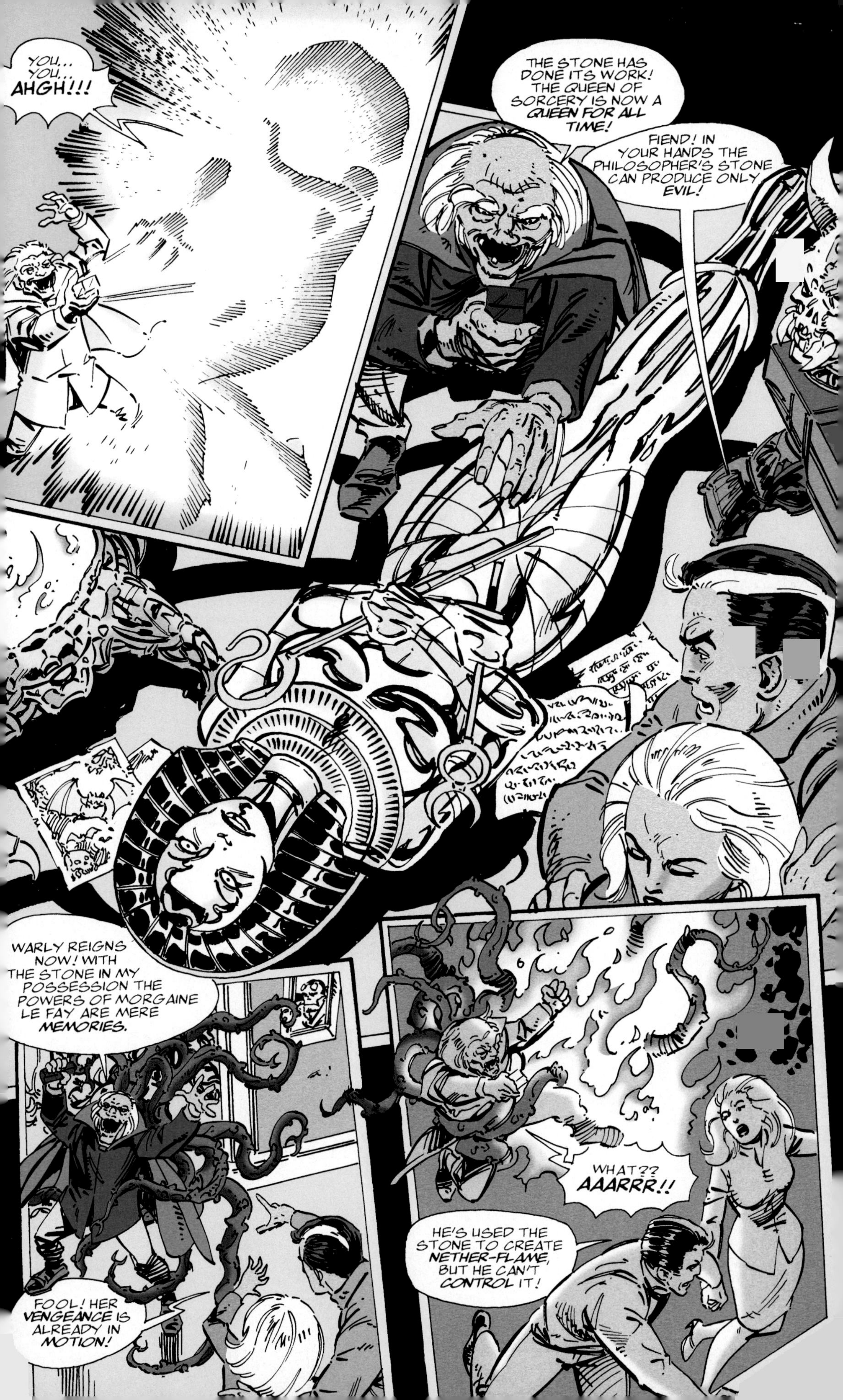
YOU... YOU... **AHGH!!!**
THE STONE HAS DONE ITS WORK! THE QUEEN OF SORCERY IS NOW A ***QUEEN FOR ALL TIME!***
FIEND! IN YOUR HANDS THE PHILOSOPHER'S STONE CAN PRODUCE ONLY ***EVIL!***
WARLY REIGNS NOW! WITH THE STONE IN MY POSSESSION THE POWERS OF MORGAINE LE FAY ARE MERE ***MEMORIES.***
FOOL! HER ***VENGEANCE*** IS ALREADY IN ***MOTION!***
WHAT?? ***AAARRR!!***
HE'S USED THE STONE TO CREATE ***NETHER-FLAME,*** BUT HE CAN'T ***CONTROL*** IT!

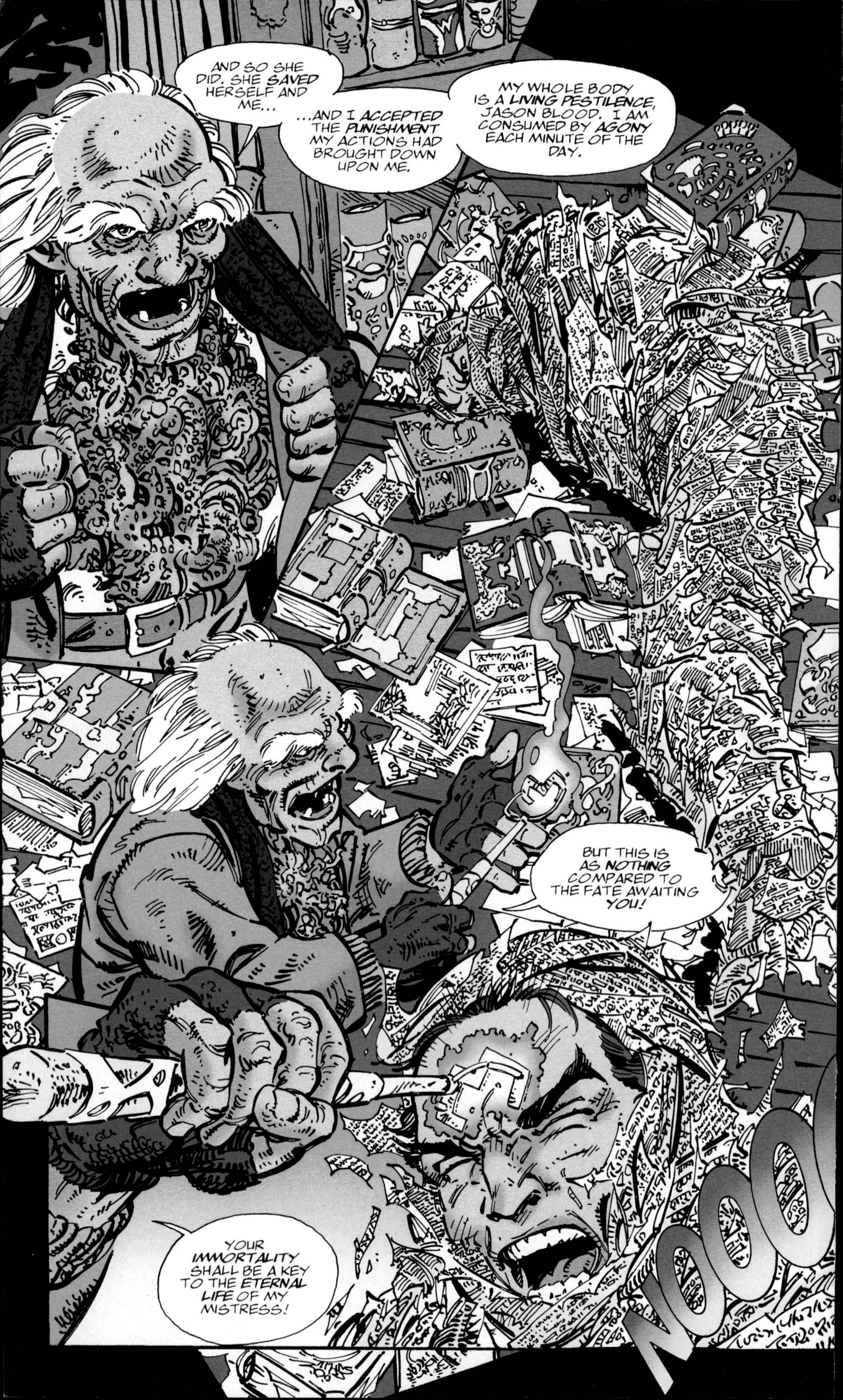
AND SO SHE DID. SHE SAVED HERSELF AND ME...
...AND I ACCEPTED THE PUNISHMENT MY ACTIONS HAD BROUGHT DOWN UPON ME.
MY WHOLE BODY IS A LIVING PESTILENCE, JASON BLOOD. I AM CONSUMED BY AGONY EACH MINUTE OF THE DAY.
BUT THIS IS AS NOTHING COMPARED TO THE FATE AWAITING YOU!
YOUR IMMORTALITY SHALL BE A KEY TO THE ETERNAL LIFE OF MY MISTRESS!
NOOOO

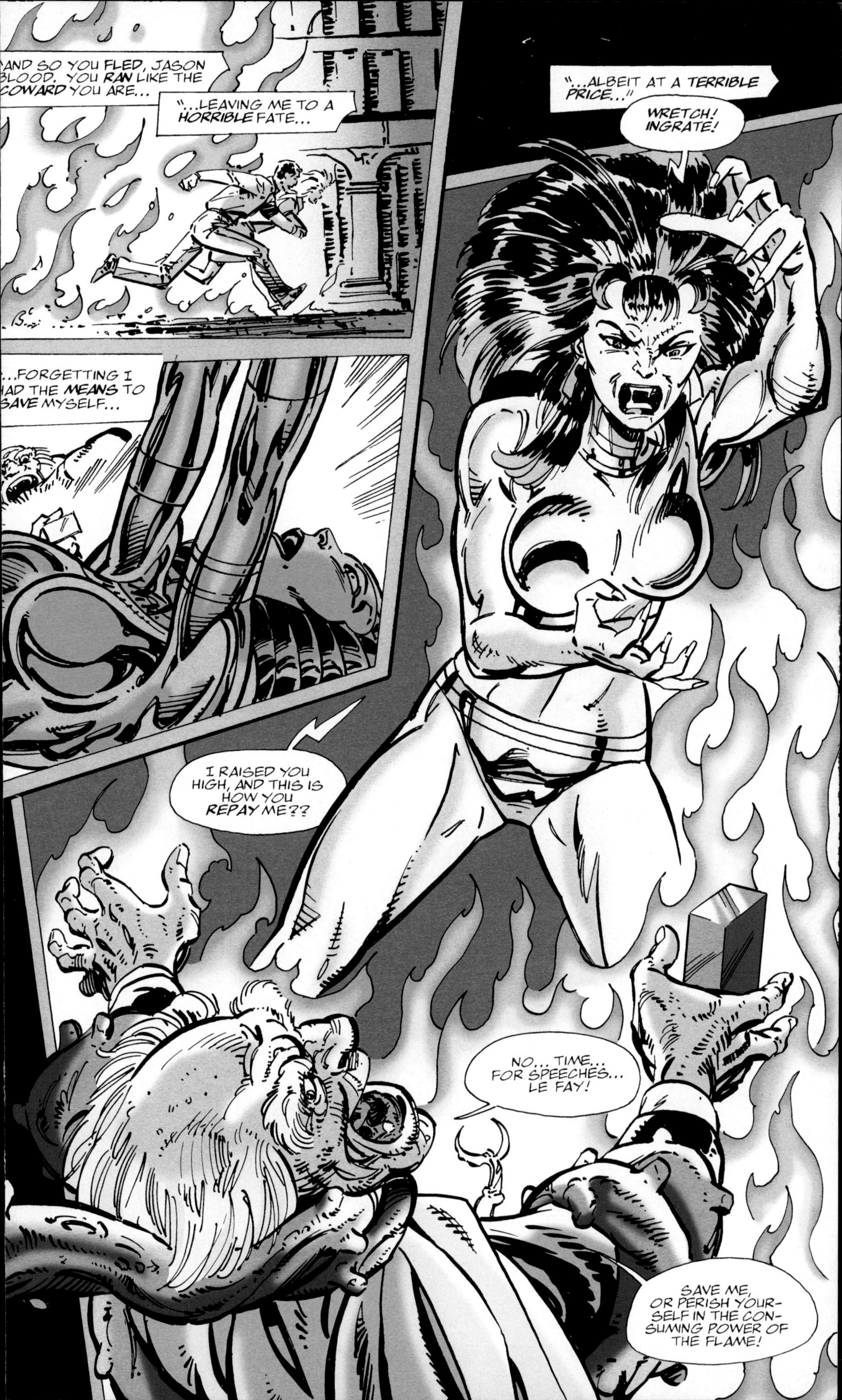

AND SO YOU FLED, JASON BLOOD. YOU RAN LIKE THE COWARD YOU ARE...
"...LEAVING ME TO A HORRIBLE FATE...
"...ALBEIT AT A TERRIBLE PRICE..."
WRETCH! INGRATE!
...FORGETTING I HAD THE MEANS TO SAVE MYSELF...
I RAISED YOU HIGH, AND THIS IS HOW YOU REPAY ME??
NO... TIME... FOR SPEECHES... LE FAY!
SAVE ME, OR PERISH YOURSELF IN THE CONSUMING POWER OF THE FLAME!

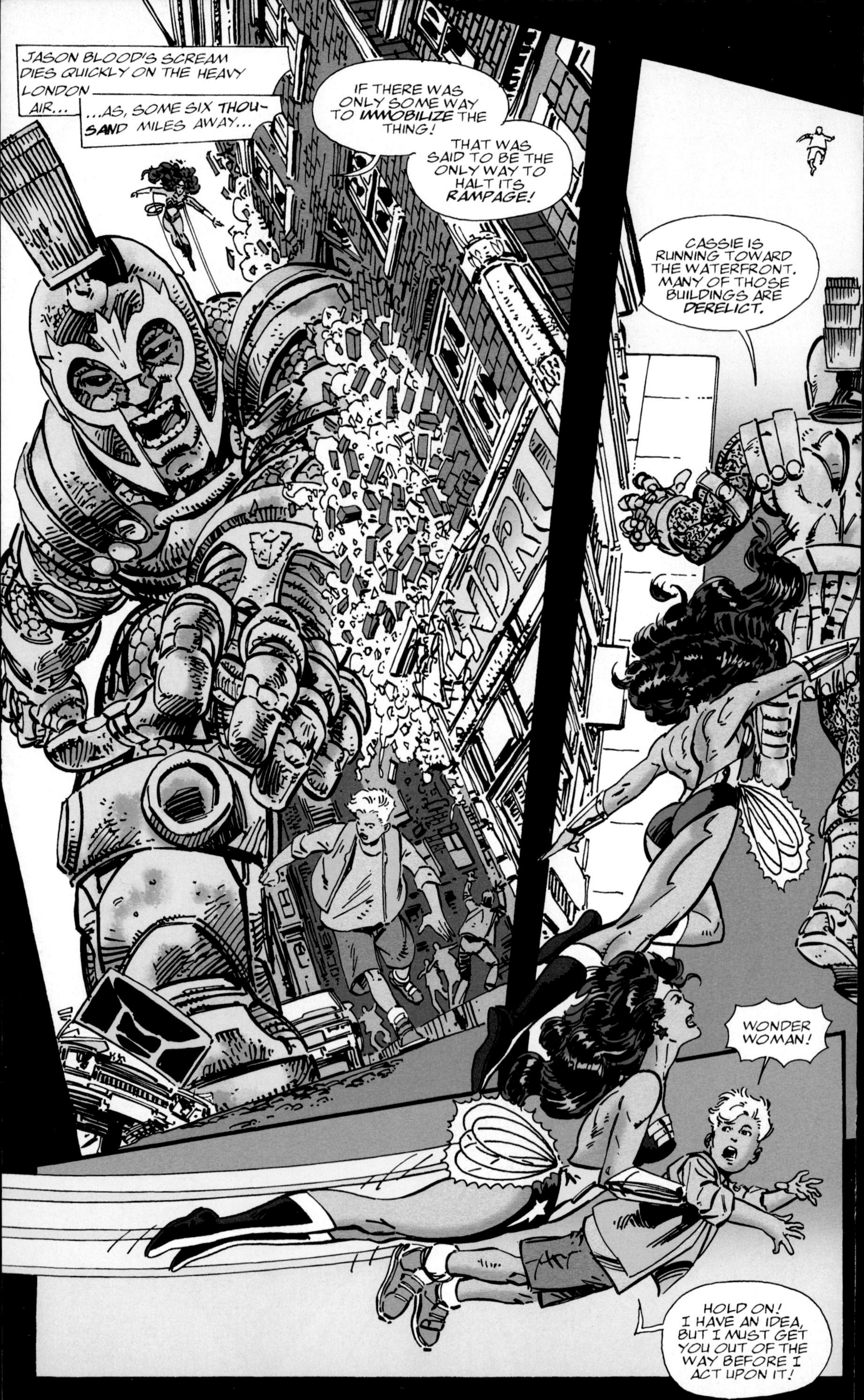
JASON BLOOD'S SCREAM DIES QUICKLY ON THE HEAVY LONDON AIR...
...AS, SOME SIX THOUSAND MILES AWAY...
IF THERE WAS ONLY SOME WAY TO IMMOBILIZE THE THING!
THAT WAS SAID TO BE THE ONLY WAY TO HALT ITS RAMPAGE!
CASSIE IS RUNNING TOWARD THE WATERFRONT. MANY OF THOSE BUILDINGS ARE DERELICT.
WONDER WOMAN!
HOLD ON! I HAVE AN IDEA, BUT I MUST GET YOU OUT OF THE WAY BEFORE I ACT UPON IT!

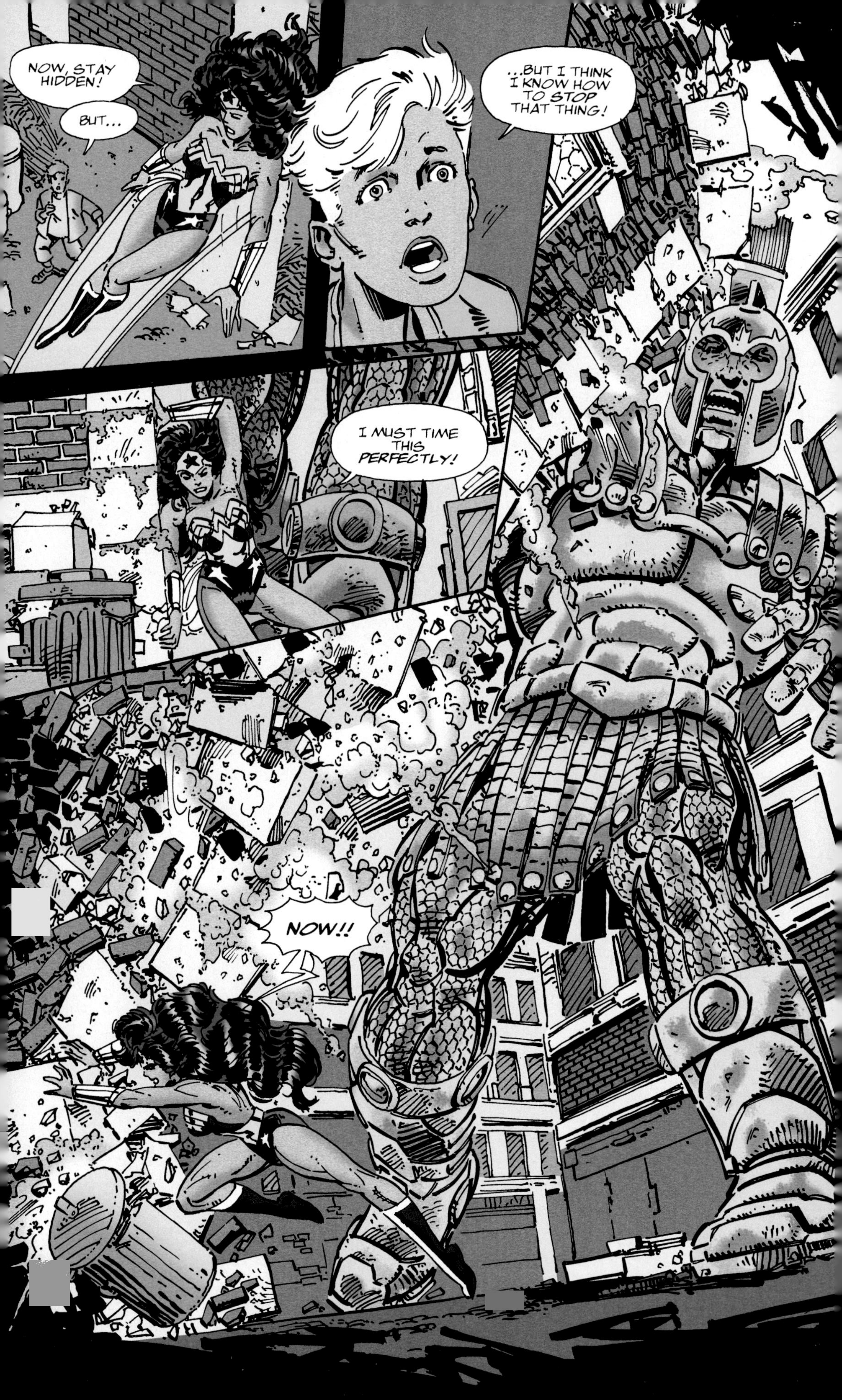
NOW, STAY HIDDEN!
BUT...
...BUT I THINK I KNOW HOW TO STOP THAT THING!
I MUST TIME THIS PERFECTLY!
NOW!!

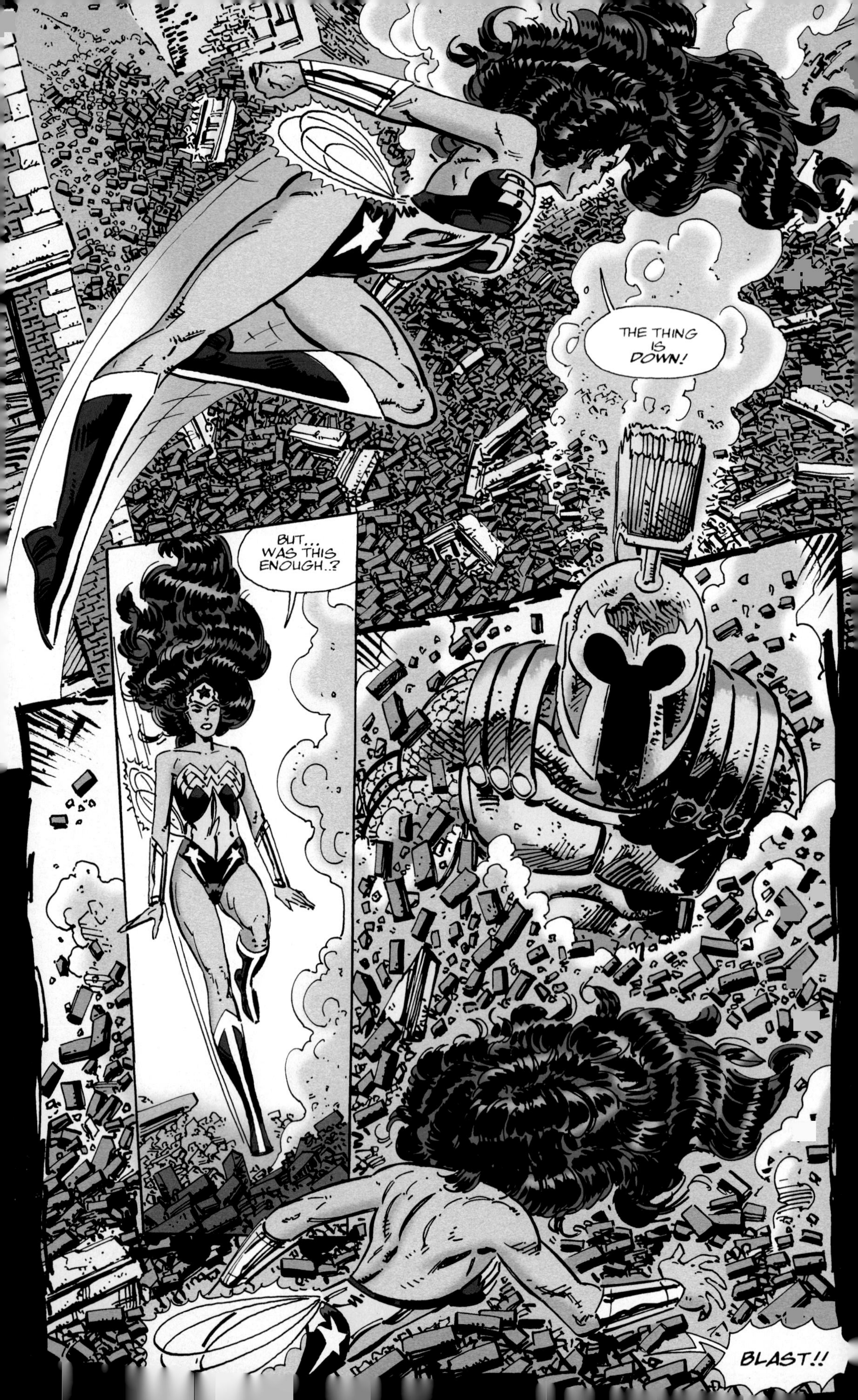
THE THING IS DOWN!
BUT... WAS THIS ENOUGH..?
BLAST!!

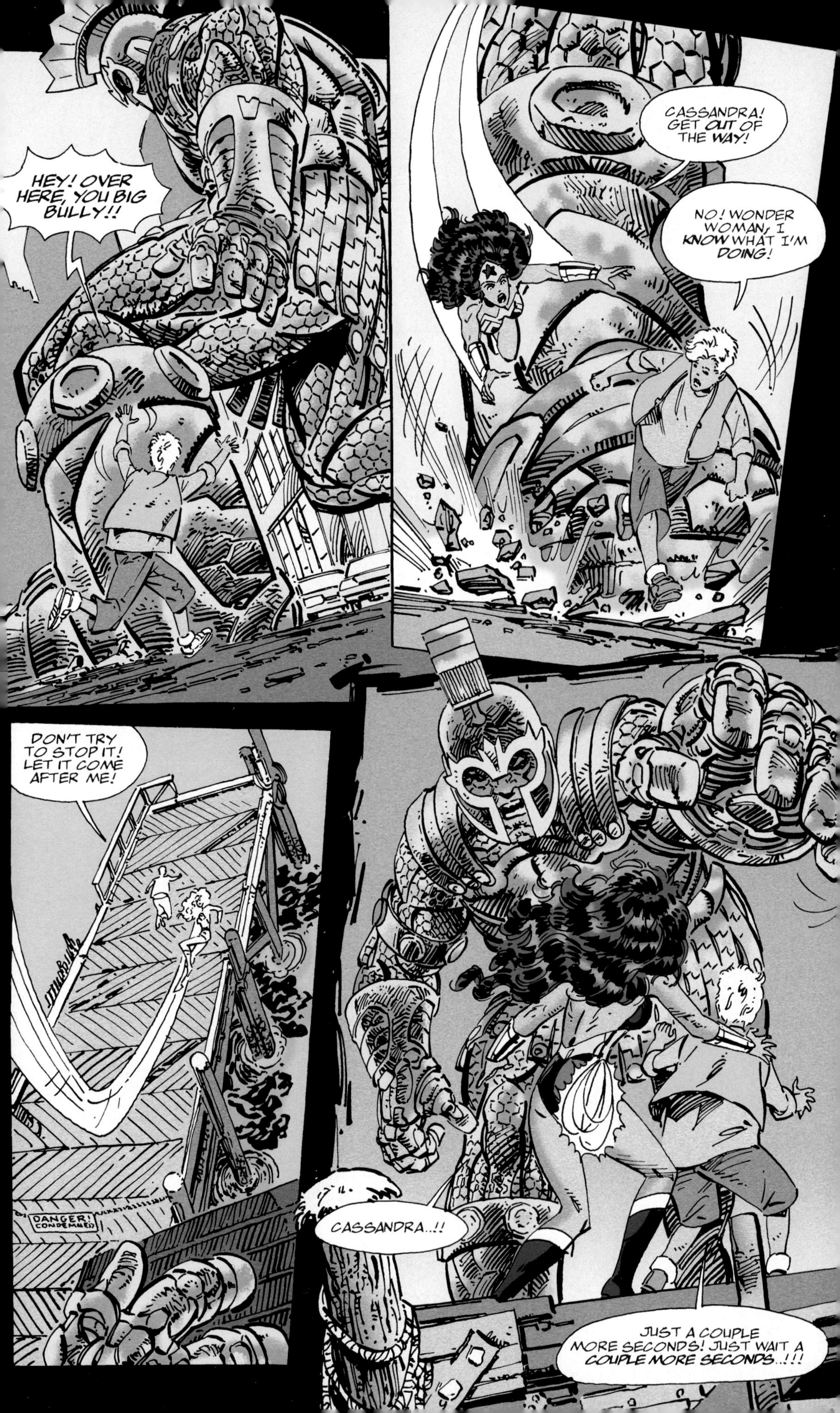
HEY! OVER HERE, YOU BIG BULLY!!
CASSANDRA! GET OUT OF THE WAY!
NO! WONDER WOMAN, I KNOW WHAT I'M DOING!
DON'T TRY TO STOP IT! LET IT COME AFTER ME!
DANGER! CONDEMNED
CASSANDRA..!!
JUST A COUPLE MORE SECONDS! JUST WAIT A COUPLE MORE SECONDS..!!!

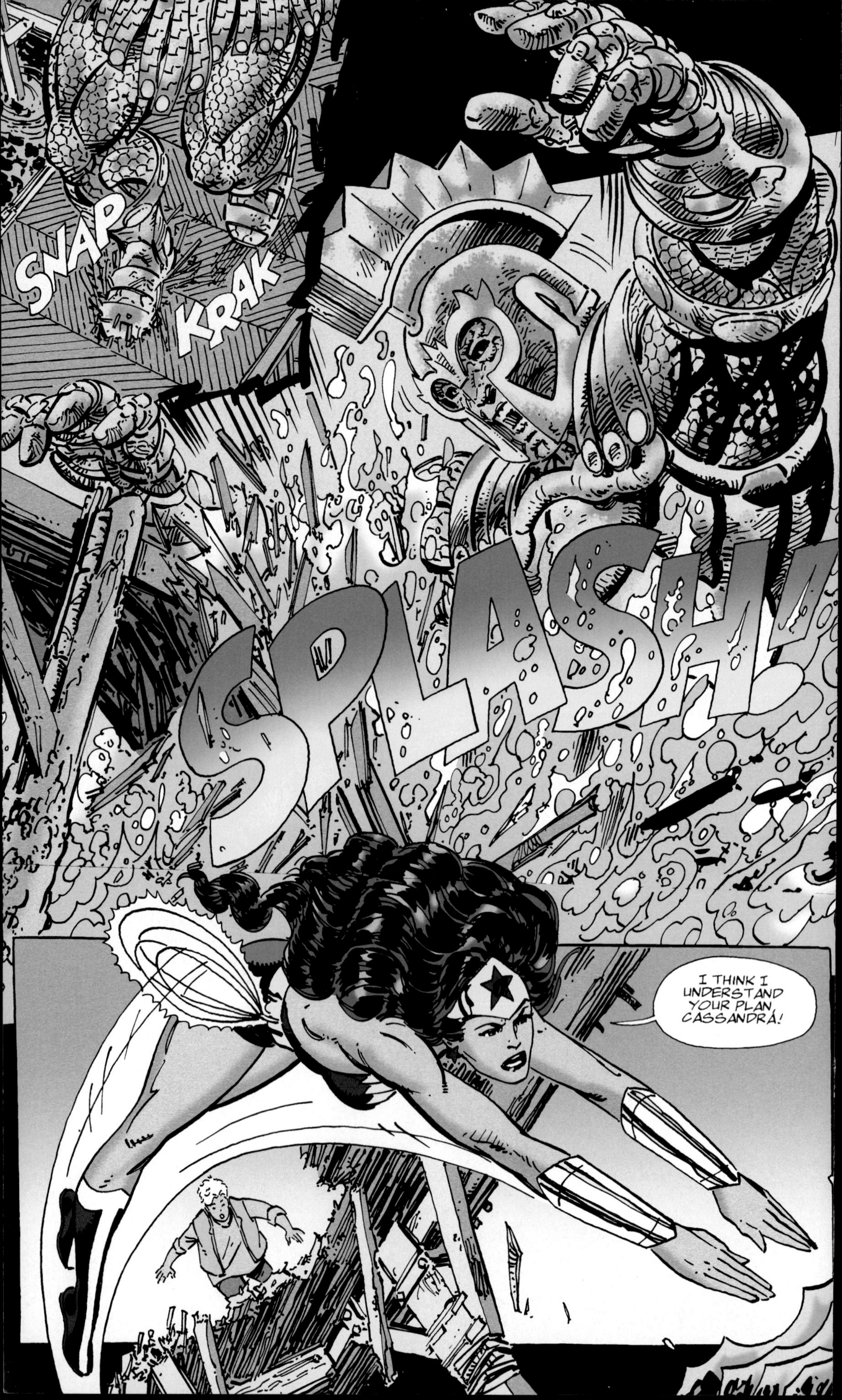
SNAP
KRAK
SPLASH!
I THINK I UNDERSTAND YOUR PLAN, CASSANDRA!

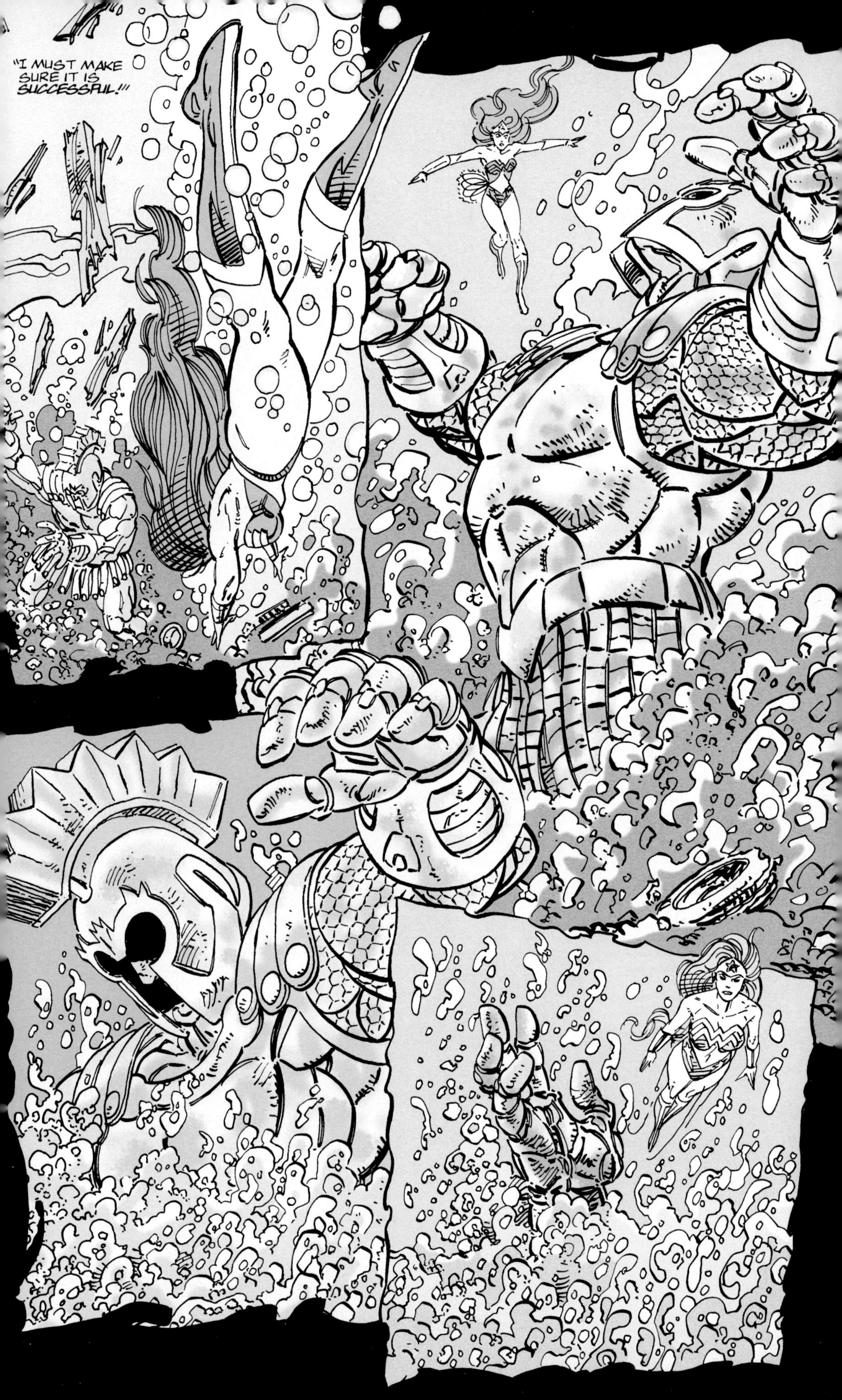
"I MUST MAKE SURE IT IS SUCCESSFUL!"

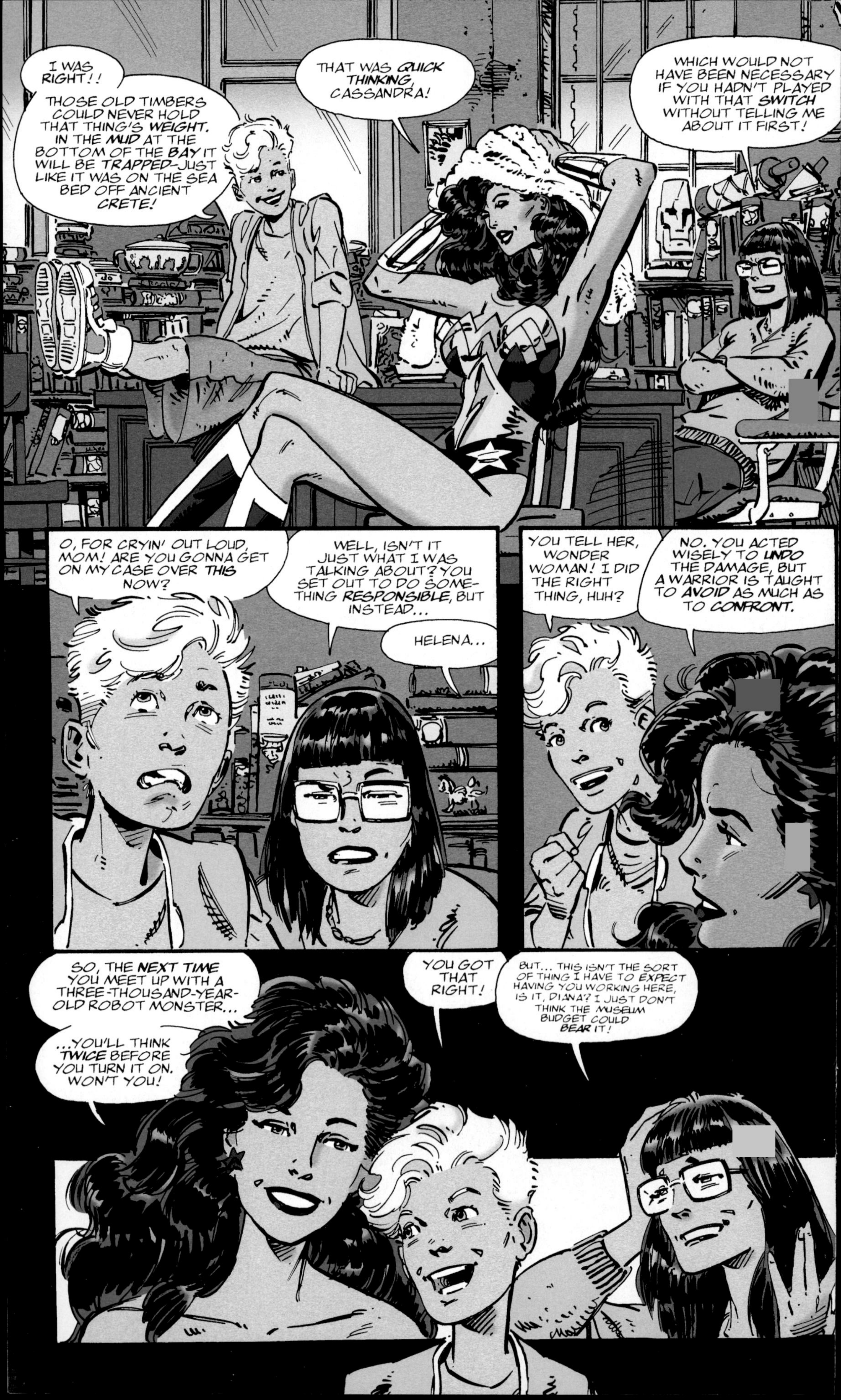

I WAS RIGHT!!
THOSE OLD TIMBERS COULD NEVER HOLD THAT THING'S WEIGHT. IN THE MUD AT THE BOTTOM OF THE BAY IT WILL BE TRAPPED--JUST LIKE IT WAS ON THE SEA BED OFF ANCIENT CRETE!
THAT WAS QUICK THINKING, CASSANDRA!
WHICH WOULD NOT HAVE BEEN NECESSARY IF YOU HADN'T PLAYED WITH THAT SWITCH WITHOUT TELLING ME ABOUT IT FIRST!
O, FOR CRYIN' OUT LOUD, MOM! ARE YOU GONNA GET ON MY CASE OVER THIS NOW?
WELL, ISN'T IT JUST WHAT I WAS TALKING ABOUT? YOU SET OUT TO DO SOMETHING RESPONSIBLE, BUT INSTEAD...
HELENA...
YOU TELL HER, WONDER WOMAN! I DID THE RIGHT THING, HUH?
NO. YOU ACTED WISELY TO UNDO THE DAMAGE, BUT A WARRIOR IS TAUGHT TO AVOID AS MUCH AS TO CONFRONT.
SO, THE NEXT TIME YOU MEET UP WITH A THREE-THOUSAND-YEAR-OLD ROBOT MONSTER...
...YOU'LL THINK TWICE BEFORE YOU TURN IT ON. WON'T YOU!
YOU GOT THAT RIGHT!
BUT... THIS ISN'T THE SORT OF THING I HAVE TO EXPECT HAVING YOU WORKING HERE, IS IT, DIANA? I JUST DON'T THINK THE MUSEUM BUDGET COULD BEAR IT!

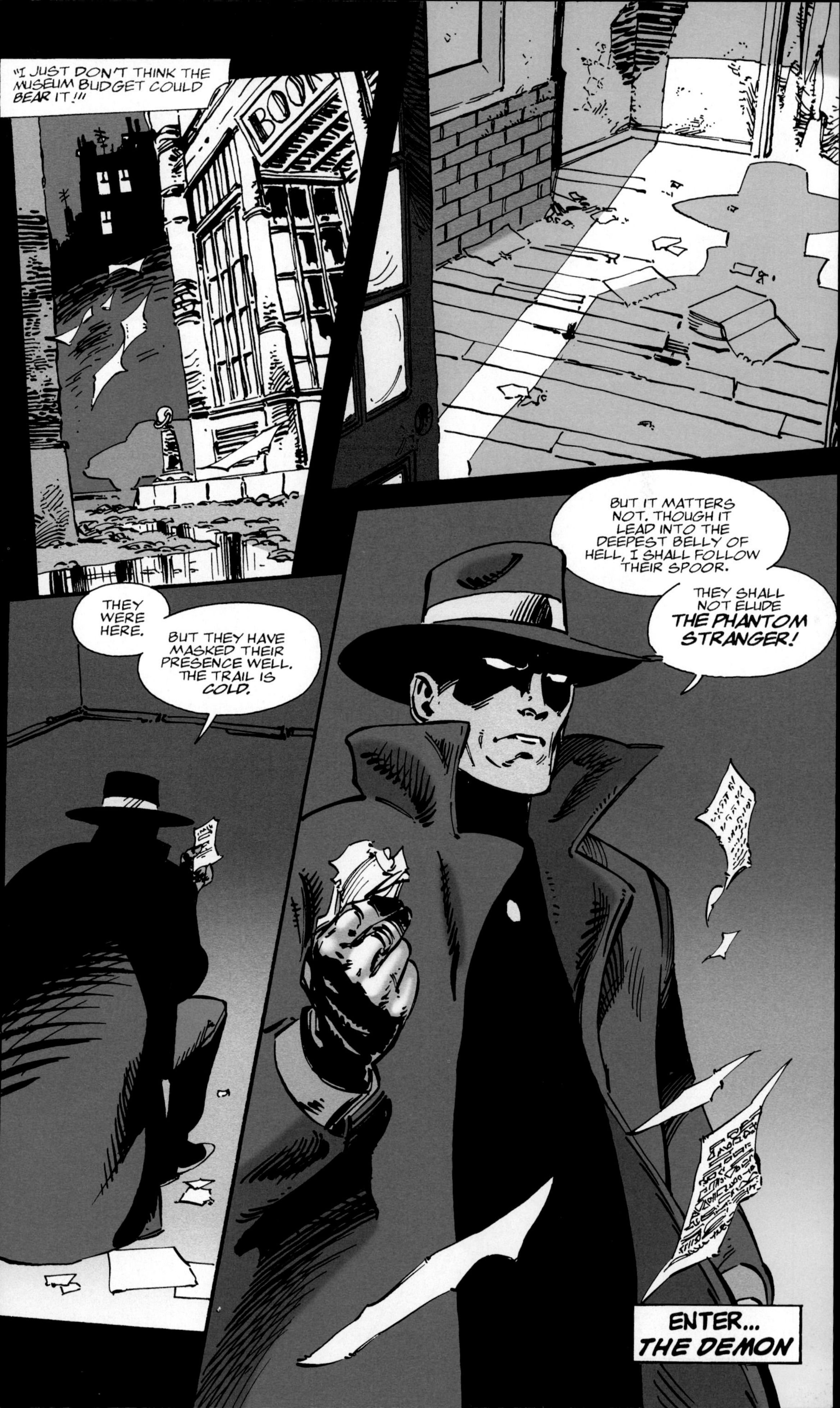
"I JUST DON'T THINK THE MUSEUM BUDGET COULD BEAR IT!!!
BOO
THEY WERE HERE.
BUT THEY HAVE MASKED THEIR PRESENCE WELL. THE TRAIL IS COLD.
BUT IT MATTERS NOT. THOUGH IT LEAD INTO THE DEEPEST BELLY OF HELL, I SHALL FOLLOW THEIR SPOOR.
THEY SHALL NOT ELUDE THE PHANTOM STRANGER!
ENTER... THE DEMON

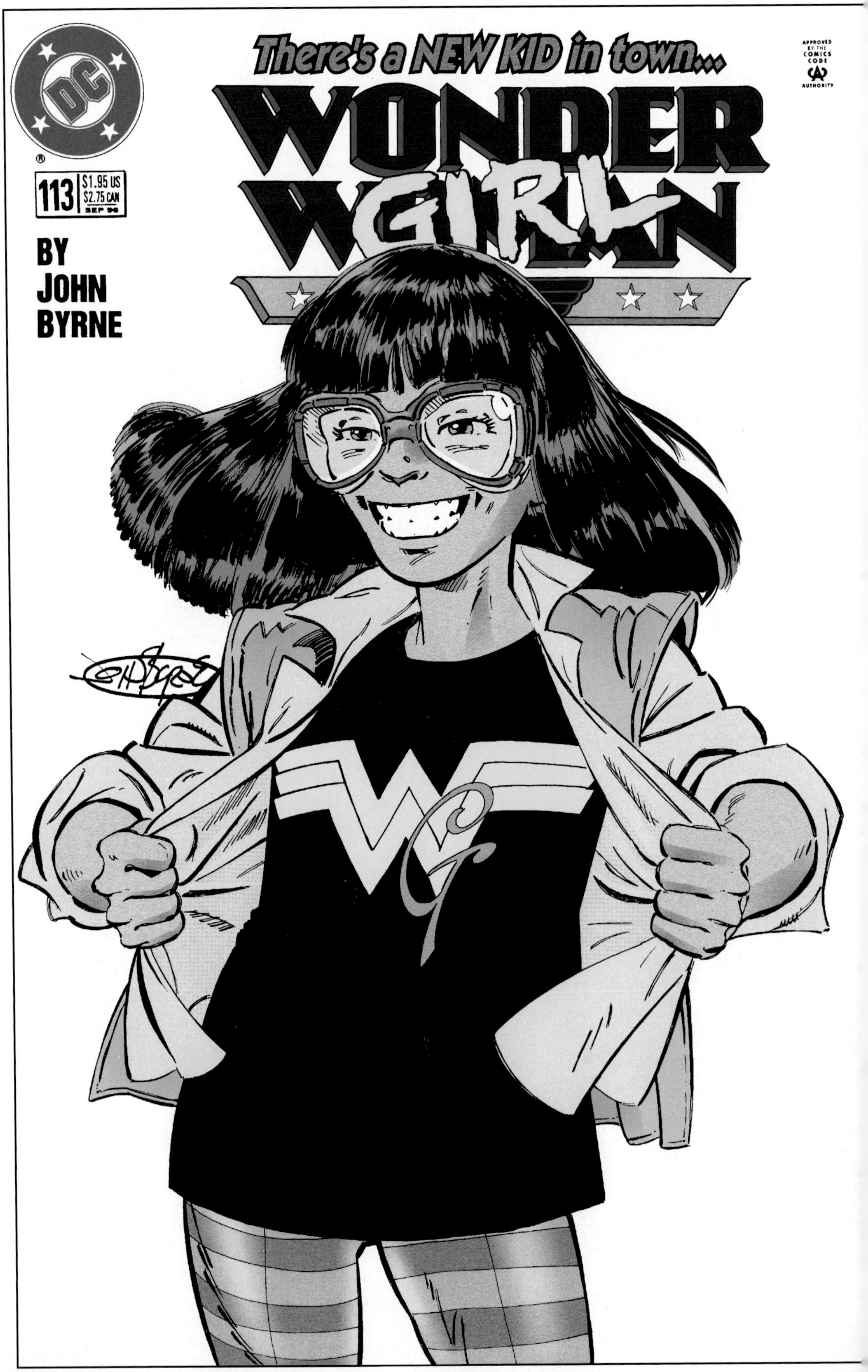

There's a NEW KID in town...
WONDER GIRL
WONDER WOMAN
113
$1.95 US
$2.75 CAN
SEP 96
BY JOHN BYRNE
APPROVED BY THE COMICS CODE AUTHORITY

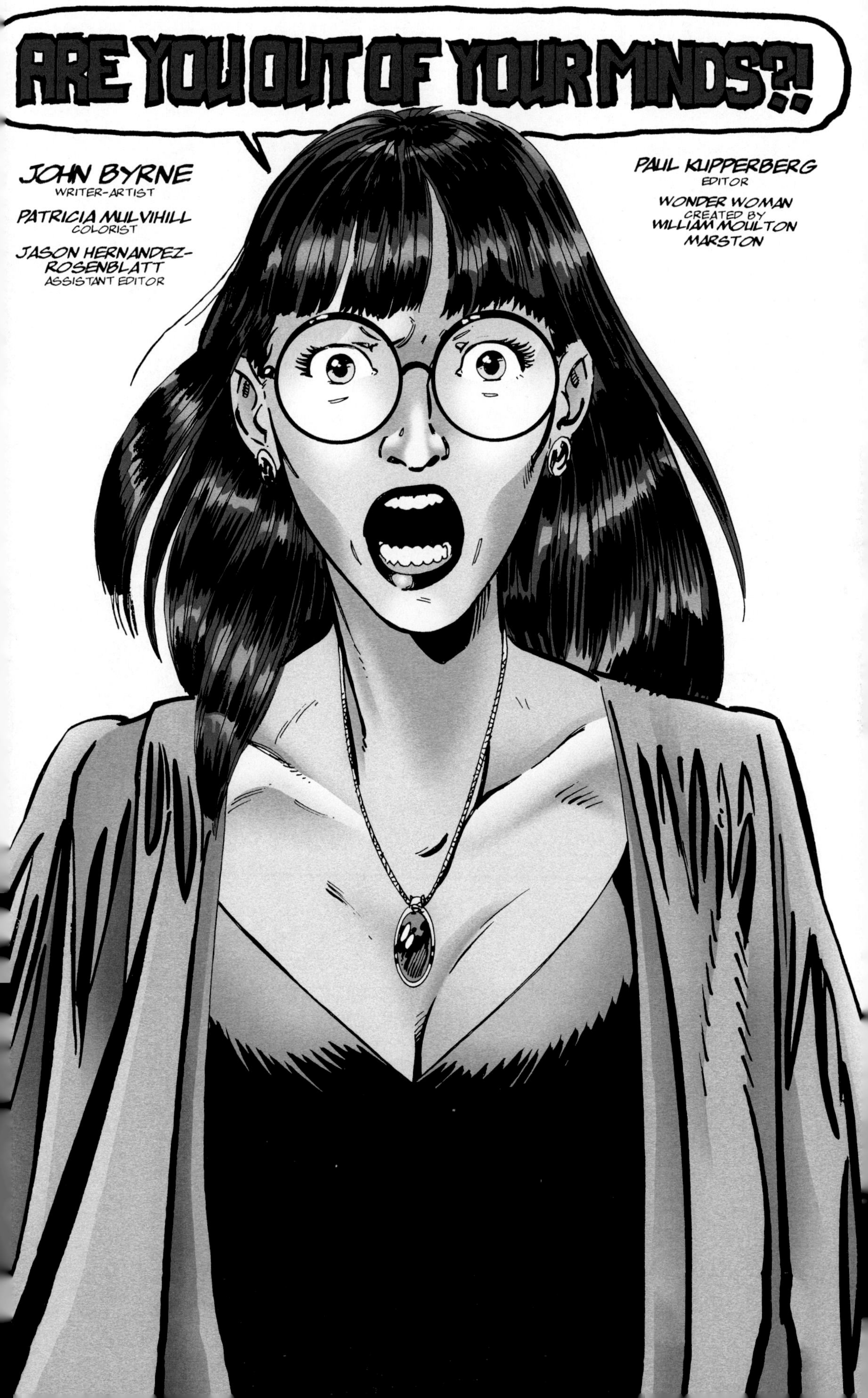
ARE YOU OUT OF YOUR MINDS?!
JOHN BYRNE
WRITER-ARTIST
PATRICIA MULVIHILL
COLORIST
JASON HERNANDEZ-ROSENBLATT
ASSISTANT EDITOR
PAUL KUPPERBERG
EDITOR
WONDER WOMAN
CREATED BY
WILLIAM MOULTON MARSTON

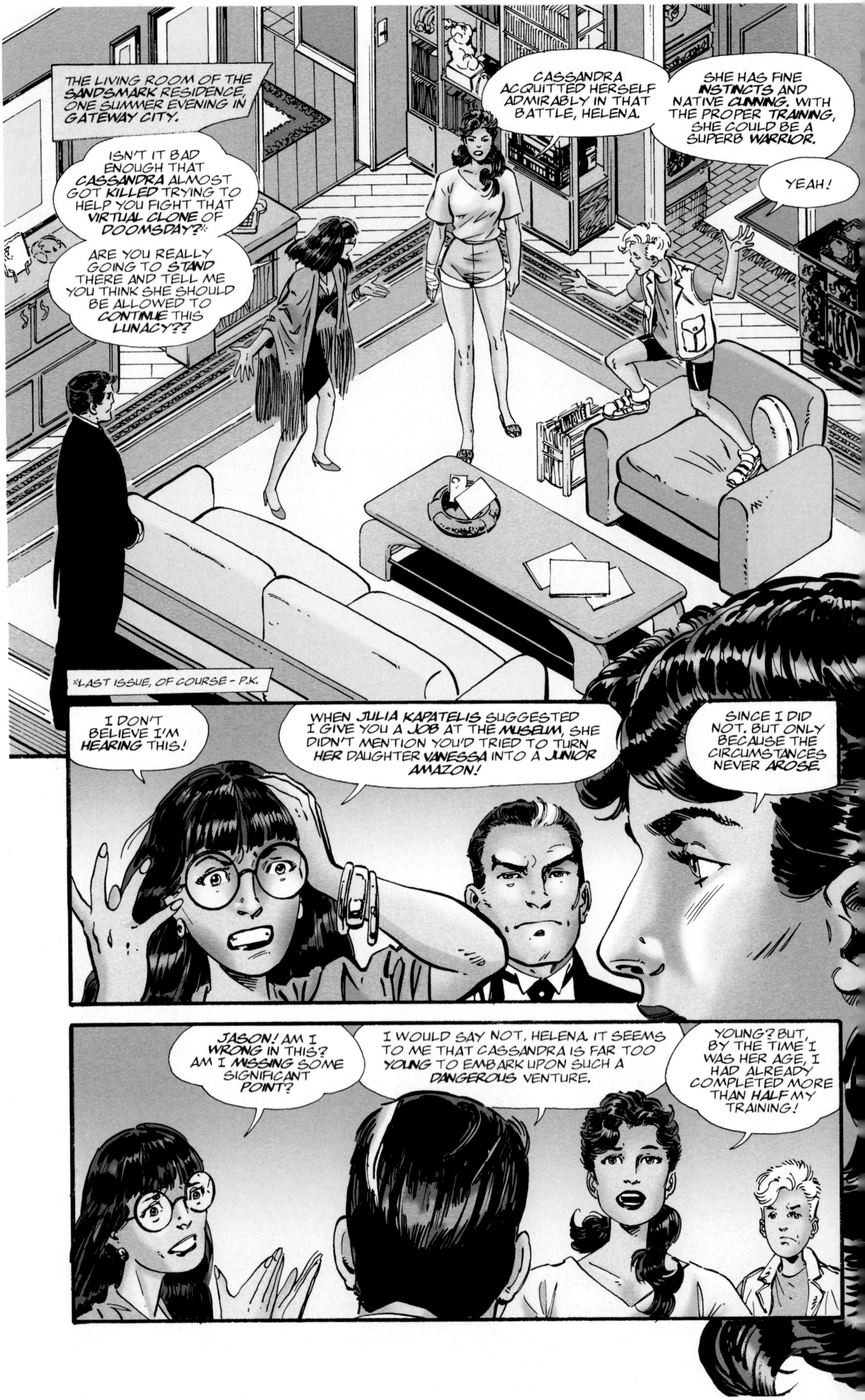
THE LIVING ROOM OF THE SANDSMARK RESIDENCE, ONE SUMMER EVENING IN GATEWAY CITY.
ISN'T IT BAD ENOUGH THAT CASSANDRA ALMOST GOT KILLED TRYING TO HELP YOU FIGHT THAT VIRTUAL CLONE OF DOOMSDAY?*
ARE YOU REALLY GOING TO STAND THERE AND TELL ME YOU THINK SHE SHOULD BE ALLOWED TO CONTINUE THIS LUNACY??
CASSANDRA ACQUITTED HERSELF ADMIRABLY IN THAT BATTLE, HELENA.
SHE HAS FINE INSTINCTS AND NATIVE CUNNING. WITH THE PROPER TRAINING, SHE COULD BE A SUPERB WARRIOR.
YEAH!
*LAST ISSUE, OF COURSE - P.K.
I DON'T BELIEVE I'M HEARING THIS!
WHEN JULIA KAPATELIS SUGGESTED I GIVE YOU A JOB AT THE MUSEUM, SHE DIDN'T MENTION YOU'D TRIED TO TURN HER DAUGHTER VANESSA INTO A JUNIOR AMAZON!
SINCE I DID NOT. BUT ONLY BECAUSE THE CIRCUMSTANCES NEVER AROSE.
JASON! AM I WRONG IN THIS? AM I MISSING SOME SIGNIFICANT POINT?
I WOULD SAY NOT, HELENA. IT SEEMS TO ME THAT CASSANDRA IS FAR TOO YOUNG TO EMBARK UPON SUCH A DANGEROUS VENTURE.
YOUNG? BUT, BY THE TIME I WAS HER AGE, I HAD ALREADY COMPLETED MORE THAN HALF MY TRAINING!

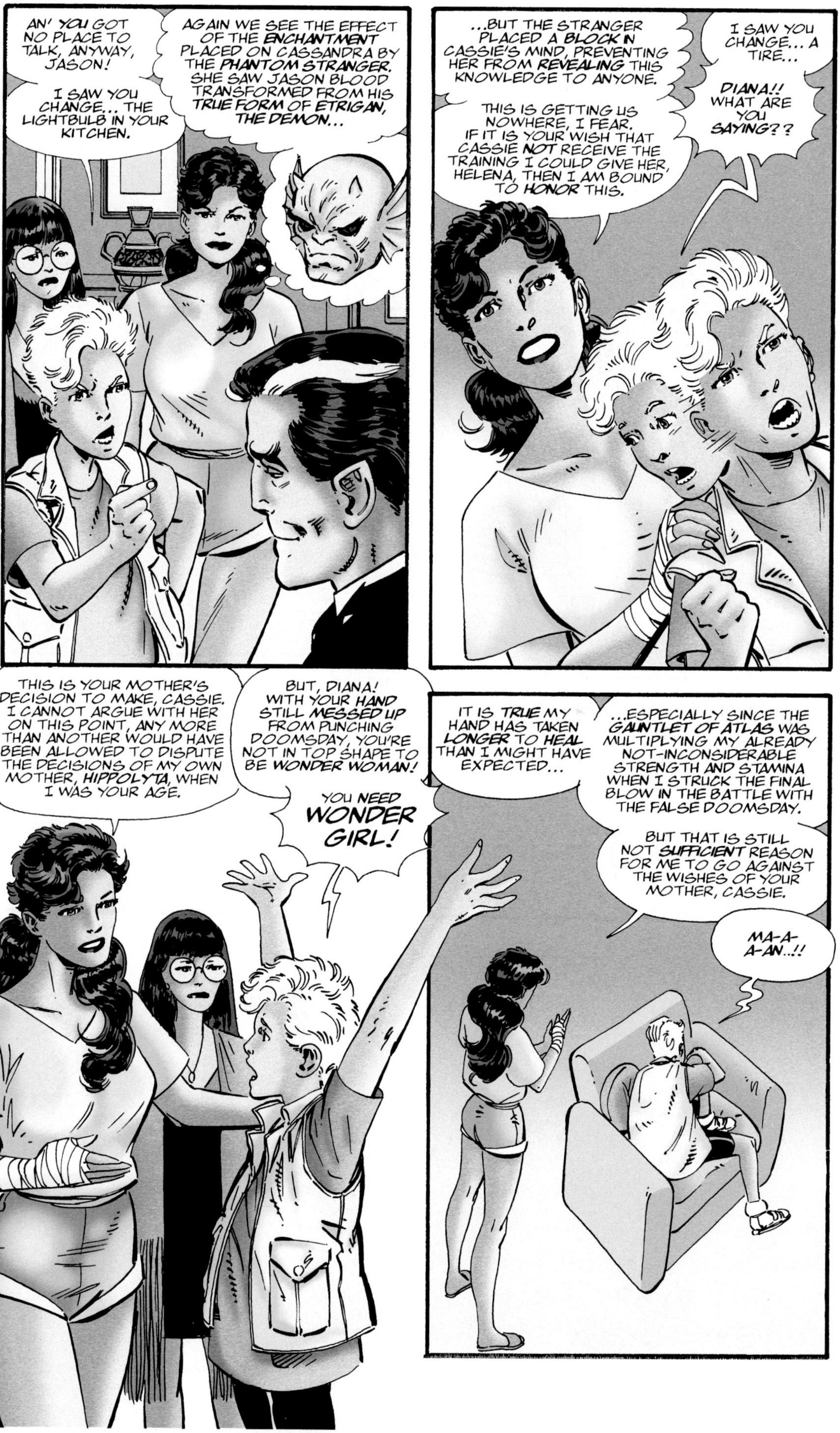
AN' YOU GOT NO PLACE TO TALK, ANYWAY, JASON!
I SAW YOU CHANGE... THE LIGHTBULB IN YOUR KITCHEN.
AGAIN WE SEE THE EFFECT OF THE ENCHANTMENT PLACED ON CASSANDRA BY THE PHANTOM STRANGER. SHE SAW JASON BLOOD TRANSFORMED FROM HIS TRUE FORM OF ETRIGAN, THE DEMON...
...BUT THE STRANGER PLACED A BLOCK IN CASSIE'S MIND, PREVENTING HER FROM REVEALING THIS KNOWLEDGE TO ANYONE.
THIS IS GETTING US NOWHERE, I FEAR. IF IT IS YOUR WISH THAT CASSIE NOT RECEIVE THE TRAINING I COULD GIVE HER, HELENA, THEN I AM BOUND TO HONOR THIS.
I SAW YOU CHANGE... A TIRE...
DIANA!! WHAT ARE YOU SAYING??
THIS IS YOUR MOTHER'S DECISION TO MAKE, CASSIE. I CANNOT ARGUE WITH HER ON THIS POINT, ANY MORE THAN ANOTHER WOULD HAVE BEEN ALLOWED TO DISPUTE THE DECISIONS OF MY OWN MOTHER, HIPPOLYTA, WHEN I WAS YOUR AGE.
BUT, DIANA! WITH YOUR HAND STILL MESSED UP FROM PUNCHING DOOMSDAY, YOU'RE NOT IN TOP SHAPE TO BE WONDER WOMAN!
YOU NEED WONDER GIRL!
IT IS TRUE MY HAND HAS TAKEN LONGER TO HEAL THAN I MIGHT HAVE EXPECTED...
...ESPECIALLY SINCE THE GAUNTLET OF ATLAS WAS MULTIPLYING MY ALREADY NOT-INCONSIDERABLE STRENGTH AND STAMINA WHEN I STRUCK THE FINAL BLOW IN THE BATTLE WITH THE FALSE DOOMSDAY.
BUT THAT IS STILL NOT SUFFICIENT REASON FOR ME TO GO AGAINST THE WISHES OF YOUR MOTHER, CASSIE.
MA-A-A-AN..!!

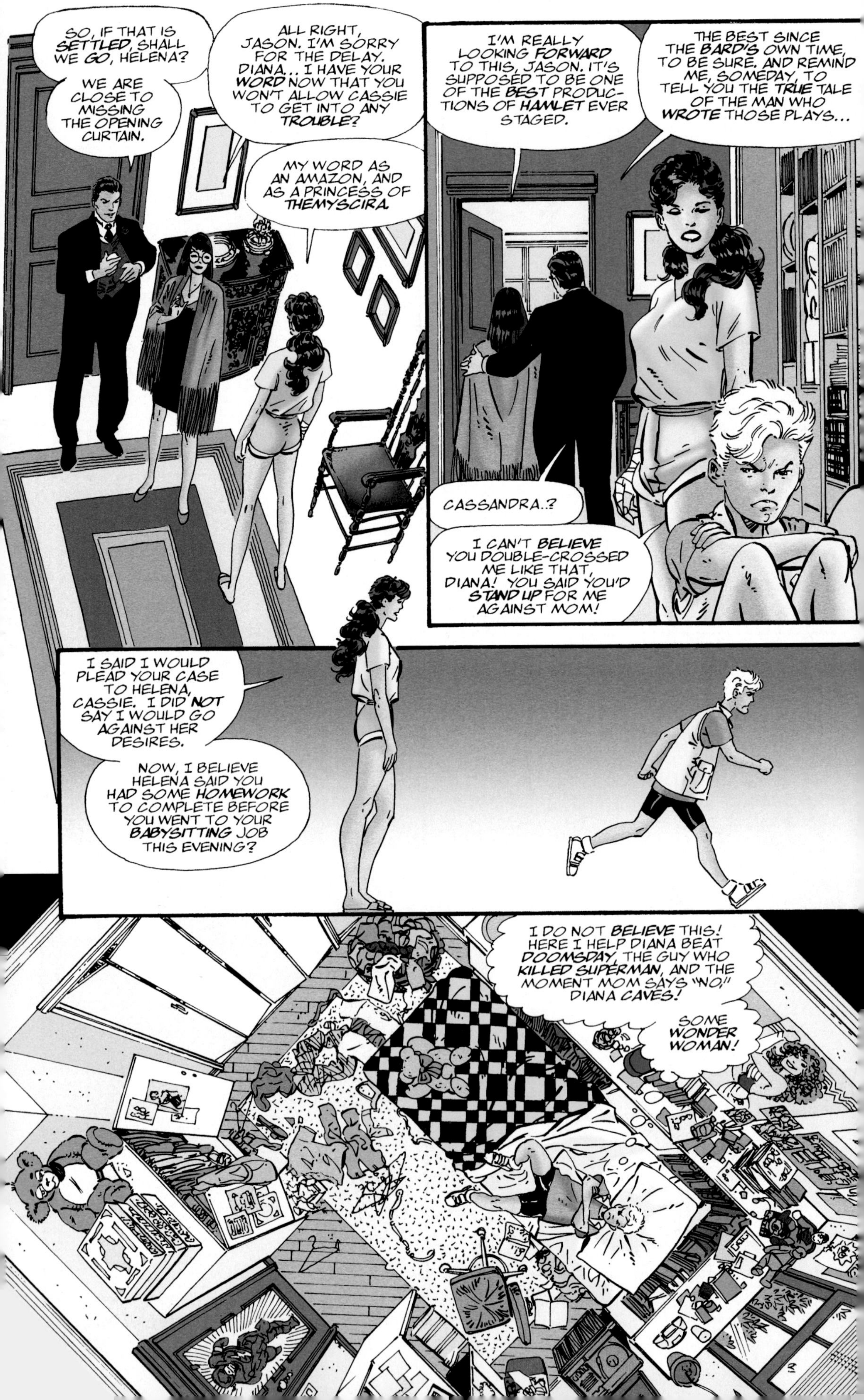
SO, IF THAT IS SETTLED, SHALL WE GO, HELENA?
WE ARE CLOSE TO MISSING THE OPENING CURTAIN.
ALL RIGHT, JASON. I'M SORRY FOR THE DELAY. DIANA... I HAVE YOUR WORD NOW THAT YOU WON'T ALLOW CASSIE TO GET INTO ANY TROUBLE?
MY WORD AS AN AMAZON, AND AS A PRINCESS OF THEMYSCIRA.
I'M REALLY LOOKING FORWARD TO THIS, JASON. IT'S SUPPOSED TO BE ONE OF THE BEST PRODUCTIONS OF HAMLET EVER STAGED.
THE BEST SINCE THE BARD'S OWN TIME, TO BE SURE. AND REMIND ME, SOMEDAY, TO TELL YOU THE TRUE TALE OF THE MAN WHO WROTE THOSE PLAYS...
CASSANDRA..?
I CAN'T BELIEVE YOU DOUBLE-CROSSED ME LIKE THAT, DIANA! YOU SAID YOU'D STAND UP FOR ME AGAINST MOM!
I SAID I WOULD PLEAD YOUR CASE TO HELENA, CASSIE. I DID NOT SAY I WOULD GO AGAINST HER DESIRES.
NOW, I BELIEVE HELENA SAID YOU HAD SOME HOMEWORK TO COMPLETE BEFORE YOU WENT TO YOUR BABYSITTING JOB THIS EVENING?
I DO NOT BELIEVE THIS! HERE I HELP DIANA BEAT DOOMSDAY, THE GUY WHO KILLED SUPERMAN, AND THE MOMENT MOM SAYS "NO," DIANA CAVES!
SOME WONDER WOMAN!

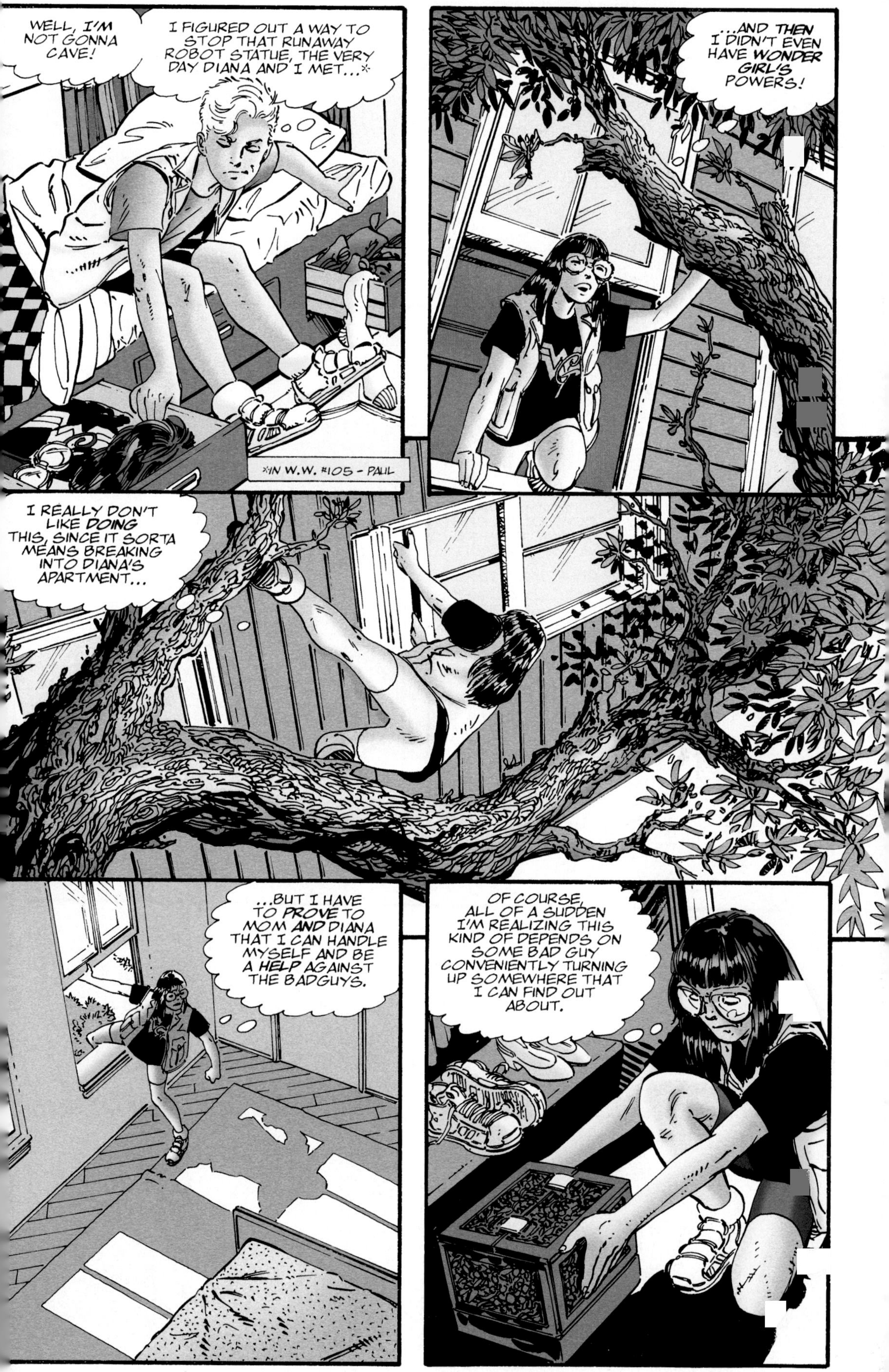

WELL, I'M NOT GONNA CAVE!
I FIGURED OUT A WAY TO STOP THAT RUNAWAY ROBOT STATUE, THE VERY DAY DIANA AND I MET...*
*IN W.W. #105 - PAUL
...AND THEN I DIDN'T EVEN HAVE WONDER GIRL'S POWERS!
I REALLY DON'T LIKE DOING THIS, SINCE IT SORTA MEANS BREAKING INTO DIANA'S APARTMENT...
...BUT I HAVE TO PROVE TO MOM AND DIANA THAT I CAN HANDLE MYSELF AND BE A HELP AGAINST THE BADGUYS.
OF COURSE, ALL OF A SUDDEN I'M REALIZING THIS KIND OF DEPENDS ON SOME BAD GUY CONVENIENTLY TURNING UP SOMEWHERE THAT I CAN FIND OUT ABOUT.

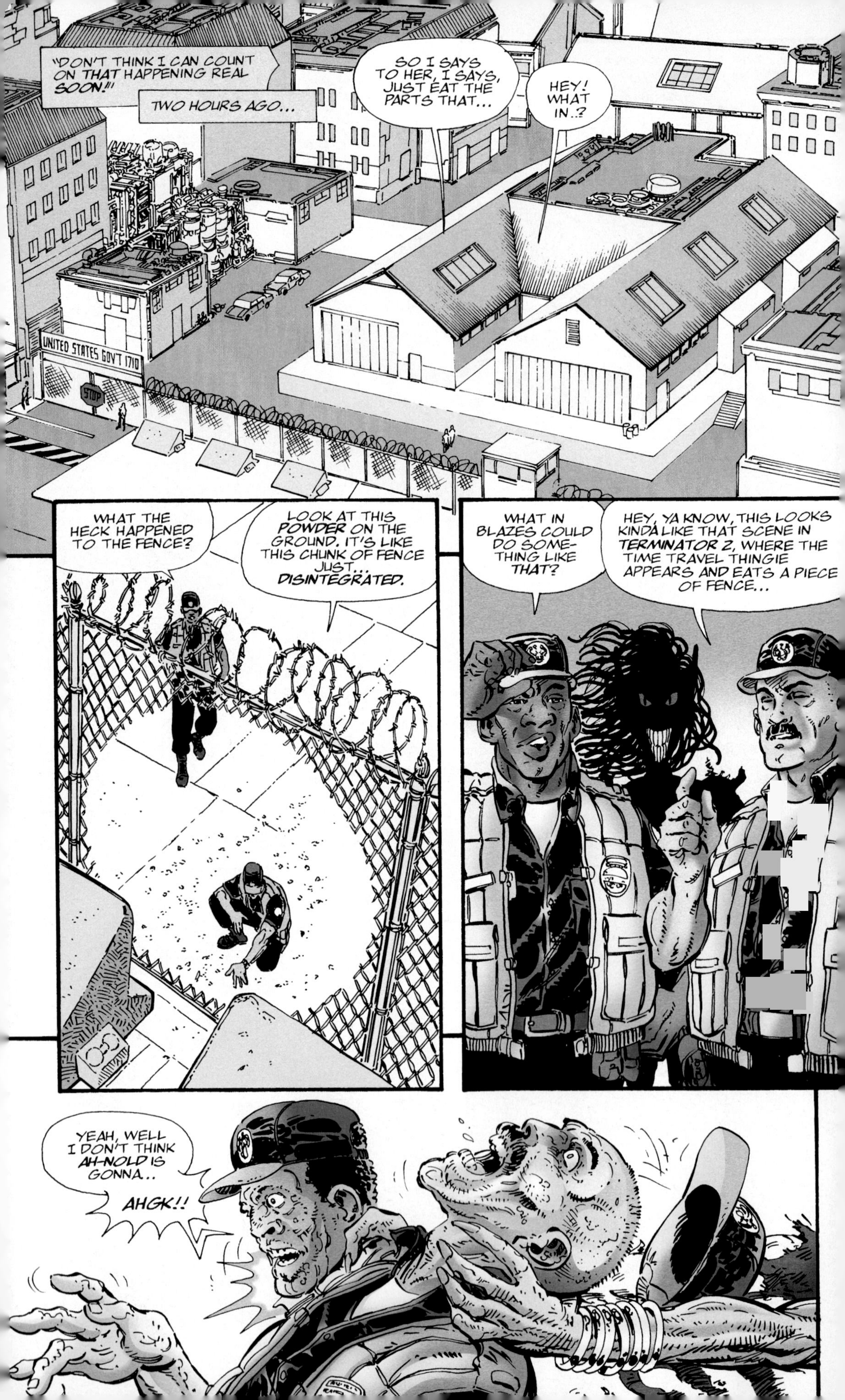
"DON'T THINK I CAN COUNT ON THAT HAPPENING REAL SOON!"
TWO HOURS AGO...
SO I SAYS TO HER, I SAYS, JUST EAT THE PARTS THAT...
HEY! WHAT IN..?
UNITED STATES GOV'T 1710
STOP
WHAT THE HECK HAPPENED TO THE FENCE?
LOOK AT THIS POWDER ON THE GROUND. IT'S LIKE THIS CHUNK OF FENCE JUST... DISINTEGRATED.
WHAT IN BLAZES COULD DO SOMETHING LIKE THAT?
HEY, YA KNOW, THIS LOOKS KINDA LIKE THAT SCENE IN TERMINATOR 2, WHERE THE TIME TRAVEL THINGIE APPEARS AND EATS A PIECE OF FENCE...
YEAH, WELL I DON'T THINK AH-NOLD IS GONNA..
AHGK!!

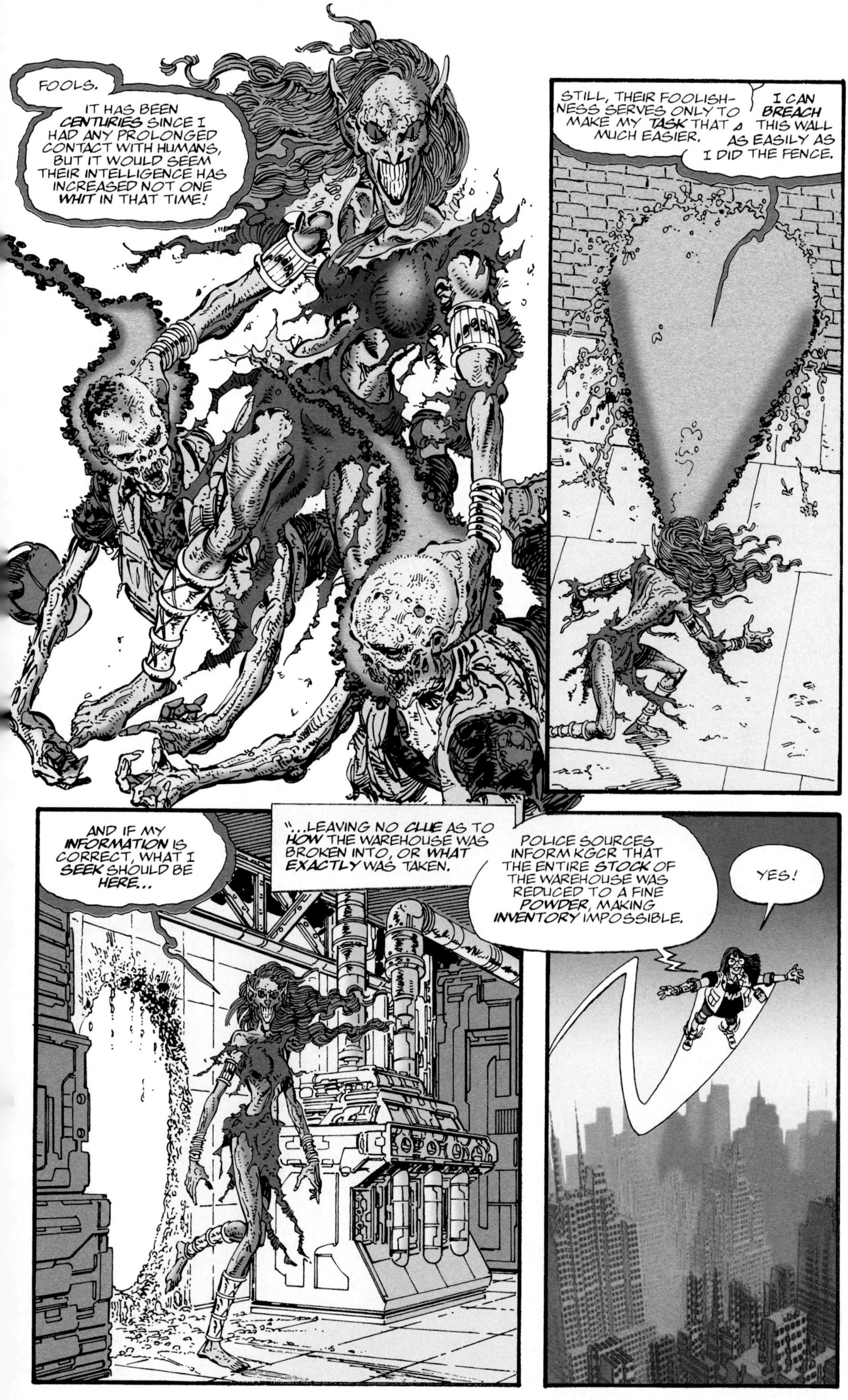
FOOLS.
IT HAS BEEN CENTURIES SINCE I HAD ANY PROLONGED CONTACT WITH HUMANS, BUT IT WOULD SEEM THEIR INTELLIGENCE HAS INCREASED NOT ONE WHIT IN THAT TIME!
STILL, THEIR FOOLISHNESS SERVES ONLY TO MAKE MY TASK THAT MUCH EASIER.
I CAN BREACH THIS WALL AS EASILY AS I DID THE FENCE.
AND IF MY INFORMATION IS CORRECT, WHAT I SEEK SHOULD BE HERE...
"...LEAVING NO CLUE AS TO HOW THE WAREHOUSE WAS BROKEN INTO, OR WHAT EXACTLY WAS TAKEN.
POLICE SOURCES INFORM KGCR THAT THE ENTIRE STOCK OF THE WAREHOUSE WAS REDUCED TO A FINE POWDER, MAKING INVENTORY IMPOSSIBLE.
YES!

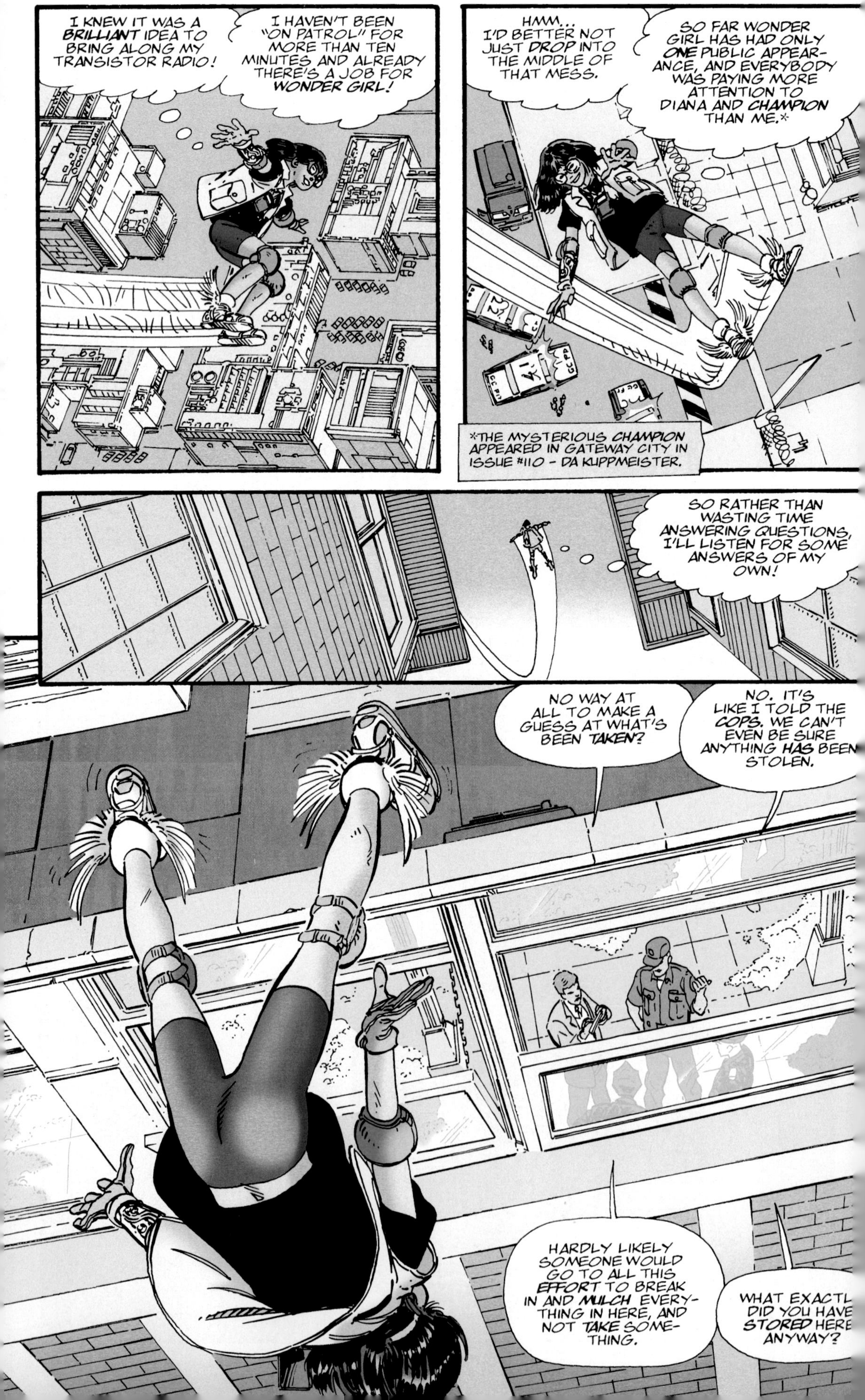
I KNEW IT WAS A BRILLIANT IDEA TO BRING ALONG MY TRANSISTOR RADIO!
I HAVEN'T BEEN "ON PATROL" FOR MORE THAN TEN MINUTES AND ALREADY THERE'S A JOB FOR WONDER GIRL!
HMM... I'D BETTER NOT JUST DROP INTO THE MIDDLE OF THAT MESS.
SO FAR WONDER GIRL HAS HAD ONLY ONE PUBLIC APPEAR-ANCE, AND EVERYBODY WAS PAYING MORE ATTENTION TO DIANA AND CHAMPION THAN ME.*
*THE MYSTERIOUS CHAMPION APPEARED IN GATEWAY CITY IN ISSUE #110 - DA KUPPMEISTER.
SO RATHER THAN WASTING TIME ANSWERING QUESTIONS, I'LL LISTEN FOR SOME ANSWERS OF MY OWN!
NO WAY AT ALL TO MAKE A GUESS AT WHAT'S BEEN TAKEN?
NO. IT'S LIKE I TOLD THE COPS. WE CAN'T EVEN BE SURE ANYTHING HAS BEEN STOLEN.
HARDLY LIKELY SOMEONE WOULD GO TO ALL THIS EFFORT TO BREAK IN AND MULCH EVERY-THING IN HERE, AND NOT TAKE SOME-THING.
WHAT EXACTL DID YOU HAVE STORED HERE ANYWAY?

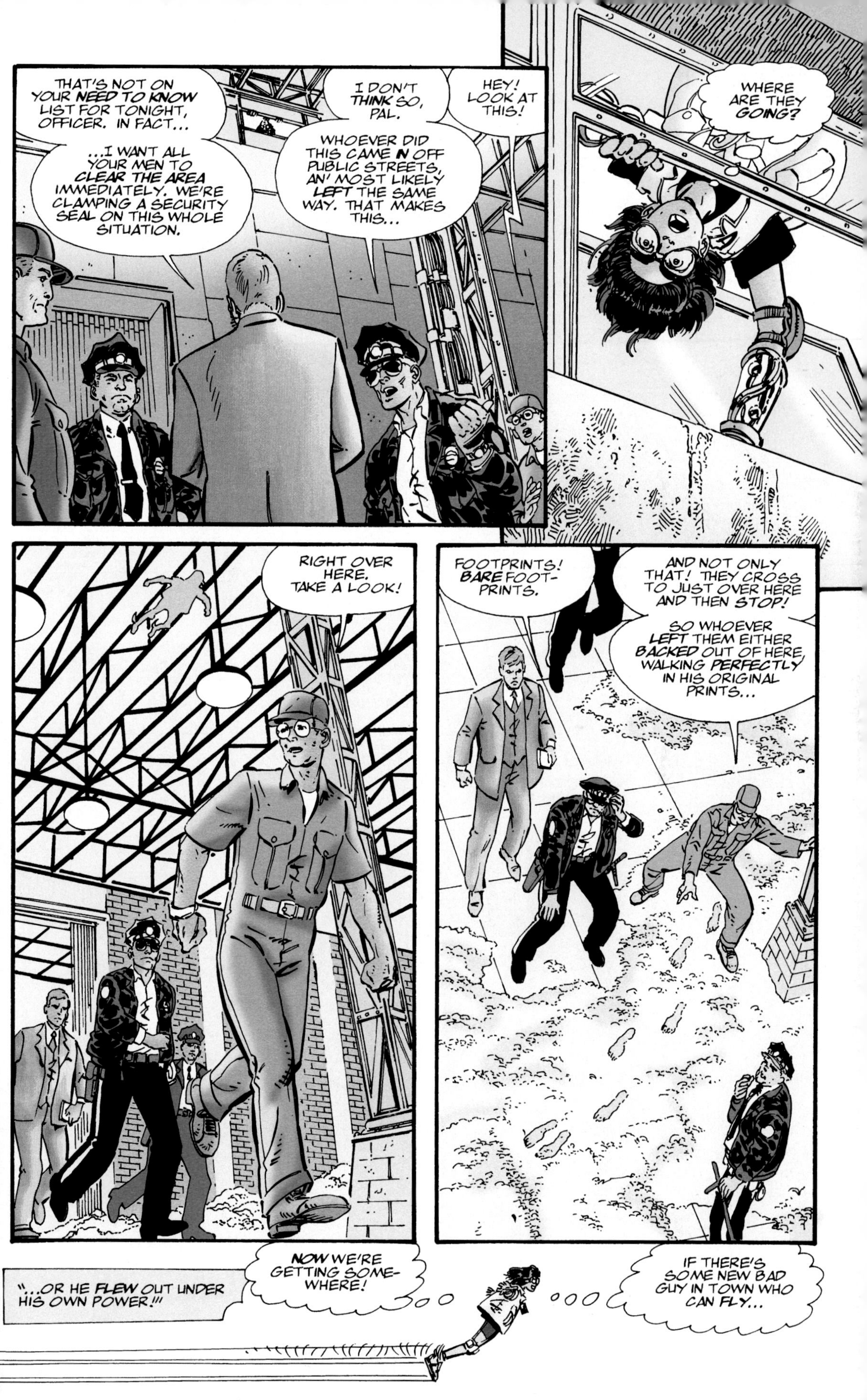

THAT'S NOT ON YOUR NEED TO KNOW LIST FOR TONIGHT, OFFICER. IN FACT...
...I WANT ALL YOUR MEN TO CLEAR THE AREA IMMEDIATELY. WE'RE CLAMPING A SECURITY SEAL ON THIS WHOLE SITUATION.
I DON'T THINK SO, PAL.
WHOEVER DID THIS CAME IN OFF PUBLIC STREETS, AN' MOST LIKELY LEFT THE SAME WAY. THAT MAKES THIS...
HEY! LOOK AT THIS!
WHERE ARE THEY GOING?
RIGHT OVER HERE. TAKE A LOOK!
FOOTPRINTS! BARE FOOT-PRINTS.
AND NOT ONLY THAT! THEY CROSS TO JUST OVER HERE AND THEN STOP!
SO WHOEVER LEFT THEM EITHER BACKED OUT OF HERE, WALKING PERFECTLY IN HIS ORIGINAL PRINTS...
"...OR HE FLEW OUT UNDER HIS OWN POWER!!"
NOW WE'RE GETTING SOME-WHERE!
IF THERE'S SOME NEW BAD GUY IN TOWN WHO CAN FLY...

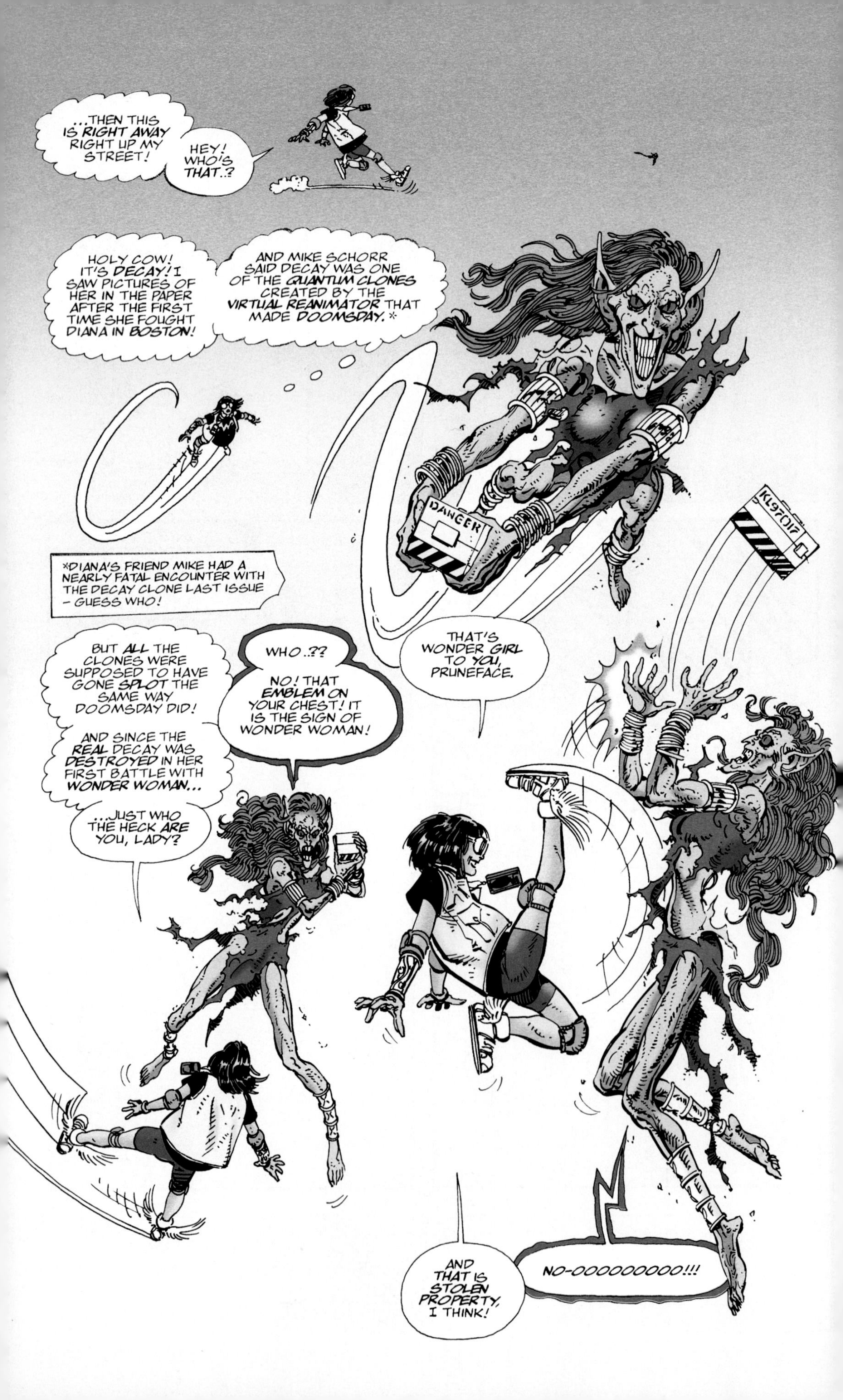
...THEN THIS IS RIGHT AWAY RIGHT UP MY STREET!
HEY! WHO'S THAT..?
HOLY COW! IT'S DECAY! I SAW PICTURES OF HER IN THE PAPER AFTER THE FIRST TIME SHE FOUGHT DIANA IN BOSTON!
AND MIKE SCHORR SAID DECAY WAS ONE OF THE QUANTUM CLONES CREATED BY THE VIRTUAL REANIMATOR THAT MADE DOOMSDAY.*
DANGER
KL9F017
*DIANA'S FRIEND MIKE HAD A NEARLY FATAL ENCOUNTER WITH THE DECAY CLONE LAST ISSUE - GUESS WHO!
BUT ALL THE CLONES WERE SUPPOSED TO HAVE GONE SPLOT THE SAME WAY DOOMSDAY DID!
AND SINCE THE REAL DECAY WAS DESTROYED IN HER FIRST BATTLE WITH WONDER WOMAN...
...JUST WHO THE HECK ARE YOU, LADY?
WHO..??
NO! THAT EMBLEM ON YOUR CHEST! IT IS THE SIGN OF WONDER WOMAN!
THAT'S WONDER GIRL TO YOU, PRUNEFACE.
AND THAT IS STOLEN PROPERTY, I THINK!
NO-OOOOOOOOO!!!

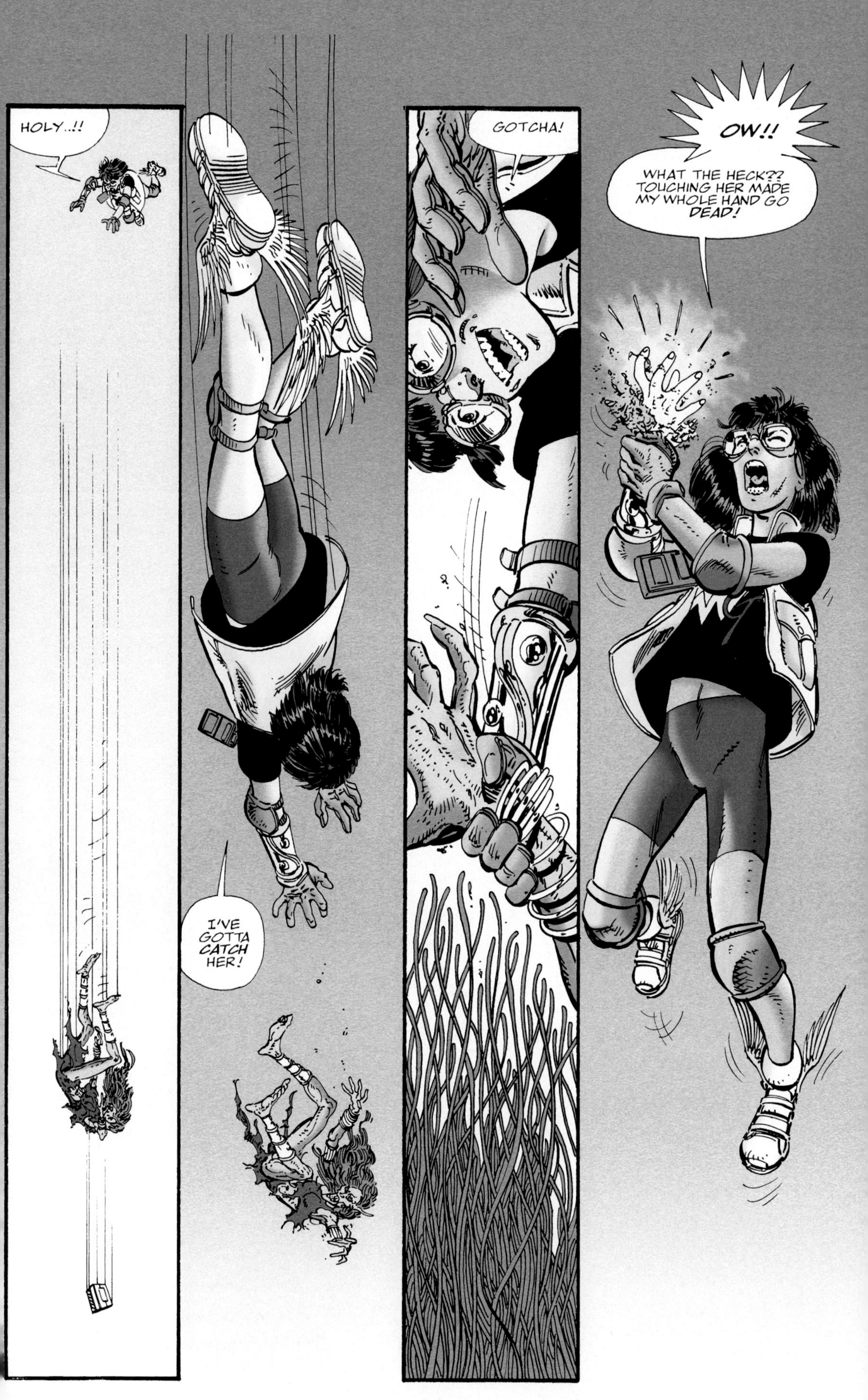
HOLY..!!
I'VE GOTTA CATCH HER!
GOTCHA!
OW!!
WHAT THE HECK?? TOUCHING HER MADE MY WHOLE HAND GO DEAD!

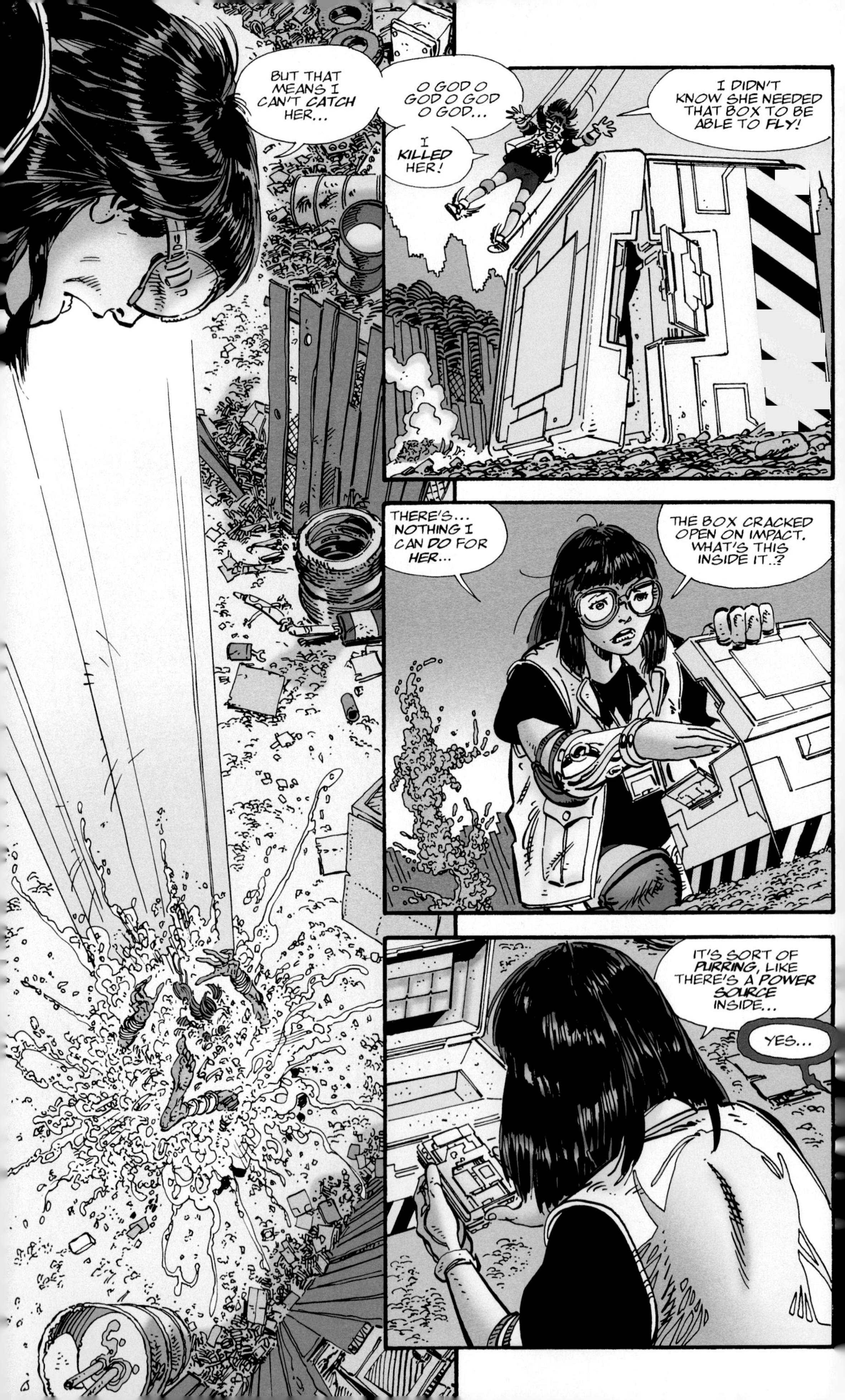
BUT THAT MEANS I CAN'T CATCH HER...
O GOD O GOD O GOD O GOD...
I KILLED HER!
I DIDN'T KNOW SHE NEEDED THAT BOX TO BE ABLE TO FLY!
THERE'S... NOTHING I CAN DO FOR HER...
THE BOX CRACKED OPEN ON IMPACT. WHAT'S THIS INSIDE IT..?
IT'S SORT OF PURRING, LIKE THERE'S A POWER SOURCE INSIDE...
YES...

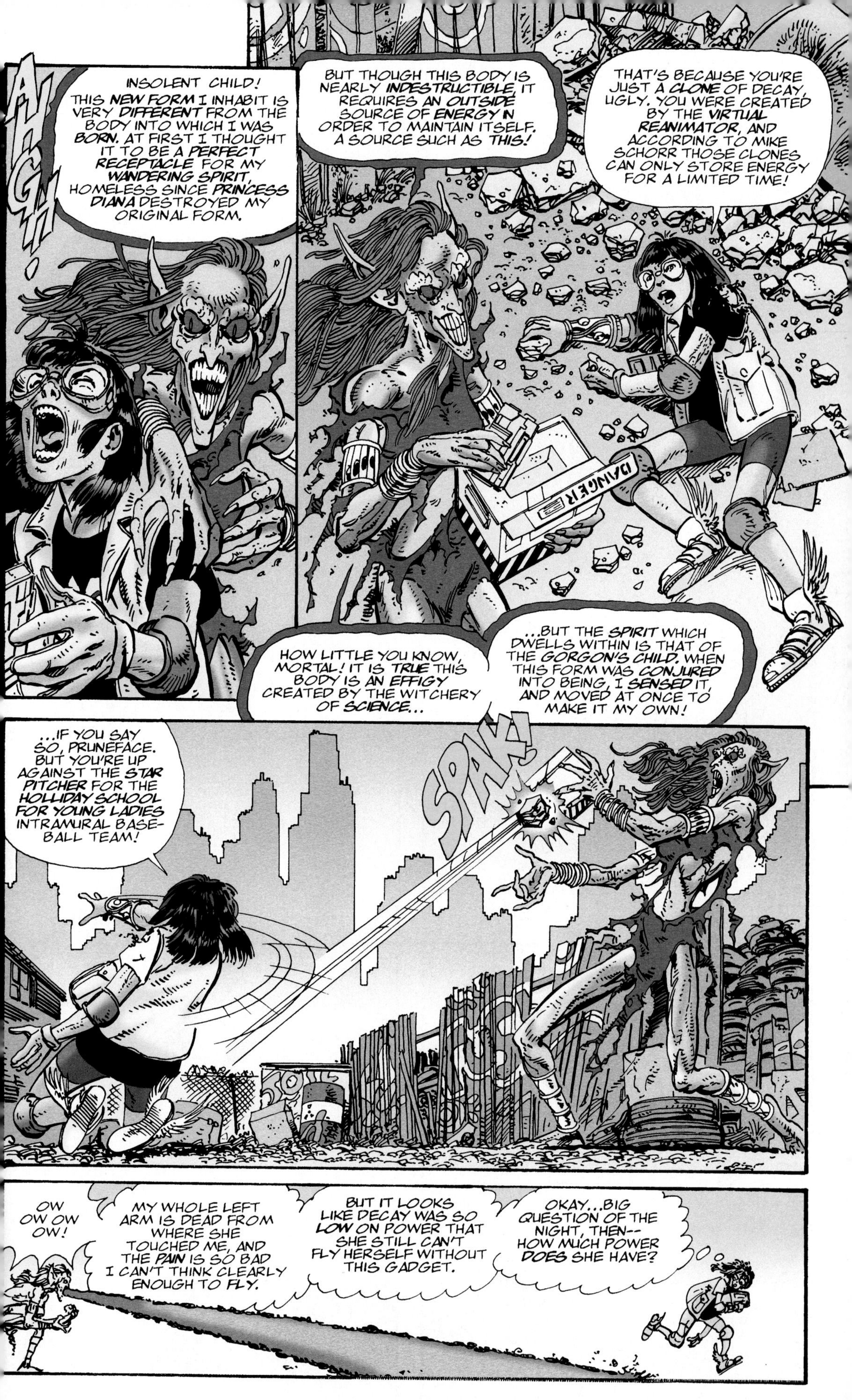
AIIGH!!
INSOLENT CHILD! THIS NEW FORM I INHABIT IS VERY DIFFERENT FROM THE BODY INTO WHICH I WAS BORN. AT FIRST I THOUGHT IT TO BE A PERFECT RECEPTACLE FOR MY WANDERING SPIRIT, HOMELESS SINCE PRINCESS DIANA DESTROYED MY ORIGINAL FORM.
BUT THOUGH THIS BODY IS NEARLY INDESTRUCTIBLE, IT REQUIRES AN OUTSIDE SOURCE OF ENERGY IN ORDER TO MAINTAIN ITSELF. A SOURCE SUCH AS THIS!
THAT'S BECAUSE YOU'RE JUST A CLONE OF DECAY, UGLY. YOU WERE CREATED BY THE VIRTUAL REANIMATOR, AND ACCORDING TO MIKE SCHORR THOSE CLONES CAN ONLY STORE ENERGY FOR A LIMITED TIME!
DANGER
HOW LITTLE YOU KNOW, MORTAL! IT IS TRUE THIS BODY IS AN EFFIGY CREATED BY THE WITCHERY OF SCIENCE...
...BUT THE SPIRIT WHICH DWELLS WITHIN IS THAT OF THE GORGON'S CHILD. WHEN THIS FORM WAS CONJURED INTO BEING, I SENSED IT, AND MOVED AT ONCE TO MAKE IT MY OWN!
...IF YOU SAY SO, PRUNEFACE. BUT YOU'RE UP AGAINST THE STAR PITCHER FOR THE HOLLIDAY SCHOOL FOR YOUNG LADIES INTRAMURAL BASE-BALL TEAM!
SPAK!
OW OW OW OW!
MY WHOLE LEFT ARM IS DEAD FROM WHERE SHE TOUCHED ME, AND THE PAIN IS SO BAD I CAN'T THINK CLEARLY ENOUGH TO FLY.
BUT IT LOOKS LIKE DECAY WAS SO LOW ON POWER THAT SHE STILL CAN'T FLY HERSELF WITHOUT THIS GADGET.
OKAY...BIG QUESTION OF THE NIGHT, THEN-- HOW MUCH POWER DOES SHE HAVE?

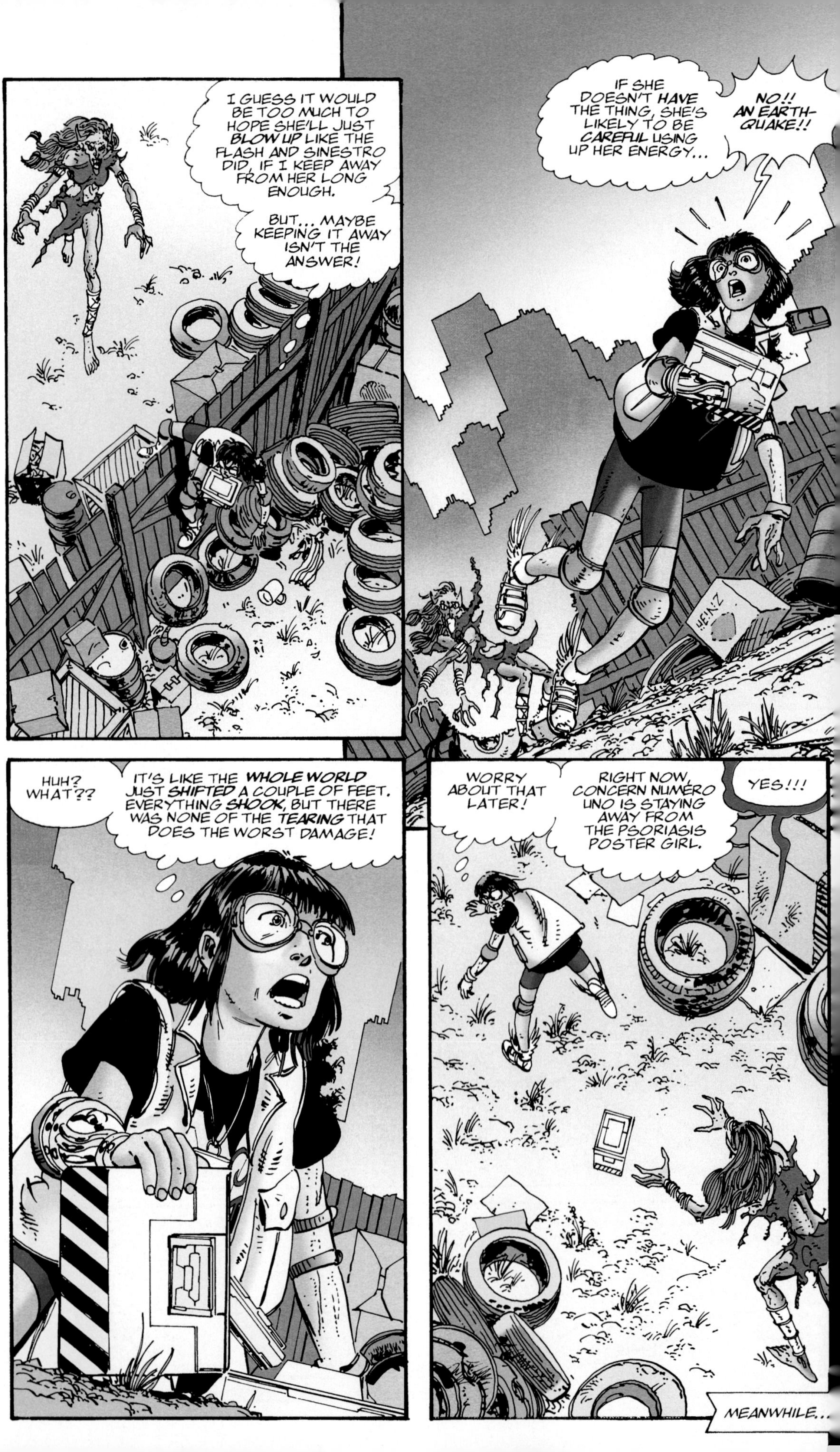
I GUESS IT WOULD BE TOO MUCH TO HOPE SHE'LL JUST BLOW UP LIKE THE FLASH AND SINESTRO DID, IF I KEEP AWAY FROM HER LONG ENOUGH.
BUT... MAYBE KEEPING IT AWAY ISN'T THE ANSWER!
IF SHE DOESN'T HAVE THE THING, SHE'S LIKELY TO BE CAREFUL USING UP HER ENERGY...
NO!! AN EARTHQUAKE!!
HEINZ
HUH? WHAT??
IT'S LIKE THE WHOLE WORLD JUST SHIFTED A COUPLE OF FEET. EVERYTHING SHOOK, BUT THERE WAS NONE OF THE TEARING THAT DOES THE WORST DAMAGE!
WORRY ABOUT THAT LATER!
RIGHT NOW, CONCERN NUMERO UNO IS STAYING AWAY FROM THE PSORIASIS POSTER GIRL.
YES!!!
MEANWHILE...

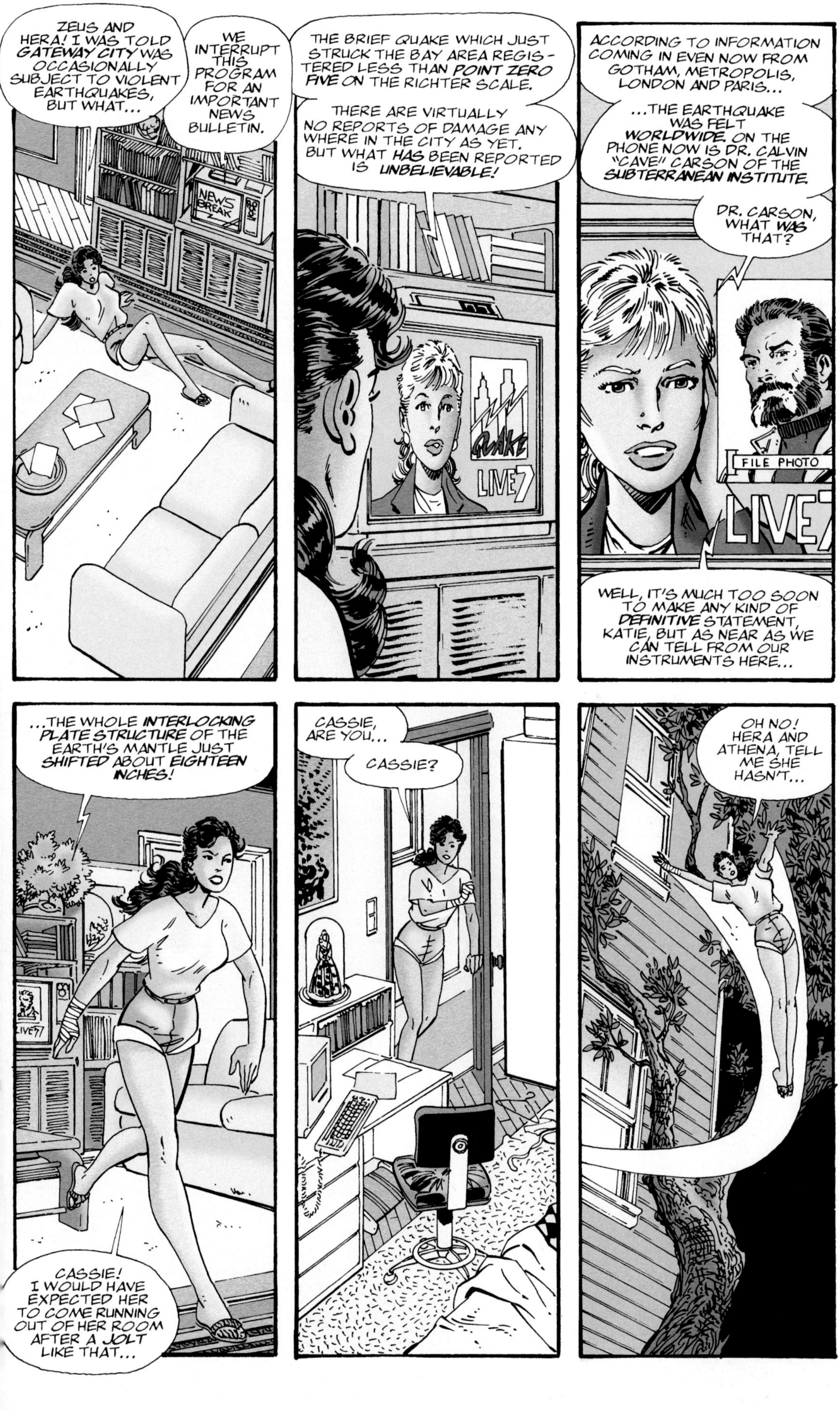
ZEUS AND HERA! I WAS TOLD GATEWAY CITY WAS OCCASIONALLY SUBJECT TO VIOLENT EARTHQUAKES, BUT WHAT...
WE INTERRUPT THIS PROGRAM FOR AN IMPORTANT NEWS BULLETIN.
NEWS BREAK
THE BRIEF QUAKE WHICH JUST STRUCK THE BAY AREA REGISTERED LESS THAN POINT ZERO FIVE ON THE RICHTER SCALE.
THERE ARE VIRTUALLY NO REPORTS OF DAMAGE ANY WHERE IN THE CITY AS YET. BUT WHAT HAS BEEN REPORTED IS UNBELIEVABLE!
QUAKE
LIVE7
ACCORDING TO INFORMATION COMING IN EVEN NOW FROM GOTHAM, METROPOLIS, LONDON AND PARIS...
...THE EARTHQUAKE WAS FELT WORLDWIDE. ON THE PHONE NOW IS DR. CALVIN "CAVE" CARSON OF THE SUBTERRANEAN INSTITUTE.
DR. CARSON, WHAT WAS THAT?
FILE PHOTO
LIVE7
WELL, IT'S MUCH TOO SOON TO MAKE ANY KIND OF DEFINITIVE STATEMENT, KATIE, BUT AS NEAR AS WE CAN TELL FROM OUR INSTRUMENTS HERE...
...THE WHOLE INTERLOCKING PLATE STRUCTURE OF THE EARTH'S MANTLE JUST SHIFTED ABOUT EIGHTEEN INCHES!
LIVE7
CASSIE! I WOULD HAVE EXPECTED HER TO COME RUNNING OUT OF HER ROOM AFTER A JOLT LIKE THAT...
CASSIE, ARE YOU...
CASSIE?
OH NO! HERA AND ATHENA, TELL ME SHE HASN'T...

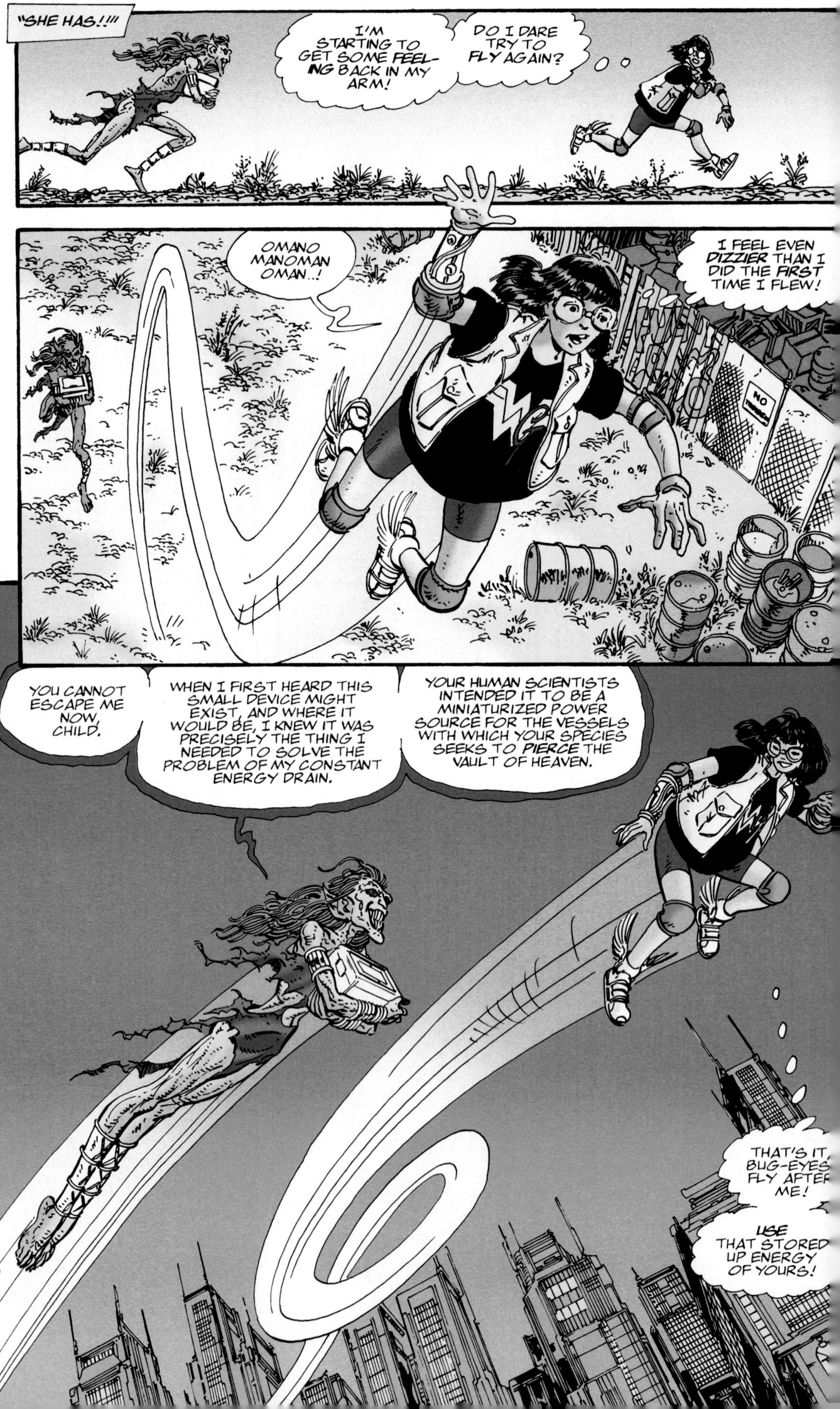
"SHE HAS!!"
I'M STARTING TO GET SOME FEELING BACK IN MY ARM!
DO I DARE TRY TO FLY AGAIN?
OMANO MANOMAN OMAN..!
I FEEL EVEN DIZZIER THAN I DID THE FIRST TIME I FLEW!
NO
YOU CANNOT ESCAPE ME NOW, CHILD.
WHEN I FIRST HEARD THIS SMALL DEVICE MIGHT EXIST, AND WHERE IT WOULD BE, I KNEW IT WAS PRECISELY THE THING I NEEDED TO SOLVE THE PROBLEM OF MY CONSTANT ENERGY DRAIN.
YOUR HUMAN SCIENTISTS INTENDED IT TO BE A MINIATURIZED POWER SOURCE FOR THE VESSELS WITH WHICH YOUR SPECIES SEEKS TO PIERCE THE VAULT OF HEAVEN.
THAT'S IT, BUG-EYES FLY AFTER ME!
USE THAT STORED UP ENERGY OF YOURS!

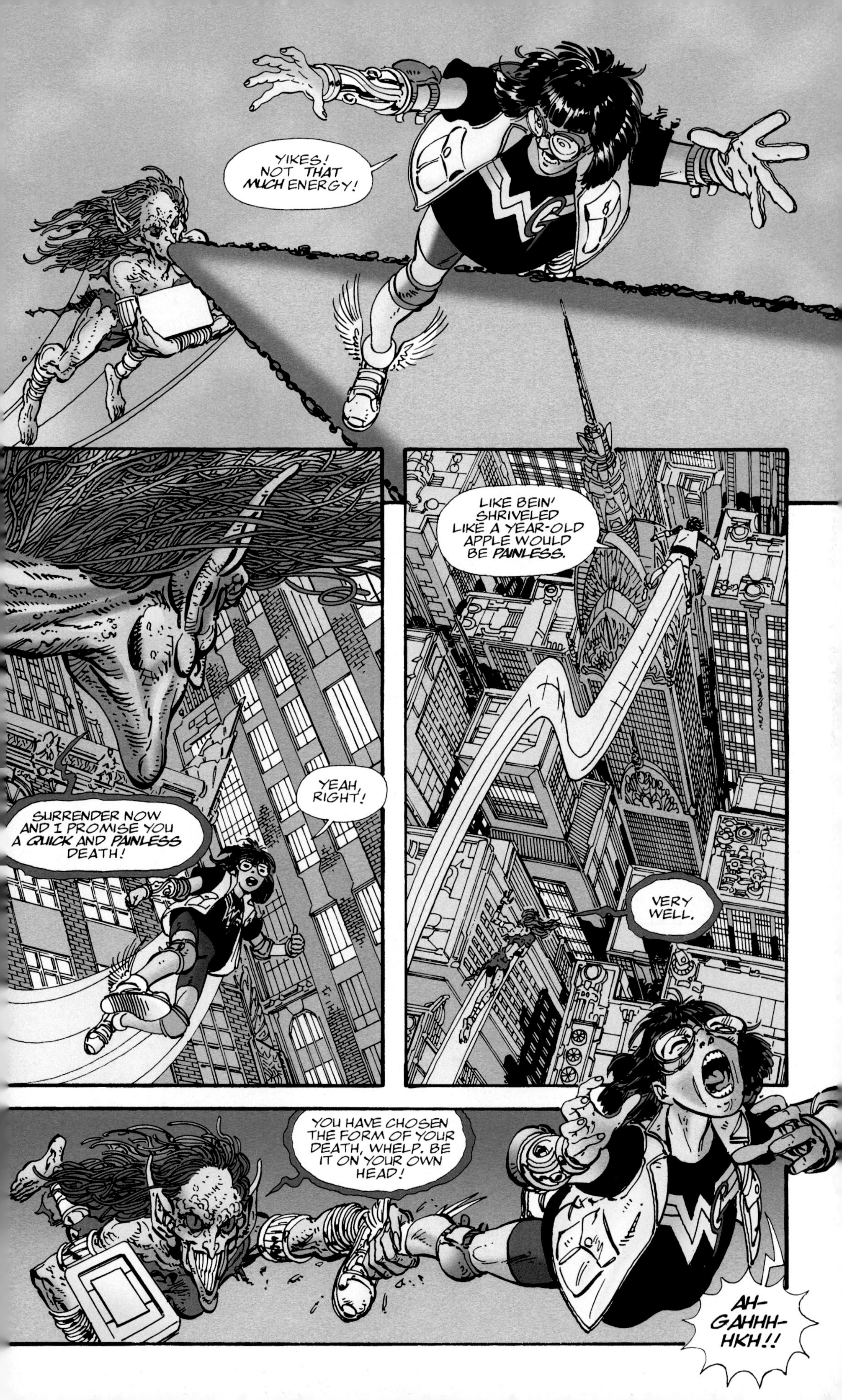
YIKES! NOT THAT MUCH ENERGY!
SURRENDER NOW AND I PROMISE YOU A QUICK AND PAINLESS DEATH!
YEAH, RIGHT!
LIKE BEIN' SHRIVELED LIKE A YEAR-OLD APPLE WOULD BE PAINLESS.
VERY WELL.
YOU HAVE CHOSEN THE FORM OF YOUR DEATH, WHELP. BE IT ON YOUR OWN HEAD!
AH-GAHHH-HKH!!

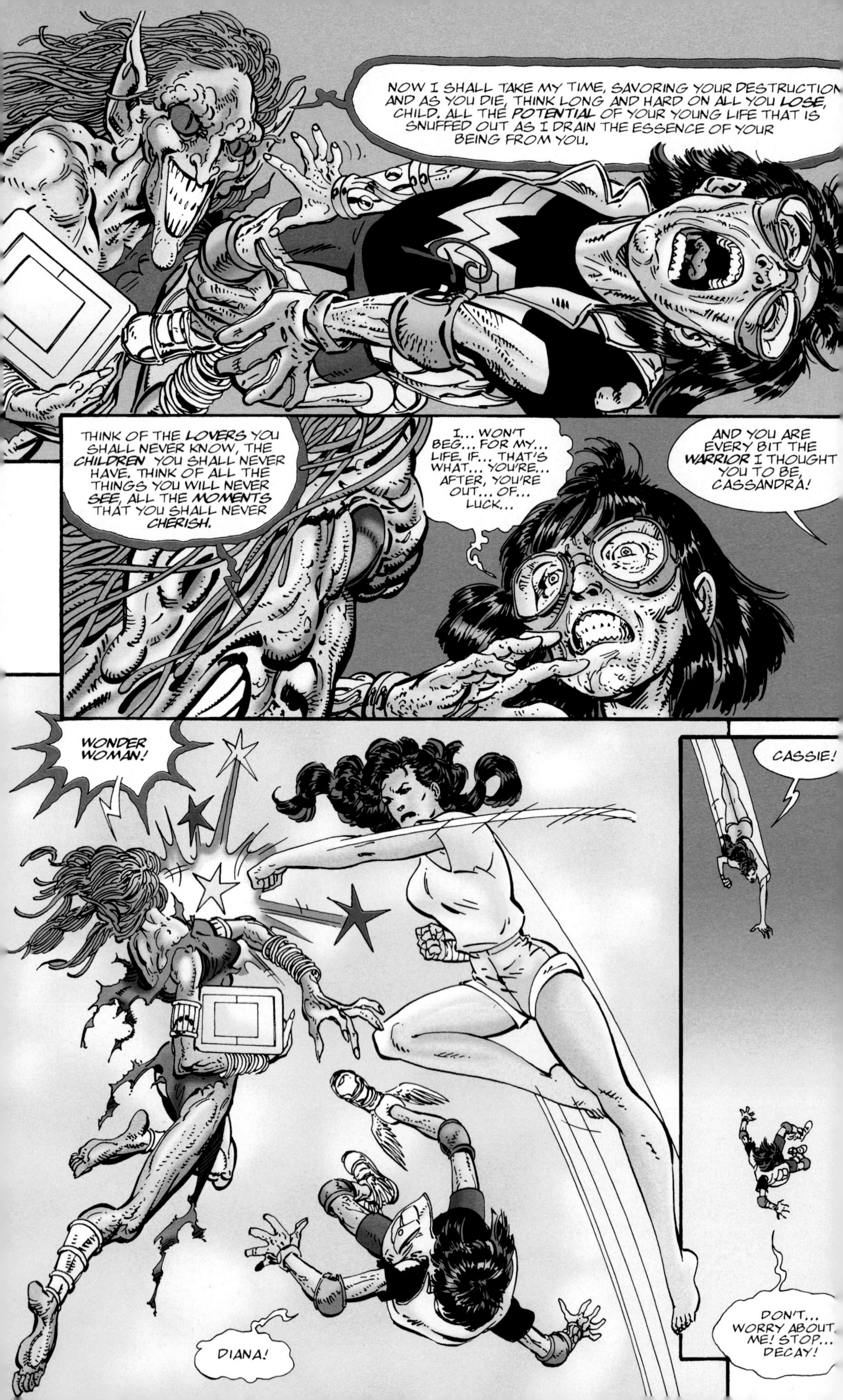
NOW I SHALL TAKE MY TIME, SAVORING YOUR DESTRUCTION AND AS YOU DIE, THINK LONG AND HARD ON ALL YOU LOSE, CHILD. ALL THE POTENTIAL OF YOUR YOUNG LIFE THAT IS SNUFFED OUT AS I DRAIN THE ESSENCE OF YOUR BEING FROM YOU.
THINK OF THE LOVERS YOU SHALL NEVER KNOW, THE CHILDREN YOU SHALL NEVER HAVE. THINK OF ALL THE THINGS YOU WILL NEVER SEE, ALL THE MOMENTS THAT YOU SHALL NEVER CHERISH.
I... WON'T BEG... FOR MY... LIFE. IF... THAT'S WHAT... YOU'RE... AFTER, YOU'RE OUT... OF... LUCK...
AND YOU ARE EVERY BIT THE WARRIOR I THOUGHT YOU TO BE, CASSANDRA!
WONDER WOMAN!
CASSIE!
DIANA!
DON'T... WORRY ABOUT ME! STOP... DECAY!

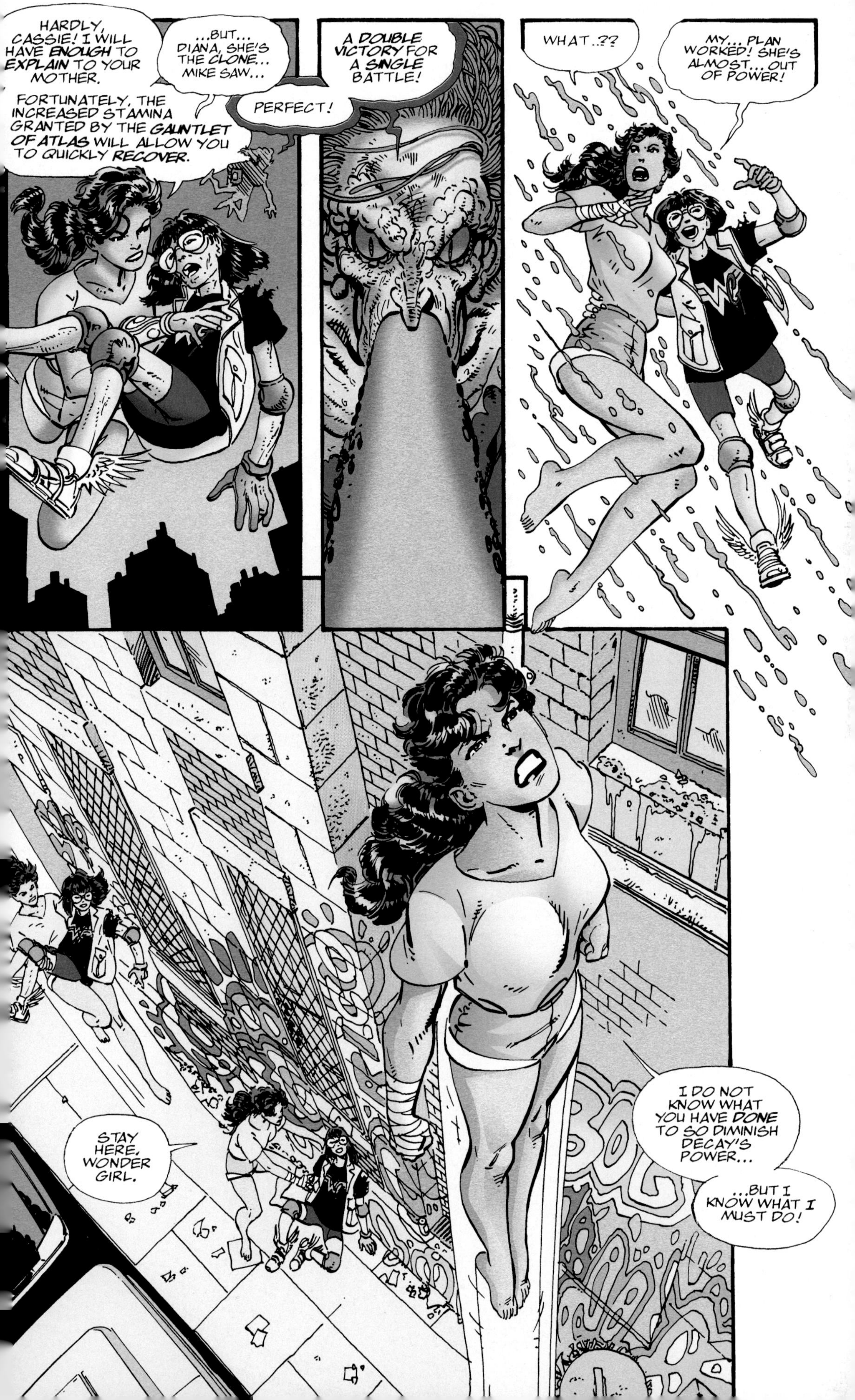

HARDLY, CASSIE! I WILL HAVE ENOUGH TO EXPLAIN TO YOUR MOTHER.
FORTUNATELY, THE INCREASED STAMINA GRANTED BY THE GAUNTLET OF ATLAS WILL ALLOW YOU TO QUICKLY RECOVER.
...BUT... DIANA, SHE'S THE CLONE... MIKE SAW...
A DOUBLE VICTORY FOR A SINGLE BATTLE!
PERFECT!
WHAT..??
MY... PLAN WORKED! SHE'S ALMOST... OUT OF POWER!
STAY HERE, WONDER GIRL.
I DO NOT KNOW WHAT YOU HAVE DONE TO SO DIMINISH DECAY'S POWER...
...BUT I KNOW WHAT I MUST DO!

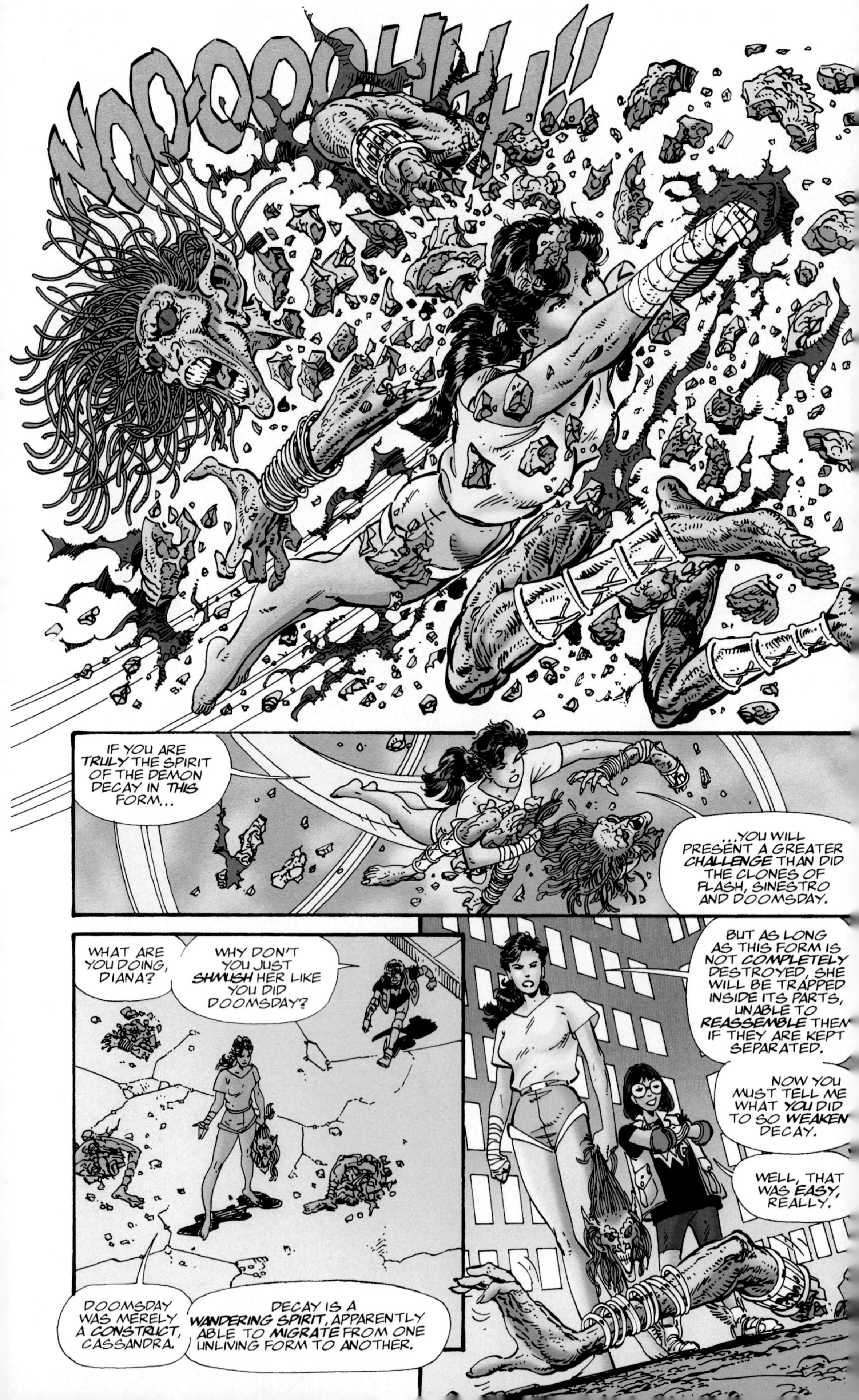
NOOOOOHHHH!!
IF YOU ARE TRULY THE SPIRIT OF THE DEMON DECAY IN THIS FORM...
...YOU WILL PRESENT A GREATER CHALLENGE THAN DID THE CLONES OF FLASH, SINESTRO AND DOOMSDAY.
WHAT ARE YOU DOING, DIANA?
WHY DON'T YOU JUST SHMUSH HER LIKE YOU DID DOOMSDAY?
DOOMSDAY WAS MERELY A CONSTRUCT, CASSANDRA.
DECAY IS A WANDERING SPIRIT, APPARENTLY ABLE TO MIGRATE FROM ONE UNLIVING FORM TO ANOTHER.
BUT AS LONG AS THIS FORM IS NOT COMPLETELY DESTROYED, SHE WILL BE TRAPPED INSIDE ITS PARTS, UNABLE TO REASSEMBLE THEM IF THEY ARE KEPT SEPARATED.
NOW YOU MUST TELL ME WHAT YOU DID TO SO WEAKEN DECAY.
WELL, THAT WAS EASY, REALLY.

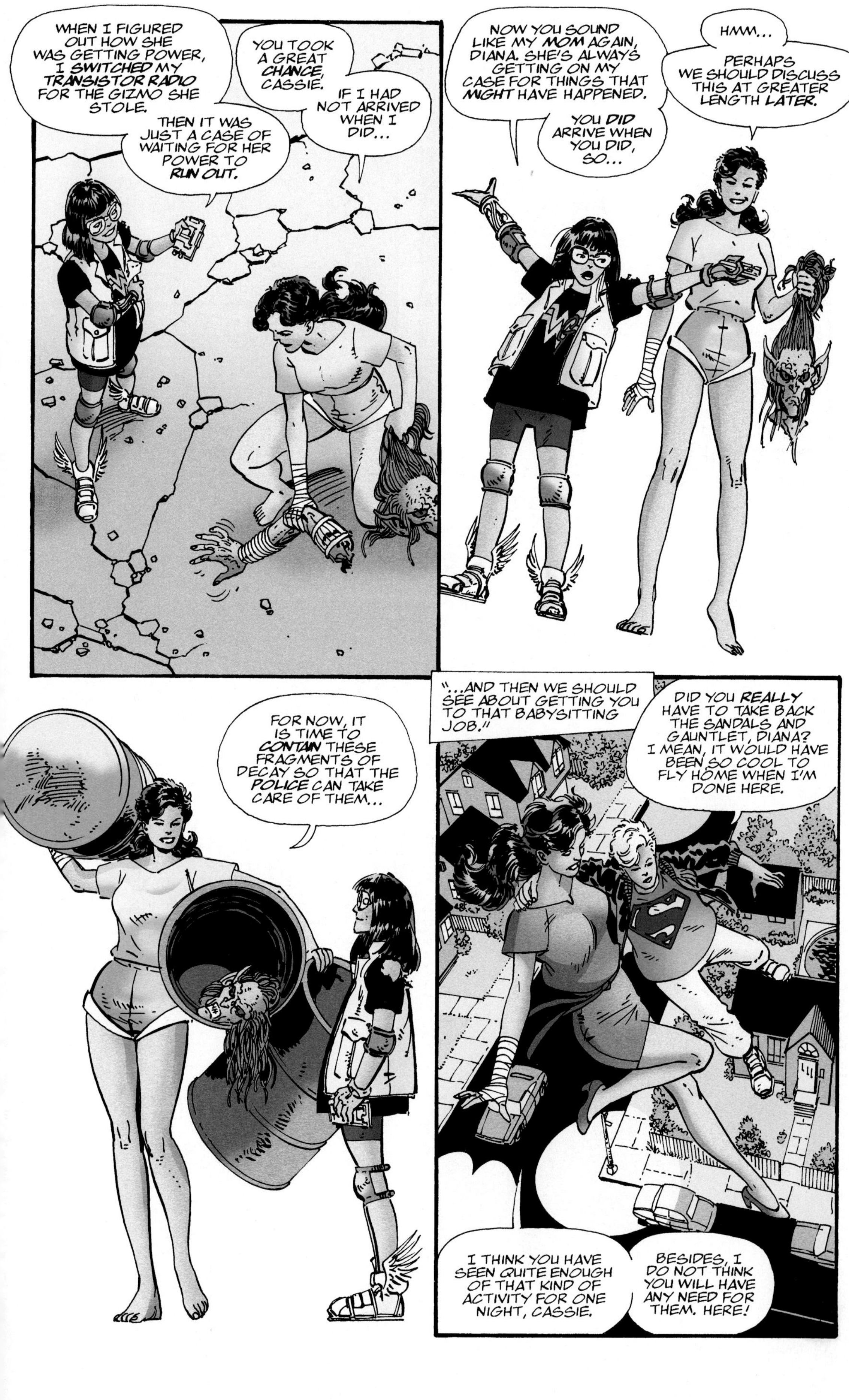
WHEN I FIGURED OUT HOW SHE WAS GETTING POWER, I **SWITCHED** MY **TRANSISTOR RADIO** FOR THE GIZMO SHE STOLE.
THEN IT WAS JUST A CASE OF WAITING FOR HER POWER TO **RUN OUT.**
YOU TOOK A GREAT **CHANCE**, CASSIE.
IF I HAD NOT ARRIVED WHEN I DID...
NOW YOU SOUND LIKE MY **MOM** AGAIN, DIANA. SHE'S ALWAYS GETTING ON MY CASE FOR THINGS THAT **MIGHT** HAVE HAPPENED.
YOU **DID** ARRIVE WHEN YOU DID, SO...
HMM...
PERHAPS WE SHOULD DISCUSS THIS AT GREATER LENGTH **LATER.**
FOR NOW, IT IS TIME TO **CONTAIN** THESE FRAGMENTS OF DECAY SO THAT THE **POLICE** CAN TAKE CARE OF THEM...
"...AND THEN WE SHOULD SEE ABOUT GETTING YOU TO THAT BABYSITTING JOB."
DID YOU **REALLY** HAVE TO TAKE BACK THE SANDALS AND GAUNTLET, DIANA? I MEAN, IT WOULD HAVE BEEN SO COOL TO FLY HOME WHEN I'M DONE HERE.
I THINK YOU HAVE SEEN QUITE ENOUGH OF THAT KIND OF ACTIVITY FOR ONE NIGHT, CASSIE.
BESIDES, I DO NOT THINK YOU WILL HAVE ANY NEED FOR THEM. HERE!

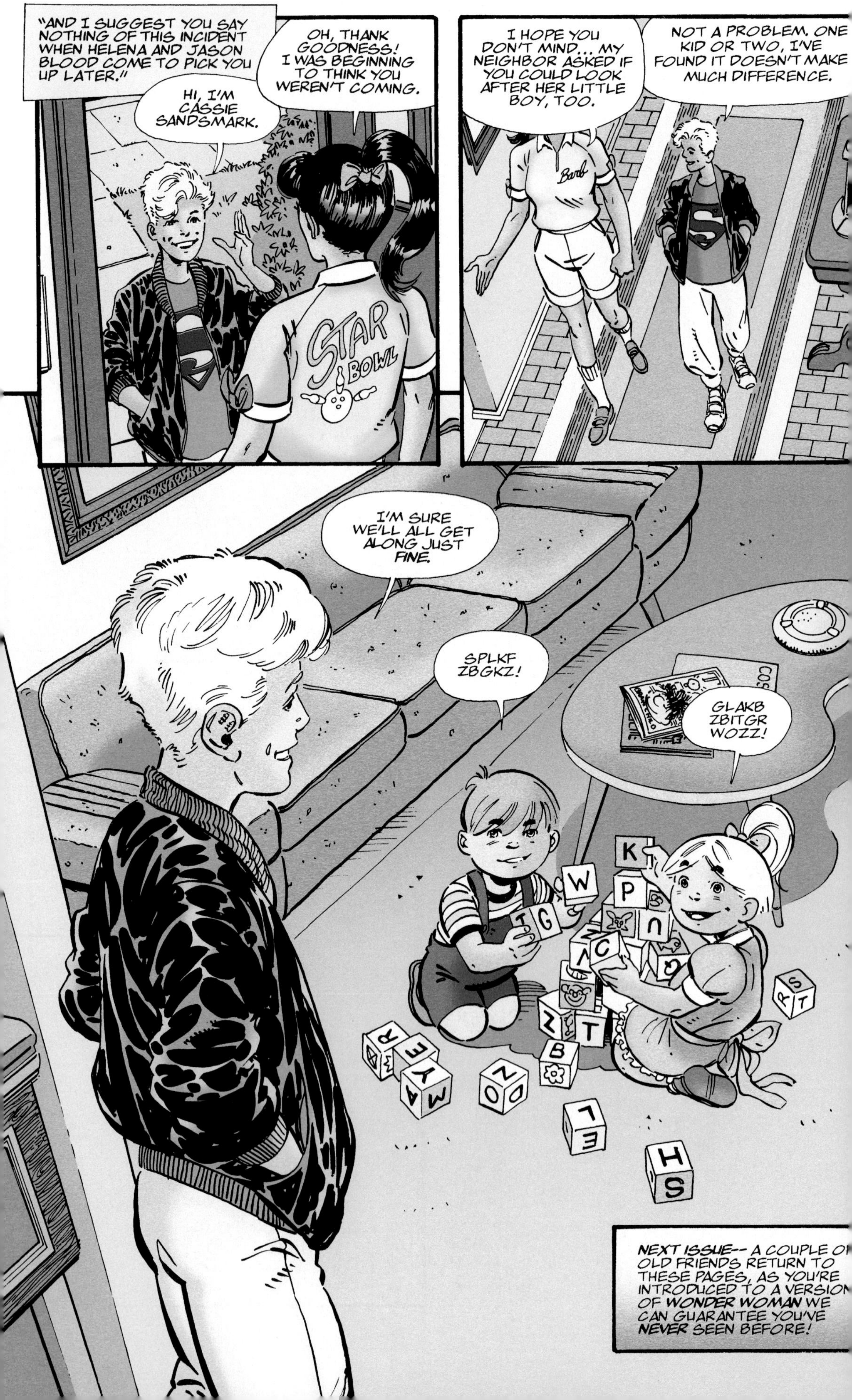
"AND I SUGGEST YOU SAY NOTHING OF THIS INCIDENT WHEN HELENA AND JASON BLOOD COME TO PICK YOU UP LATER."
HI, I'M CASSIE SANDSMARK.
OH, THANK GOODNESS! I WAS BEGINNING TO THINK YOU WEREN'T COMING.
STAR BOWL
I HOPE YOU DON'T MIND... MY NEIGHBOR ASKED IF YOU COULD LOOK AFTER HER LITTLE BOY, TOO.
NOT A PROBLEM. ONE KID OR TWO, I'VE FOUND IT DOESN'T MAKE MUCH DIFFERENCE.
I'M SURE WE'LL ALL GET ALONG JUST FINE.
SPLKF ZBGKZ!
GLAKB ZBITGR WOZZ!
NEXT ISSUE-- A COUPLE OF OLD FRIENDS RETURN TO THESE PAGES, AS YOU'RE INTRODUCED TO A VERSION OF WONDER WOMAN WE CAN GUARANTEE YOU'VE NEVER SEEN BEFORE!

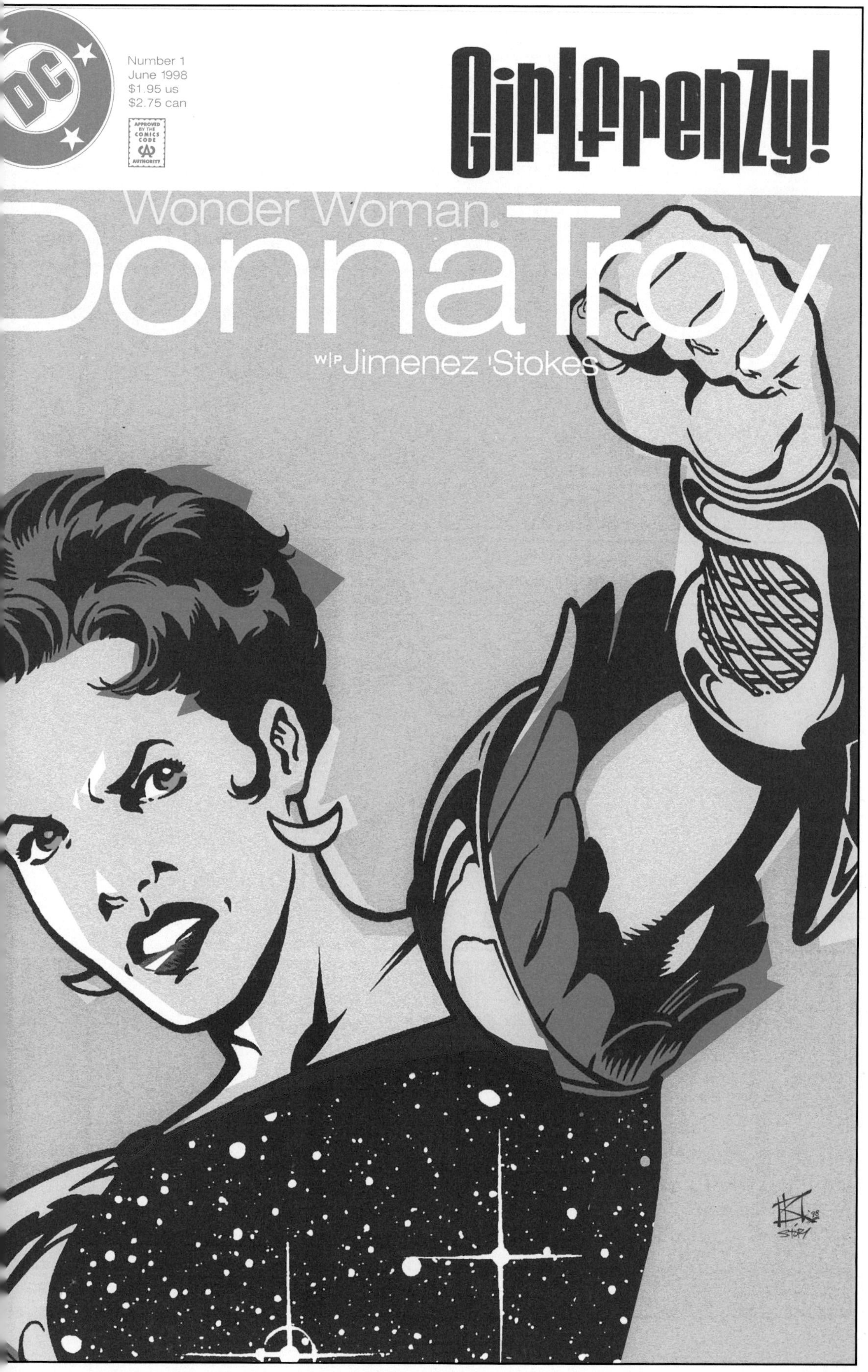

Number 1
June 1998
$1.95 us
$2.75 can
APPROVED BY THE COMICS CODE AUTHORITY
GirlFrenzy!
Wonder Woman.
Donna Troy
w|p Jimenez |Stokes

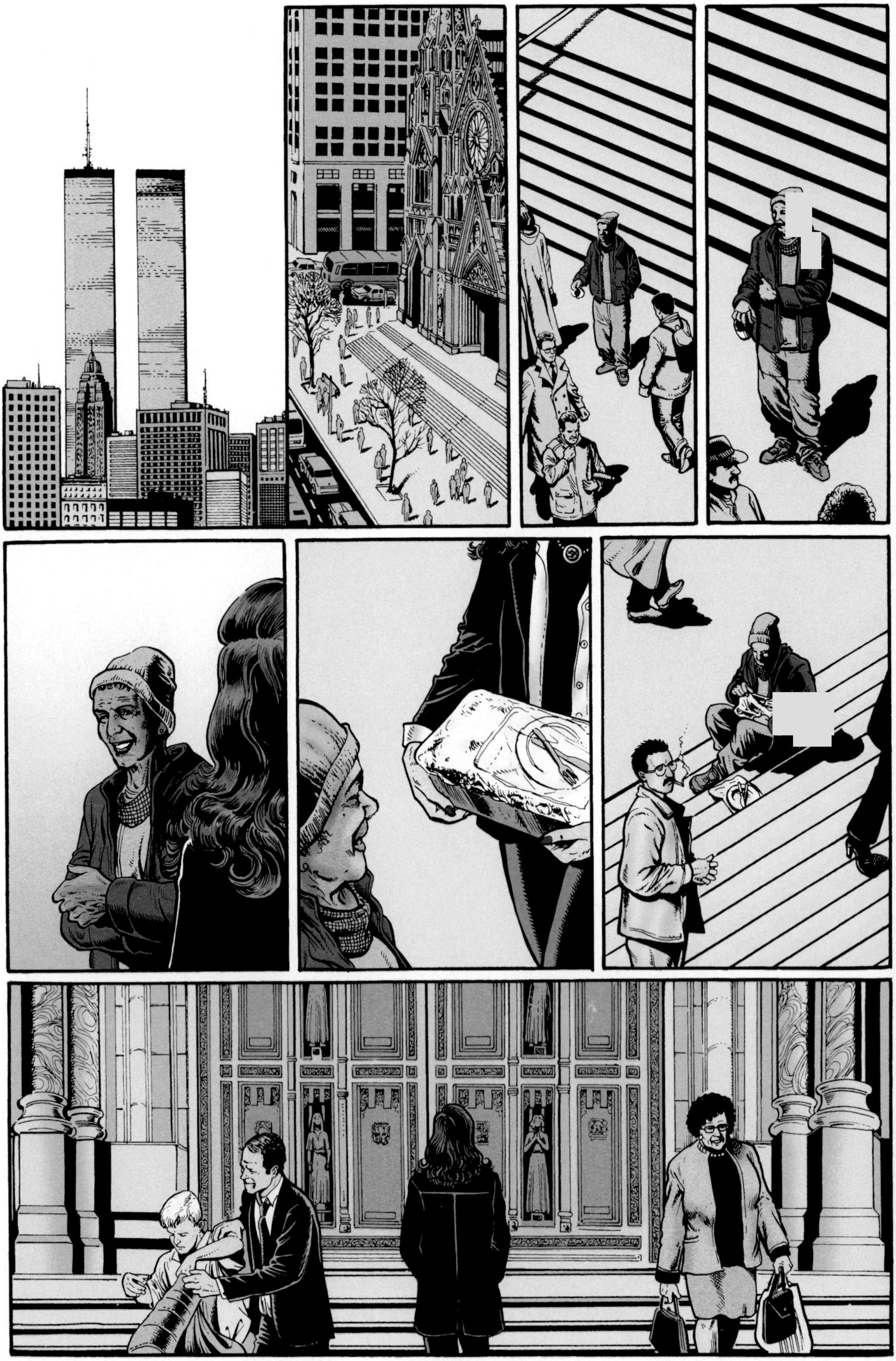

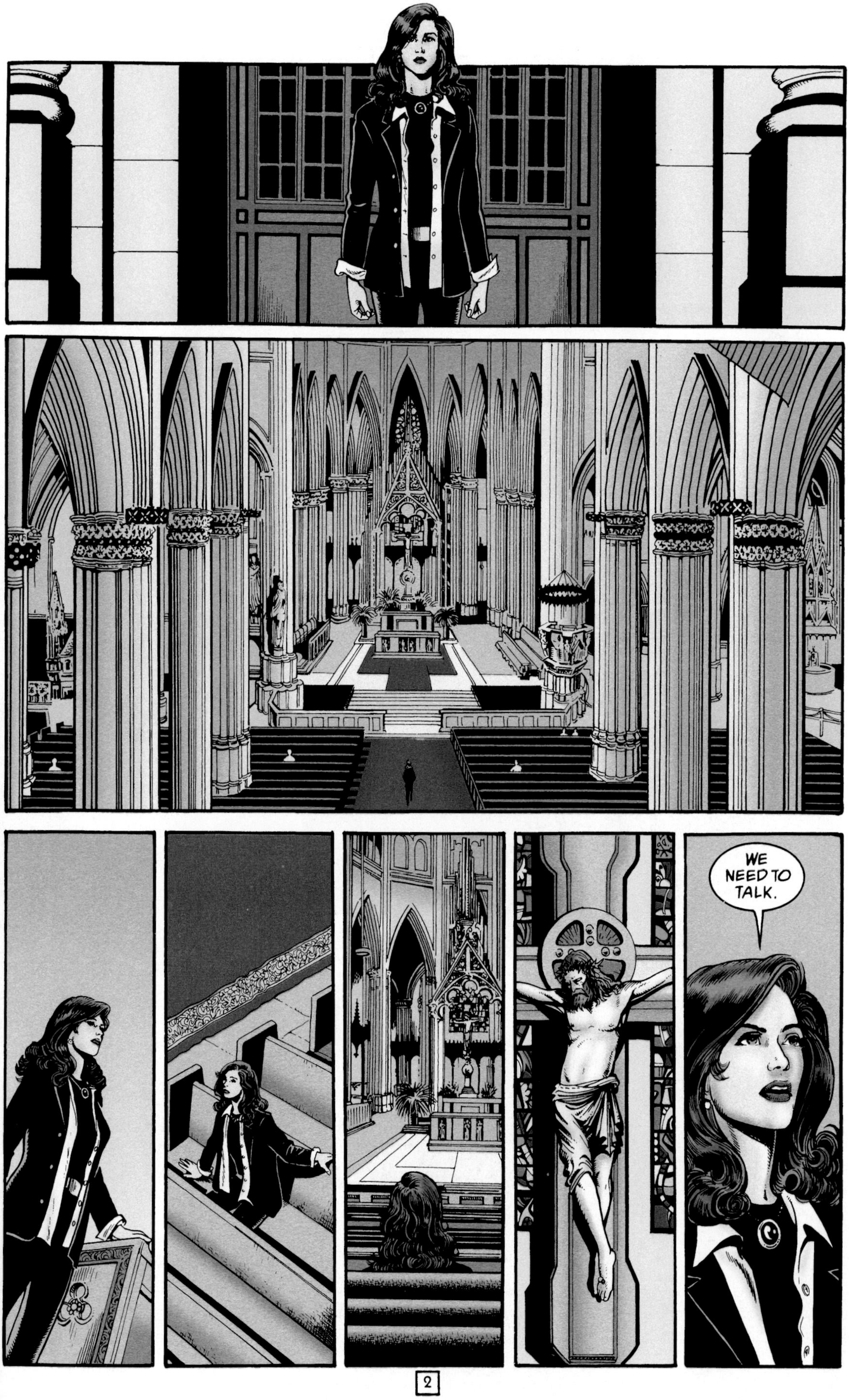
WE NEED TO TALK.

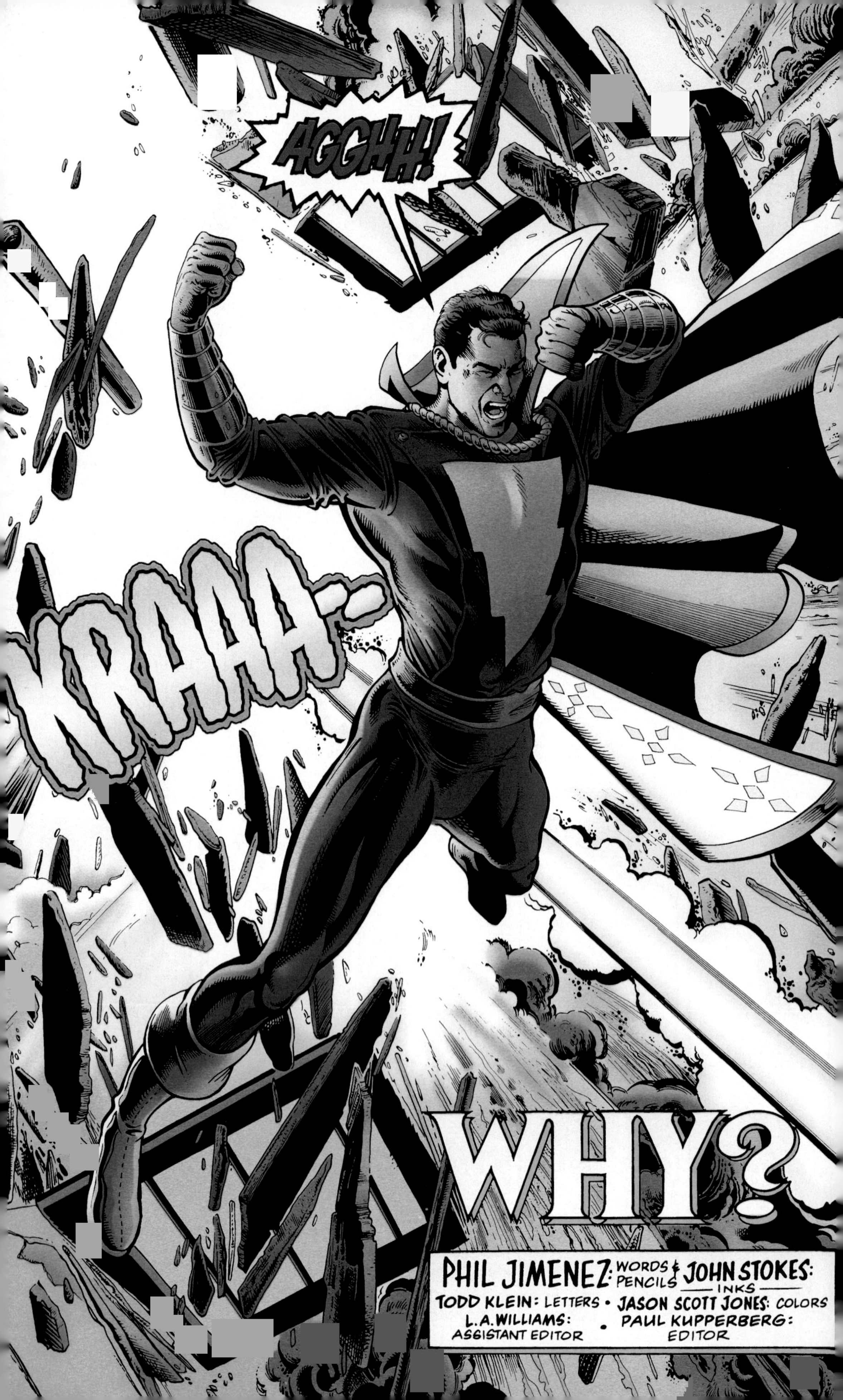
AGGHH!
KRAAA-
WHY?
PHIL JIMENEZ: WORDS & PENCILS
JOHN STOKES: INKS
TODD KLEIN: LETTERS
JASON SCOTT JONES: COLORS
L.A. WILLIAMS: ASSISTANT EDITOR
PAUL KUPPERBERG: EDITOR

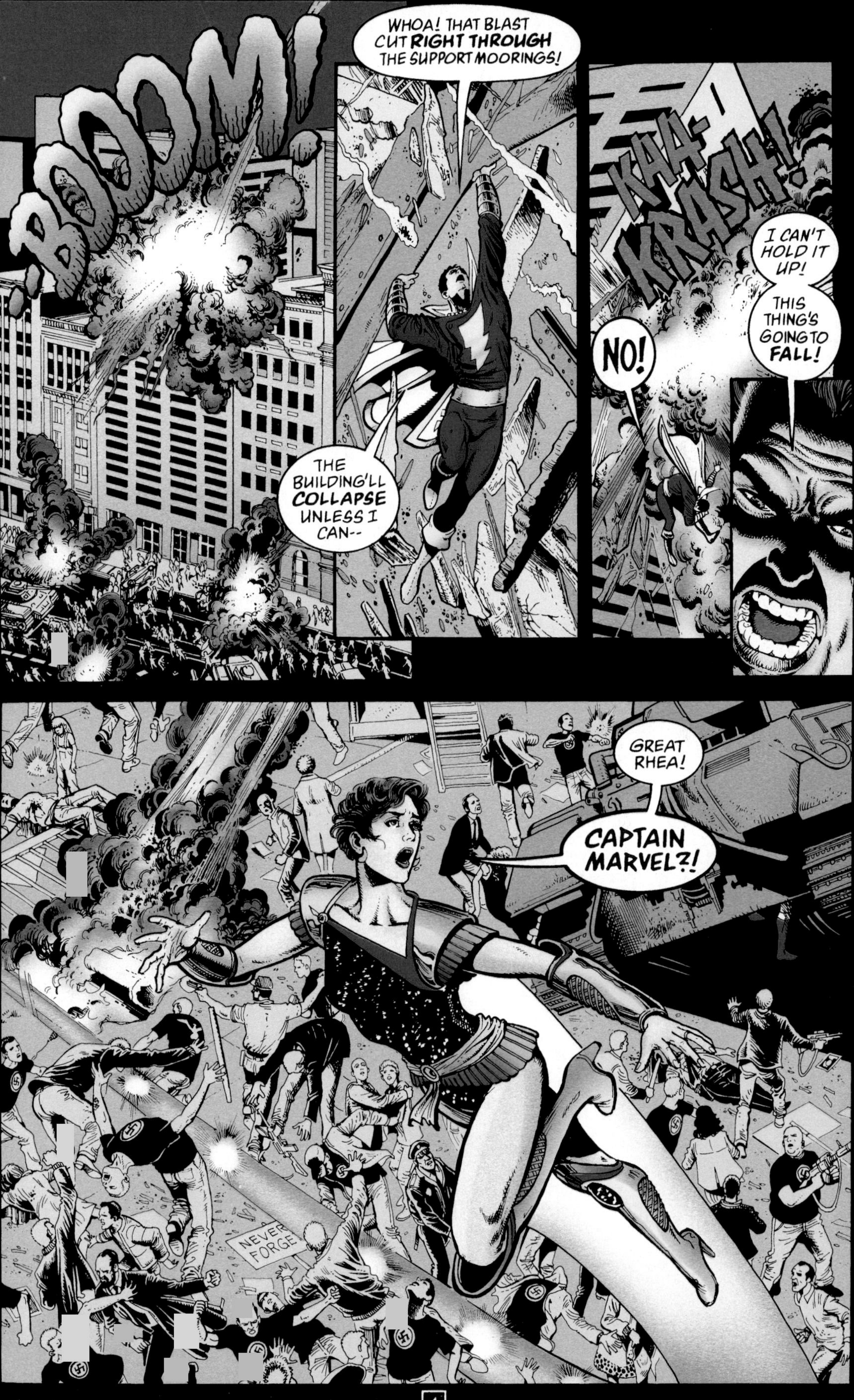
BOOOM!
WHOA! THAT BLAST CUT RIGHT THROUGH THE SUPPORT MOORINGS!
THE BUILDING'LL COLLAPSE UNLESS I CAN--
KAA-KRASH!
NO!
I CAN'T HOLD IT UP!
THIS THING'S GOING TO FALL!
GREAT RHEA!
CAPTAIN MARVEL?!
NEVER FORGE

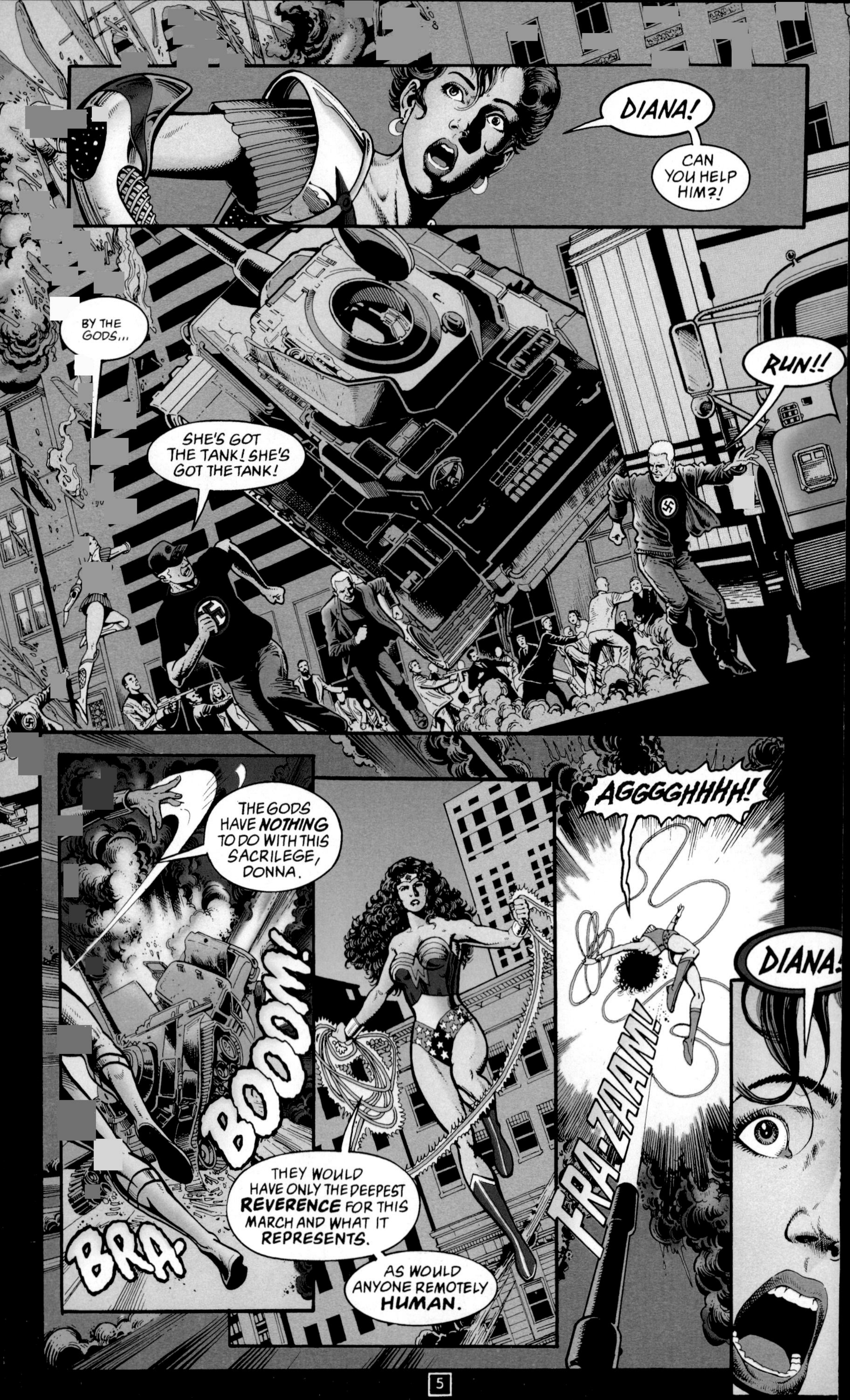

DIANA!
CAN YOU HELP HIM?!
BY THE GODS...
SHE'S GOT THE TANK! SHE'S GOT THE TANK!
RUN!!
THE GODS HAVE NOTHING TO DO WITH THIS SACRILEGE, DONNA.
THEY WOULD HAVE ONLY THE DEEPEST REVERENCE FOR THIS MARCH AND WHAT IT REPRESENTS.
AS WOULD ANYONE REMOTELY HUMAN.
BRA-BOOOM!
AGGGGHHHH!
FRA-ZAAM!
DIANA!

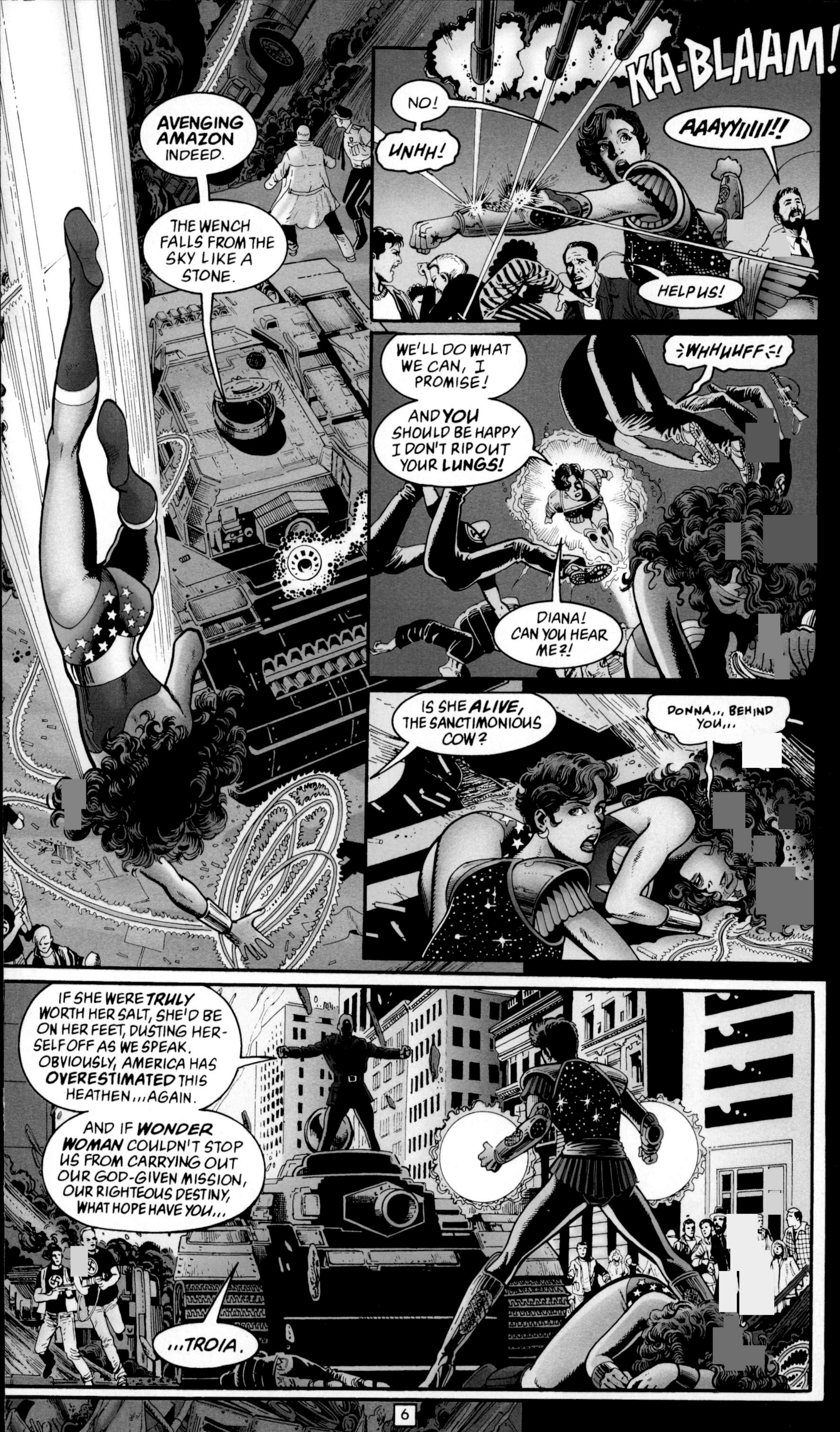
AVENGING AMAZON INDEED.
THE WENCH FALLS FROM THE SKY LIKE A STONE.
KA-BLAAM!
NO!
UNHH!
AAAYYIIIII!!
HELP US!
WE'LL DO WHAT WE CAN, I PROMISE!
AND YOU SHOULD BE HAPPY I DON'T RIP OUT YOUR LUNGS!
WHHUUFF!
DIANA! CAN YOU HEAR ME?!
IS SHE ALIVE, THE SANCTIMONIOUS COW?
DONNA... BEHIND YOU...
IF SHE WERE TRULY WORTH HER SALT, SHE'D BE ON HER FEET, DUSTING HERSELF OFF AS WE SPEAK. OBVIOUSLY, AMERICA HAS OVERESTIMATED THIS HEATHEN... AGAIN.
AND IF WONDER WOMAN COULDN'T STOP US FROM CARRYING OUT OUR GOD-GIVEN MISSION, OUR RIGHTEOUS DESTINY, WHAT HOPE HAVE YOU...
...TROIA.

"ARE YOU THERE, GOD? IT'S ME, *DONNA TROY.*"

SORRY. BAD JOKE.

I HOPE I'M NOT BEING *RUDE.*

I'M HERE BECAUSE I NEED TO *TALK* TO SOMEONE.

AND WITH *MY* GODS BEYOND MY REACH...

...I THOUGHT *THIS* MIGHT BE THE PLACE TO GO.

I FOUND THIS, GOING THROUGH *TERRY'S* OLD THINGS.

...and of Titan Hospitalized After Bias Attack

New York -- Terry Long, husband of Donna Troy, the New Titan known as Troia, was brutally beaten along with his friend Christopher Jacobs last night in what is reported as an anti-... attack. Lon... ...ish, was a... ...hil...

POOR TERRY. EVEN THEN, HE COULDN'T ESCAPE IT. MY *LUCK.*

I WON'T ASK WHY YOU *TOOK* HIM FROM ME, OR MY *BABY BOY.* I'VE SEEN ENOUGH TO KNOW THAT I WON'T HAVE THE ANSWERS TO THOSE QUESTIONS UNTIL I *JOIN* THEM.

BUT I HOPE YOU KNOW HOW MUCH I *MISS* BOTH OF THEM...

...AND I HOPE YOU KNOW HOW MUCH IT *HURTS.*

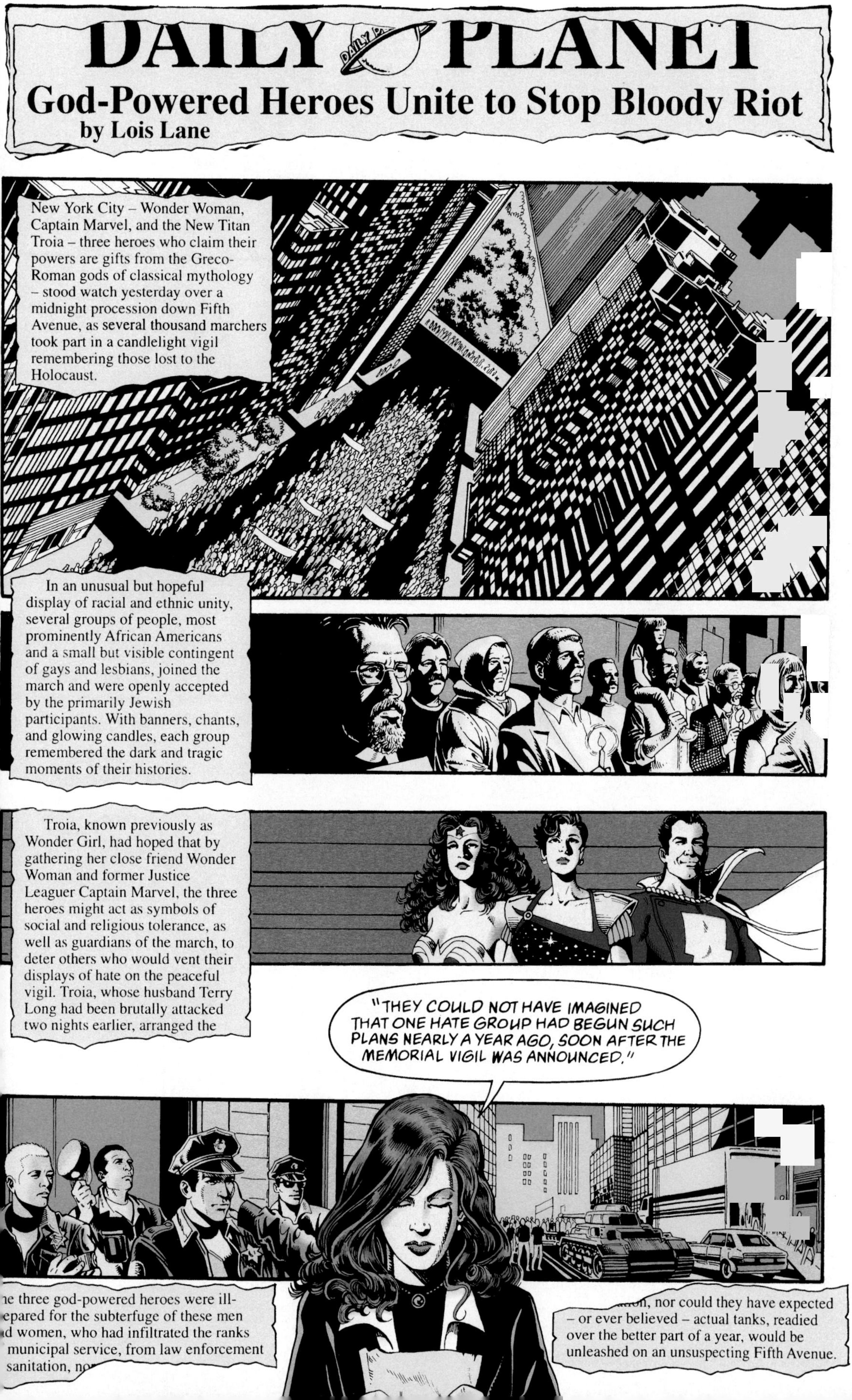

DAILY PLANET
DAILY PLANET
God-Powered Heroes Unite to Stop Bloody Riot
by Lois Lane
New York City – Wonder Woman, Captain Marvel, and the New Titan Troia – three heroes who claim their powers are gifts from the Greco-Roman gods of classical mythology – stood watch yesterday over a midnight procession down Fifth Avenue, as several thousand marchers took part in a candlelight vigil remembering those lost to the Holocaust.
In an unusual but hopeful display of racial and ethnic unity, several groups of people, most prominently African Americans and a small but visible contingent of gays and lesbians, joined the march and were openly accepted by the primarily Jewish participants. With banners, chants, and glowing candles, each group remembered the dark and tragic moments of their histories.
Troia, known previously as Wonder Girl, had hoped that by gathering her close friend Wonder Woman and former Justice Leaguer Captain Marvel, the three heroes might act as symbols of social and religious tolerance, as well as guardians of the march, to deter others who would vent their displays of hate on the peaceful vigil. Troia, whose husband Terry Long had been brutally attacked two nights earlier, arranged the
"THEY COULD NOT HAVE IMAGINED THAT ONE HATE GROUP HAD BEGUN SUCH PLANS NEARLY A YEAR AGO, SOON AFTER THE MEMORIAL VIGIL WAS ANNOUNCED."
ne three god-powered heroes were ill-epared for the subterfuge of these men d women, who had infiltrated the ranks municipal service, from law enforcement sanitation, no
, nor could they have expected – or ever believed – actual tanks, readied over the better part of a year, would be unleashed on an unsuspecting Fifth Avenue.

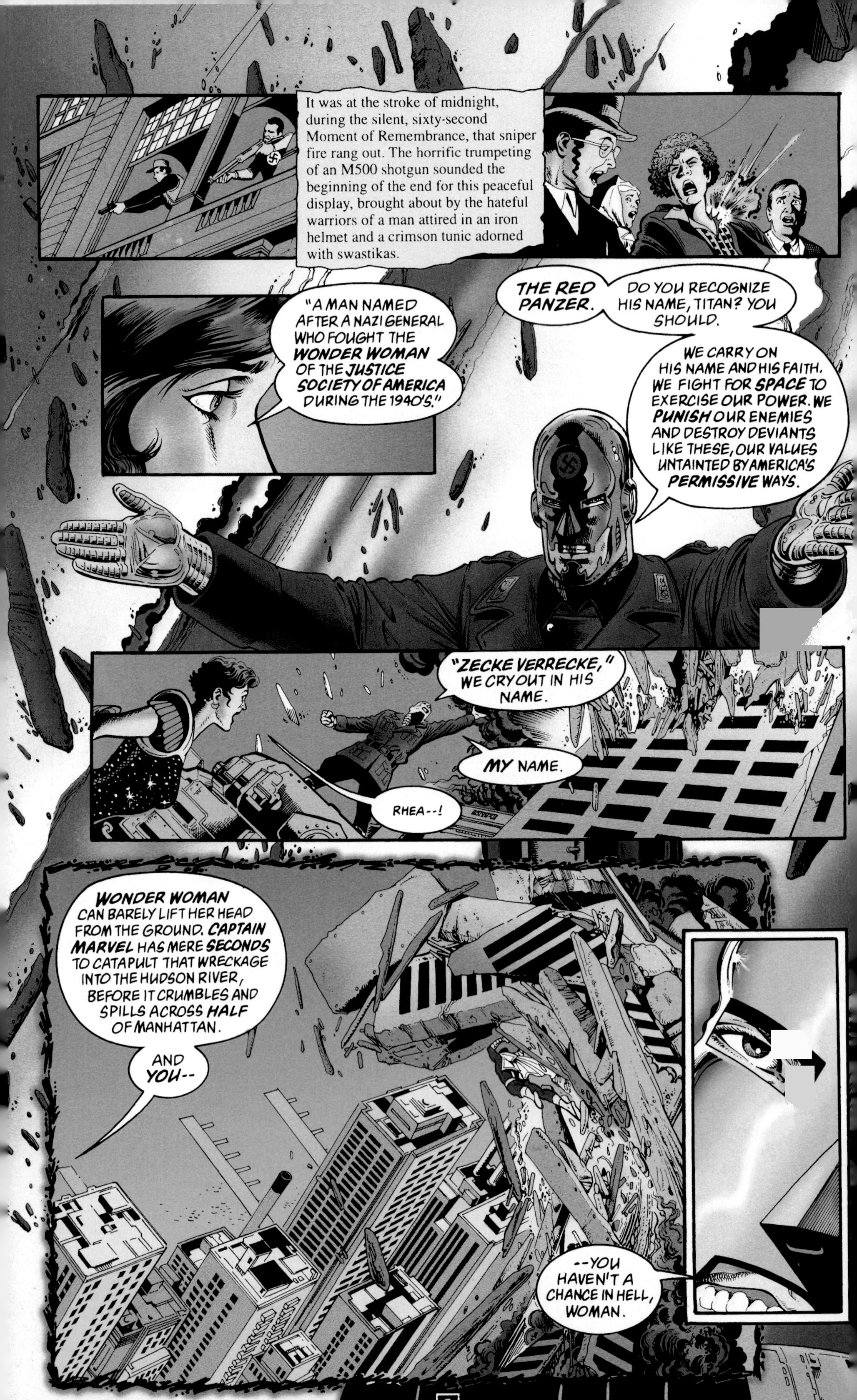

It was at the stroke of midnight, during the silent, sixty-second Moment of Remembrance, that sniper fire rang out. The horrific trumpeting of an M500 shotgun sounded the beginning of the end for this peaceful display, brought about by the hateful warriors of a man attired in an iron helmet and a crimson tunic adorned with swastikas.
"A MAN NAMED AFTER A NAZI GENERAL WHO FOUGHT THE WONDER WOMAN OF THE JUSTICE SOCIETY OF AMERICA DURING THE 1940'S."
THE RED PANZER.
DO YOU RECOGNIZE HIS NAME, TITAN? YOU SHOULD.
WE CARRY ON HIS NAME AND HIS FAITH. WE FIGHT FOR SPACE TO EXERCISE OUR POWER. WE PUNISH OUR ENEMIES AND DESTROY DEVIANTS LIKE THESE, OUR VALUES UNTAINTED BY AMERICA'S PERMISSIVE WAYS.
"ZECKE VERRECKE," WE CRY OUT IN HIS NAME.
MY NAME.
RHEA--!
WONDER WOMAN CAN BARELY LIFT HER HEAD FROM THE GROUND. CAPTAIN MARVEL HAS MERE SECONDS TO CATAPULT THAT WRECKAGE INTO THE HUDSON RIVER, BEFORE IT CRUMBLES AND SPILLS ACROSS HALF OF MANHATTAN.
AND YOU--
--YOU HAVEN'T A CHANCE IN HELL, WOMAN.

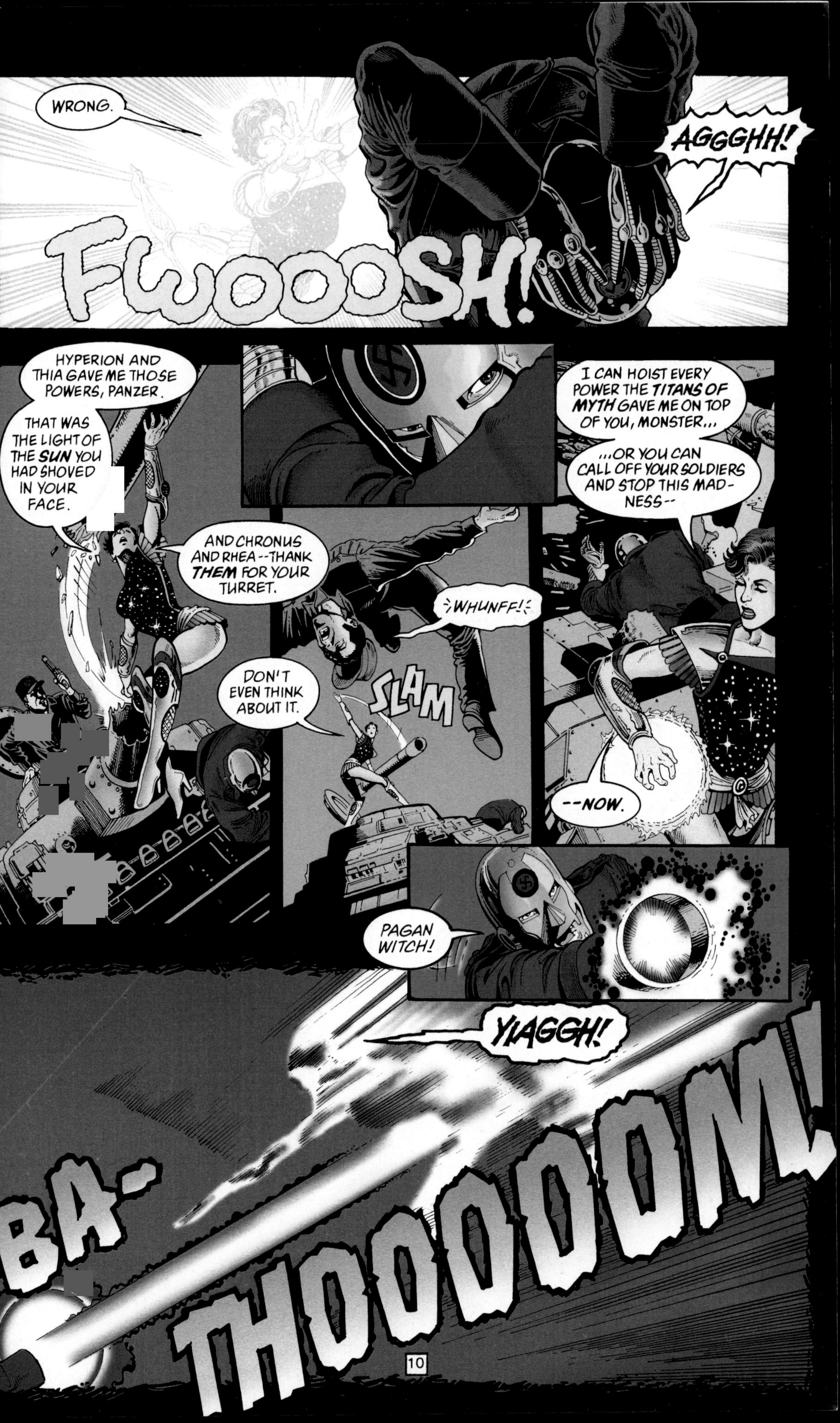
WRONG.
AGGGHH!
FWOOOSH!
HYPERION AND THIA GAVE ME THOSE POWERS, PANZER.
THAT WAS THE LIGHT OF THE SUN YOU HAD SHOVED IN YOUR FACE.
AND CHRONUS AND RHEA--THANK THEM FOR YOUR TURRET.
WHUNFF!
SLAM
DON'T EVEN THINK ABOUT IT.
I CAN HOIST EVERY POWER THE TITANS OF MYTH GAVE ME ON TOP OF YOU, MONSTER...
...OR YOU CAN CALL OFF YOUR SOLDIERS AND STOP THIS MAD-NESS--
--NOW.
PAGAN WITCH!
YIAGGH!
BA-THOOOOOM!

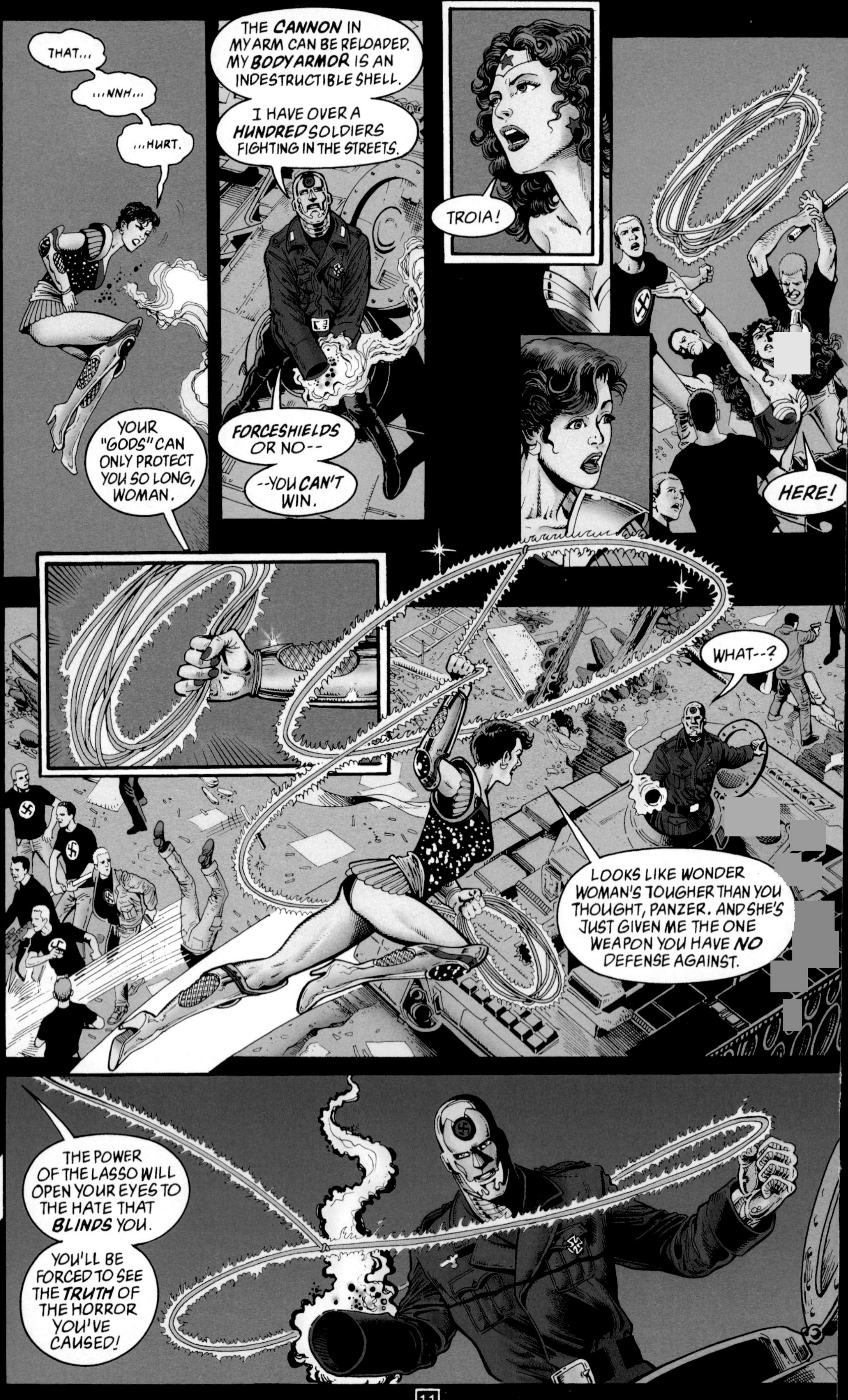
THAT...
...NNH...
...HURT.
YOUR "GODS" CAN ONLY PROTECT YOU SO LONG, WOMAN.
THE CANNON IN MY ARM CAN BE RELOADED. MY BODY ARMOR IS AN INDESTRUCTIBLE SHELL.
I HAVE OVER A HUNDRED SOLDIERS FIGHTING IN THE STREETS.
FORCESHIELDS OR NO--
--YOU CAN'T WIN.
TROIA!
HERE!
WHAT--?
LOOKS LIKE WONDER WOMAN'S TOUGHER THAN YOU THOUGHT, PANZER. AND SHE'S JUST GIVEN ME THE ONE WEAPON YOU HAVE NO DEFENSE AGAINST.
THE POWER OF THE LASSO WILL OPEN YOUR EYES TO THE HATE THAT BLINDS YOU.
YOU'LL BE FORCED TO SEE THE TRUTH OF THE HORROR YOU'VE CAUSED!

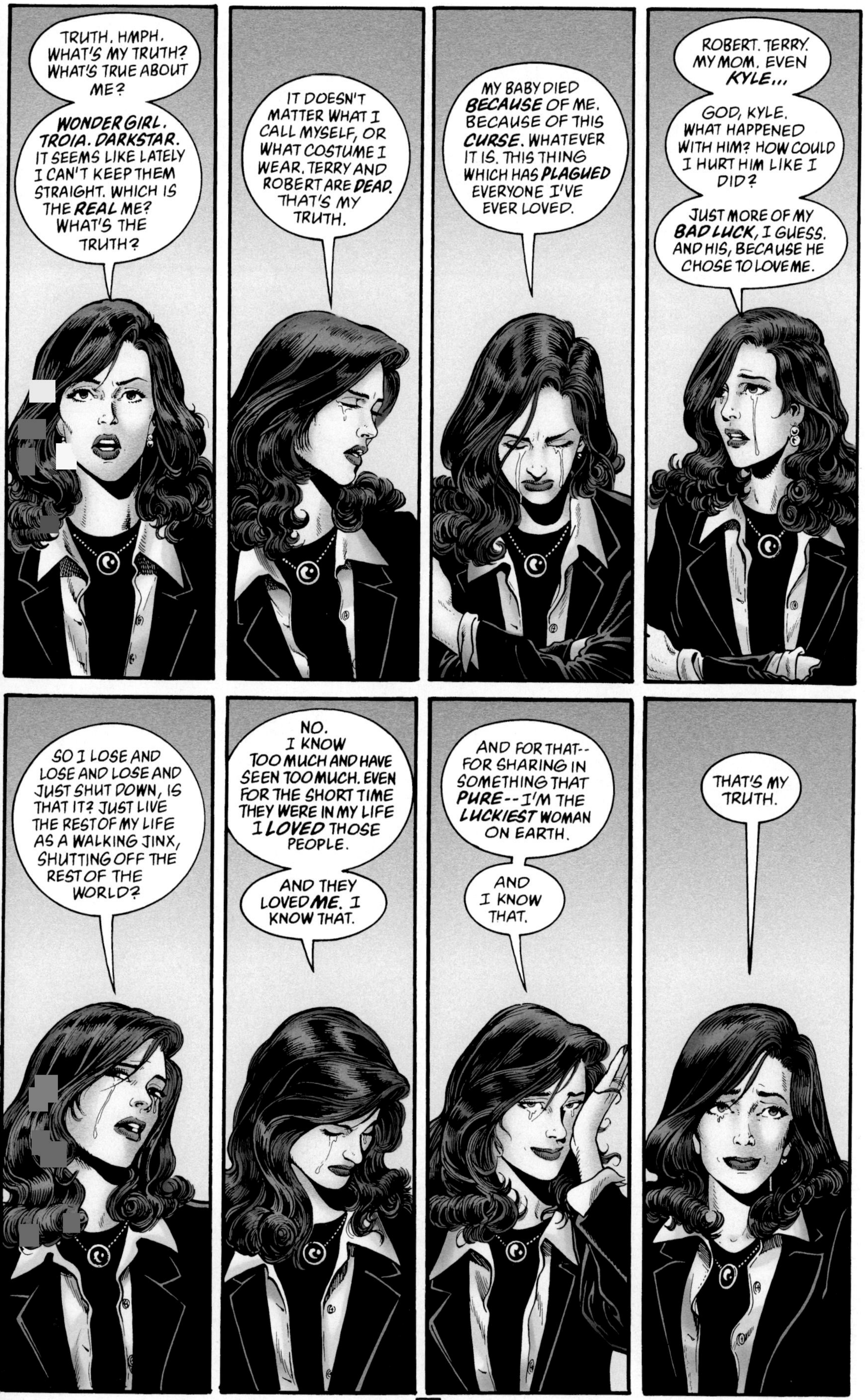
TRUTH. HMPH. WHAT'S MY TRUTH? WHAT'S TRUE ABOUT ME?
WONDER GIRL. TROIA. DARKSTAR. IT SEEMS LIKE LATELY I CAN'T KEEP THEM STRAIGHT. WHICH IS THE REAL ME? WHAT'S THE TRUTH?
IT DOESN'T MATTER WHAT I CALL MYSELF, OR WHAT COSTUME I WEAR. TERRY AND ROBERT ARE DEAD. THAT'S MY TRUTH.
MY BABY DIED BECAUSE OF ME. BECAUSE OF THIS CURSE. WHATEVER IT IS. THIS THING WHICH HAS PLAGUED EVERYONE I'VE EVER LOVED.
ROBERT. TERRY. MY MOM. EVEN KYLE...
GOD, KYLE. WHAT HAPPENED WITH HIM? HOW COULD I HURT HIM LIKE I DID?
JUST MORE OF MY BAD LUCK, I GUESS. AND HIS, BECAUSE HE CHOSE TO LOVE ME.
SO I LOSE AND LOSE AND LOSE AND JUST SHUT DOWN, IS THAT IT? JUST LIVE THE REST OF MY LIFE AS A WALKING JINX, SHUTTING OFF THE REST OF THE WORLD?
NO. I KNOW TOO MUCH AND HAVE SEEN TOO MUCH. EVEN FOR THE SHORT TIME THEY WERE IN MY LIFE I LOVED THOSE PEOPLE.
AND THEY LOVED ME. I KNOW THAT.
AND FOR THAT-- FOR SHARING IN SOMETHING THAT PURE--I'M THE LUCKIEST WOMAN ON EARTH.
AND I KNOW THAT.
THAT'S MY TRUTH.

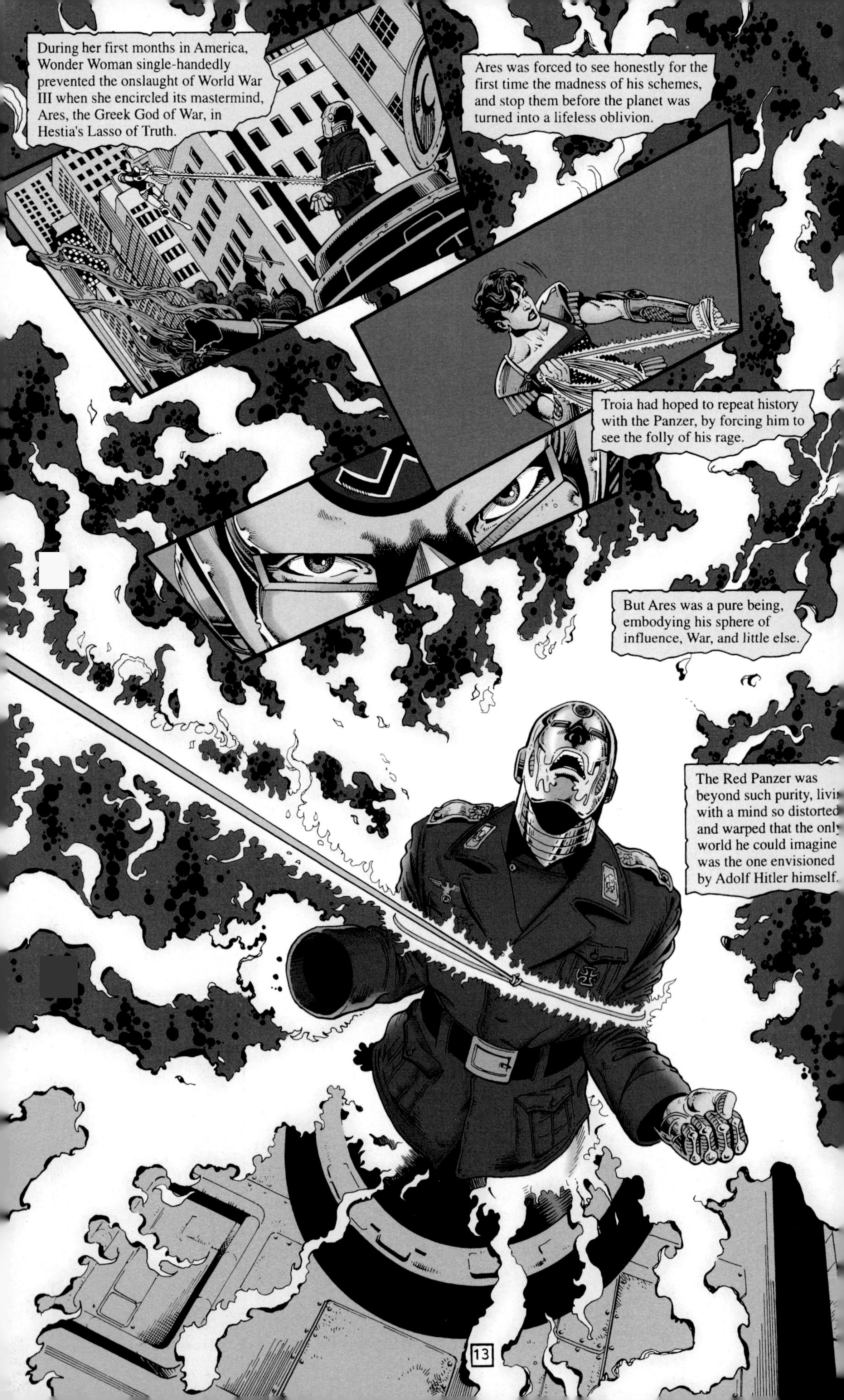
During her first months in America, Wonder Woman single-handedly prevented the onslaught of World War III when she encircled its mastermind, Ares, the Greek God of War, in Hestia's Lasso of Truth.
Ares was forced to see honestly for the first time the madness of his schemes, and stop them before the planet was turned into a lifeless oblivion.
Troia had hoped to repeat history with the Panzer, by forcing him to see the folly of his rage.
But Ares was a pure being, embodying his sphere of influence, War, and little else.
The Red Panzer was beyond such purity, livi with a mind so distorted and warped that the onl world he could imagine was the one envisioned by Adolf Hitler himself.

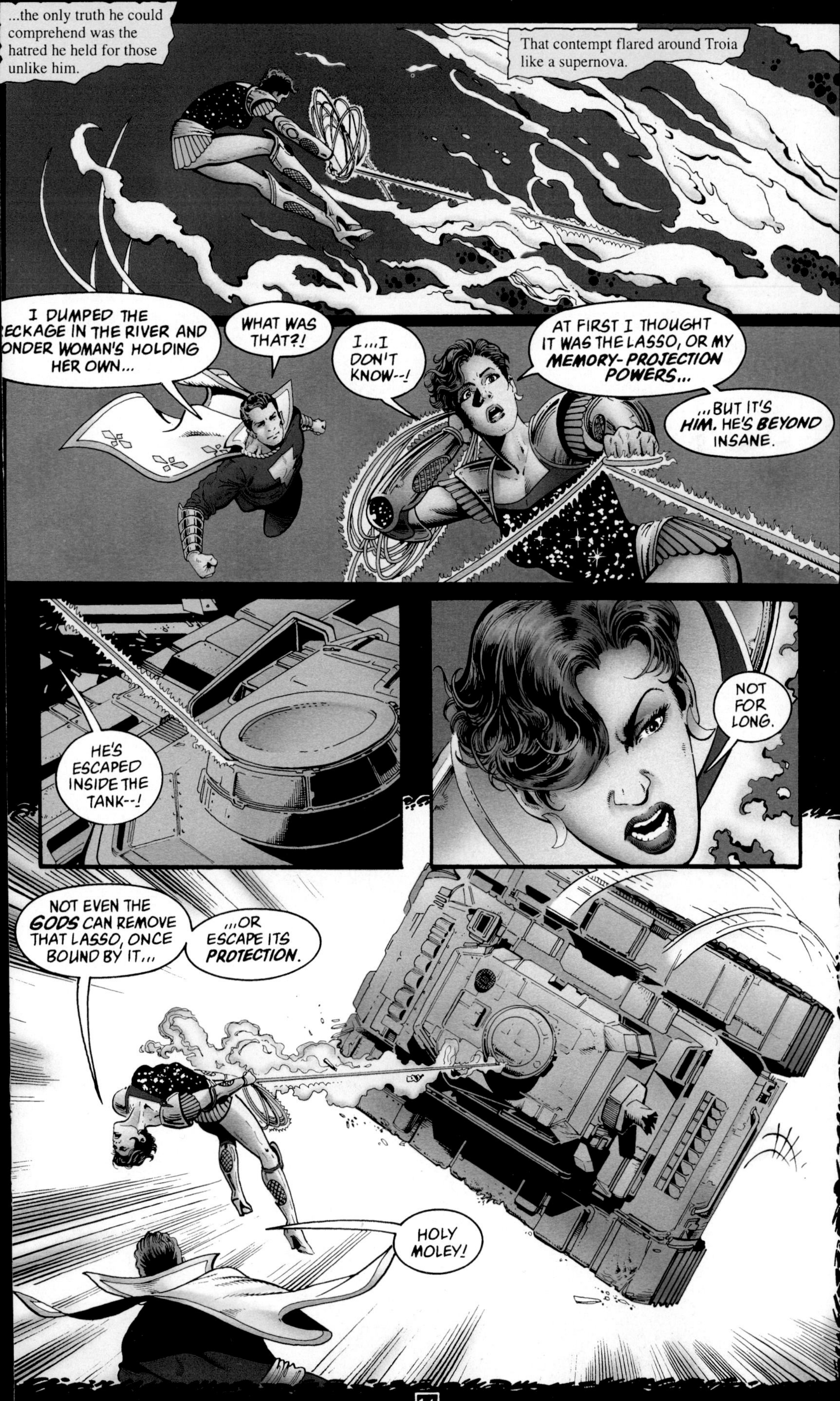
...the only truth he could comprehend was the hatred he held for those unlike him.
That contempt flared around Troia like a supernova.
I DUMPED THE RECKAGE IN THE RIVER AND ONDER WOMAN'S HOLDING HER OWN...
WHAT WAS THAT?!
I...I DON'T KNOW--!
AT FIRST I THOUGHT IT WAS THE LASSO, OR MY MEMORY-PROJECTION POWERS...
...BUT IT'S HIM. HE'S BEYOND INSANE.
HE'S ESCAPED INSIDE THE TANK--!
NOT FOR LONG.
NOT EVEN THE GODS CAN REMOVE THAT LASSO, ONCE BOUND BY IT...
...OR ESCAPE ITS PROTECTION.
HOLY MOLEY!

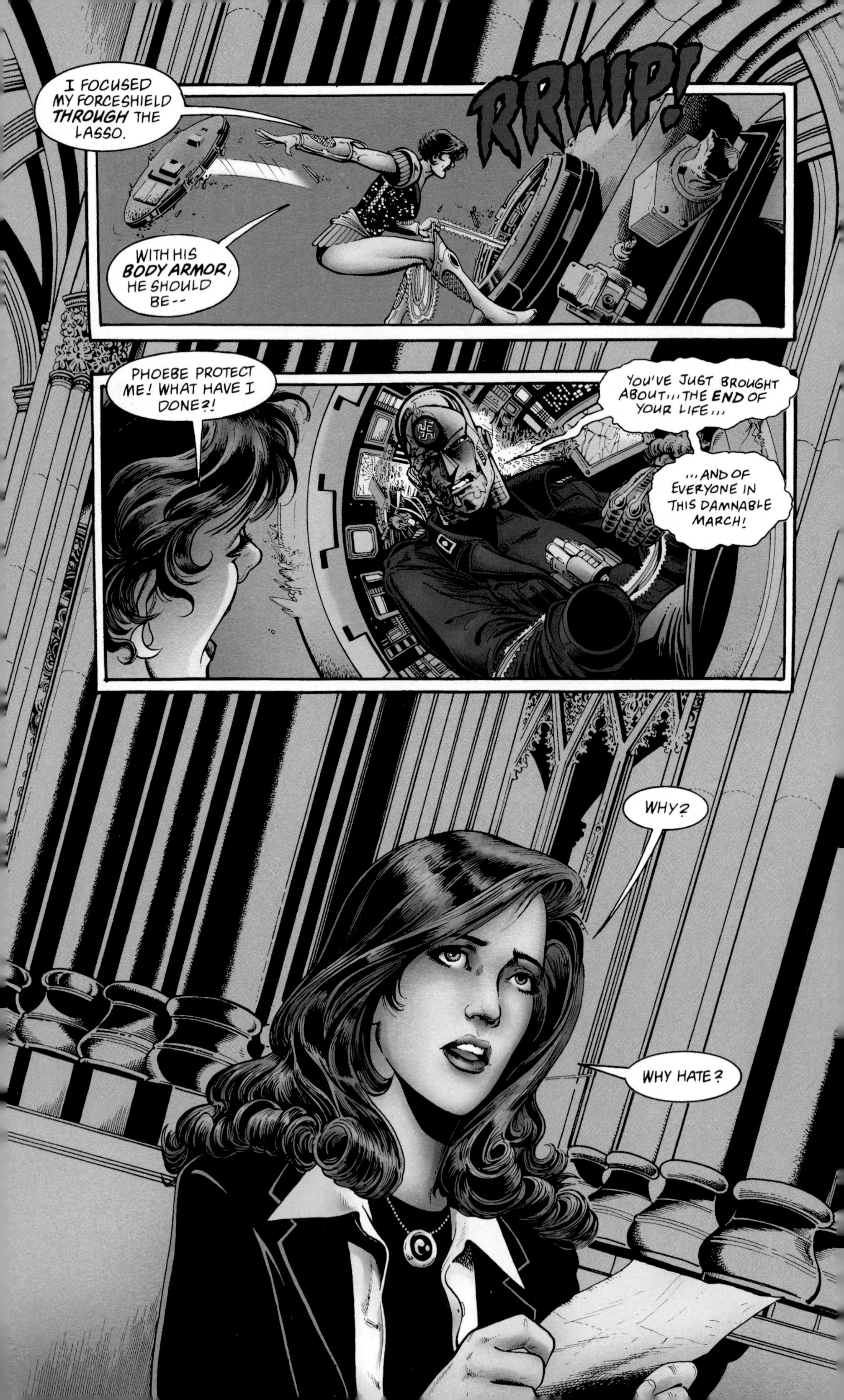
I FOCUSED MY FORCESHIELD THROUGH THE LASSO.
RRIIIP!
WITH HIS BODY ARMOR, HE SHOULD BE--
PHOEBE PROTECT ME! WHAT HAVE I DONE?!
YOU'VE JUST BROUGHT ABOUT... THE END OF YOUR LIFE...
...AND OF EVERYONE IN THIS DAMNABLE MARCH!
WHY?
WHY HATE?

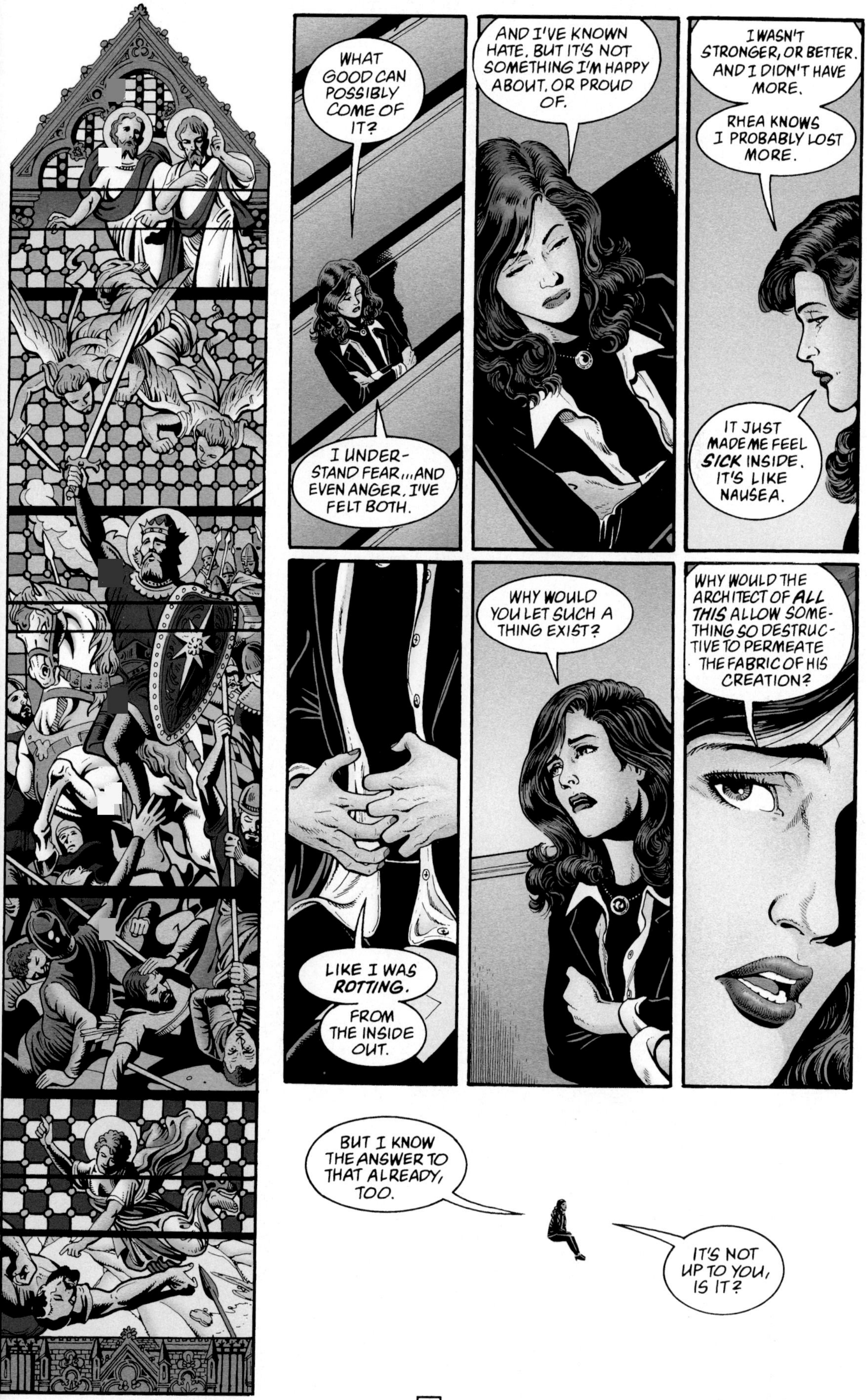
WHAT GOOD CAN POSSIBLY COME OF IT?
I UNDER-STAND FEAR...AND EVEN ANGER. I'VE FELT BOTH.
AND I'VE KNOWN HATE. BUT IT'S NOT SOMETHING I'M HAPPY ABOUT, OR PROUD OF.
I WASN'T STRONGER, OR BETTER. AND I DIDN'T HAVE MORE.
RHEA KNOWS I PROBABLY LOST MORE.
IT JUST MADE ME FEEL **SICK** INSIDE. IT'S LIKE NAUSEA.
LIKE I WAS **ROTTING.**
FROM THE INSIDE OUT.
WHY WOULD YOU LET SUCH A THING EXIST?
WHY WOULD THE ARCHITECT OF **ALL THIS** ALLOW SOME-THING SO DESTRUC-TIVE TO PERMEATE THE FABRIC OF HIS CREATION?
BUT I KNOW THE ANSWER TO THAT ALREADY, TOO.
IT'S NOT UP TO YOU, IS IT?

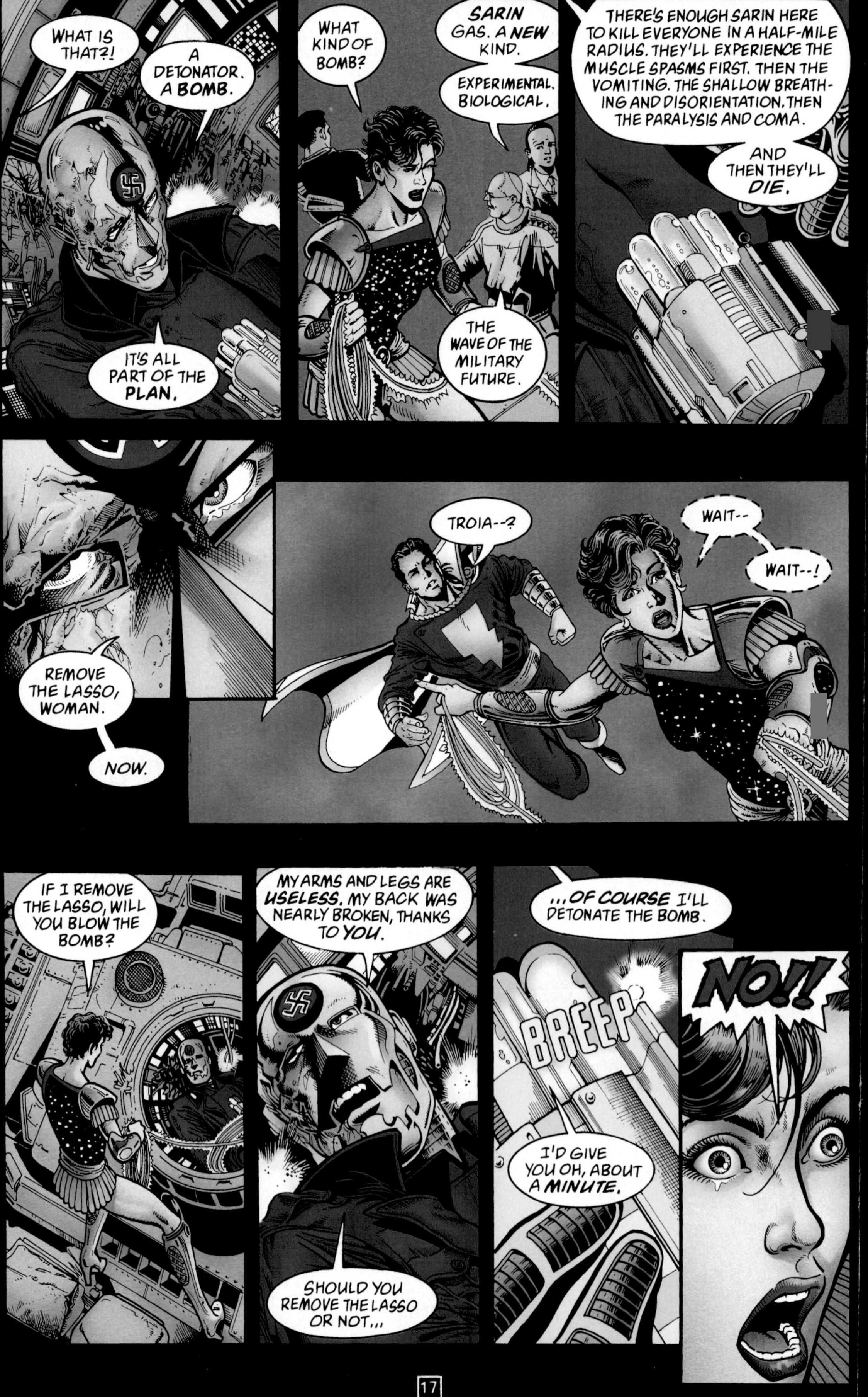
WHAT IS THAT?!
A DETONATOR. A BOMB.
IT'S ALL PART OF THE PLAN.
WHAT KIND OF BOMB?
SARIN GAS. A NEW KIND.
EXPERIMENTAL. BIOLOGICAL.
THE WAVE OF THE MILITARY FUTURE.
THERE'S ENOUGH SARIN HERE TO KILL EVERYONE IN A HALF-MILE RADIUS. THEY'LL EXPERIENCE THE MUSCLE SPASMS FIRST. THEN THE VOMITING. THE SHALLOW BREATHING AND DISORIENTATION. THEN THE PARALYSIS AND COMA.
AND THEN THEY'LL DIE.
REMOVE THE LASSO, WOMAN.
NOW.
TROIA--?
WAIT--
WAIT--!
IF I REMOVE THE LASSO, WILL YOU BLOW THE BOMB?
MY ARMS AND LEGS ARE USELESS. MY BACK WAS NEARLY BROKEN, THANKS TO YOU.
SHOULD YOU REMOVE THE LASSO OR NOT...
...OF COURSE I'LL DETONATE THE BOMB.
BREEP
I'D GIVE YOU OH, ABOUT A MINUTE.
NO!!

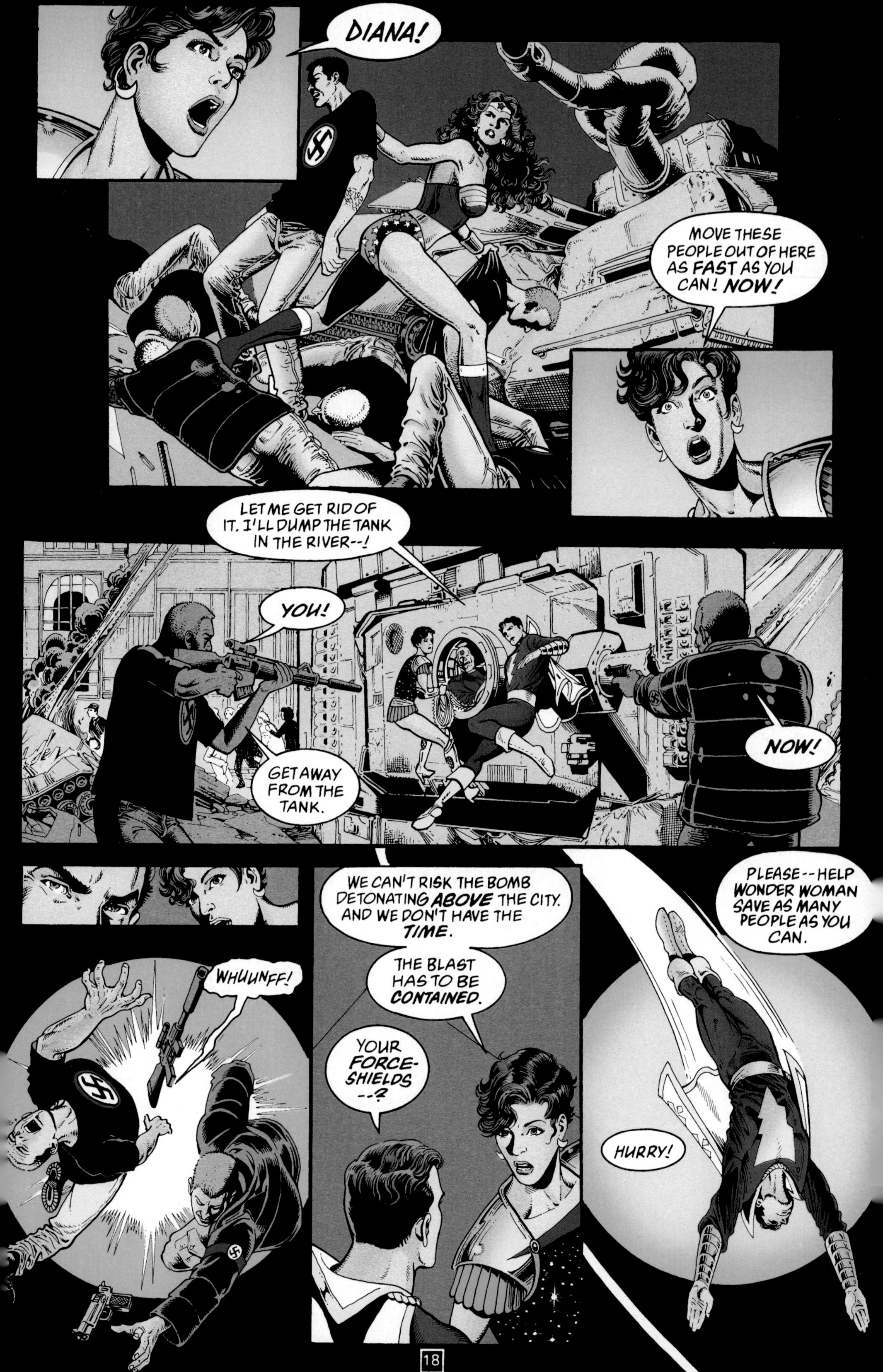
DIANA!
MOVE THESE PEOPLE OUT OF HERE AS FAST AS YOU CAN! NOW!
LET ME GET RID OF IT. I'LL DUMP THE TANK IN THE RIVER--!
YOU!
GET AWAY FROM THE TANK.
NOW!
WHUUNFF!
WE CAN'T RISK THE BOMB DETONATING ABOVE THE CITY. AND WE DON'T HAVE THE TIME.
THE BLAST HAS TO BE CONTAINED.
YOUR FORCE-SHIELDS --?
PLEASE--HELP WONDER WOMAN SAVE AS MANY PEOPLE AS YOU CAN.
HURRY!

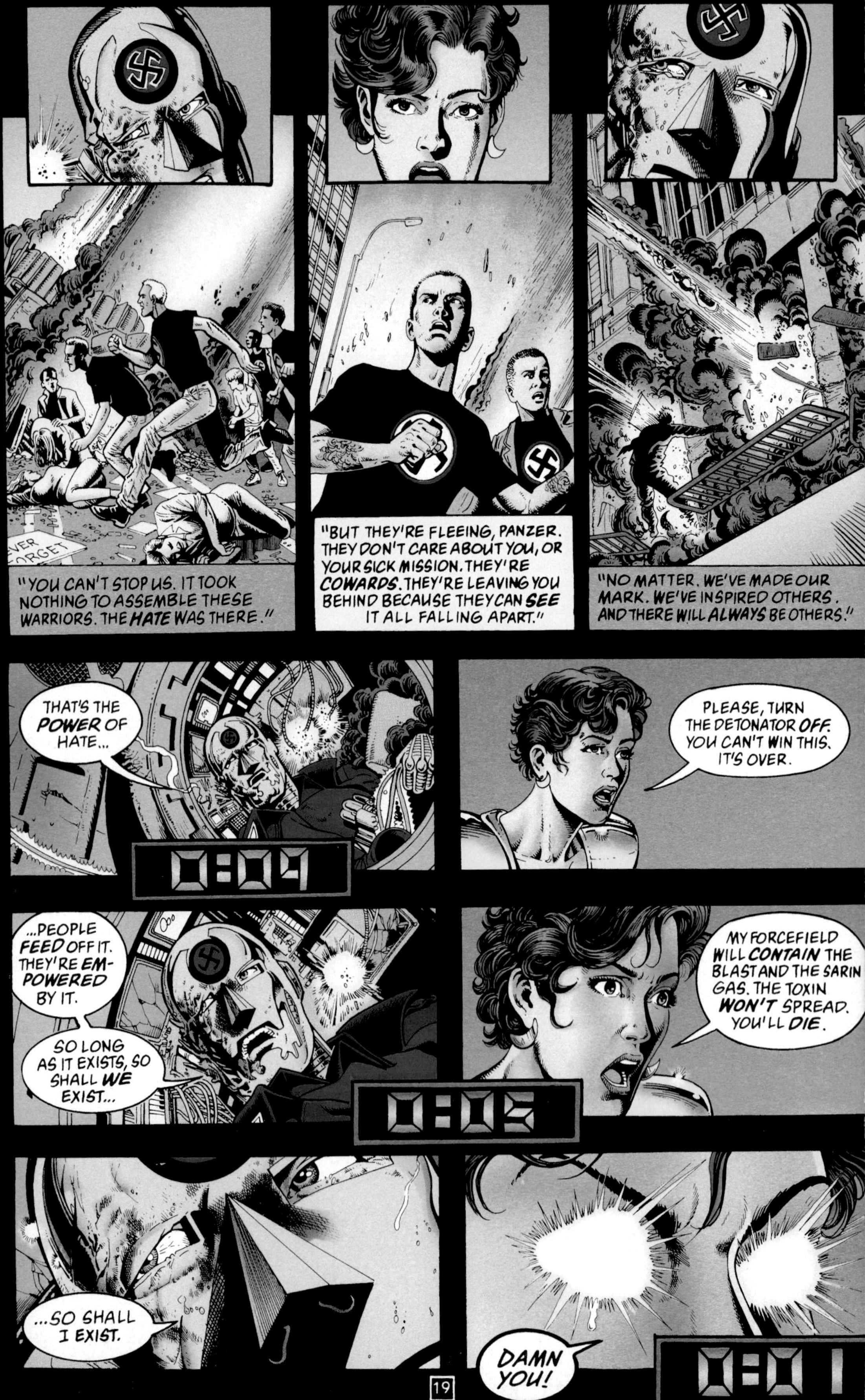
NEVER FORGET
"YOU CAN'T STOP US. IT TOOK NOTHING TO ASSEMBLE THESE WARRIORS. THE HATE WAS THERE."
"BUT THEY'RE FLEEING, PANZER. THEY DON'T CARE ABOUT YOU, OR YOUR SICK MISSION. THEY'RE COWARDS. THEY'RE LEAVING YOU BEHIND BECAUSE THEY CAN SEE IT ALL FALLING APART."
"NO MATTER. WE'VE MADE OUR MARK. WE'VE INSPIRED OTHERS. AND THERE WILL ALWAYS BE OTHERS."
THAT'S THE POWER OF HATE...
0:04
PLEASE, TURN THE DETONATOR OFF. YOU CAN'T WIN THIS. IT'S OVER.
...PEOPLE FEED OFF IT. THEY'RE EMPOWERED BY IT.
SO LONG AS IT EXISTS, SO SHALL WE EXIST...
0:05
MY FORCEFIELD WILL CONTAIN THE BLAST AND THE SARIN GAS. THE TOXIN WON'T SPREAD. YOU'LL DIE.
...SO SHALL I EXIST.
DAMN YOU!
0:01

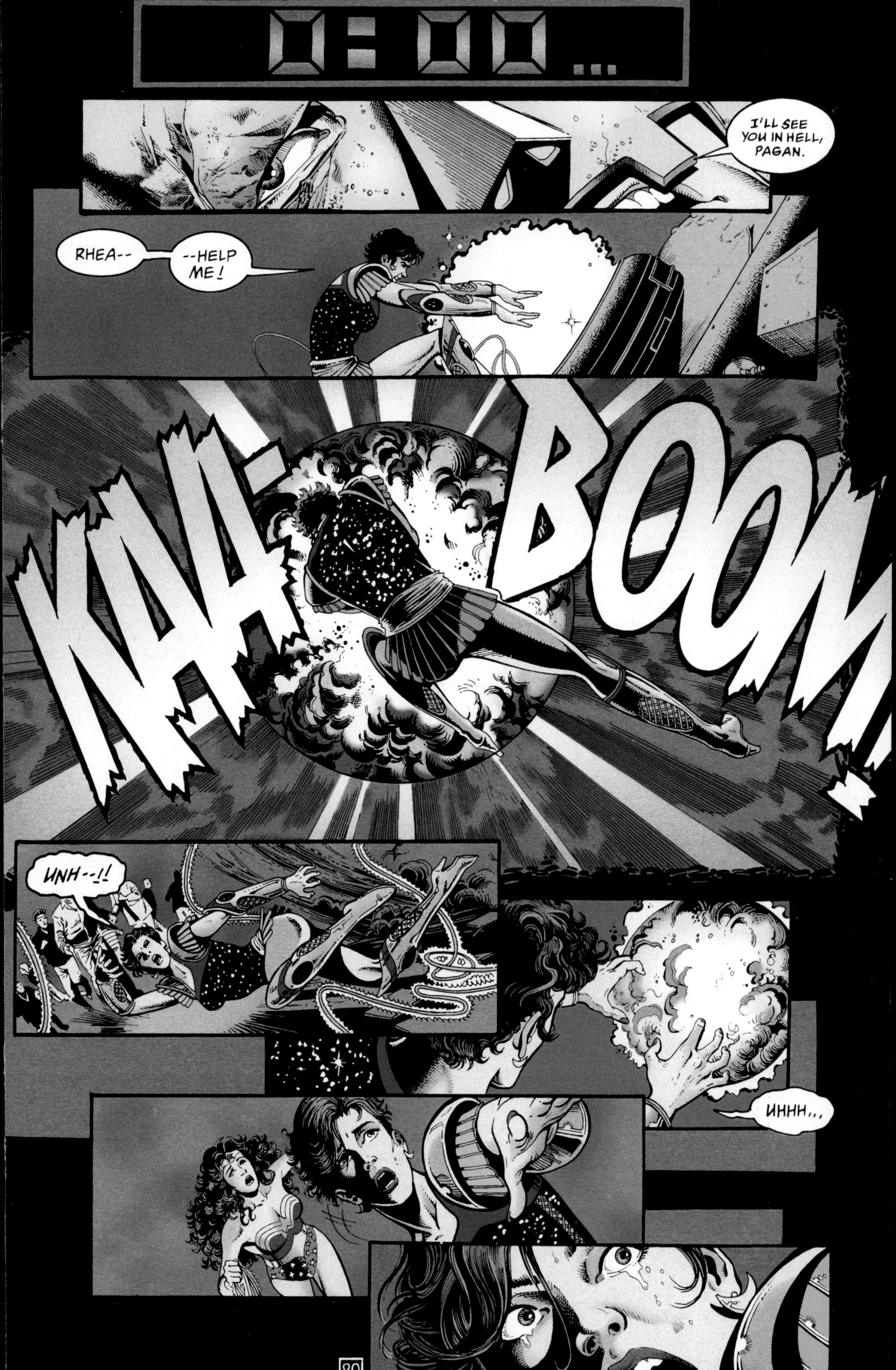

0:00...
I'LL SEE YOU IN HELL, PAGAN.
RHEA--
--HELP ME!
KAA-BOOM!
UNH--!!
UHHH...

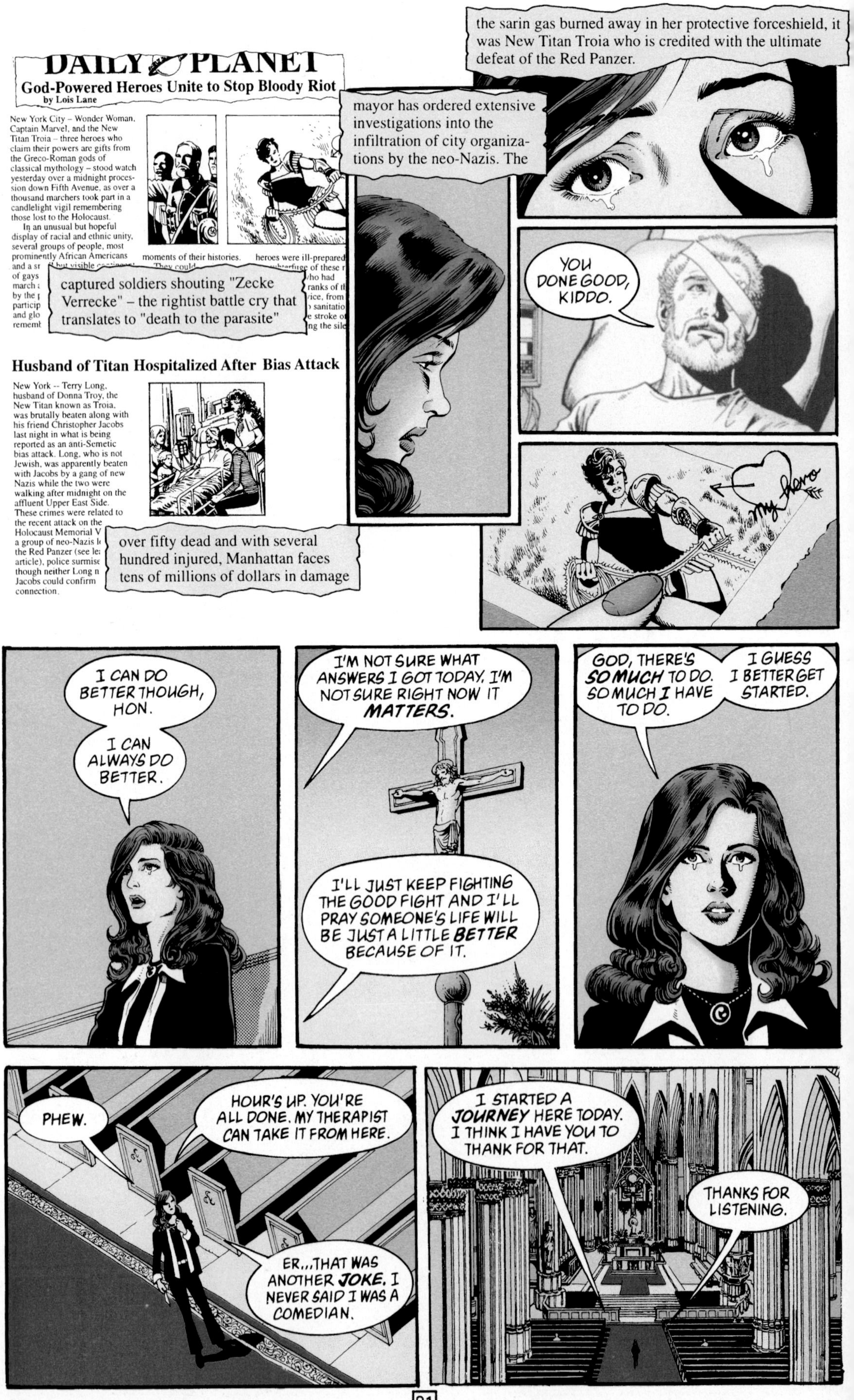

DAILY PLANET
God-Powered Heroes Unite to Stop Bloody Riot
by Lois Lane
New York City – Wonder Woman, Captain Marvel, and the New Titan Troia – three heroes who claim their powers are gifts from the Greco-Roman gods of classical mythology – stood watch yesterday over a midnight procession down Fifth Avenue, as over a thousand marchers took part in a candlelight vigil remembering those lost to the Holocaust.
In an unusual but hopeful display of racial and ethnic unity, several groups of people, most prominently African Americans
moments of their histories.
heroes were ill-prepared
captured soldiers shouting "Zecke Verrecke" – the rightist battle cry that translates to "death to the parasite"
Husband of Titan Hospitalized After Bias Attack
New York -- Terry Long, husband of Donna Troy, the New Titan known as Troia, was brutally beaten along with his friend Christopher Jacobs last night in what is being reported as an anti-Semetic bias attack. Long, who is not Jewish, was apparently beaten with Jacobs by a gang of new Nazis while the two were walking after midnight on the affluent Upper East Side. These crimes were related to the recent attack on the Holocaust Memorial V
over fifty dead and with several hundred injured, Manhattan faces tens of millions of dollars in damage
mayor has ordered extensive investigations into the infiltration of city organizations by the neo-Nazis. The
the sarin gas burned away in her protective forceshield, it was New Titan Troia who is credited with the ultimate defeat of the Red Panzer.
YOU DONE GOOD, KIDDO.
my hero
I CAN DO BETTER THOUGH, HON.
I CAN ALWAYS DO BETTER.
I'M NOT SURE WHAT ANSWERS I GOT TODAY. I'M NOT SURE RIGHT NOW IT MATTERS.
I'LL JUST KEEP FIGHTING THE GOOD FIGHT AND I'LL PRAY SOMEONE'S LIFE WILL BE JUST A LITTLE BETTER BECAUSE OF IT.
GOD, THERE'S SO MUCH TO DO. SO MUCH I HAVE TO DO.
I GUESS I BETTER GET STARTED.
PHEW.
HOUR'S UP. YOU'RE ALL DONE. MY THERAPIST CAN TAKE IT FROM HERE.
ER...THAT WAS ANOTHER JOKE. I NEVER SAID I WAS A COMEDIAN.
I STARTED A JOURNEY HERE TODAY. I THINK I HAVE YOU TO THANK FOR THAT.
THANKS FOR LISTENING.

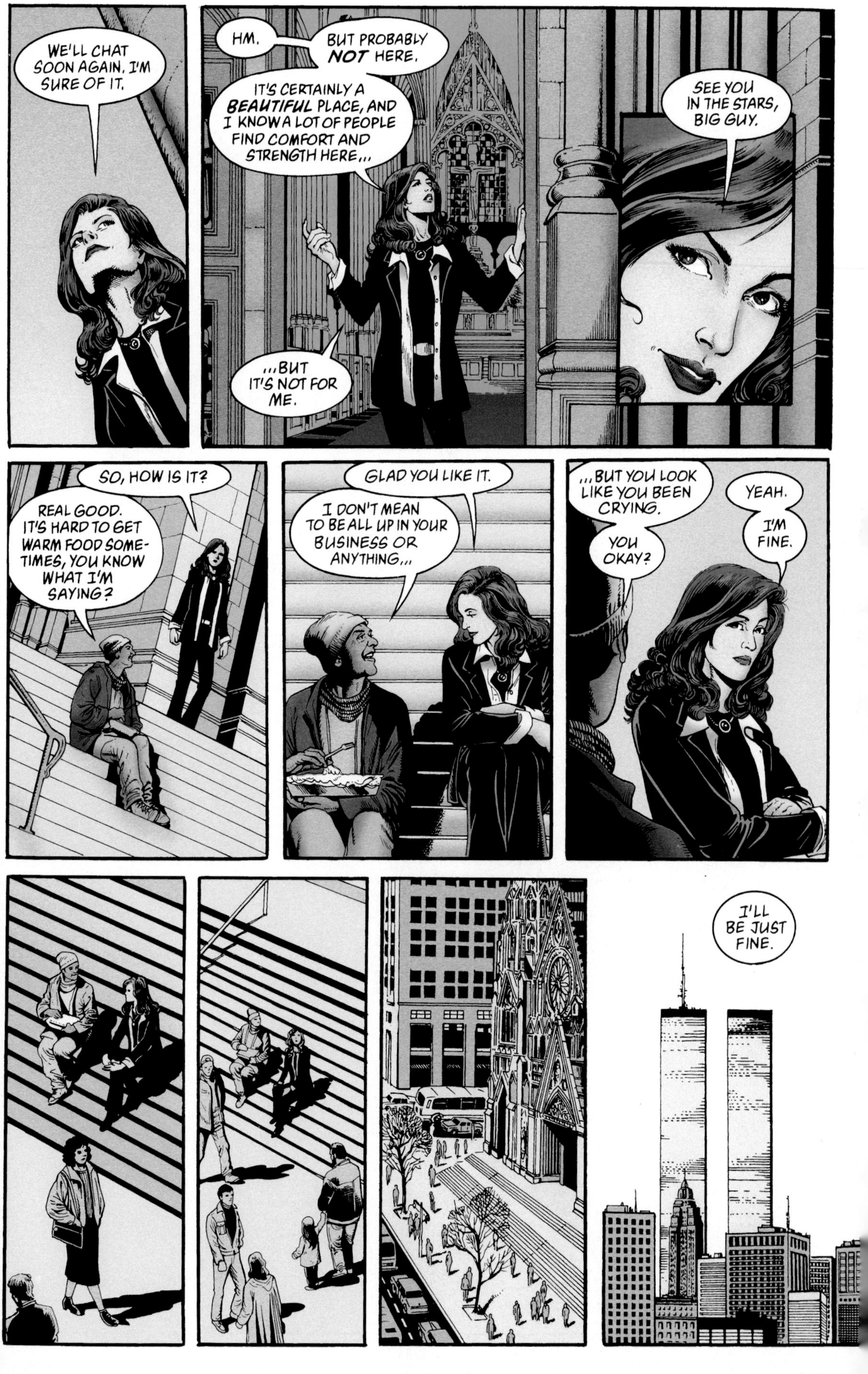
WE'LL CHAT SOON AGAIN. I'M SURE OF IT.
HM.
BUT PROBABLY NOT HERE.
IT'S CERTAINLY A BEAUTIFUL PLACE, AND I KNOW A LOT OF PEOPLE FIND COMFORT AND STRENGTH HERE...
...BUT IT'S NOT FOR ME.
SEE YOU IN THE STARS, BIG GUY.
SO, HOW IS IT?
REAL GOOD. IT'S HARD TO GET WARM FOOD SOME-TIMES, YOU KNOW WHAT I'M SAYING?
GLAD YOU LIKE IT.
I DON'T MEAN TO BE ALL UP IN YOUR BUSINESS OR ANYTHING...
...BUT YOU LOOK LIKE YOU BEEN CRYING.
YOU OKAY?
YEAH.
I'M FINE.
I'LL BE JUST FINE.

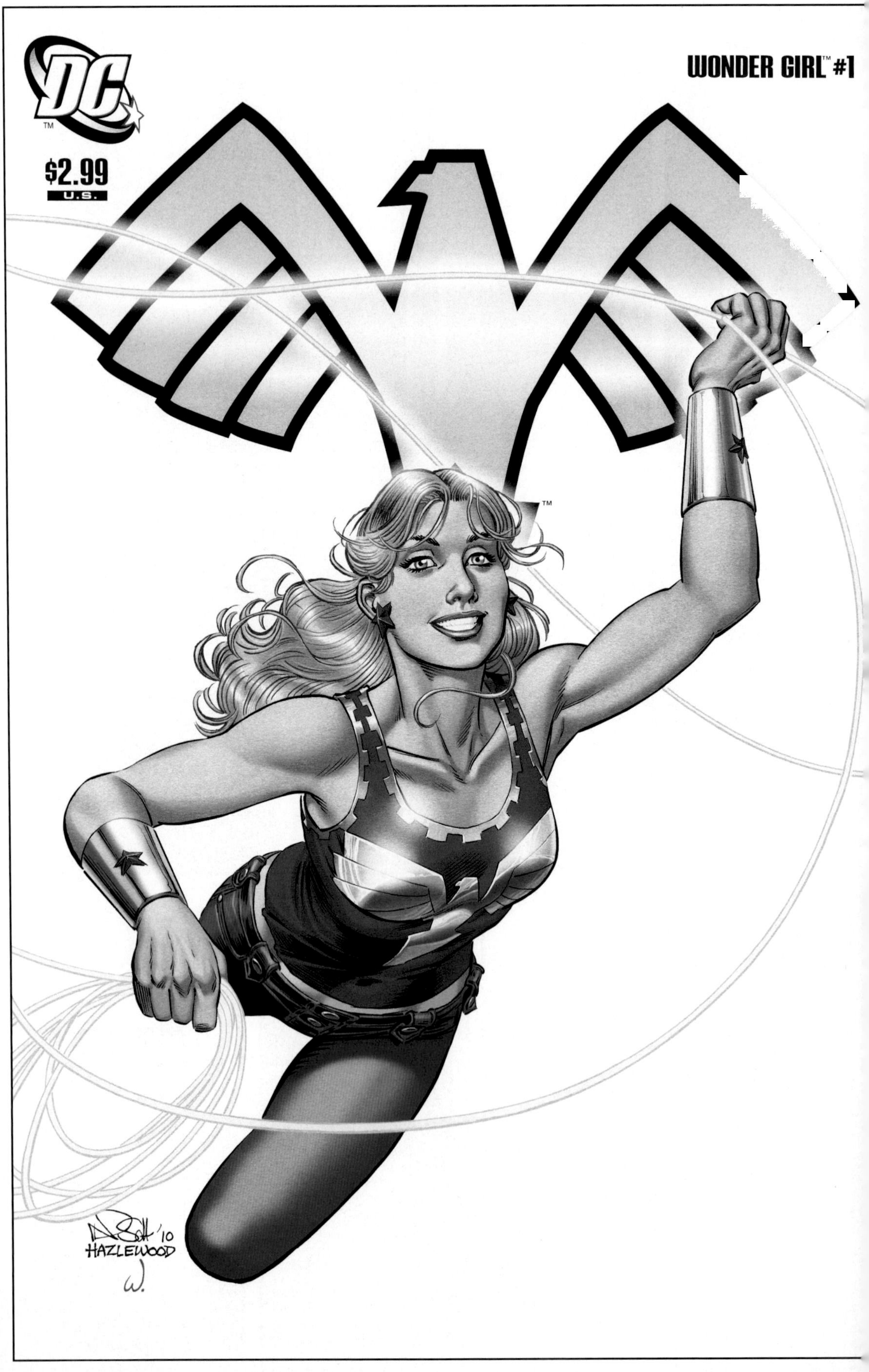
WONDER GIRL™ #1
$2.99
U.S.
HAZLEWOOD

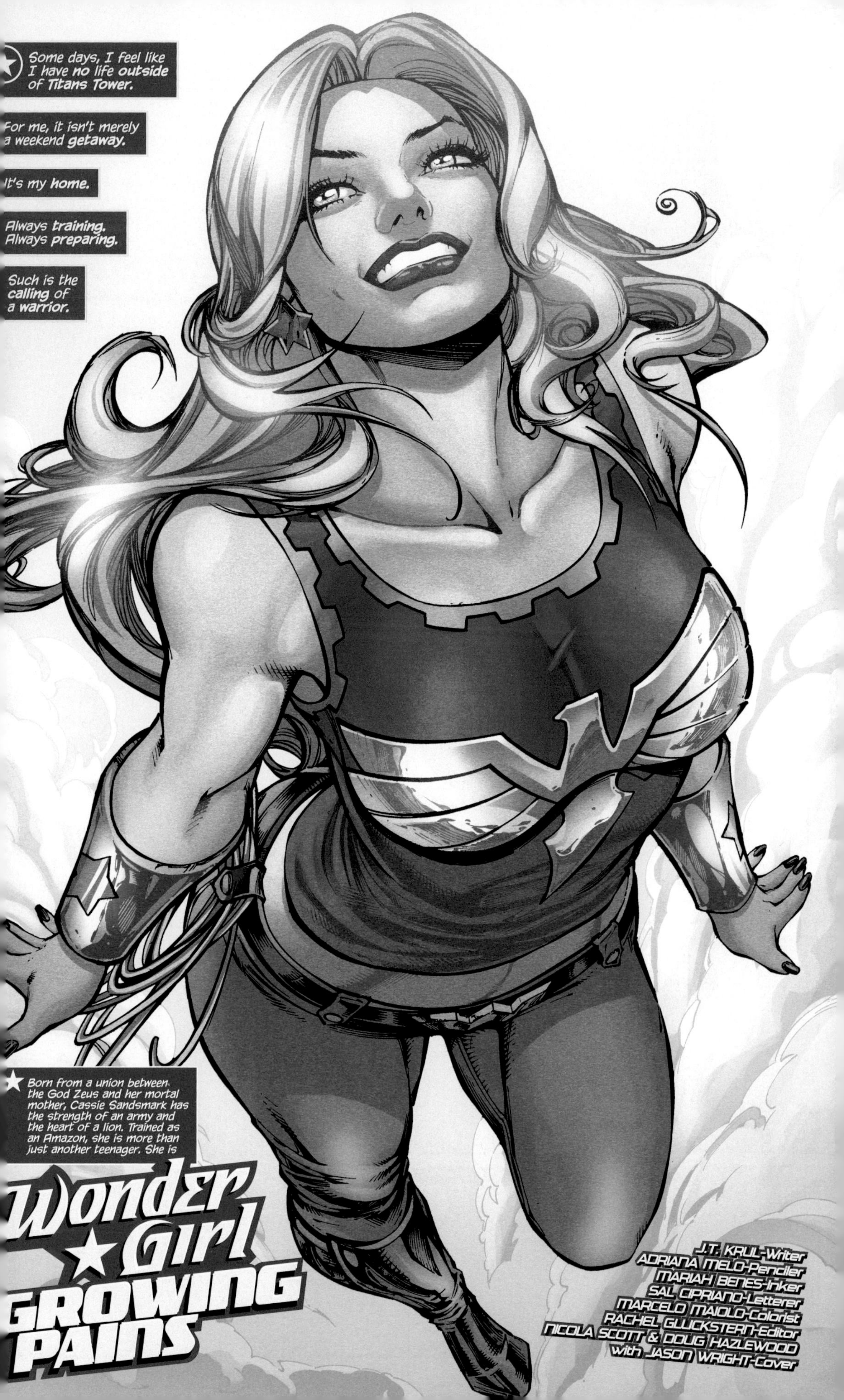

Some days, I feel like I have no life outside of Titans Tower.
For me, it isn't merely a weekend getaway.
It's my home.
Always training. Always preparing.
Such is the calling of a warrior.
Born from a union between the God Zeus and her mortal mother, Cassie Sandsmark has the strength of an army and the heart of a lion. Trained as an Amazon, she is more than just another teenager. She is
Wonder Girl
Growing Pains
J.T. KRUL-Writer
ADRIANA MELO-Penciler
MARIAH BENES-Inker
SAL CIPRIANO-Letterer
MARCELO MAIOLO-Colorist
RACHEL GLUCKSTERN-Editor
NICOLA SCOTT & DOUG HAZLEWOOD with JASON WRIGHT-Cover

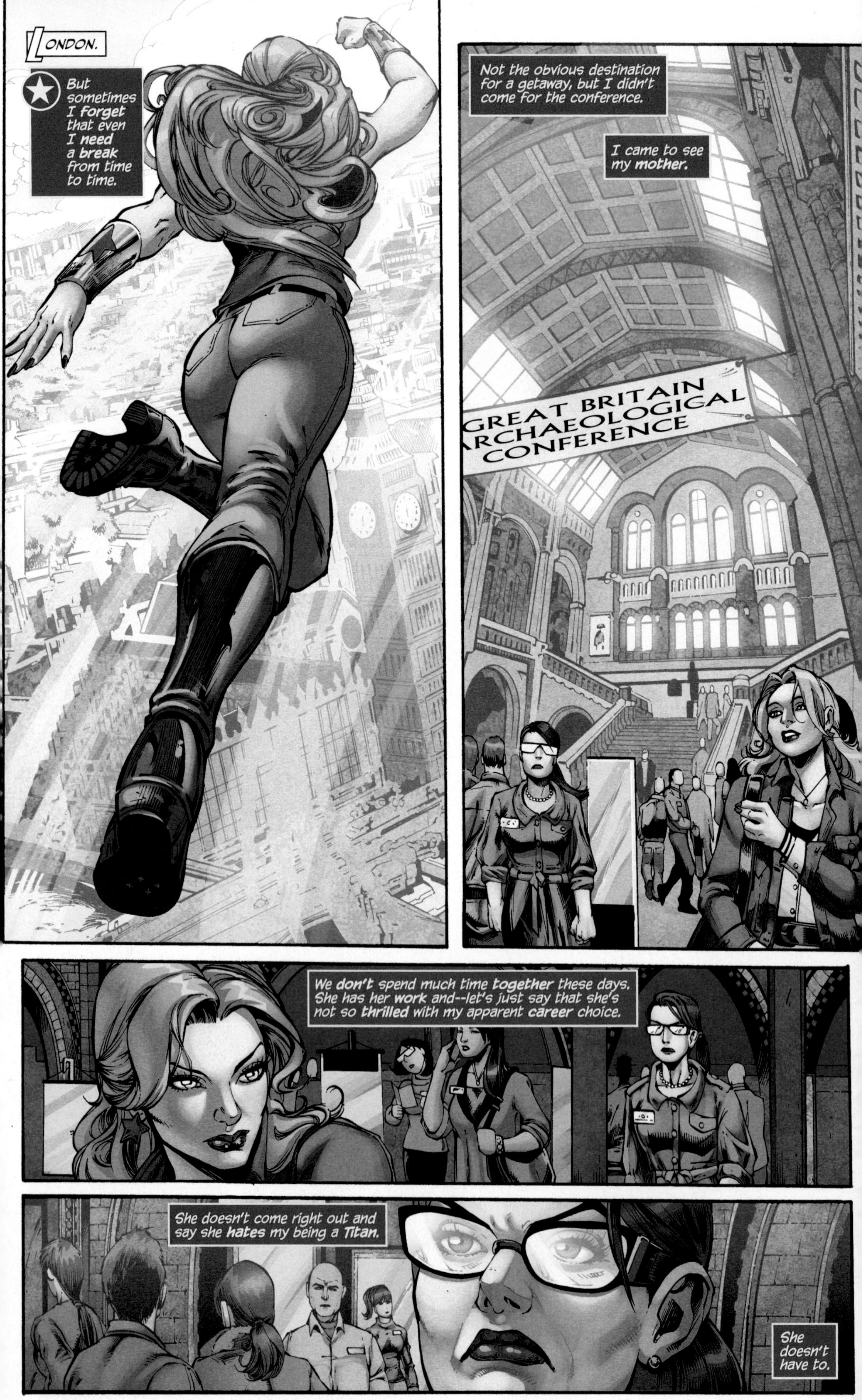
LONDON.
But sometimes I forget that even I need a break from time to time.
Not the obvious destination for a getaway, but I didn't come for the conference.
I came to see my mother.
GREAT BRITAIN ARCHAEOLOGICAL CONFERENCE
We don't spend much time together these days. She has her work and--let's just say that she's not so thrilled with my apparent career choice.
She doesn't come right out and say she hates my being a Titan.
She doesn't have to.

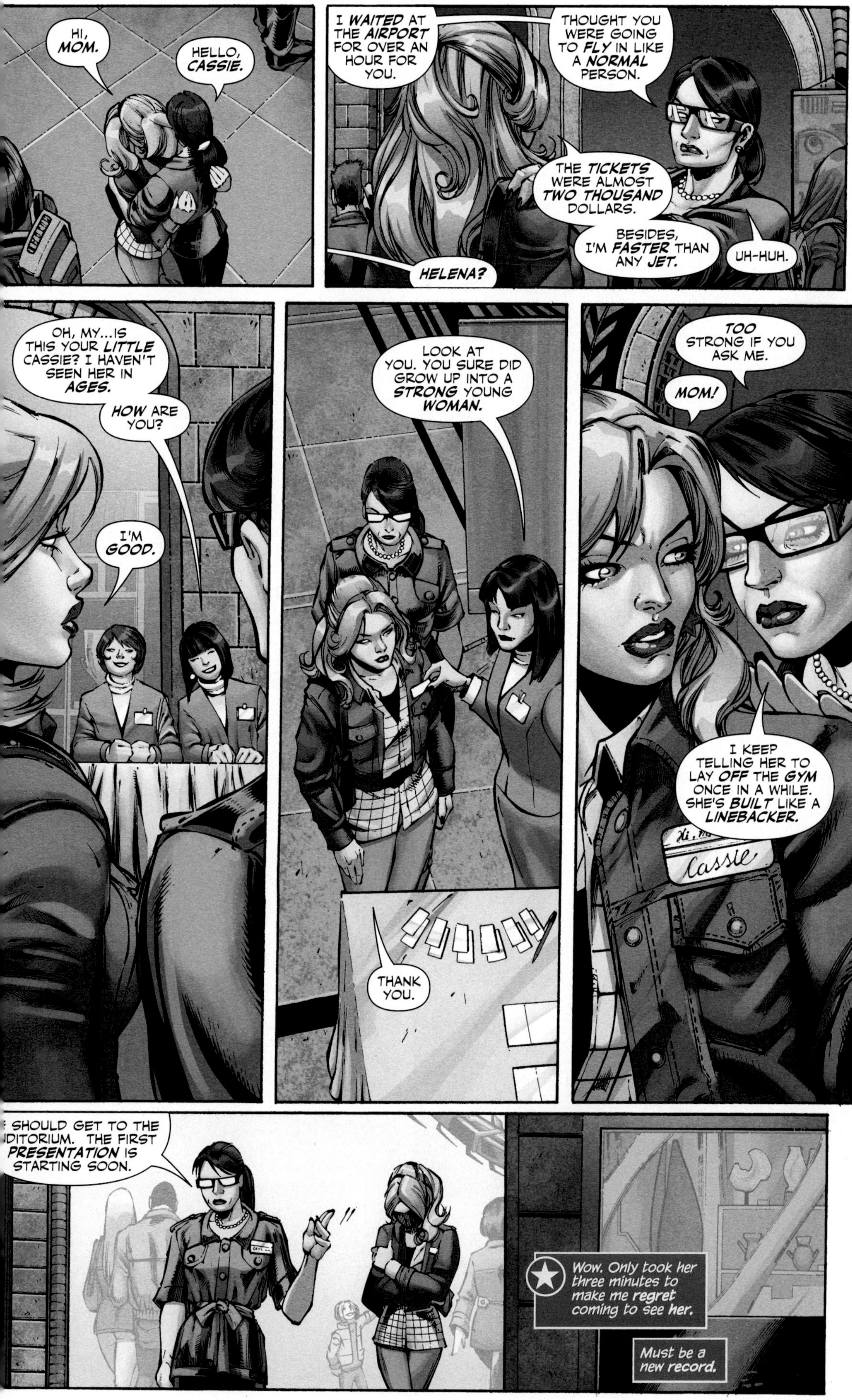
HI, MOM.
HELLO, CASSIE.
I WAITED AT THE AIRPORT FOR OVER AN HOUR FOR YOU.
THOUGHT YOU WERE GOING TO FLY IN LIKE A NORMAL PERSON.
THE TICKETS WERE ALMOST TWO THOUSAND DOLLARS.
BESIDES, I'M FASTER THAN ANY JET.
UH-HUH.
HELENA?
OH, MY...IS THIS YOUR LITTLE CASSIE? I HAVEN'T SEEN HER IN AGES.
HOW ARE YOU?
I'M GOOD.
LOOK AT YOU. YOU SURE DID GROW UP INTO A STRONG YOUNG WOMAN.
THANK YOU.
TOO STRONG IF YOU ASK ME.
MOM!
I KEEP TELLING HER TO LAY OFF THE GYM ONCE IN A WHILE. SHE'S BUILT LIKE A LINEBACKER.
Cassie
E SHOULD GET TO THE UDITORIUM. THE FIRST PRESENTATION IS STARTING SOON.
Wow. Only took her three minutes to make me regret coming to see her.
Must be a new record.

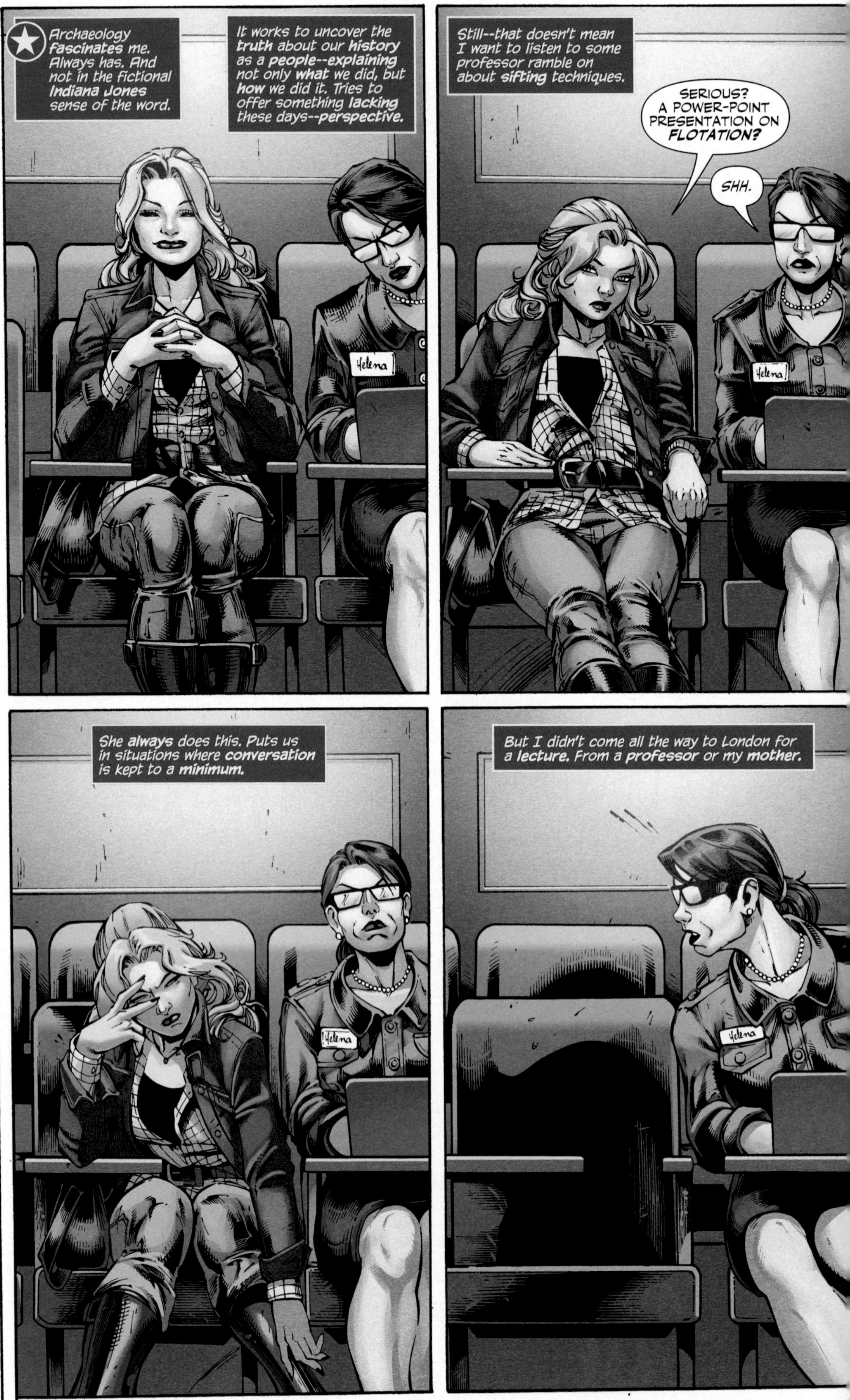
Archaeology **fascinates** me. Always has. And not in the fictional **Indiana Jones** sense of the word.
It works to uncover the **truth** about our **history** as a **people--explaining** not only **what** we did, but **how** we did it. Tries to offer something **lacking** these days--**perspective.**
Helena
Still--**that** doesn't mean I want to listen to some professor ramble on about **sifting** techniques.
SERIOUS? A POWER-POINT PRESENTATION ON ***FLOTATION?***
SHH.
Helena
She **always** does this. Puts us in situations where **conversation** is kept to a **minimum.**
Helena
But I didn't come all the way to London for a **lecture.** From a **professor** or my **mother.**
Helena

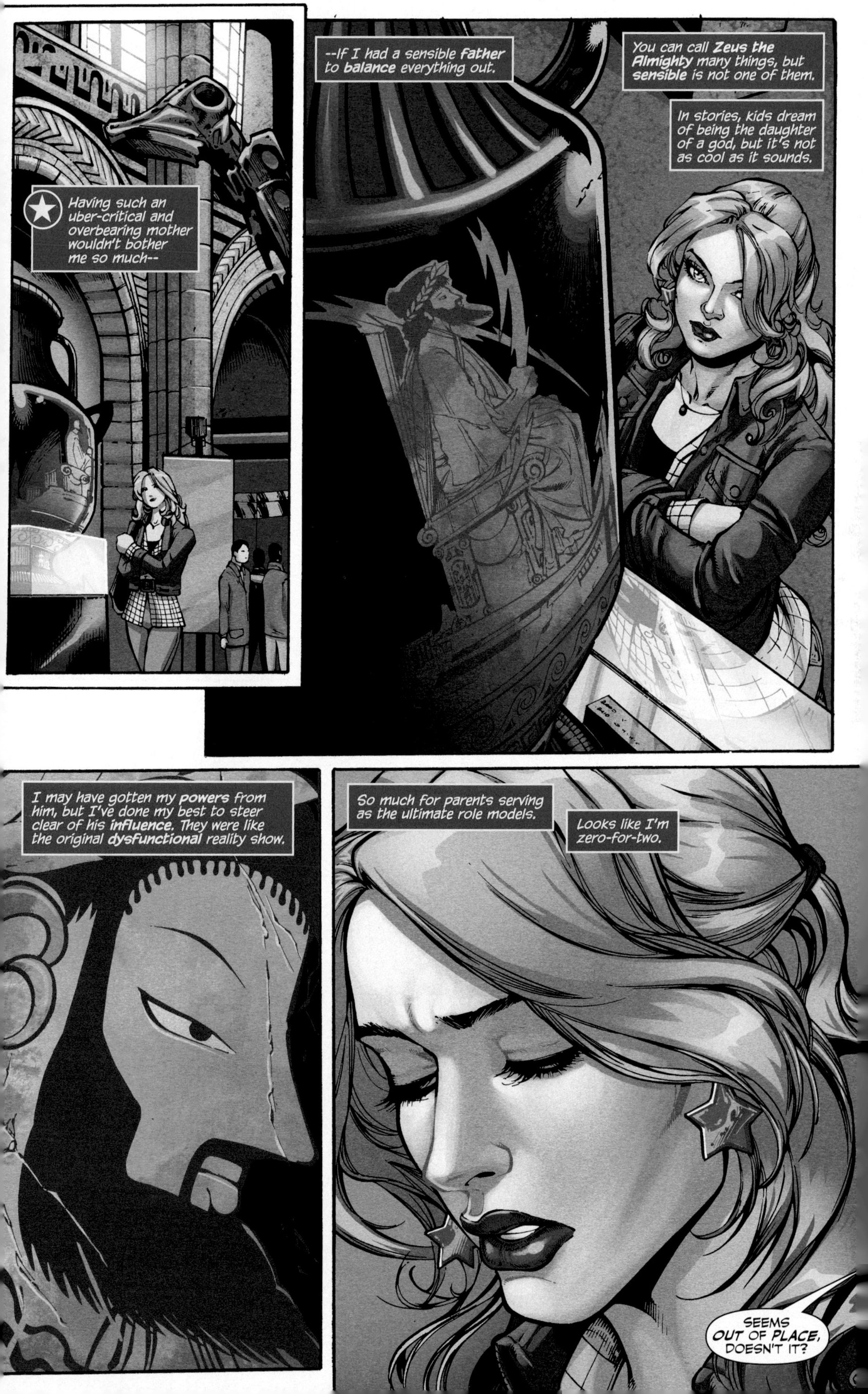
Having such an uber-critical and overbearing mother wouldn't bother me so much--
--If I had a sensible father to balance everything out.
You can call Zeus the Almighty many things, but sensible is not one of them.
In stories, kids dream of being the daughter of a god, but it's not as cool as it sounds.
I may have gotten my powers from him, but I've done my best to steer clear of his influence. They were like the original dysfunctional reality show.
So much for parents serving as the ultimate role models.
Looks like I'm zero-for-two.
SEEMS OUT OF PLACE, DOESN'T IT?

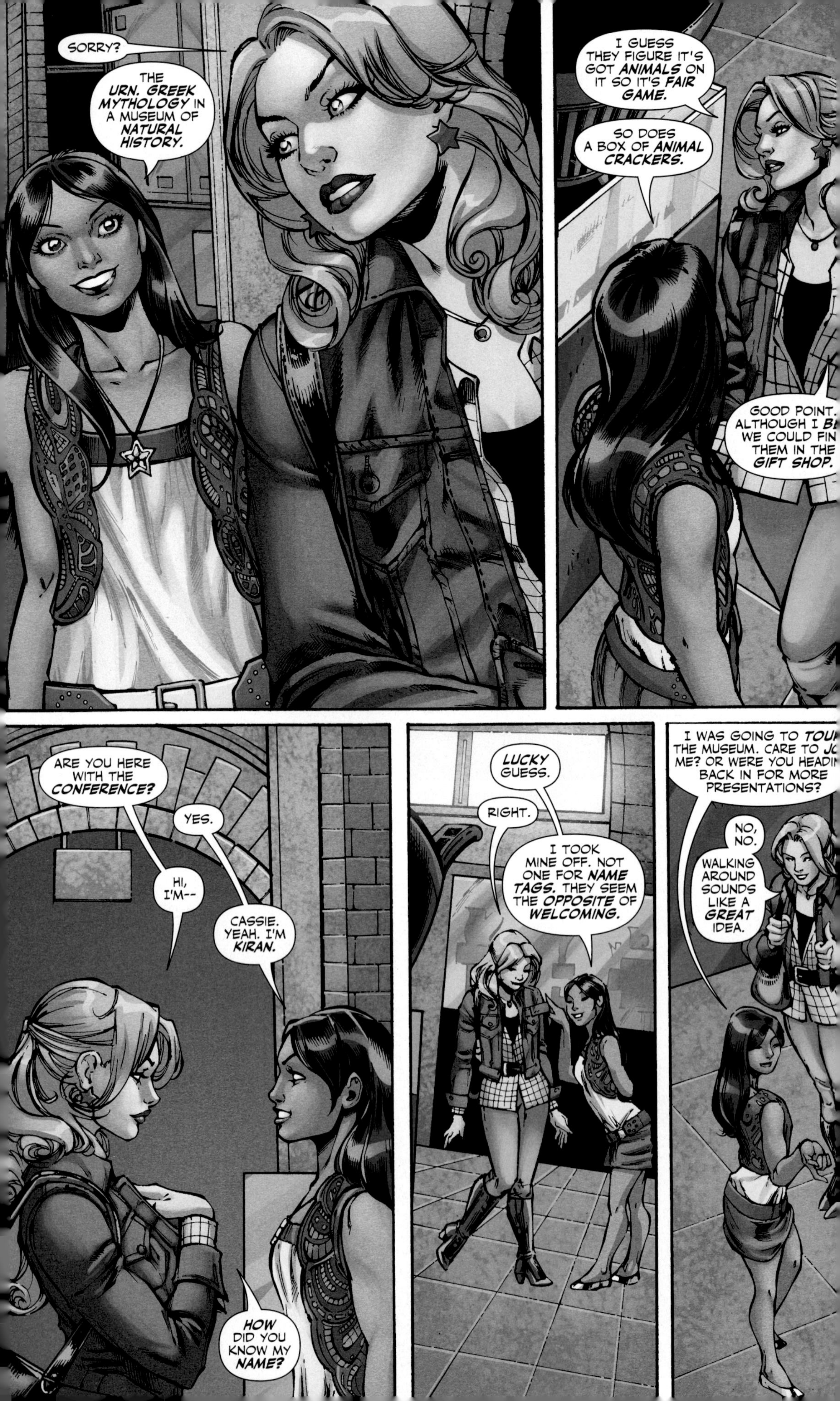

SORRY?
THE URN. GREEK MYTHOLOGY IN A MUSEUM OF NATURAL HISTORY.
I GUESS THEY FIGURE IT'S GOT ANIMALS ON IT SO IT'S FAIR GAME.
SO DOES A BOX OF ANIMAL CRACKERS.
GOOD POINT. ALTHOUGH I B WE COULD FIN THEM IN THE GIFT SHOP.
ARE YOU HERE WITH THE CONFERENCE?
YES.
HI, I'M--
CASSIE. YEAH. I'M KIRAN.
HOW DID YOU KNOW MY NAME?
LUCKY GUESS.
RIGHT.
I TOOK MINE OFF. NOT ONE FOR NAME TAGS. THEY SEEM THE OPPOSITE OF WELCOMING.
I WAS GOING TO TOU THE MUSEUM. CARE TO J ME? OR WERE YOU HEADI BACK IN FOR MORE PRESENTATIONS?
NO, NO.
WALKING AROUND SOUNDS LIKE A GREAT IDEA.

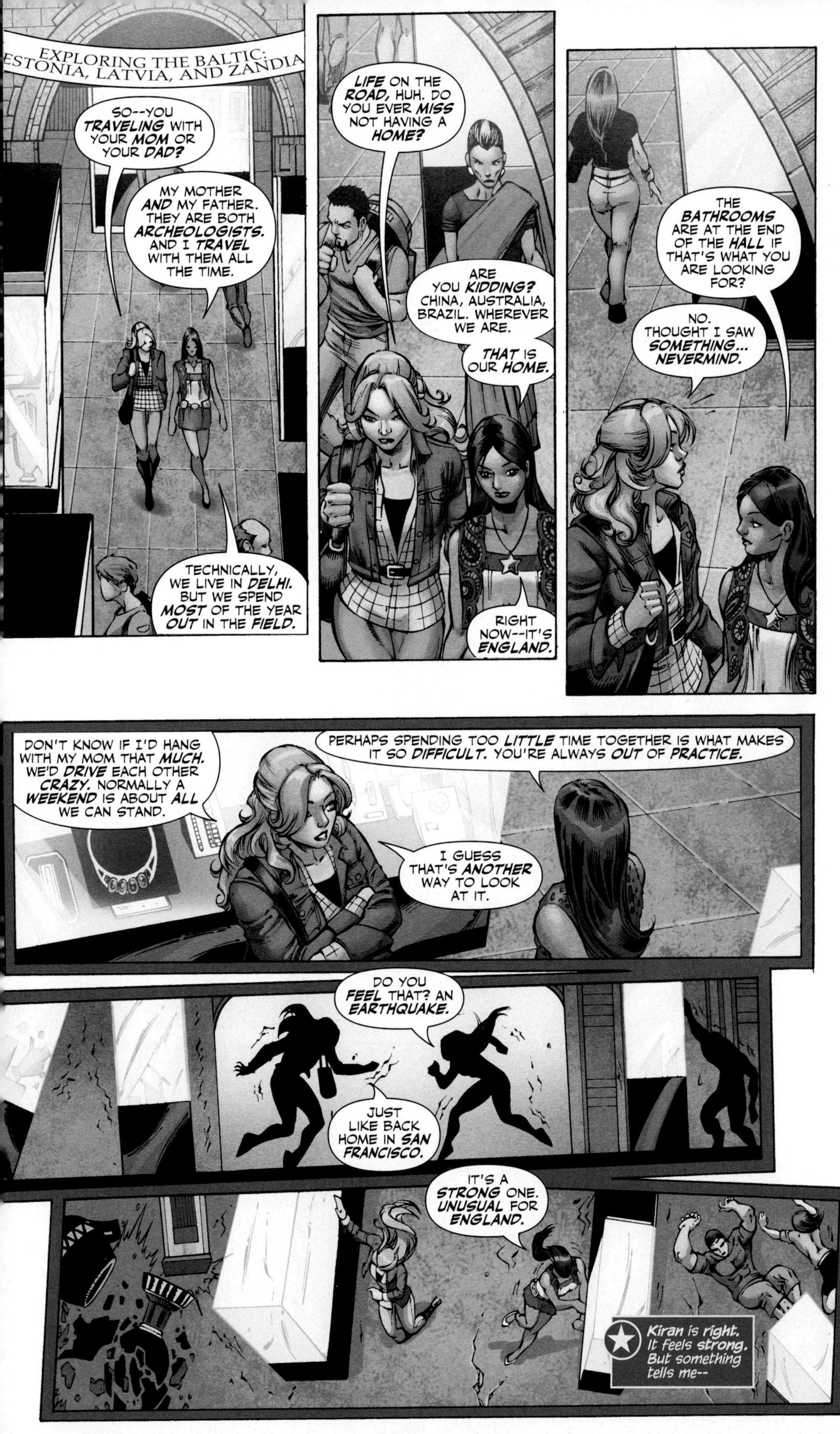
EXPLORING THE BALTIC: ESTONIA, LATVIA, AND ZANDIA
SO--YOU TRAVELING WITH YOUR MOM OR YOUR DAD?
MY MOTHER AND MY FATHER. THEY ARE BOTH ARCHEOLOGISTS. AND I TRAVEL WITH THEM ALL THE TIME.
TECHNICALLY, WE LIVE IN DELHI. BUT WE SPEND MOST OF THE YEAR OUT IN THE FIELD.
LIFE ON THE ROAD, HUH. DO YOU EVER MISS NOT HAVING A HOME?
ARE YOU KIDDING? CHINA, AUSTRALIA, BRAZIL. WHEREVER WE ARE.
THAT IS OUR HOME.
RIGHT NOW--IT'S ENGLAND.
THE BATHROOMS ARE AT THE END OF THE HALL IF THAT'S WHAT YOU ARE LOOKING FOR?
NO. THOUGHT I SAW SOMETHING... NEVERMIND.
DON'T KNOW IF I'D HANG WITH MY MOM THAT MUCH. WE'D DRIVE EACH OTHER CRAZY. NORMALLY A WEEKEND IS ABOUT ALL WE CAN STAND.
PERHAPS SPENDING TOO LITTLE TIME TOGETHER IS WHAT MAKES IT SO DIFFICULT. YOU'RE ALWAYS OUT OF PRACTICE.
I GUESS THAT'S ANOTHER WAY TO LOOK AT IT.
DO YOU FEEL THAT? AN EARTHQUAKE.
JUST LIKE BACK HOME IN SAN FRANCISCO.
IT'S A STRONG ONE. UNUSUAL FOR ENGLAND.
Kiran is right. It feels strong. But something tells me--

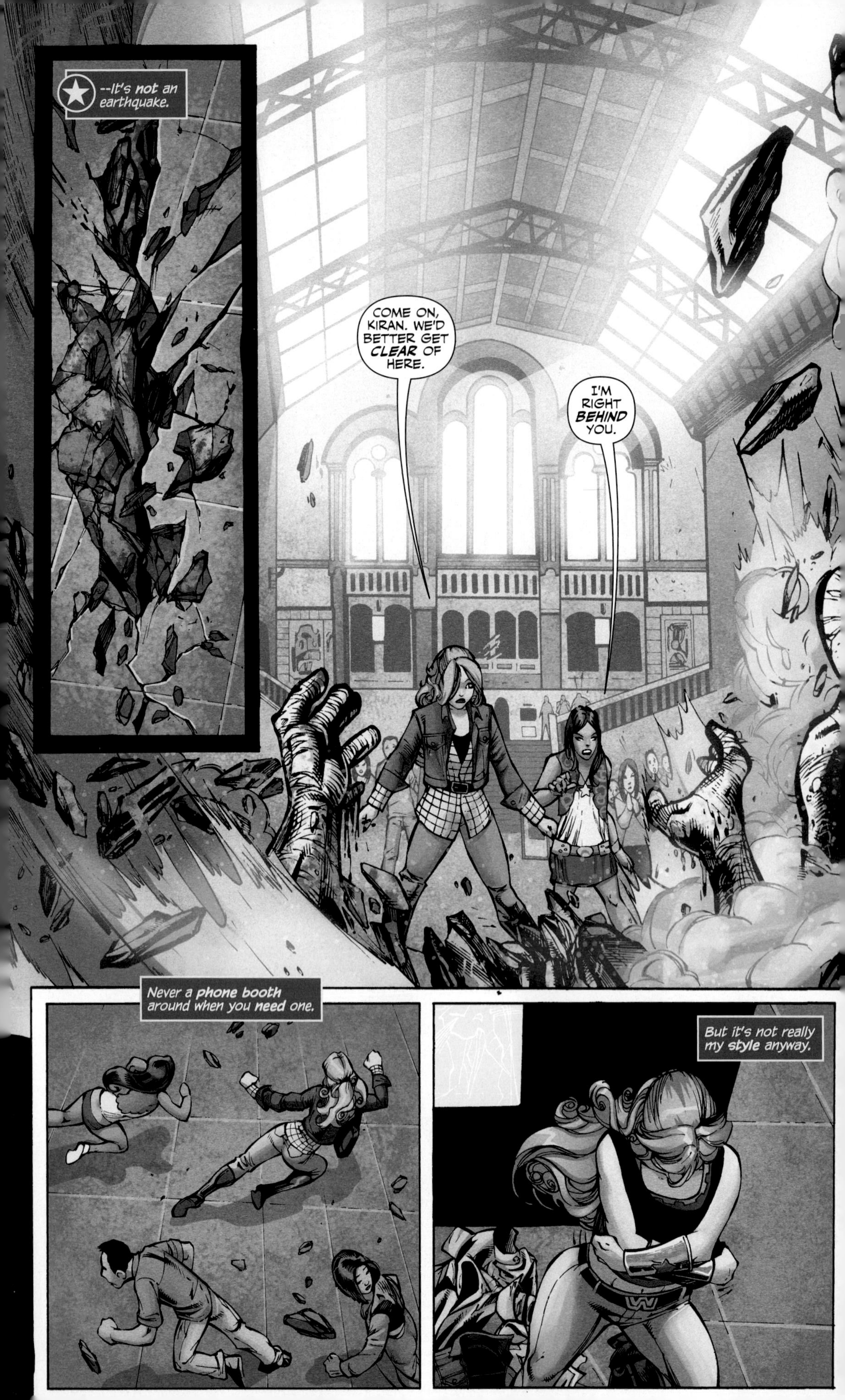
--It's not an earthquake.
COME ON, KIRAN. WE'D BETTER GET CLEAR OF HERE.
I'M RIGHT BEHIND YOU.
Never a phone booth around when you need one.
But it's not really my style anyway.

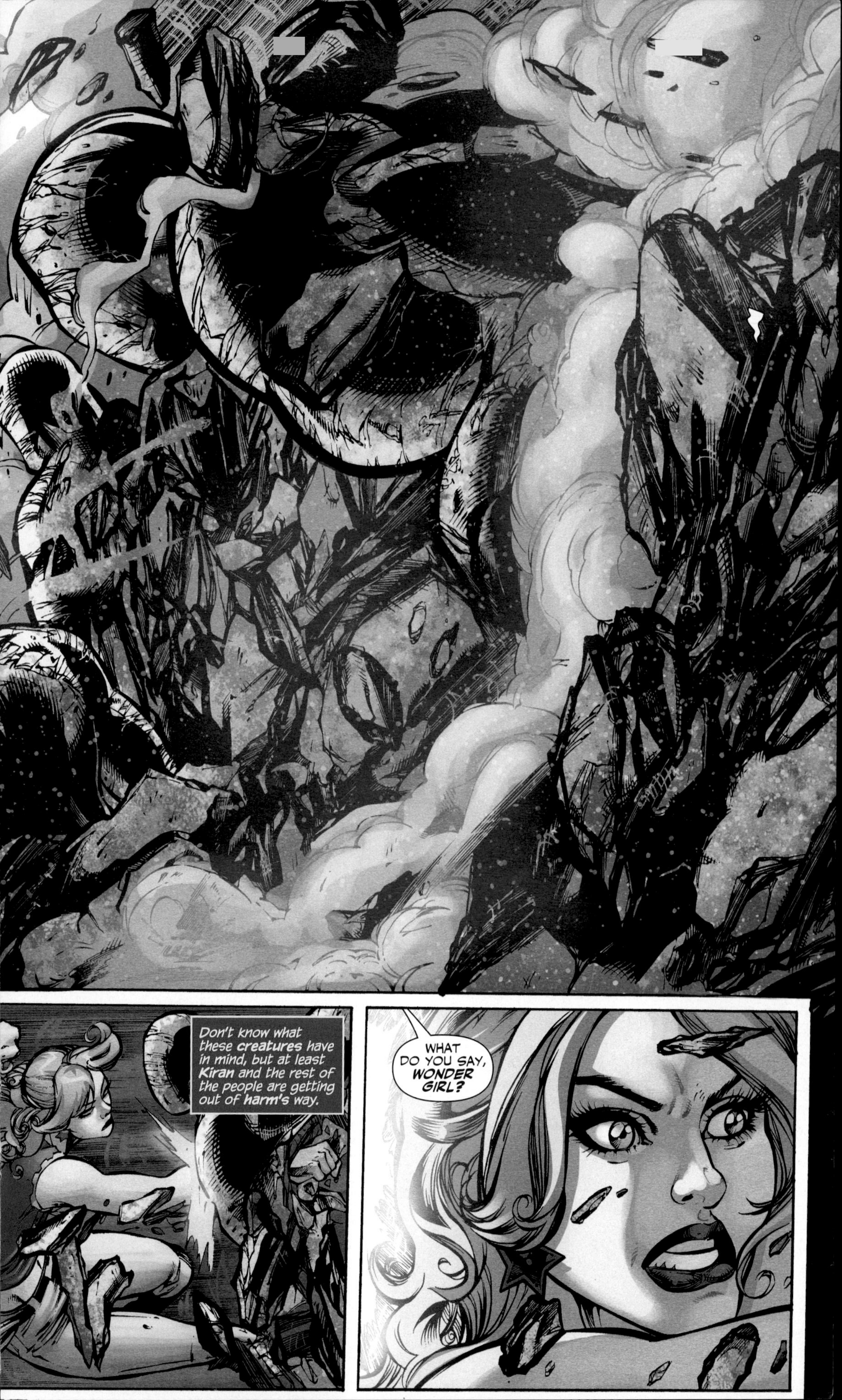
Don't know what these creatures have in mind, but at least Kiran and the rest of the people are getting out of harm's way.
WHAT DO YOU SAY, WONDER GIRL?

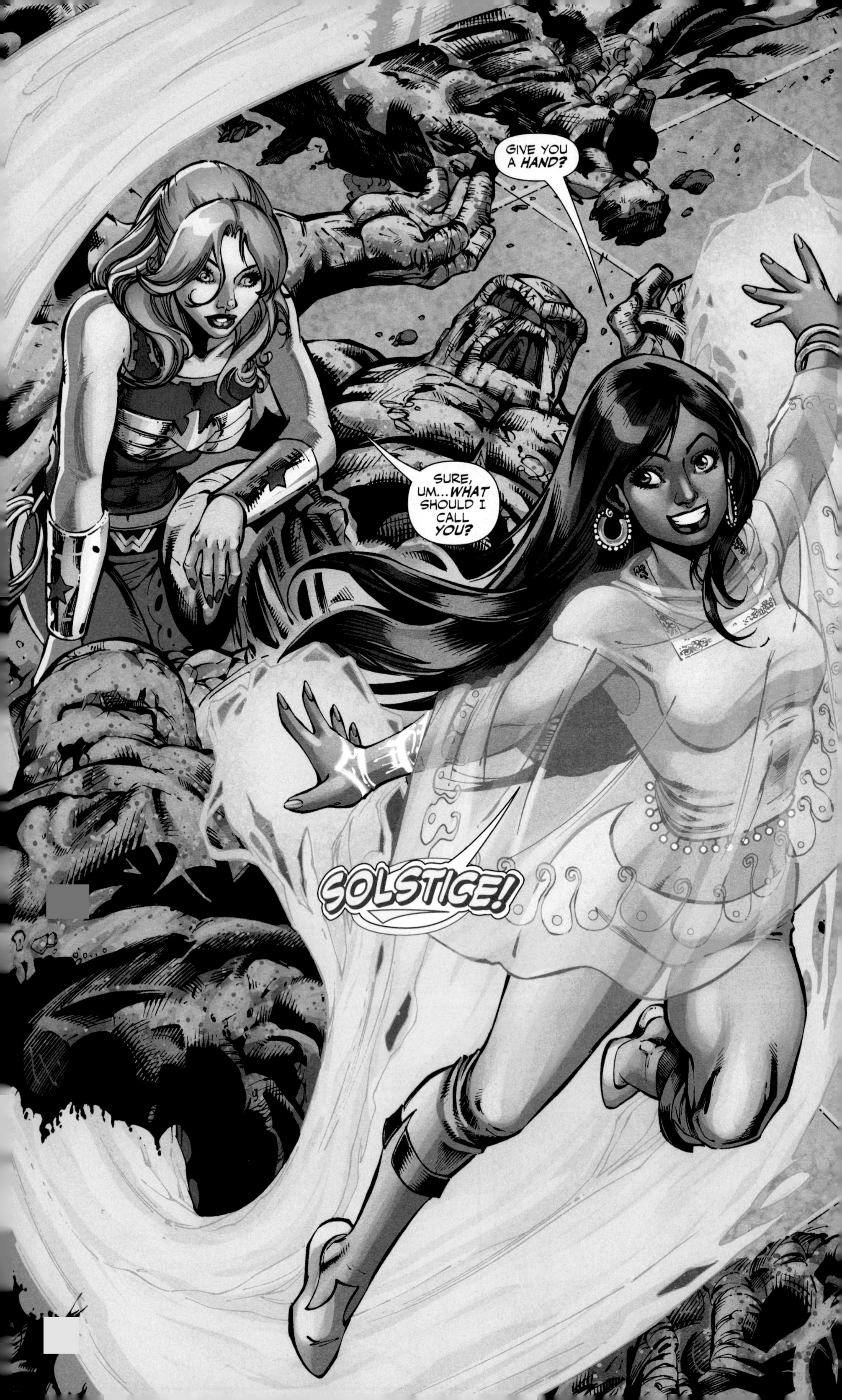
GIVE YOU A HAND?
SURE, UM...WHAT SHOULD I CALL YOU?
SOLSTICE!

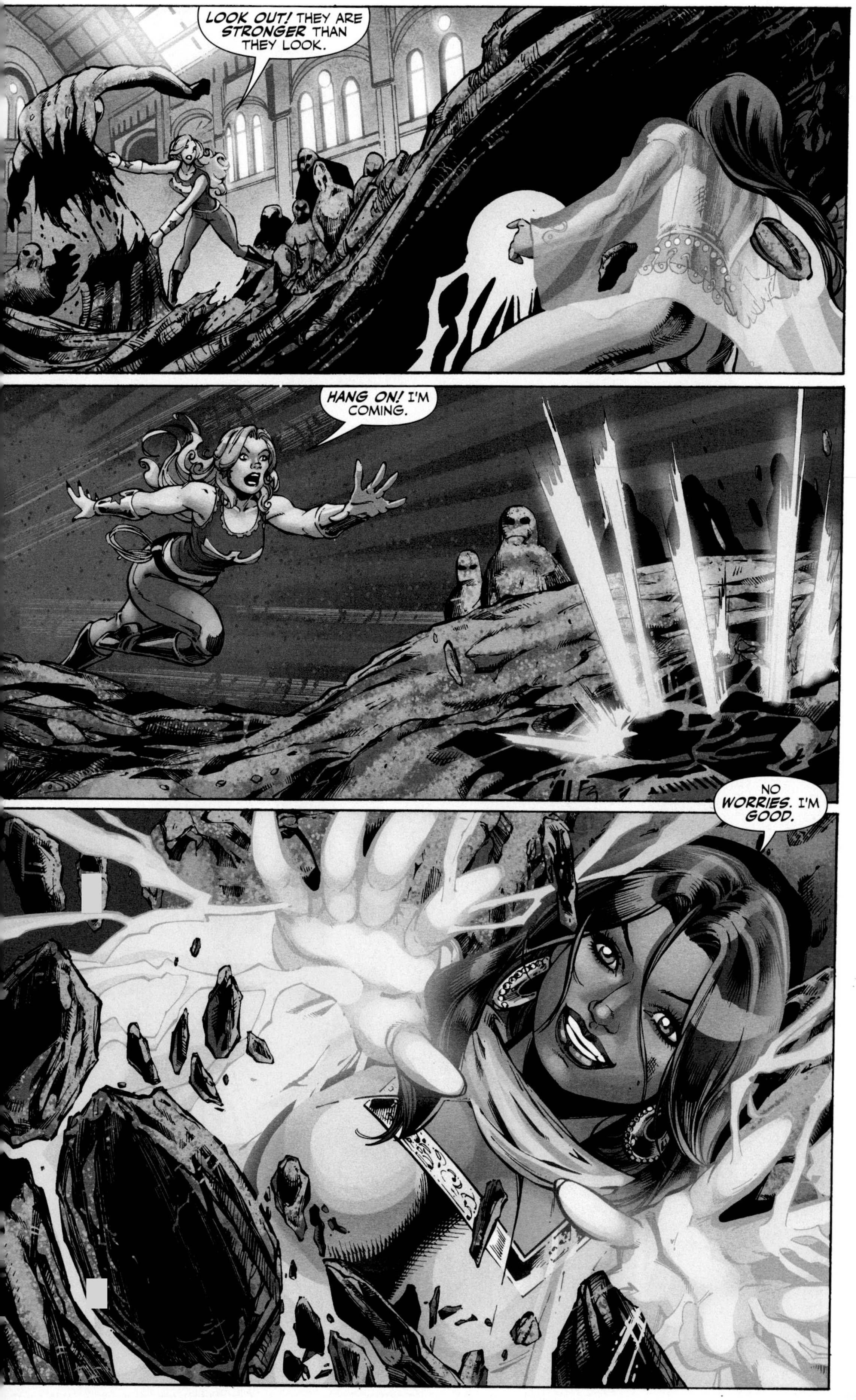
LOOK OUT! THEY ARE STRONGER THAN THEY LOOK.
HANG ON! I'M COMING.
NO WORRIES. I'M GOOD.

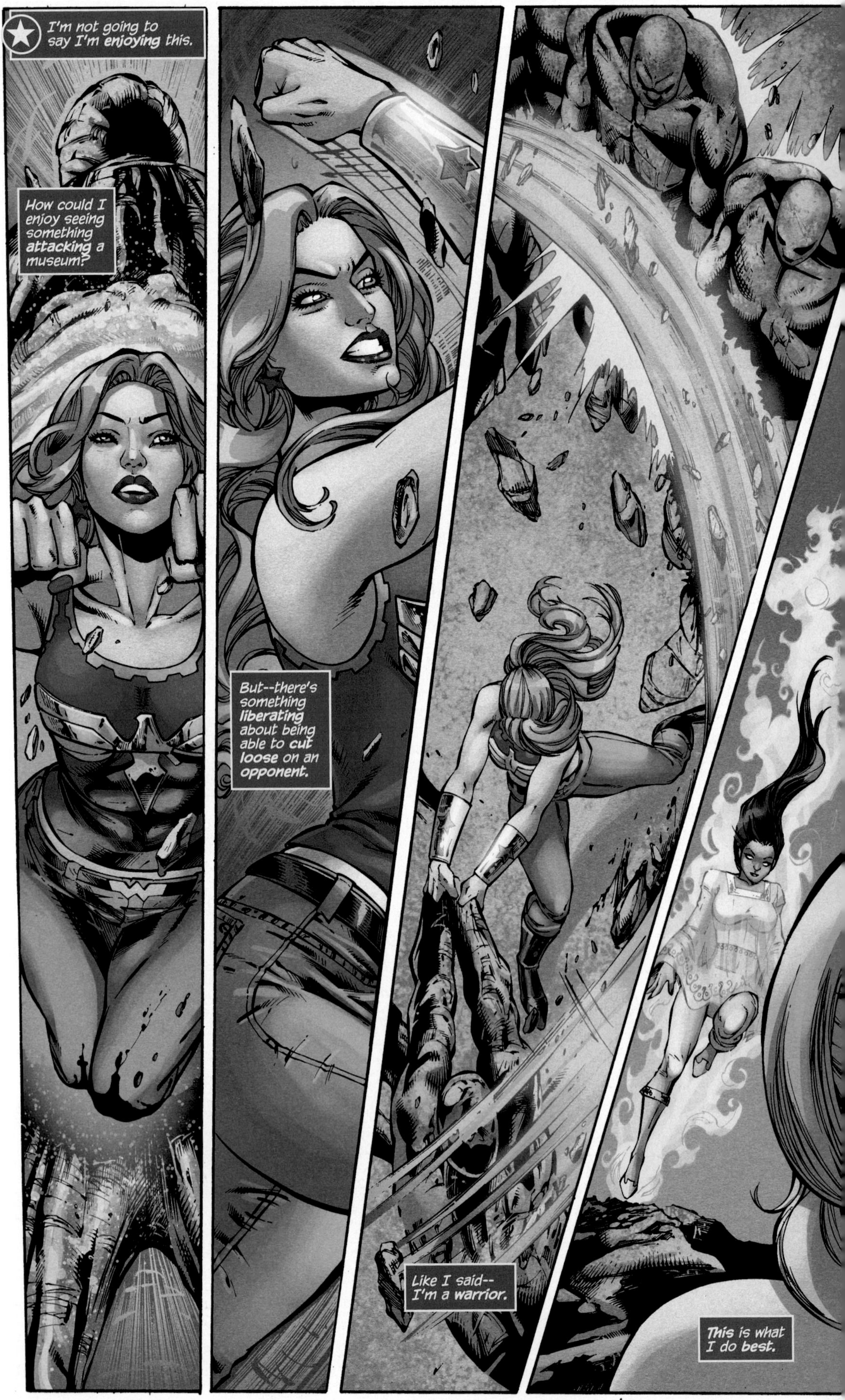
I'm not going to say I'm **enjoying** this.
How could I enjoy seeing something **attacking** a museum?
But--there's something **liberating** about being able to **cut loose** on an **opponent.**
Like I said-- I'm a **warrior.**
This is what I do **best.**

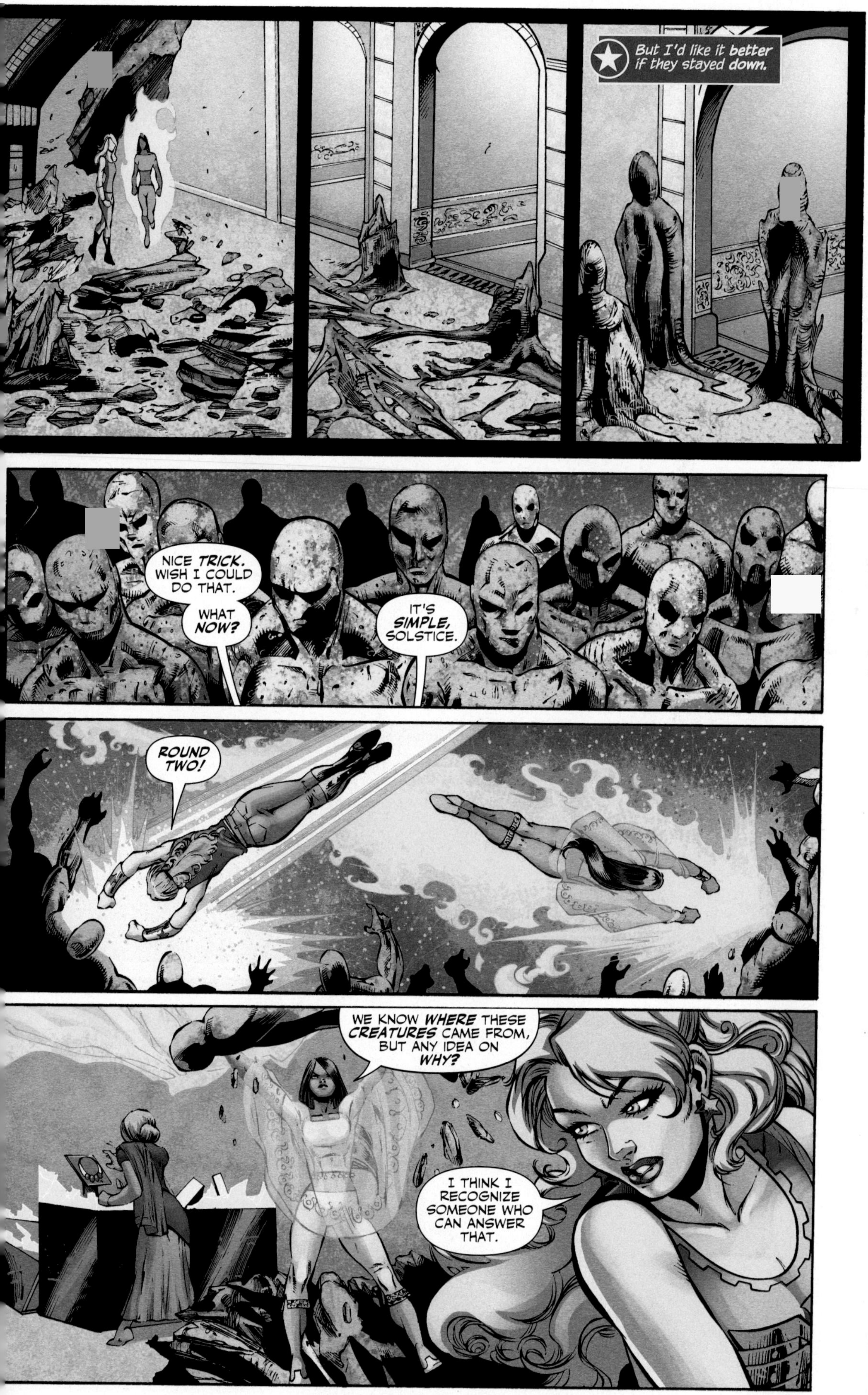
But I'd like it better if they stayed down.
NICE TRICK. WISH I COULD DO THAT.
WHAT NOW?
IT'S SIMPLE, SOLSTICE.
ROUND TWO!
WE KNOW WHERE THESE CREATURES CAME FROM, BUT ANY IDEA ON WHY?
I THINK I RECOGNIZE SOMEONE WHO CAN ANSWER THAT.

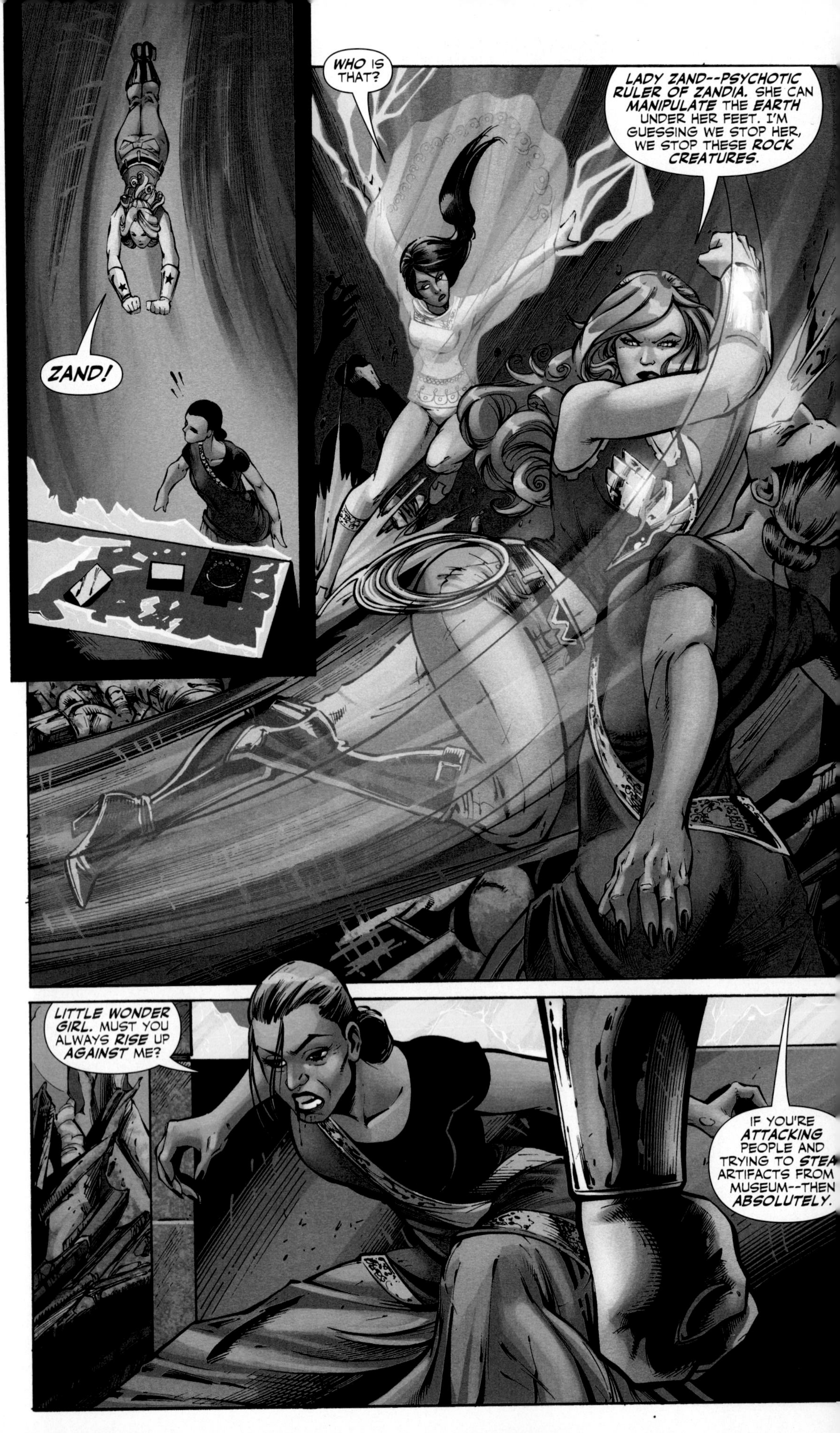
ZAND!
WHO IS THAT?
LADY ZAND--PSYCHOTIC RULER OF ZANDIA. SHE CAN MANIPULATE THE EARTH UNDER HER FEET. I'M GUESSING WE STOP HER, WE STOP THESE ROCK CREATURES.
LITTLE WONDER GIRL. MUST YOU ALWAYS RISE UP AGAINST ME?
IF YOU'RE ATTACKING PEOPLE AND TRYING TO STEA ARTIFACTS FROM MUSEUM--THEN ABSOLUTELY.

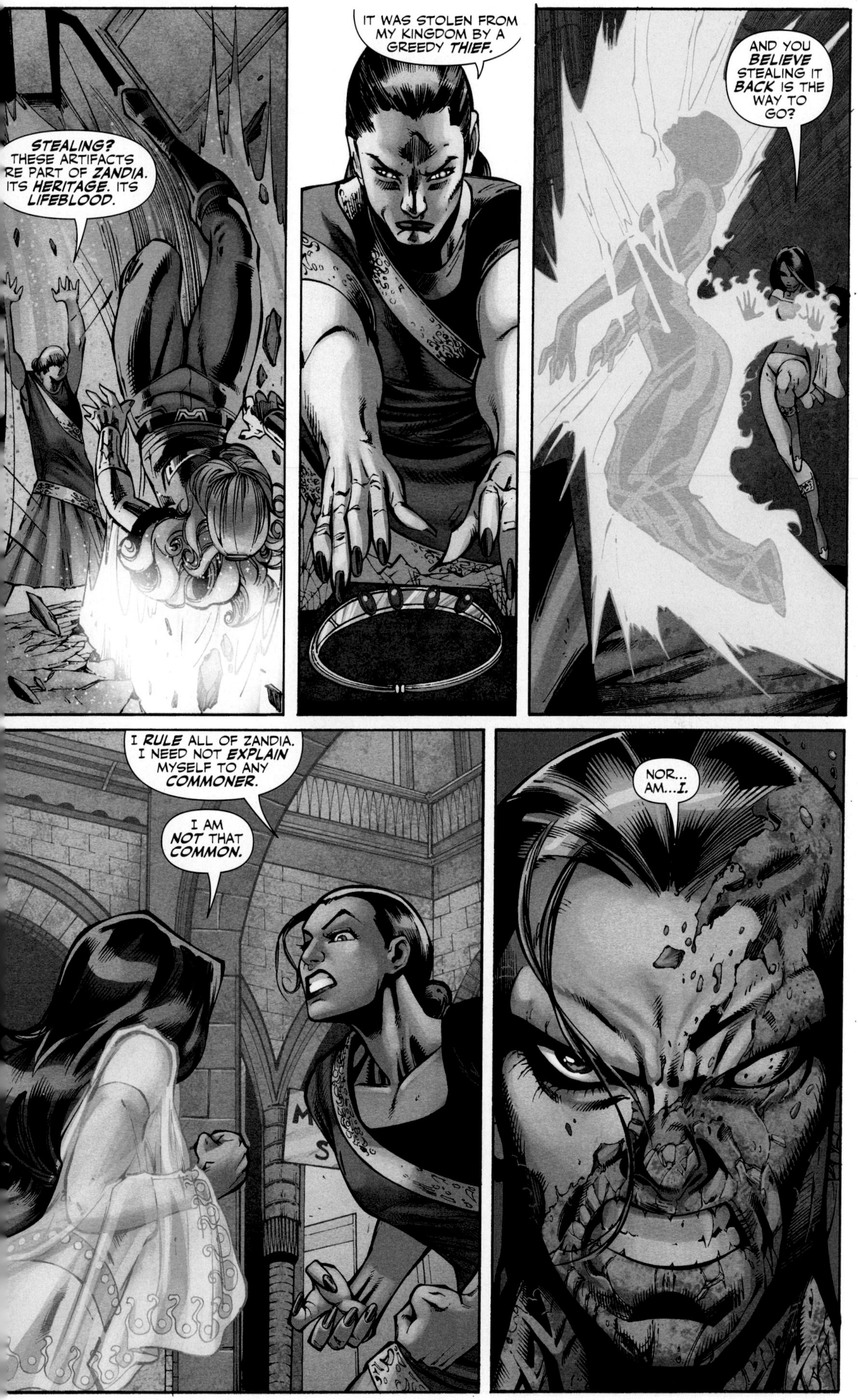

STEALING? THESE ARTIFACTS RE PART OF ZANDIA. ITS HERITAGE. ITS LIFEBLOOD.
IT WAS STOLEN FROM MY KINGDOM BY A GREEDY THIEF.
AND YOU BELIEVE STEALING IT BACK IS THE WAY TO GO?
I RULE ALL OF ZANDIA. I NEED NOT EXPLAIN MYSELF TO ANY COMMONER.
I AM NOT THAT COMMON.
NOR... AM... I.

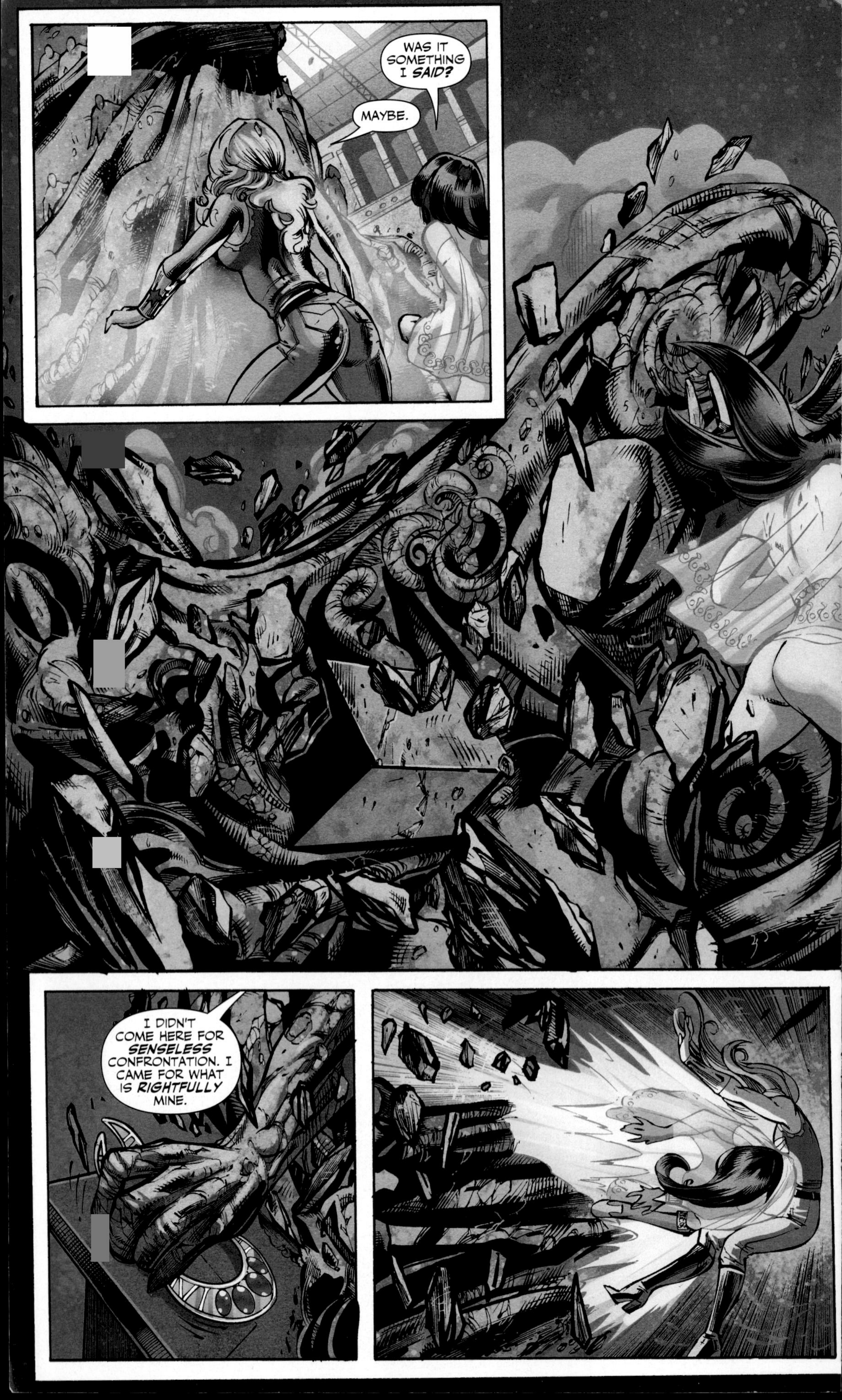
WAS IT SOMETHING I SAID?
MAYBE.
I DIDN'T COME HERE FOR SENSELESS CONFRONTATION. I CAME FOR WHAT IS RIGHTFULLY MINE.

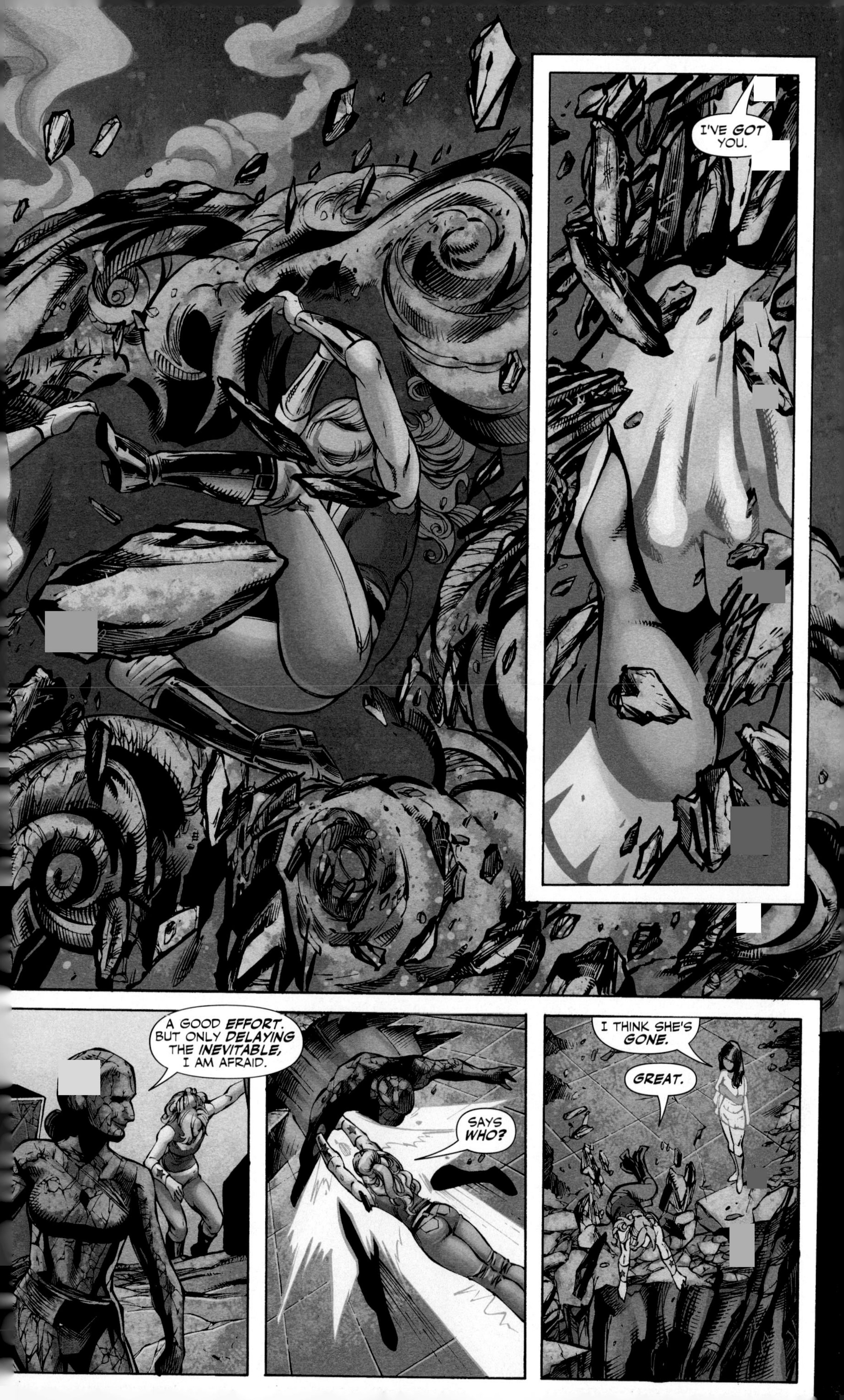
I'VE GOT YOU.
A GOOD EFFORT. BUT ONLY DELAYING THE INEVITABLE, I AM AFRAID.
SAYS WHO?
I THINK SHE'S GONE.
GREAT.

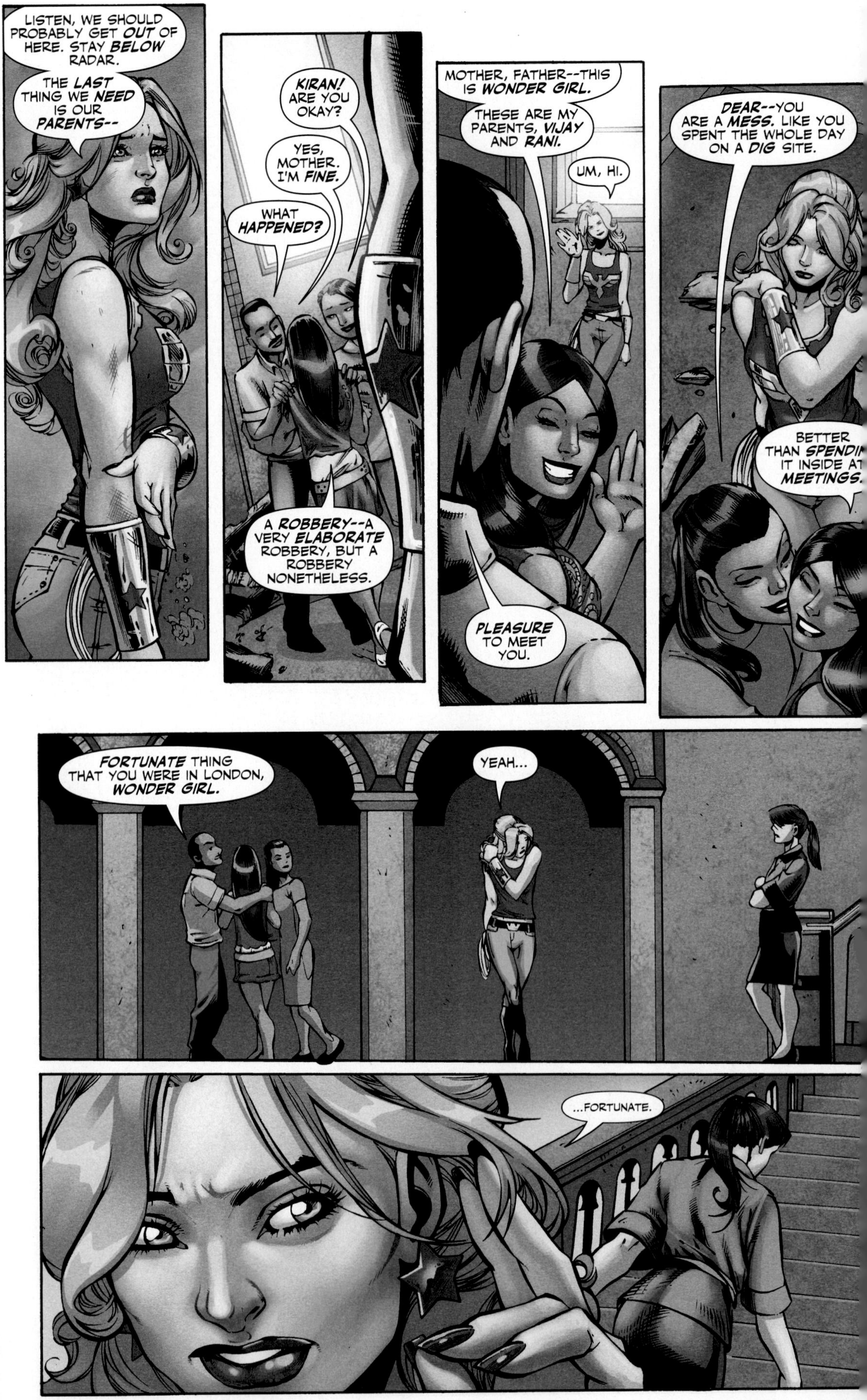
LISTEN, WE SHOULD PROBABLY GET OUT OF HERE. STAY BELOW RADAR.
THE LAST THING WE NEED IS OUR PARENTS--
KIRAN! ARE YOU OKAY?
YES, MOTHER. I'M FINE.
WHAT HAPPENED?
A ROBBERY--A VERY ELABORATE ROBBERY, BUT A ROBBERY NONETHELESS.
MOTHER, FATHER--THIS IS WONDER GIRL.
THESE ARE MY PARENTS, VIJAY AND RANI.
UM, HI.
PLEASURE TO MEET YOU.
DEAR--YOU ARE A MESS. LIKE YOU SPENT THE WHOLE DAY ON A DIG SITE.
FORTUNATE THING THAT YOU WERE IN LONDON, WONDER GIRL.
YEAH...
...FORTUNATE.

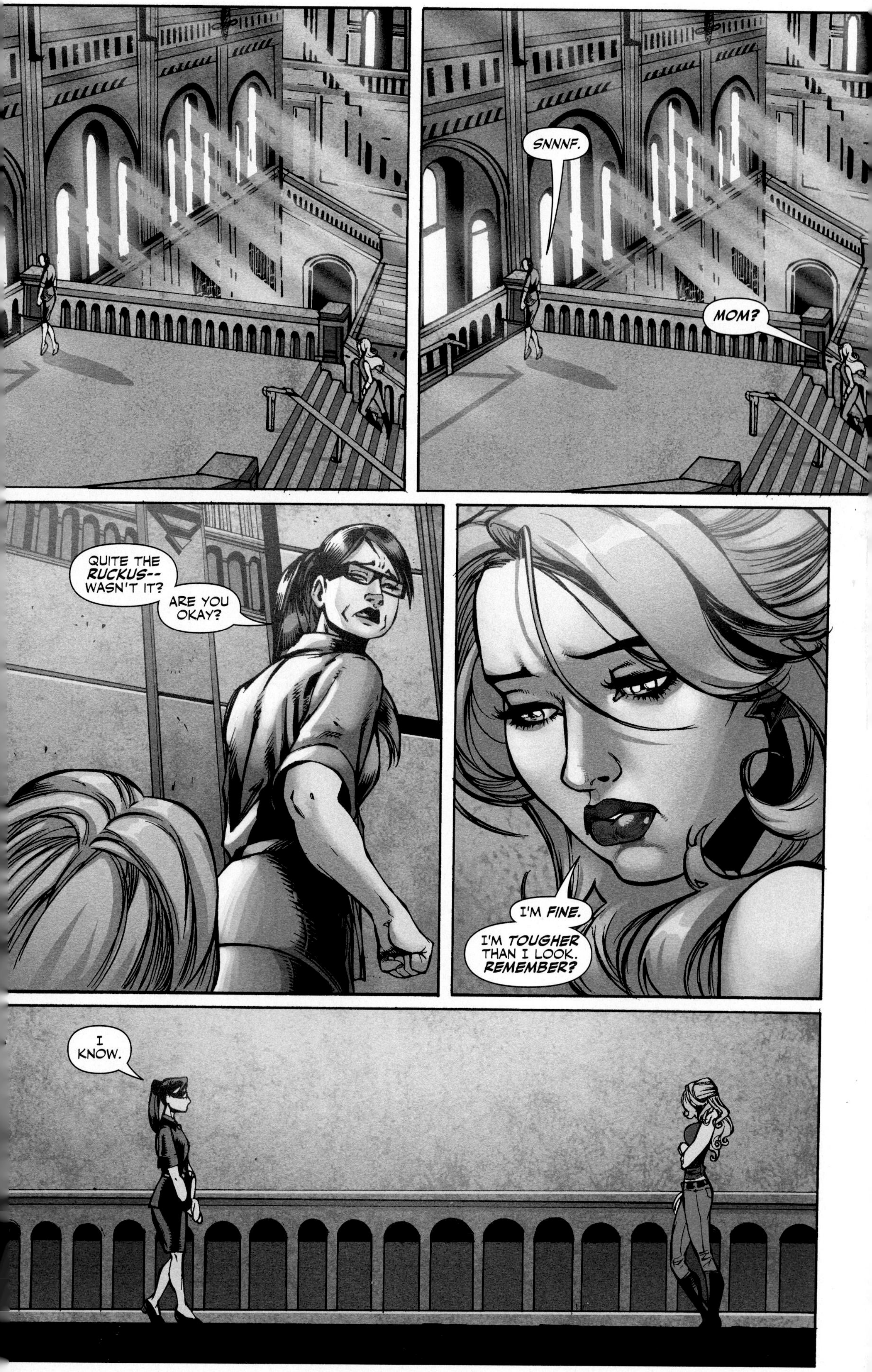
SNNNF.
MOM?
QUITE THE RUCKUS--WASN'T IT?
ARE YOU OKAY?
I'M FINE.
I'M TOUGHER THAN I LOOK. REMEMBER?
I KNOW.

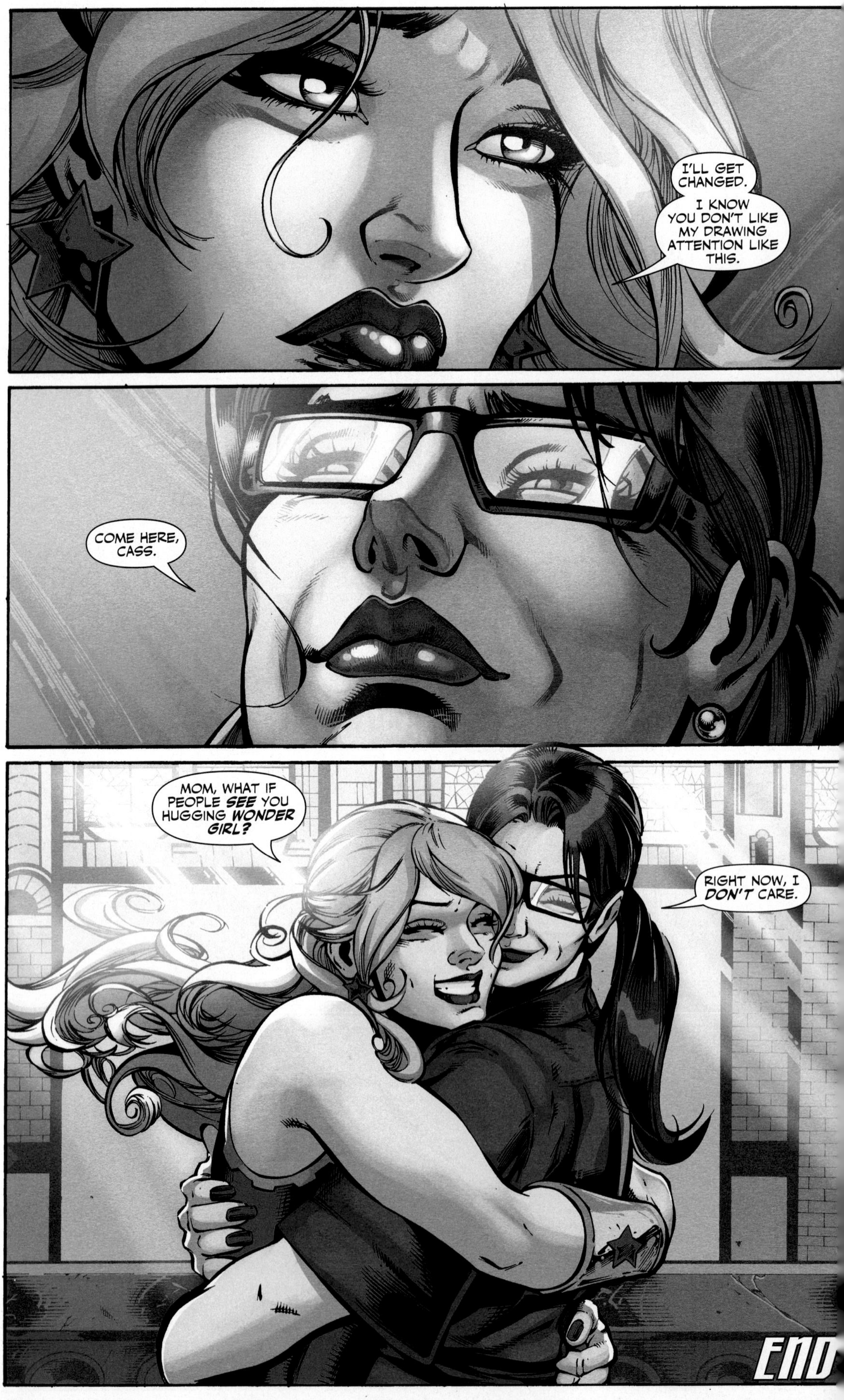
I'LL GET CHANGED.
I KNOW YOU DON'T LIKE MY DRAWING ATTENTION LIKE THIS.
COME HERE, CASS.
MOM, WHAT IF PEOPLE SEE YOU HUGGING WONDER GIRL?
RIGHT NOW, I DON'T CARE.
END

DC UNIVERSE REBIRTH

WONDER WOMAN

VOL. 1: THE LIES

GREG RUCKA
with LIAM SHARP

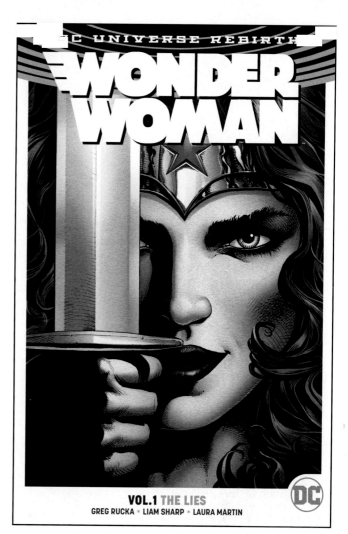

VOL. 1 THE LIES
GREG RUCKA * LIAM SHARP * LAURA MARTIN

JUSTICE LEAGUE VOL. 1:
THE EXTINCTION MACHINES

SUPERGIRL VOL. 1:
REIGN OF THE SUPERMEN

BATGIRL VOL. 1:
BEYOND BURNSIDE

"One of the best writers for Wonder Woman in the modern era."
– NERDIST

WONDER WOMAN BY
GREG
RUCKA
with J.G. JONES
& DREW JOHNSON

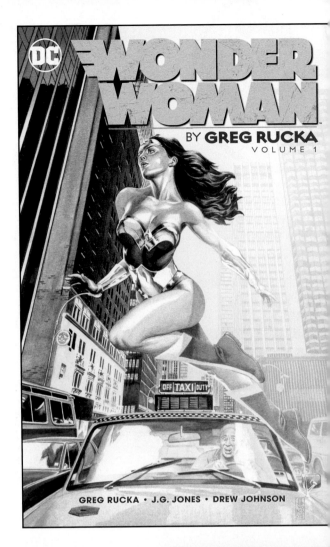

BATWOMAN: ELEGY
with J.H. WILLIAMS III

52 VOL. 1
with VARIOUS ARTISTS

GOTHAM CENTRAL BOOK ONE
with ED BRUBAKER
& MICHAEL LARK

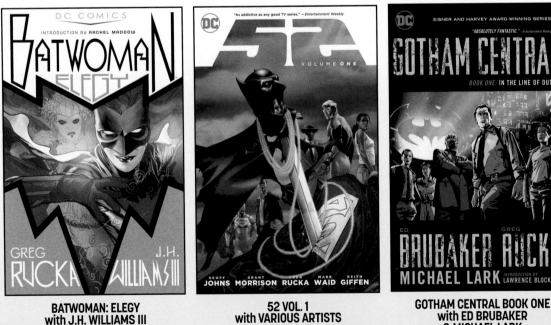

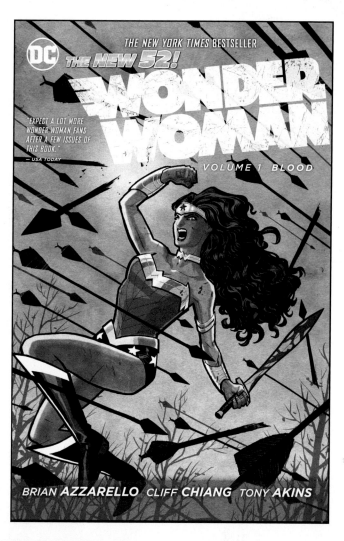

"Clear storytelling at its best. It's an intriguing concept and easy to grasp."
– THE NEW YORK TIMES

"Azzarello is rebuilding the mythology of Wonder Woman."
– CRAVE ONLINE

WONDER WOMAN

VOL. 1: BLOOD

BRIAN AZZARELLO
with CLIFF CHIANG

THE NEW YORK TIMES BESTSELLER
THE NEW 52!
WONDER WOMAN
"EXPECT A LOT MORE WONDER WOMAN FANS AFTER A FEW ISSUES OF THIS BOOK."
— USA TODAY
VOLUME 1 BLOOD
BRIAN AZZARELLO CLIFF CHIANG TONY AKINS

THE NEW YORK TIMES BEST-SELLING SERIES
THE NEW 52!
WONDER WOMAN
VOLUME 2 GUTS
AZZARELLO CLIFF CHIANG TONY AKINS

WONDER WOMAN
VOL. 2: GUTS

THE #1 NEW YORK TIMES BESTSELLING SERIES
THE NEW 52!
WONDER WOMAN
"[AZZARELLO] HAS REJUVENATED THE CHARACTER AND MADE WONDER WOMAN ONE OF THE STANDOUT BOOKS OF THE NEW 52."
— THE ONION/A.V. CLUB
VOLUME 3 IRON
BRIAN AZZARELLO CLIFF CHIANG

WONDER WOMAN
VOL. 3: IRON

READ THE ENTIRE EPIC!

WONDER WOMAN VOL. 4: WAR

WONDER WOMAN VOL. 5: FLESH

WONDER WOMAN VOL. 6: BONES

WONDER WOMAN VOL. 7: WAR-TORN

WONDER WOMAN VOL. 8: A TWIST OF FATE

WONDER WOMAN VOL. 9: RESURRECTION

Get more DC graphic novels wherever comics and books are sold!

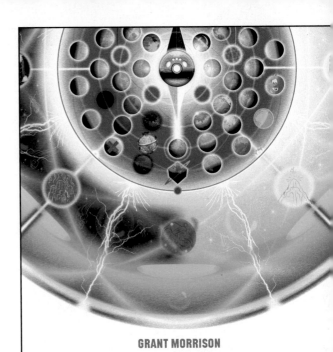